The Open Court
Library of Philosophy

EUGENE FREEMAN, Editor

San Jose State College

Hegel's *Phenomenology:*

Dialogues on The Life of Mind

J. LOEWENBERG

Hegel's *Phenomenology:*

Dialogues on The Life of Mind

La Salle, Illinois · 1965 · The Open Court Publishing Co. · Established 1887

Library of Congress Catalog Card Number: 65-15621

HEGEL'S *PHENOMENOLOGY:* DIALOGUES ON THE LIFE OF MIND

© 1965 by The Open Court Publishing Company

Printed in the United States of America

Preface

Something needs to be said in justification of a new book on Hegel. Much has been written on his philosophy, and nothing fresh, it would seem, could now be added to the bulk of Hegelian scholarship. But the present volume, I hasten to state, is not designed to offer one more interpretation of Hegel's system. I propose neither to praise Hegel nor to bury him. My chief purpose is to afford a suitable approach to but one of Hegel's works which, as Windelband characterized it, is perhaps the most difficult treatise in the history of philosophy.

The *Phenomenology of Mind,* published in 1807, was Hegel's first major work. Bewildering in matter and forbidding in manner, this early treatise has remained subject to conflicting valuations. To some it represents the very essence of Hegelianism, to others it exhibits a superseded position, the later writings alone constituting the true canon.

The treatise has not been without panegyrists. William Wallace, for example, in a note introductory to his translation of Hegel's *Logic,* quotes with approval the dictum of David Strauss that the *Phenomenology* "is the Alpha and Omega of Hegel, and his later writings only extracts from it"; and but here, as Wallace continues,

the Pegasus of mind soars free through untrodden fields of air, and tastes the joys of first love and the pride of fresh discovery in the quest for truth. . . . The mood is Olympian, far above the turmoil and bitterness of lower earth. . . . But the *Phenomenology* is a key which needs consummate patience and skill to use with advantage. If it commands a larger view [than the *Encyclopaedia*], it demands a stronger wing of him who would voyage through the atmosphere of thought up to its purest empyrean.

Hyperbolic language, this. Yet, in spite of the extravagant figures of speech, the statement intimates a side of Hegel not unjustly deemed esoteric. In the *Phenomenology* there may indeed lie, as Wallace maintains, the "royal road" to Hegel's lofty thought, but few, alas, are blessed with the "kingly soul" requisite for the journey.

To speak of it in such terms is to leave the *Phenomenology* virtually inaccessible save to those with a special aptitude for sharing its secret.

But what a labyrinth the text must seem to those not so gifted! There is in it no dearth of pages baffling as regards content and tortuous in expression. For the antiquarian and the exegete it serves as a happy hunting ground. How elusive are the sundry allusions to defunct ideas and beliefs, and how sinuous is the course of the dialectic! Some of the issues broached are too arcane for lay consideration. Caviare to the general, they had better be left to those with a particular penchant for them.

Fortunately, however, the treatise presents another side which is distinctly exoteric. Here Hegel moves in an atmosphere considerably below the empyrean. The subject he is concerned with is the life of mind on earth. Not remote is the analogy, as Royce pointed out in his *Lectures on Modern Idealism,* between Hegel's early work and a literary biography. This analogy, which occurs in Royce as but a passing suggestion, deserves to be taken more seriously. A clear though oblique light falls on Hegel's recondite product when the analogy, adopted as a working hypothesis, is painstakingly carried into detail. Those able to peruse it as a document of perennial import will perceive in the *Phenomenology* a confluence of the major persuasions of mankind, present in universal array, redolent of actuality. The recurrent forms of consciousness, so Hegel calls the persuasions, appear in the text as a graded series, each laying claim to exclusive paramountcy, as it cannot avoid doing in accordance with its special perspective. Hegel exhibits the inevitable tendency of each form of consciousness to grow overweening and to overreach itself, thus necessarily passing into its opposite. In impugning the excessive claims made for any and every special perspective ultimately consists the progressive task of his dialectic. Told here in an altogether unique way is the tragicomic story of mind's generic patterns of belief and comportment. To read the *Phenomenology* as involving such a story is to bring it down from the clouds to the plane of human experience.

It has been my ambition for some time to write a book with the intent of capturing without its letter the spirit of the humanism pervading the *Phenomenology.* To divorce what Hegel says from his way of saying it is to invite censure for rashness. Although in eschewing his idiom completely one runs the risk of miscomprehension, strict fidelity to it incurs the greater risk of incomprehension. From this dilemma no writer on Hegel can escape entirely. Be that as it may, in writing this book I have deliberately striven for a prose capable of being intelligible as well as readable.

My book has a twofold aim. One, though not the foremost, is to provide a convenient mode of ingress into a work the unassisted study of which is apt to produce a sense of frustration. Some initiation, no matter how one-sided, may render the initial encounter with it less formidable. But no introduction to Hegel could be adjudged satisfactory if it failed to follow without deviation his method of tracing in the *Phenomenology* the order and connection of the various stages in the development of mind. In no other work does the method evince so pliant and so original a use. On the assumption that the heart of Hegel's thought is to be found more in the method than in the results achieved by it, emphasis on the former is not misplaced. Before grappling therefore with the dialectical logic of the abstract categories, one should first observe the logic at work in the less rigorous and the more imaginative version to which the early treatise owes its construction. But there are more things in the treatise than are dreamt of by the professional student. Liberated from the author's odd and obscure locutions, it emerges as a treasure house of challenging ideas rich in variety and wide in range. Behind its technical trappings one may espy a synoptic vision of the multiform career of human consciousness. It is indeed a chronicle, Homeric in scale, of man's spiritual odyssey. To give an intimation of this has been my primary aim.

The 'secret' of Hegel, whether contained in the *Phenomenology* or in the later writings, is one, as some wit has declared, which seems to have been well kept. Of keys to that secret the choice has proved quite embarrassing. The specialists, bent on explaining the author's varied utterances, explain them, alas, differently, and in ways often no less inscrutable. The pregnant insights embodied in the early treatise would appear to have a greater claim to general consideration than the dark diction in which they lie embedded.

A critical examination of the text, a task devolving upon the learned commentators, is thus not to be looked for in the following quasi-lay conversations. Although the themes treated, some more fully than others, parallel those marshalled by Hegel, the parallelism is but selective, many matters he dilates on being too technical or too minute for inclusion in a discussion free of exegesis. Yet it was hardly possible to reconstruct the logical sequence and development of Hegel's themes without reproducing the structural framework within which his dialectic operated. I have thus faithfully adhered to the division of the text into its main sections. With some of the subsections alone I have taken certain liberties. But the changes made in them, whether affecting their order or titles, involved no essential change in Hegel's architectonic. Missing from my book are the usual paraphernalia of academic scholarship. There are no footnotes. Quotations are brief and few, and such only as appeared necessary for accentuating or clinching some crucial point, without intruding on the spontaneous discourse of the interlocutors.

What is novel in my treatment of Hegel's work is the attempt to adapt it to the dialogue form. Apart from the affinity of the dialectical logic with the Socratic-Platonic method of discussion by dialogue, the form chosen has seemed to me particularly suited for sharpening as well as deepening the inner tensions and incongruities which Hegel's diagnosis of every type of consciousness brings to light. The two speakers, viewing the same themes from different angles of the mind, reflect the interplay of point and counterpoint which lends to the *Phenomenology* its dramatic quality. For the work exemplifies a tremendous debate, the subject debated upon being the claim to exclusive truth on the part of every human persuasion. Carried on by a method which requires successive shifts of position, the debate is in essence a continuous dialogue, susceptible of translation into an interchange of conversation. In another sense, too, it seemed appropriate to use this form: in addition to debating on the subjects provided *by* Hegel, the speakers dispute also over subjects generated by questions *about* Hegel, to wit, questions about the nature of his inquiry, the validity of his method, the truth of his conclusions. Dialogue has the advantage over disquisition in uniting in integral fashion exposition and criticism. Recurrent alternation of advocacy and rebuttal, such as the participants in an actual debate concretely illustrate, imparts to Hegel's dialectic in the pages that follow a lively and focalized mobility, showing at the same time the extent to which his method is both defensible and vulnerable. But the proof of all this lies ahead and needs here no further elaboration.

The names of the persons of the dialogues have no special significance. I created the characters bearing the names in a book devoted to a consideration of issues in aesthetics and criticism published some time ago under the title *Dialogues from Delphi* (University of California Press). I have retained the characters here, though I might have invented others, partly because I like them, but mainly because their association with a previous discussion broadly conceived may lend emphasis to the equal breadth of view characteristic of the present volume.

It should be mentioned that Dialogues 1 and 2 contain in modified form some excerpts from two printed articles on Hegel (*Mind,* Vol. XLIII, N.S., No. 172, and Vol. XLIV, N.S., No. 173).

I am grateful to my friend Dr. Stanley Moore for reading the manuscript. He has helped to reduce the number of stylistic infelicities. And I wish to thank my nephew Professor Bert James Loewenberg for much-needed aid in connection with the book's publication.

J. L.

Berkeley, California, 1963

Contents

Preface ix
Dialogue 1. The Problem of Starting Point 1
  1. Hegel's Preface to the *Phenomenology* 2
  2. Hegel's Introduction to the *Phenomenology* 8

PART I   CONSCIOUSNESS 23
Dialogue 2. Sense-Certainty 24
  1. The Initial Experiment 24
  2. The Interrogatory Procedure 28
  3. Gesticulatory Immediacy 34
Dialogue 3. Perception 41
  1. The Thing and its Properties 41
  2. Perception as Reception 46
  3. Perception and Reflection 50
  4. Perception with Reservations 54
Dialogue 4. Understanding 59
  1. The Concept of Force 59
  2. The Play of Forces and the Kingdom of Laws 64
  3. The Locus of Necessity 68

PART II   SELF-CONSCIOUSNESS 75
Dialogue 5. Self-Certainty 76
Dialogue 6. Independence and Freedom of Self-Consciousness . . 84
  1. Self-Consciousness and Solipsism 84
  2. Master and Slave 86
  3. The Stoic 91
  4. The Sceptic 93
Dialogue 7. The Unhappy Consciousness 97
  1. The Schizophrenic 97
  2. The Mystic 100
  3. The Adolescent 104

4. The Monastic 106
5. Transition to Reason 110

PART III   REASON 113

Dialogue 8. Reason's Certainty and Truth 114
Dialogue 9. Rational Observation of Nature 120
   1. Observation as an Activity of Reason 120
   2. Observation of Inorganic Nature 123
   3. Observation of Organic Nature 128
Dialogue 10. Rational Observation of Human Nature 136
   1. Logical Laws and the Logic of Observation. 136
   2. Observational Psychology and its Issues 139
   3. The Individual and the Environment 140
   4. Mind's Perceptible Traits 142
   5. The Physical Seat of Mind 145
Dialogue 11. Reason and Individual Aspiration 150
   1. Preliminary Remarks on Individualism 150
   2. Pleasure and Necessity 154
   3. The Law of the Heart 158
   4. Virtue and the Course of the World 162
Dialogue 12. The Individual and the Universal 167
   1. Pseudo-Objective Individualism 167
   2. Animal Behavior in the Realm of Reason 168
   3. Reason as Lawgiver 174
   4. Reason as Judge 178

PART IV   SPIRIT 185

Dialogue 13. The Ethical World and the Rule of Custom 186
   1. Transition to Spirit 186
   2. The Ingenuous Society and the Two Laws 189
   3. The Tragedy of Conflicting Imperatives 195
Dialogue 14. Condition of Right and Legal Personality 202
Dialogue 15. Self-Alienation Through Culture 207
   1. Preface to the Cultural Process 207
   2. The Artificial Society and the Factitious Individual . . . 209
   3. The Twin Pillars of Culture 213
   4. The Noble and the Base 216
   5. Heroism of Flattery and the Language of Disintegration . . . 221
Dialogue 16. Culture and Enlightenment 226
   1. Belief and Insight 226
   2. The Struggle with Alleged Superstition 231
   3. The Distortive Effect of Clarification 235
   4. The Rise of Enlightened Belief 238

Contents

Dialogue 17. The Truth of Enlightenment. 242
Dialogue 18. Absolute Freedom and Terror 249
Dialogue 19. The Moral Consciousness 258
   1. The Concept of Morality 258
   2. The Moral Postulates 260
   3. The Moral Makeshifts 266
Dialogue 20. Conscience 273
   1. Morality without Postulates 273
   2. Moral Judgment 279
   3. The Beautiful Soul 283
   4. Evil and its Forgiveness 287
Dialogue 21. The Religious Consciousness 292
   1. The Concept of Religion 292
   2. The Structure of Religion 296
Dialogue 22. Natural Religion 303
Dialogue 23. Religion of Art 310
   1. Concentric Spheres of Art and Religion 310
   2. The Abstract Work of Art 313
   3. The Living Work of Art 318
   4. The Spiritual Work of Art 320
Dialogue 24. Tragedy and Comedy 326
   1. Decline of the Gods 326
   2. Departure of the Gods 331
Dialogue 25. Revealed Religion 334
   1. The Ambivalence of Revelation 334
   2. The Stages of Revelation 339
   3. Revelation of God as Trinitarian 344
   4. Christianity and Hegelianism 348
Dialogue 26. The Philosophical Consciousness 354
   1. A Chapter in the Life of Mind 354
   2. The Ambiguous Subject of Absolute Knowledge 359
   3. The Twofold Ontology 363
   4. The Anomalies of Absoluteness 366
Index 372

The Problem of Starting Point

Hardith: I have been reflecting of late with some care on your method of dealing with the themes and issues that formed the contents of our former conversations. Do you recall how often I accused you of going to dialectical extremes at the bidding of your love of paradox? The loose and pejorative sense in which I used the word 'dialectical' revealed prejudice on my part rather than understanding. I now wish to make amends by a more sympathetic approach to the method you followed with such admirable skill. I am but an amateur philosopher full of preconceived notions and my opinion adverse to Hegel is probably quite unjust. Yet even the little I could glean from his speculations struck me as too important to be ignored. You have been devoting, I know, considerable time to a painstaking study of the *Phenomenology of Mind,* a work said to exemplify the dialectical method on a grand scale. I wonder whether you would be willing to enter upon a discussion, but in a language adapted to the lay mind, of the salient features of the Hegelian method as embodied principally in that early text.

Meredy: I always like to talk about Hegel, so much so that I have frequently been mistaken for a disciple of his. The *Phenomenology,* insufficiently explored by competent scholars, is perhaps his greatest achievement. But it is certainly forbidding. How bizarre is the idiom in which insights so profound lie so deeply buried! The relative neglect of it, as compared with the author's later products, is thus not at all surprising. Your suggestion that we discuss Hegel in intelligible prose is a tremendous challenge. Is it possible to meet the challenge? To reproduce his method without his language is to sacrifice profundity, to reproduce the method with it is to remain lost in obfuscation. The dilemma—surrender of depth or surrender to obscurity—seems inescapable. So significant, however, is the *Phenomenology* that an approach to its dialectic without an abstruse dialect, so to speak, may

1

nevertheless prove rewarding. Gain in actual relevance may compensate for loss of esoteric subtlety. But tell me, Hardith, how do you propose that we begin our task?

1. *Hegel's Preface to the* Phenomenology

Hardith: We should, I suppose, begin at the beginning. And is there a better beginning than the book's Preface? But, alas, "all hope abandon ye who enter here". Unlike any other preface known to me, Hegel's is apparently designed rather to mystify than to enlighten. The purpose of a prefatory statement to acquaint the reader with the conclusions to be arrived at and with the principles underlying them, Hegel considers superfluous and unsuitable. For philosophic results, he declares, are but dogmatic assurances in the absence of the arguments adduced in their support. His own preface—and it is very long and very difficult—contains the reasons for discrediting a priori the attempt to set forth at the outset the final outcome of his philosophy. Yet, throwing consistency to the winds, Hegel proceeds to write the very preface he condemns. How paradoxical to enter so deliberately upon a task for the very purpose of denying its necessity!

Meredy: The Preface as written is scarcely fit to serve as introduction to the author's undertaking. As prophecy of the shape of his philosophy to come, Hegel's foreword is entirely inadequate: it is couched in the idiom that takes for granted the doctrine awaiting exposition and justification. No paradox, however, is involved in showing the impossibility of indicating in summary fashion a position the meaning of which depends on the progressive phases contributing to its development. That a persuasion is without validity as an abstract epitome, since its systematic articulation alone can have a claim on truth, this is precisely what the sequel is intended to demonstrate. One must bear in mind that the Preface belongs to the kind of pronouncement required to be read as epilogue instead of as prologue. In actual composition, most such statements, Hegel's not excepted, follow rather than precede completion of the author's creative task. When thus understood, Hegel's indirect approach to the *Phenomenology,* in the terms in which he chose to formulate it, becomes highly important.

Hardith: Why not then ignore the foreword altogether? Could we not proceed as if it had no bearing at all on the subject matter of the treatise? Why such an elaborate initial posture when its use as initiation into the ensuing investigation is so candidly rejected?

Meredy: No, the Preface cannot be dismissed as irrelevant. Its intent is to afford a comprehensive view of Hegel's position as a whole, the *Phenomenology* being, in accordance with the author's original plan, a preliminary entrance upon it. In the absence of the Preface, we should have no inkling of the universal applicability which Hegel attributes to the dialectical method. What he places in the foreground, therefore, is a summary and vindication of the nature and function of philosophic knowledge. This assumes the form of a manifesto unique as regards the ruthlessness of the polemic and the audacity of the asseverations. In the name of 'science', of which he proposes to furnish the only tenable conception, Hegel attacks his predecessors and contemporaries, branding them in turn as dreamers, simpletons, formalists, dogmatists. Impugning as naïve or sterile methods hitherto followed— namely, the inductive, the empirical, the analytical, the mathematical— he promises to institute a new procedure designed to transcend the traditional dichotomy of truth and error. This procedure, the dialectical, will reveal conflicting ideas or beliefs not as disjunctions but as conjoined. A theory of truth will emerge in radical opposition to the prevailing one. Truth will appear as dramatic and organic, each of its phases both false and necessary, false in isolation but necessary as determining its course of evolution. Of truth as thus envisaged, involving its own opposite as an integral aspect of itself, the *Phenomenology* is to offer an exposition and defense, the metaphors Hegel uses to convey his meaning being drawn from biology. The growth and continuity of truth, comparable to that of an organism, requires different stages, the latter supplanting yet completing the earlier. As bud and blossom are related to each other in the total life of the plant, the latter fulfilling the former by superseding it, so, too, in the total life of reason, when conceived in dynamic terms, incompatible ideas or beliefs lose their wonted opposition and become mutually implicative. To facilitate the reader's attempt to comprehend a work so revolutionary (for the uninitiated as difficult as the attempt 'to walk on his head') the Preface anticipates in condensed shape the outcome of the inquiry to follow. Hegel concedes, however, that in advance of the dialectical deduction the predicted result can have no probative force.

Hardith: The question is not so much of proof as of intelligibility. The promised result, communicated through a vocabulary downright occult, can mean nothing to those to whom the 'new' philosophy is to be introduced. Hegel manipulates his crucial terms, which presuppose the doctrine justifying them, in reckless oblivion of their uselessness to serve the purpose he uses them for. Ordinary thought is simply unable to ascend to a vision so singularly unfamiliar. The 'ladder' provided— the expression is Hegel's—is too slippery and insecure. Statements couched in language so esoteric must leave the reader utterly bewildered.

Meredy: This is true enough. The Preface does announce the program of a philosophic system demanding for articulation a technical idiom especially contrived for and adapted to it. The idiom and the system are indeed bound each to each in circular fashion: neither can be understood without reference to the other. Despite its esoteric features, the Preface contains certain exoteric pronouncements, and these might well be regarded as constituting a sort of oblique introduction to the *Phenomenology.* To prove my point, let me briefly speak of them.

Hardith: Can you really cull from Hegel's manifesto some dicta sufficiently clear to serve as clues to the nature of his work? What precisely have you in mind?

Meredy: I should like to single out as having particular importance the famous utterance that "the truth is the whole." Epitomizing the basic contention developed in the system, the proposition may afford to the uninitiated perhaps the most convenient ingress into the argument of the *Phenomenology.* Its implication is double-edged. The whole alone being wholly true, any claim to truth short of the whole represents, as it were, an epicene species, neither true nor untrue; it is the aim of the dialectic to show that every truth-claim has a truth-value, but only within and not without an organic system of ideas or beliefs. In other words, particular or partial claims to truth are at once valid and invalid, the former as mutually implicated and the latter as mutually sundered. This simply follows upon the analogy Hegel invokes between the life of reason and the life of an organism. The different stages or phases of truth, not unlike those of plant or animal, though distinguishable, are never isolable; for only as reciprocally related can they condition its sequential process and continuous growth. Of the view that truth depends for its coherent integrity upon an ordered series of incomplete and incompatible claims the *Phenomenology* purports to be the original demonstration.

Hardith: But is the proposition you mention more than an apothegm? That *das Wahre ist das Ganze*—this is of course unexceptionable if not 'loaded' with a special theory. There is hardly a votary of philosophy or science who does not think of truth's wholeness as an ideal desideratum. The proposition has the earmarks of a truism. But Hegel does not announce it as such; with the notions of truth and wholeness phrased in esoteric fashion, the truism becomes a paradox. For we are bidden in the Preface to accept as credible without any proof whatever that truth is not truth unless error forms an integral part of it, and that wholeness consists of a hierarchy of errors which, since they are requisite for its process and growth, shed thereby their actual erroneousness. The whole truth is likened at the outset to a "baccha-

4

nalian revel wherein everyone of the participants is intoxicated." The sobriety of ultimate truth, so to speak, thus depends on the toxic condition with which all proximate truth is infected. How strange a simile and how unintelligible! What an intolerable strain upon our credulity is the demand that the beginning be made with an egregious paradox! We are of course at liberty to withhold assent from a proposition appearing simply as an article of faith and voiced in a diction alien to ordinary thought. The proposition would thus seem to hinder instead of to help initial understanding of Hegel's task.

Meredy: The intent of the *Phenomenology* can obviously not be compressed within the compass of a single formula. Yet the one chosen, considered in conjunction with others, clearly reveals the aim of the argument to be propounded. The dictum concerning truth must be supplemented by the assertion, with which it is indeed equatable, that knowledge becomes philosophic only when it appears as result reached by an evolutionary process. Hegel epitomizes this by using as synonymous the terms 'science' and 'system'; no true *Wissen,* accordingly, without systematic *Wissenschaft.* Unfortunately, the word science (as well as its German equivalent) has been preempted by specialists who labor in separate fields of inquiry. A modern reader, therefore, accustomed as he is to associate the word with any discipline concerned with the study of matters of fact by techniques avowedly nonphilosophic, will look askance at Hegel's ambition to demonstrate as scientific the fruits of his speculation. In the broadest sense, however, scientific knowledge does connote knowledge that is discriminative and organized, cohesive and generalized. The attempt to raise speculation from the level of vague intuitions or loose reflections to the plane of systematic thought by a mode of procedure suited for search for connection and discovery of order, this for Hegel is the same as the attempt to turn philosophy into science. That truth is whole and that true philosophy is science are propositions not only mutually implicative but virtually interchangeable.

Hardith: Here again we should distinguish between the exoteric and the esoteric. That knowledge has philosophic merit only when it acquires the form of a systematic science remains unexceptionable if the general reader is not required to assume that there is but one conception of science and that a particular system is its only true embodiment. After all, science and system are familiar terms; ordinary thought is free to use them for different products of human intelligence achieved in various ways. To be sure, Hegel expressly warns us against the confusion of the familiar with the intelligible. But if familiarity with the notion of science is no clue to its true nature, Hegel's strange view of it,

5

stated in tortuous language, has no lien on our acquiescence. So startling indeed is the view that it strikes us "as if shot out of a pistol," to turn against Hegel a phrase he employs in disparagement of speculations differing from his. What are we to understand by a science in which the moving spirit is the power of negativity productive of organic wholeness? We are given no reasons for reserving the eulogistic name of science for knowledge amenable to the dialectical process. In the Preface there is and obviously can be no evidence for equating science with dialectic and system solely with Hegel's speculative undertaking. All this remains but asseveration with no claim upon our acceptance.

Meredy: After what you have been saying, your comment on the next statement will, I fear, be especially censorious. This is the statement that what is true must be grasped and expressed not only in terms of substance but in terms of subject as well. The allusion is clearly to Spinoza whose philosophy Hegel sets in contrast with his own. To exalt substance by identifying it with God must appear shocking if not revolting, so Hegel contends, simply because in such exaltation self-consciousness becomes submerged. Quite apart from his cryptic polemic against Spinoza, what Hegel here insists upon is the primacy of mind as source of truth. How indeed conceive of claims to truth, irrespective of the objects involved, unless conceived as claims made by a subject? To the subjective origin of truth the investigation of the *Phenomenology* is explicitly directed, its subject matter being mind as truth-claiming subject. Exhibited throughout as incorrigibly volatile and protean, mind advances by dialectical necessity from claim to claim, and their nexus is such that every claim contains within it a negative element which the succeeding claim assimilates. All claims thus related constitute the complex to which alone complete truth belongs. In this complex, representing the entire system or science of subjective claims, the career of truth reveals the logical rhythm intrinsic to it: recurrent passage from extreme to extreme. Absolute truth, in other words, is the totality of relative truths, each of which attains self-realization through the process of oscillation between self-assertion and self-alienation. The three statements mentioned thus hang together and serve as intimations of the argument to be justified, to wit, that truth is not true unless viewed as holistic, consisting of an organic concatenation of claims, all successively affirmed and recanted and absorbed by a dynamic subject.

Hardith: Yes, the words are clear and not lacking in sense until forced to assume recondite meanings. I do not intend to be captious. I am simply bewildered by attempts made to divest certain terms of the significance they enjoy in communicable discourse. It is thus that platitudes come to parade as paradoxes. What more commonplace than the distinction between the completely true and the partially true or the distinction between scientific knowledge and unscientific? But that truth is sublimation of error and science dialectical speculation must at first sight seem anomalous. Equally without subtlety but here appearing anomalous is the notion of mind as knowing subject. Of course, no cognition in the absence of mind affected by or reacting to objects: observation implies an observer and inquiry an inquirer. But subject does not exclusively connote a knowing mind. Apart from signifying the knower in contrast with the knowable object, the subject signifies also the term of a proposition about which something is asserted, the term distinct from it being predicate. The subject, alas, has another and less neutral sense; in certain quarters its connotation is that of spirit with a religious halo, in opposition to it being any term, such as matter or substance, underlying or transcending mind. Now struggle as we may, we are unable to distinguish the diverse senses which in the Preface Hegel imputes to the concepts of subject and substance; possessing such divergent meanings, seemingly arbitrary until defended, these concepts produce confusion stultifying the intent to lighten by means of them the task of comprehension. And so when Hegel lays down the proposition that truth must be conceived and stated not as substance but as subject, we remain uninstructed and unpersuaded. Why should substance be disparaged as immediate, simple, undifferentiated, inert, abstract, unreal? And why should subject be considered something honorific, the epitome of all that is living and actual and concrete? We have nothing but Hegel's assurance, which we are under no compulsion to share, that one of the concepts is higher and the other lower.

Meredy: Your emphasis on the difficulties inherent in the Preface is not misplaced; the document before us ill succeeds in paving an accessible road to the *Phenomenology*. It affords a better approach to the system than to the initial stage of it which the treatise was intended for. Of Hegel's philosophy, it is safe to say, no epitome, Hegel's own included, can escape being distortive. For Hegel's thought and the language in which it is clothed constitute, as remarked earlier, a vicious circle; to grasp the meaning of his peculiar nomenclature an understanding of his system must already be in one's possession, yet the system defies utterance without the strange idiom in which it appears. Equally circular is the relation between the result of his speculation and the method chosen for reaching it; the dialectical procedure prescribes what is to ensue from its application, and the end sought cannot be attained save by the dialectical process generated for the very pur-

7

pose of achieving it. That such circularity is not conducive to win from those inured to traditional ways of thinking appreciation of a new philosophy goes without saying. This Hegel himself could hardly fail to recognize. Mastery of the system can supervene only upon painstaking study of all the relevant texts in which it is embodied. Yet, a beginning must somehow be made. I still insist that the Preface contains certain theses serviceable as guide posts to the *Phenomenology*. These are (a) that truth must always appear in the shape of asserted claims the roots of which are in the mind of a knowing subject; (b) that truth is without philosophic value unless exhibited as a system of claims and counterclaims; and (c) that only truth as thus exhibited comports with the criterion of wholeness, the whole truth being the synthesis of antagonistic claims grown mutually implicative. To be sure, theses so summarily put forward, though helpful, scarcely suffice for the task of embarking upon Hegel's inquiry. Much more needs to be asked. What, for example, is here the preemptive subject matter? And to what modes of procedure is exploration of this subject matter amenable? With these questions the Introduction and not the Preface is directly concerned.

2. *Hegel's Introduction to the* Phenomenology

Hardith: If the office of an Introduction is to introduce, what Hegel says under this head, though he says it in his magisterial manner, certainly provides a more appropriate access to his undertaking. For here we are made acquainted with the nature of a special investigation such that does not explicitly presuppose as context the entire system in which it may *eventually* be shown to play an important part. It is an investigation the specificity of which the very title explicitly indicates. Phenomenology has a subject matter not identical with the subject matter of any other discipline. Phenomenology is not logic or ontology or psychology or history. What precisely is it? The Introduction, unless I miss its drift, does not preclude assimilating phenomenology with epistemology. Am I right?

Meredy: I wonder. If phenomenology involves a theory of knowledge, the theory is markedly unique. For Hegel takes pains to assert at the outset that the knowledge he is investigating is not knowledge in general. Abstract epistemologies run riot in anomalies. Should knowledge, for example, be conceived as instrument through which the real is attained or as medium in which the real is reflected? However knowledge be viewed, whether as active vehicle or as passive mirror, the dualism between being and knowing becomes a fundamental postulate, precipitating at once the question of their logical distinction and actual relation, a question susceptible of inducing distrust of truth, for in one case the role of knowledge is magnified and in the other belittled. If we regard knowledge as having an active part in the formation of its object, we banish beyond our ken the intrinsic nature of the real; and if knowledge is assumed to possess no power to shape and modify its object, serving merely as a diaphanous veil for it, knowledge becomes an otiose redundancy. Either anomaly, the anomaly of allowing knowledge to tamper with the real or the anomaly of divesting knowledge of all activity, renders precarious the search for truth. But, Hegel asks, need we face such a dilemma? Why begin with stereotyping knowledge as instrument or medium? Neither alternative can be maintained without a host of assailable assumptions. Once the assumptions are impugned—and what assumptions respecting knowledge are unexceptionable?—the epistemologies resting on them become a prey of doubt. But the scepticism which certain theories of knowledge engender may be always escaped through skepticism of these theories. There is no reason, Hegel holds, why distrust of truth should not itself be distrusted. It is thus that he approaches the perennial problem of knowledge. To whom does he here allude? The question, of interest to the connoisseurs of Hegel, does not concern us. Of importance for us is his emphatic declaration that an examination of knowledge may be inaugurated without prior assumptions about its nature.

Hardith: The clarity with which you are able to paraphrase Hegel's thought has my unstinted admiration. The clarity is of course yours and not the philosopher's. But if you have not altered his thought by making it so intelligible, what am I to understand by an attempt to deal with a subject matter without any assumption regarding its nature? What makes it the subject matter it is? In examining knowledge, what precisely are we supposed to examine?

Meredy: Your question touches the nerve of the problem. What Hegel does is to reduce to the level of mere assurances all assumptions; one assurance, he maintains, is as good as another. More than assurance, however, is the fact that knowledge occurs; if it failed to occur we should have nothing to examine. What is this occurrence? In what manner does it appear, under what conditions, in what shapes? All this is open to critical study. We are bidden by the author to lay aside our prepossessions and to take knowledge as a phenomenon; the fact of its appearing being, as it were, an empirical datum. We are of course unable to discover its characters and relations save by an investigation pursued by a method claiming to dispense with assumptions. But prior to such investigation, nothing that we say about knowledge can have philosophic value. This at all events is the view voiced in the Introduction.

9

Hardith: And yet Hegel indulges in many an unwarrantable assumption of his own. I recall the sentence, uttered as if it conveyed an axiom, to the effect that "the absolute alone is true or the true is alone the absolute." Should not such a pontifical proposition be dismissed as falling under his own ban of barren assurances? Is this not the very sort of *trockenes Versichern* he insists should be eschewed?

Meredy: Yes, the sentence seems out of place, belonging, together with others like it, more to the Preface than the Introduction. Phenomenological subject matter is knowledge such as it appears to a consciousness Hegel describes as natural, the adjective being here synonymous with nonphilosophic. Hegel makes adroit use of the word's etymology in characterizing natural knowledge as *erscheinend*. The meanings which he ascribes to it are analogous to those borne by the English term 'apparent'. Depending on the context, the term may signify that which appears or that which is evident or that which is specious. Even in the Introduction we encounter Hegel's penchant for expressions we may speak of as polysynthetic. He defines natural knowledge as apparent in all the three senses of the word, representing it as a phenomenon seemingly obvious but ultimately unreal, for no knowledge deserves to be considered genuine unless supported by rational evidence. Here is an expression subtly trivalent by means of which Hegel manages to indicate the starting-place of his inquiry as well as its direction and halting-place. The theme of the *Phenomenology* being apparent knowledge, the treatise will begin with a form of knowledge first in the order of seeming obviousness and certitude; it will reveal the spuriousness of the first appearance of knowledge by rendering insecure its putative claim to truth; the process of challenging the claim must lead to a second appearance, more inclusive but no less vulnerable; and this process of showing that higher appearances of knowledge emerge from criticism of lower ones will continue until a point is reached where knowledge, as Hegel declares, "is no longer compelled to go beyond itself." Such knowledge alone, as the synthesis of all the previous phenomenal forms, will then cease being natural or apparent and become scientific or real. Thus apposite is the compendious term chosen by Hegel to intimate the object and the objective of the inquiry.

Hardith: To make a term mean so much, not to say too much, constitutes indeed a great feat of condensation. But terminological dexterity apart, the intent of the *Phenomenology,* admitting it to be the elaboration of a singular theory of knowledge, is to seek anchorage in cognition as a natural phenomenon. This phenomenon, occurring in minds prior to their cultivation by speculative reason, we must regard as subject to an evolutionary process ever passing into and moving beyond different phases, the highest phase in which the process culminates being a system of philosophy, exclusively Hegel's own, and to this alone the honorific name of science appertains. What an audacious thesis! But can the generic concept of evolution be preempted for a particular species of progressive order such as Hegel imposes upon the phenomenal forms of cognition? And is the gradual advance from natural to philosophic forms, which he promises to exhibit in the text to follow, interpretable as taking place in time? Such questions, though not strictly relevant at present, I cannot refrain from raising if I am to enter without too much confusion upon Hegel's task.

Meredy: I doubt whether the word evolution is here altogether appropriate. Post-Hegelian in origin, its biological connotation has acquired a certain paramountcy. The sequence of cognitive forms treated in the text is due to a process of selection more philosophical than natural, in the sense Hegel gives to these terms. Nor can their logical succession be always made to tally with their historical. But this is a topic hardly germane to our present discussion. The main point now demanding attention, though in but a preliminary way, is the nature of the subject matter covered in the treatise together with the method governing its development. Incidentally, the concept of development has the advantage over that of evolution in being more comprehensive and thus more neutral. At any rate, let us postpone queries that cannot be dealt with until we observe Hegel's method at work.

Hardith: Very well! In precipitating issues clearly premature, what chiefly excited my interest was the method deliberately designed for the study of the forms of knowledge in their intermutation; and it matters greatly whether the advance from one form to another could or could not be shown to represent a temporal process. For the time being, however, let that pass. That the method is to be called dialectical we glean from the Preface. But the Introduction accords to it special consideration and prepares the ground for its detailed application. How should the contents of Hegel's work be envisaged as generative of situations under dialectical direction and control? Of this we must have some grasp however tenuous.

Meredy: If the study we are to engage in is of knowledge as it flourishes 'naturally', the method pertinent to it is dictated by the description of such knowledge as apparent, a term exceedingly useful in indicating the *via negativa,* so to speak, followed throughout the *Phenomenology.* For the method is one of doubt if apparent knowledge is to cease being so in one sense (as obviously true) and is to remain apparent in another sense (as speciously true), the method as sceptical

11

having for its aim the demonstration that what initially appears self-evident must appear subsequently self-inconsistent. There is in the text a sentence which tersely declares that philosophic endeavor consists in achieving the *bewusste Einsicht in die Unwahrheit des erscheinenden Wissens*. This is a wonderful epitome of scepticism as a necessary antidote to the supposititious claim that the only true knowledge is seeming knowledge.

Hardith: The sentence is so extreme in condemnation as 'untruth' of all 'apparent' knowledge that the 'insight' prescribed goes far beyond mere scepticism. Is not the word a misnomer? Taken at face value, the epigram, if regarded as such, may be used in support of complete nihilism, so sweeping is the denial of the claim to truth for any persuasion bred in natural consciousness.

Meredy: A pertinent comment, Hardith, but again somewhat premature. Yet what you say accurately represents the feelings of those whose tendency to identify the apparent with the evident is so natural. The method can hardly strike ordinary thought as anything but maliciously negative, the purpose being to induce in it doubt or despair regarding everything such thought is in the habit of taking for granted. (Hegel's tendency to pun is worth noting; the words here played upon are *Zweifel* and *Verzweiflung*.) But from the standpoint of the philosophic critic, apt as he is to equate the apparent with the specious, the method is not only salutary but indispensable. For it is this method alone which can show that the true course of knowledge is not straightforward but one to which untrue ways are essential. As for scepticism, Hegel is careful to note that what he advocates, though offensive to natural consciousness, is the very leaven of philosophic activity. Negation of the apparent (recognition as specious of the seemingly evident) implies affirmation of the nonapparent (acknowledgement as genuine of what often contravenes ordinary thought). "The exhibition of untrue consciousness in its untruth," as Hegel insists, "is not merely a negative process." That scepticism which culminates in wholesale negation, being a sort of blind alley into which men are led by yielding without resistance to the seductive power of doubt, is one of the reflective experiments to be tried and overcome in the course of the *Phenomenology*. The scepticism urged by Hegel is not an impasse but an expedient; it is a tentative *way* which constructive reason must follow and not a final *state* in which it can rest. Such scepticism is specific or qualified (Hegel characterizes it as determinate); it is addressed to particular forms of human persuasion whose claims to truth are shown to be false claims, and, accordingly, must not be confused with universal or unqualified scepticism inimical to all truth.

Hardith: Am I to think then of the method as one which is both negative and constructive, being, like Shelley's West Wind, "destroyer and preserver"? It is a strange procedure that depends for its use on operations so mutually exclusive.

Meredy: No, not mutually exclusive but mutually implicative. The acts of subverting and rebuilding Hegel considers complementary. Real knowledge is but another name for apparent knowledge purged of presumption and transfigured into truth. Exclusive emphasis on the purgative operation ignores the regenerative power Hegel ascribes to the principle of negativity. Scepticism of one form of apparent knowledge entails of necessity transition to a new form in which the meaning of the old survives. The dialectical development of every stage of knowledge signifies both its supersession and rebirth, so that in the entire movement of truth nothing is fixed and nothing is lost. Of this fertile method, which is able to save appearances by negating them, the *Phenomenology* is designed to furnish a detailed exposition and justification.

Hardith: One aspect of the sceptico-positive method, to name it thus, still baffles me. Since it is a method for examining the claims of apparent knowledge some standard is clearly requisite for guiding the examination. Could claims to truth be tested in the absence of a valid criterion? If there is no such criterion at all, the testing of knowledge becomes a useless exercise. If the criterion is but assumed, its validity is merely that of a dogmatic assurance always open to criticism. In the light of Hegel's animadversion upon all assumptions and presuppositions the problem becomes crucial. How begin with a standard not reducible to conjecture or caprice?

Meredy: The difficulty you express is formidable, and one which appears insurmountable from the standpoint of abstract epistemology. Hegel circumvents the difficulty by his approach to knowledge as given, and given, as it were, in standardized form. Instead of testing knowledge in relation to a criterion posited in advance, a procedure manifestly precluded without assuming as legitimate the chosen criterion, Hegel accepts the standard inherent in apparent knowledge, and with reference to that standard, and to it alone, he asks whether the alternative is truth or untruth. Dismissing as futile the question of whether this or that standard be accorded supremacy, he simply disengages the tests to which adherents of apparent knowledge themselves would be willing to submit their claims. This procedure enables Hegel to remain inside the circle of apparent knowledge, assuming nothing except what such knowledge itself assumes, and judging such knowledge by means of norms not imported from without. The dialectical method, as Hegel

13

conceives it, is thus essentially, if I may say so, a method of boring from within, and what it delves into is the complex of knowledge as a phenomenon one of whose constituents is the criterion of its own truth.

Hardith: What an ingenious attempt to look in the phenomenon of knowledge itself for a criteriology indigenous to it! But precisely what is the criterion said to be empirically given with the very occurrence of knowledge?

Meredy: The answer is not simple. We must bear in mind that the cognitive situation involves as such a certain relation between some given 'object' and the 'conception' formed of it. About the real nature of the relation and of the terms in that relation no true statement is initially possible; at the beginning of the inquiry, if we are to follow Hegel's procedure, we must take the cognitive situation just as it *appears*. Now it is natural consciousness, whose point of view we are here to adopt, which, in claiming to *have* knowledge, claims also that its knowledge is *true*. And what can such claim rest on if not the affirmation that between object and conception the relation is one of concordance or congruity (or correspondence, if the word be used in a sense rather neutral than doctrinary)? Here then is the standard which natural consciousness itself invokes for appraising the truth of its presumptive knowledge: it is a standard not superimposed upon the cognitive situation from without but one latent in every appearance of it. The claim to true knowledge, whenever and however the claim is made, can thus mean nothing else than the claim that a certain conception agrees with its object. Accordingly, if it could be shown that the conception is such as to demand a different object or the object a different conception, the original claim would collapse, resulting in the emergence of a new situation in which object and conception must appear in a revised shape. And it is precisely the aim of the dialectic to effect in natural consciousness, in conformity with its own standard, continual shifts of position with respect to the content and form of knowledge. Given the phenomenon called knowledge, which represents a conscious linkage of two terms proffered as inalienable because of their alleged mutual adequacy, all the dialectic has to do is to alienate the two terms from each other by showing that the reciprocal congruity claimed for them is in fact purely specious. Not extraneous, therefore, is the test by the sceptico-positive method, for it consists in examining the allegation of compatibility between object and conception, these being the factors of which the cognitive situation is the resultant, an allegation coeval with the appearance of knowledge as its own measure of truth.

14

Hardith: As you interpret the method, its application would seem to presuppose a certain attitude difficult to assume. What I mean may be stated quite simply. Consider the standard of truth immanent in every appearance of knowledge. How can the standard's putative validity be made to reveal its inherent speciousness? Not unless we initially adopt the standard as if it were our own, approaching it with sympathy as well as with detachment. For only such a posture can induce us to lay aside our prepossessions for the sake of discovering what is indigenous to every cognitive situation soliciting inquiry. Yes, our own fancies and opinions, Hegel demands, must ever be kept at bay. Indeed, true impartiality, granting the philosopher's desire for it, must rest on the dual capacity to view a thing from within and from without—capacity to enter into its singular states and movements and capacity to occupy a position from which to survey the conditions and consequences of its behavior. To see it entirely from within is to disregard the point of view of the disinterested onlooker; to contemplate it completely from without is to miss what intimate experience alone can vouch for. Impartiality thus conceived hinges on a sort of rhythmic alternation of intuition and observation, the first bent upon the inwardness of the appearance, the second upon watching its comportment. Am I right in thinking that none but minds capable of such alternation can pursue the dialectical method?

Meredy: You have hit the nail on the head. The method does call for the alternation you speak of but you speak of it in an idiom not quite conducive to bring out fully Hegel's contention. The word 'experimental' suggests, I think, better than any other, the alternation in question if we choose to extend its application to products of the intellect, such as the Germans include under the name of *Gedankenexperimente.* For thought may obviously subject to trial a specific work of thought. Indeed, we always do this whenever we attend to an argument asserted to be valid. How arrive at an opinion concerning its validity unless we first seek to understand the argument by yielding to its standpoint, adhering to its premises, reproducing its context, making it, in short, for the time being our own? Only after having seized the argument from within may doubt arise concerning its claim to truth, provided the evidence for the claim, as appraised from without, be found wanting in adequacy. The invitation to heed an argument is an invitation to perform a reflective experiment, entailing alternation of two acts, the alternation of appreciative insight and deliberate vigilance. An experimental attitude of this sort Hegel requires that we assume before we approach the subject matter of the *Phenomenology,* prescribing that no idea or belief be considered untrue unless we first preempt it vicariously or that

15

every idea or belief be grasped from its own perspective as precedent condition of criticism.

Hardith: Choice of the word 'experimental' must have been prompted by your desire to emphasize the undogmatic nature of the dialectic. We gather from the Introduction that the urge to examine on its merits every appearance of knowledge cannot be satisfied by means of prior assurances which Hegel dismisses as barren. One assurance rebuking another may in turn be impugned by a third, each a matter of faith or bias. The experimentalism you associate with the dialectic seemingly serves as antidote to dogmatism. The investigation of knowledge, if conceived as proceeding under the direction and control of the experimental mode of procedure, might thus be set free from challengeable assumptions. If Hegel's theory of knowledge depends for its deduction not on first principles deemed axiomatic but on the sequence of progressive operations instead, might not the method requisite for establishing the theory be called experimental rather than dialectical? Descriptive as they are of the same procedure, the two adjectives become virtually interchangeable.

Meredy: A pertinent point, this, but hardly debatable at present. For the moment we are only concerned with a preliminary approach to the text as indicated for our guidance in the Introduction. The clue to that approach lies in the subject matter conceived as natural knowledge, and in the injunction not to read into it our prejudices. We are called upon to accept at their face value the ways of cognition such as they appear with the stamp of truth upon them in the course of human experience. What induces consequent criticism as well as revision of these appearances is the discovery, made in the process of testing them by their own standard, that their claims to truth are illusory claims. Thus crucial is the role of the experimenter: in the laboratory of his mind, so to speak, he must reconstruct specific phenomena in order to watch their modes of behavior.

Hardith: The experimenter is of course Hegel or anyone else choosing to engage in the same inquiry by the same method. Can it seriously be maintained that operations performed in the laboratory of one's mind, to use your arresting phrase, are uninfluenced by what induces them or by that to which they are conducive? The phenomenological argument seems to be generable without overt presuppositions or predictive consequences. But this only seems so. Indispensable is always some hypothesis setting any experiment in motion and some prophecy of the result definitive of its success. Hegel's dialectical experimentation, if such it be, is no exception; it too is begotten of surmise of ends in view. It involves two complementary acts, to wit, reconstruction of the phenomena to be observed and observation of the phenomena thus reconstructed. *How* should their reconstruction be achieved and *what* is to be discerned in them? Here as elsewhere some prior notion of the manner in which and the objectives for which experiments are instituted would seem to be necessary.

Meredy: You have your finger on a critical issue touching the nature of Hegel's methodology. Hegel does scant justice to a subject so central. The Introduction conveys his meaning too tersely and in the terms of the very argument in behalf of which the method is to be employed. Nevertheless, if in the light of some foreknowledge of the text, we substitute for his special idiom a diction less obscure and more flexible, we may, after a fashion, succeed in clarifying as well as deepening the dialectical process. As regards your query, namely, how an appearance of cognition is to be reproduced and what we should discern in it, the language of art, and especially dramatic art, would clearly be a more suitable medium for dealing with it than the language of science on which you set so much store.

Hardith: I find it difficult to attach much sense to the idea of experimentation when deprived of its affiliation with scientific procedure. It is but by the grace of analogy that the dialectical method may be construed as experimental. Unless viewed as comparable to an operation designed for confirming a scientific hypothesis, the operation usually performed within the precinct of a physical laboratory, the word is obviously a misnomer. The laboratory of the mind—the felicitous metaphor is yours—to what can it be likened if not to a workroom, as it were, set aside for testing hypotheses by trial and error?

Meredy: Ah, but you forget that mind serves as laboratory in which the experiments performed are not strictly analogous to scientific. The manner of reproducing the phenomenon of knowledge, the phenomenon in each case being a unique persuasion, is comparable more to the actor's part of impersonation than to laboratorial behavior of the scientist. The actor's performance, described as histrionic, involves an experiment in vicariousness. Concealing his real self behind an alien mask, and assuming with fidelity the appearance of another being, the actor is required, as the saying goes, to play a part. He must mimic a personality not his own, and in this consists the histrionic experiment. It is an experiment deemed successful only if, seizing a given character from within, the actor is able to identify himself for the moment with the inner life of the dramatis persona he is called upon to portray. In the illusion of identity between himself and his role lies the test of the actor's performance, an illusion dispelled only when, the play being over, he appears without his assumed mask to receive the plaudits for his deft experiment in simulation.

17

Hardith: May I interrupt to ask how the illusion of identity induced by histrionic effort differs from the sort of illusion belonging to the very essence of the impersonated phenomenon of cognition, the illusion of being true in accordance with its own criterion of truth? One thing is illusion created by art, quite another is natural illusion, so to speak, to which every particular form of cognition is subject.

Meredy: You are anticipating. Our present task is but to see how the various appearances of cognition are reproducible as objects of critical study. The illusion of identity between the actor and his part suggests one aspect of Hegel's method, the phenomenological investigator having no other subject matter than the apparent ways of knowing successively enactable in verisimilar fashion. Without intrusion of his own predilections and preferences, he must reconstruct his phenomena in the manner in which they appear to themselves, as it were, 'suiting the action to the word and the word to the action'. Running throughout the *Phenomenology* is the distinction between what a thing is 'for itself' and what it is 'for us'. What it is *für uns,* the external critics, is not the measure of its intrinsic nature; before passing judgment, we must first discover what it is *für sich.* Accordingly, requisite for relevant criticism is always provisional congruence with the object of it. Suppose, for example, the empiricism grounded in the immediacy of sense-experience is what we are bent upon examining. The outsider's conception of it can scarce be accepted as authentic. The only true version of empiricism is the empiricist's. To perceive things as he does, we must see them through his eyes, react to them in his ways, accommodate our words to his impressions, and adapt our meanings to his ideas. Unless we vicariously assume his characteristic position our understanding of the empiricist as he appears to himself remains precluded. And this is precisely Hegel's endeavor. He delineates an extreme type of empiricism (with the impersonation of which the *Phenomenology* begins) in its own idiom, representing it as if speaking 'for itself'. The simulation of identity between the impersonator and the impersonated continues until the very histrionic effort leads to the exhibition of the empirical persuasion's inward discrepancy. What is true of empiricism is true of every subsequent persuasion. Each to be understood must first be impersonated, and only as histrionically recreated can its inherent self-inconsistency be made manifest.

Hardith: I am somewhat disturbed by the theatrical metaphor you are inclined to press so hard. The illusion of identity, achievement of which may indeed characterize the actor's endeavor in relation to his part, is a phrase open to misunderstanding when made to apply to a philosophic method. The epithet 'illusion', generally used in a pejorative sense, cannot be associated with Hegel's dialectic without courting prejudice. Should it be said of his mode of procedure that its employment demands experiments in deceit? How reconcile with intellectual integrity specious vindications of specious truth-claims? Why not express the matter in terms less extravagant and not quite so liable to criticism? I have in mind the notion of the 'as if', upon which Kant's dialectic depends, a notion fictional (feigned) without being fictitious (deceptive). There is no scandal in make-believe as a methodological device; its operation is pervasive, and its value pragmatic. Who does not on occasion and for argument's sake readily entertain as if credible beliefs patently doubtful or even downright false? All this may possibly strike you as but verbal punctiliousness.

Meredy: Your allusion to Kant is quite apposite. You tend, however, to draw too sharp a contrast between illusion and fiction. Between Kant's dialectic and Hegel's there are similarities as well as differences. But this is a topic not strictly relevant here. Yet, I must remind you of Kant's reduction to illusions, though he describes them as 'transcendental', of all doubtful persuasions adhered to as if demonstrably true. Such persuasions, being for Kant species of make-believe, become fictitious instead of fictional, to borrow your apt distinction, whenever they are extended beyond theoretically permissible limits, an extension which he holds to be both inevitable and incorrigible. Fiction and illusion are thus terms not inequatable in meaning. Be that as it may, Hegel's dialectic may be regarded as hinging on two distinct kinds of illusion. One is histrionic, a form of make-believe, phenomenological inquiry demanding that every persuasion examined be impersonated as if true. The other is the illusion inherent in every impersonated persuasion, its truth-claim being provably specious by its own standard of truth. No persuasion can satisfy the criterion that between the object and the idea of it the relation exhibits complete congruity.

Hardith: The word congruity seems well chosen to throw an oblique light on the sorts of illusion you speak of. Deliberately contrived, histrionic illusion lies in the feigned identity between the impersonation of persuasions, and the persuasions impersonated. But the mutual correspondence of object and idea, the alleged basis of every persuasion's claim to truth, is an illusion not created but discovered. I am beginning to see the relevance of your theatrical image. Whereas the method of impersonating given persuasions, comparable to the actor's method in relation to his parts, requires that they be initially portrayed as if self-consistent and self-sufficient, the method of disclosing their latent tensions and conflicts demands that the direction be reversed and that their putatively credible self-sufficiency and self-

19

consistency be discredited as fictitious. Recreation of persuasions in their native hue, so to speak, is one thing, another is exhibition of their covert incongruities. In its first function the dialectic resembles histrionic art, in its second comic art. If it is the intent of the dialectic to impersonate the incongruous, the logic of the *Phenomenology* would seem to be the logic of comedy par excellence. Is this view tenable?

Meredy: Admirable, Hardith, admirable! Yes, the word comic fittingly describes the sequence of situations generated by the dialectical method. The Introduction clearly intimates what the *Phenomenology* is headed for: it is to disclose the incongruous features latent in particular claims to incontrovertible truth. And if all comedy has for its aim disclosure of the incongruous in human character and comportment, the *Phenomenology,* judged as literary product, strange though the application of the adjective be to Hegel's style, designedly reflects a vision of the life of mind seen in comic perspective, a vision encyclopedic in scope and singular in detachment. For it devolves upon the dialectic to uncover the absurdity of the particular masquerading as universal and to unmask the folly of drawing the whole to the scale of the part; the power that makes for organic unity lies in the very method of exposing to ridicule persuasions put forward as exclusive or privileged. But the logical illusion inherent in partial or prerogative claims to truth furnishes, as it were, its own logical catharsis: recognition of self-contradiction must perforce be followed by retraction. This Socratic postulate, governing the construction of comedy when deeply conceived, dominates Hegel's method. The *Phenomenology* is a sort of comedy of errors ingeniously devised to serve as 'deduction' of organic truth. And in Hegel's comedy, too, the incongruities exposed are visible, not to those who enact them, but only to those watching them as spectators. Comic figures, not perceiving what goes on "behind their backs," to use Hegel's expression, are unaware of their own folly. The absurdity of their ways, so transparent to us, is not apparent to them. Successive impersonation of types of persuasion as comic, comic because they betray to us the contradictions hidden from their adherents, this is the task Hegel assigns to the dialectical method.

Hardith: Serious thinkers, apt to look askance at the Comic Muse, will not be pleased with such an unwonted if not wanton treatment of Hegel's dialectic. The specialists in particular will scornfully dismiss it as travesty. But our lay undertaking, seeking to make Hegel's 'caviare to the general' generally palatable, can of course not compete with the exegetical labors of the learned. Besides, there is a saying of Socrates at the end of the *Symposium* that the genius of tragedy and of comedy is the same. If Hegel's *Phenomenology* is likened to comedy soberly construed, there is no scandal in the comparison, and we may proceed without fear of pedantic criticism. This, however, is not the point that needs to be raised at present. What now does call for clarification is Hegel's cryptic equation made in the Introduction between dialectic and experience. Surely, the term cannot be used without qualification. If the dialectical movement consists in alternation of histrionic reproduction and comic observation, is it not a movement that only a special kind of experience can exemplify? That all experience, taken in a universal sense, involves a process of rational transition and growth, in which objects and conceptions become progressively modified in accordance with the method of trial and supersedure, this is either an assumption or a deduction. If the former, it is clearly inadmissible; Hegel himself condemns every assumption as mere assurance without intrinsic worth. If the latter, it has no probative force prior to its development, the initial statement being in fact indistinguishable from an assumption. If Hegel's method is to be followed, any advance view of experience as a whole would seem gratuitous and impertinent. What then does it mean to speak of the dialectic as a dialectic of experience?

Meredy: Once again you focus attention on a critical matter. Hegel's statement touching on the dialectic of experience is indeed without warrant if the dialectic is what in the Introduction he says it is. The only experience that can be experienced as dialectical is the experience of the investigator. He it is who in examining the appearances of persuasion must broach them in alternate ways. The consciousness wedded to specious truth-claims can obviously not qualify as dialectical, unaware as it is of the speciousness detectable only by 'us' and 'behind its back'. Dialectical experience, in short, is a supervenient one, supervening, that is, upon a singular mode of experimentation, that embodied in the impersonation of types of consciousness ignorant of their inherent fallaciousness, and only in this kind of experience is the power of negativity triumphant, scepticism becoming the road to truth and comedy the vehicle of reason. Nothing is here so important as the distinction between the consciousness of the experimenter and the consciousness experimented with, the latter being completely unconscious of cutting a comic figure in the eyes of the former. Only the experimenter has the awareness that his 'subject' is self-deceived and that self-deception is both inevitable and sublatable. And if none but an experience enjoying such awareness may be called dialectical, it is an experience clearly reserved for the 'subject' conducting the experiment and not for the 'subject' submitted to it. The thesis, even if finally defensible, that an absolute subject expresses itself in all the incongruous forms of natural consciousness, and that the dialectical exposition of these forms in

21

the *Phenomenology* constitutes a replica of the experience of a super-human mind, is not relevant for the purpose of setting in motion Hegel's experiment. That experiment, be the outcome what it may, is initially Hegel's and not God's, and it is not God but Hegel who lays down the conditions for its proper execution, these being histrionic intuition and comic analysis. To conform to them one must alternately be actor and spectator. Nothing else than such alternation renders experience dialectical. And where should we look for its occurrence if not in a consciousness able to make the experiment in the manner prescribed by Hegel?

Hardith: Our preliminary task, I take it, has now been accomplished and we now pass from the general to the specific. Hegel's prefatory and introductory remarks, though important, are after all extraneous. His method, however explained in comprehensive fashion, has no validity prior to its application to the subject matter proposed for inquiry. The initial experiment conducted in the *Phenomenology* by a method so singular calls for particular scrutiny. Here if anywhere the first step is decisive. I am now prepared to move into the text, seeking to grasp the incipient argument on its own terms.

Meredy: I am glad we need discuss no further the problem of Hegel's starting point. In attempting to understand what the treatise actually begins with, we must, if I may say so, accept it *on* but not *in* its terms. Above all, we must avoid predetermining the validity of the result. Thus to follow in the wake of Hegel's voyage of discovery, allowing neither his bias nor our own to influence the issue, is to proceed in the true spirit of intellectual adventure.

PART I

CONSCIOUSNESS

Sense-Certainty

1. The Initial Experiment

Hardith: I have carefully perused the opening section devoted to the experiment with a type of consciousness purely sensuous. Hegel's name for it is *Die sinnliche Gewissheit* for which the hyphened expression sense-certainty must serve as English equivalent. The initial type of experience seems as if made to order for exemplifying in impressive fashion the operation of the dialectical method. The analysis is governed by the histrionic illusion between actual and vicarious experience, and the section may thus not inaccurately be read as a dialogue carried on between a defender of the faith in the senses and a critic of such faith. The interchange of positions regarding the meaning and validity of sensory awareness constitutes the contrapuntal pattern upon which the comedy of the situation chiefly depends: the positions advanced in the face of opposition turn out to be progressively unstable and hence untenable. The interlocution, in other words, is between sense-certainty as if speaking 'for itself' and what it signifies 'for us'. But before going into this further, I should like to raise the question of priority. Why must sense-certainty head the series of cognitive phenomena? To what does it owe its choice as initial experiment? Is it first in the order of time or first in the order of evidence? If the *Phenomenology* is concerned not with historical genesis but with dialectical generation, whose arguments for sense-certainty is he impersonating? Whence the necessity of stating the arguments in the terms in which Hegel chooses to state them?

Meredy: The first section, though providing a clear example of the dialectic in its histrionic function, is indeed crucial. The impersonation of sense-certainty as a distinct form of human persuasion is not without verisimilitude so long as we do not confuse phenomenology with history or psychology, both disciplines having for their determinate subject matter specific facts or events. The subject matter of Hegel's work, as will be shown later, is deeply rooted in the generic; such extreme empiricism, for example, as treated at the outset, represents a persuasion encountered in different versions and in different contexts always and everywhere.

Incidentally, I suggest that we think of persuasion as a concept extensible to the ideas and beliefs forming the contents of the *Phenomenology*. What Hegel explores, as the title indicates, is mind, but mind as a generic subject involved in every kind of persuasion. It is convenient to have a single concept comprehending under it not only the varieties of experience commonly considered cognitive but also such from which the votaries of certain abstract theories of knowledge have seen fit to withdraw the adjective. In the *Phenomenology* knowledge and experience are held to be virtually interchangeable, awareness or feeling *of* anything having a cognitive import. Persuasions in the realm of art and religion, for instance, will later be found to be ways of experience with truth-claims, claims based on the alleged congruity between object and idea. But the topic cannot be broached at present.

You ask, to return to your question, why the experiment with sense-certainty should enjoy priority. But with what else, having regard to Hegel's undertaking, should the work have begun? In the absence of first principles, disavowed in the Introduction, what cognition could take precedence over immediate awareness? It is natural for natural consciousness, so to speak, to yield to the suasion of direct experience. 'Seeing is believing', a cliché as well as a dogma, epitomizes a cognitive security impervious to reflection and doubt. If the area of inquiry is the area Hegel defines as natural consciousness, sense-certainty has presumptive primacy, not on grounds of actual genesis or logical proof, but only on grounds of simplicity and artlessness. Sense-certainty, in a word, may be said to outrank all human persuasions in complacent credulity. Prior to experimentation with persuasions less gullible or more sophisticated, the comedy of immediacy, latent in sense purged of thought, must first be brought to light.

Hardith: There is of course nothing comic in the belief—or persuasion, if you like—that the senses are the original vehicles of experience, no matter how the word 'original' be construed. And as such the senses do actually appear to us when by an effort of the will we succeed in keeping abeyant judgment and inference. But seldom if ever can the senses function in pure isolation. What you speak of as sense 'purged of thought' does not appear to be an authentic phenomenon of natural consciousness. When is the immediacy of sensations or impressions not invaded or disturbed by other mental events? How impersonate such

25

immediacy? And whose defense of its claim to truth is the impersonation to be modeled on?

Meredy: The purity of sensuous cognition may be related to the act of reduction as well as to that of reproduction. Hence the difficulty you register. What we are bidden to impersonate is a state of mind as if it could be enjoyed either before reflection has appeared on the scene or after it has been deliberately suspended. The experiment with natural consciousness reduced to the sensory level is a speculative experiment. And to reproduce sense-certainty in supposititious isolation, we must examine it from within, without importing into it elements drawn from prior or subsequent ideation. We should distort sense-certainty if we failed to represent it as singularly concrete and indubitably true. For the empiricist's contention is precisely this, that there is nothing more palpable than objects open to sensibility, and nothing more veridical than direct awareness of them. Achievement of histrionic verisimilitude requires that, abandoning all interpretation, we naïvely accept whatever happens to impinge upon our sensibility here and now. To be is to be sensibly present, as it were, and nothing can thus vie with sensuous cognition in richness and fullness. The world does indeed continually flood our senses with new impressions, there being no limits to the permanent possibility of sensations save the limits of space and time.

Hardith: A philosopher pretending to be naïve—what a remarkable pose! Yet such is the pose exacted by the histrionic method of assuming the attitude of another mind and of simulating a character actually alien. Feigning a consciousness not one's own, a consciousness reduced to a sensorium, the attempt must be made to draw the world to its scale and to acquiesce without question in the deliverances of immediate awareness. This if carried out in detail, as the *Phenomenology* fails to do, would reveal the life of mind at a sub-ideational level seldom seriously broached. George Santayana, in *Scepticism and Animal Faith,* superbly performs this feat: the theme of immediacy, culminating in what he calls "the solipsism of the present moment," appears in his work with sundry variations conveyed through empathetic and mellifluous prose. Hegel is not so impartial as you present him. He is interested more in the comedy than the impersonation of this type of experience, and the comedy seemingly dictates the terms of its reduction and reproduction.

Meredy: Impartiality, my dear fellow, is a *rara avis* among philosophers. Who does not, consciously or unconsciously, distort other men's ideas when rendering them in his own idiom to serve his purpose? But this is beside the point. Hegel, it is true, impersonates sensuous cognition in a manner suitable for the disclosure of its inherent comedy.

26

How incongruous is the boast of concreteness and fullness attributed to it! As a matter of fact, no experience is so abstract and so vacuous as that which is said to occur at the level of pure immediacy. For an experience from which thought is excluded—and its exclusion distinguishes the certainty of sense *as* sensuous—can never be certain (and this is the irony) *what* it is certain of. Ascription of characters is the work of judgment here suspended. Precluded from qualifying its object, the certainty of sense is the certainty of nothing specific. Until thought supervenes, the content of sensuous experience must needs remain amorphous. All that one can do in its presence is to stare and exclaim— Here it *is!* There is *this!* What swims into one's ken is but the indeterminate being of something without local or temporal relations. Nothing indeed can describe it except the auxiliary verb reduced to its present tense. It just *is*.

The same applies to the mind aware of its objects whose indefinite being constitutes their sole nature. The word 'I' by which a mind affirms its existence indicates a particular individual, one specimen among many, with a describable characteristic nature. Here, too, we must presuppose discernment of differences and comparison of affinities, acts clearly reflective, before the word can acquire any such meaning. No mind conceived as mere sensorium could possibly avail itself of the term 'I'. At the level of pure sense, the vagueness of the object and the vagueness of the subject are completely matched. Since consciousness of the specific depends upon thought, a consciousness from which thought is absent remains but a sensitive register of unspecifiable impressions. One *this* dimly aware of another *this*—thus, according to Hegel, must sensuousness be described by us when in histrionic fashion we identify ourselves with its alleged position. Only in language—and in this lies the comedy—most abstract and poverty-stricken can we express a mode of experience presumed to flaunt its concreteness and wealth.

Hardith: Whence the necessity of impersonating sense-certainty as comic? The dialectic foreshadowed would seem to hinge on nothing else than a factitious dialect, so to speak, for rendering sensuousness inevitably incongruous. Sensuousness is not comic except for us when through the medium of discourse the dice are loaded against it from the start. In translating sensuousness in the locution of thought we force it deliberately into contradiction; so to translate it is simply to abolish its immediacy. Immediacy transferred to the plane of discourse is patently absurd but the absurdity lies in the attempted transference. How could an experience be convicted out of its own mouth if it remains speechless? We who speak for it commit the fallacy of holding

27

sensuousness responsible for the implications of a language to which it need not be committed. In other words, sensuousness is untenable only when reproduced through a nonsensuous medium.

2. The Interrogatory Procedure

Meredy: You show with considerable force how wide is the gap between what sensuousness is 'for itself' and what it is 'for us'. Not in sense-experience as such is the comic to be detected but only in the alleged contention of its certainty, a contention repeatedly advanced in sundry forms. Hegel simply collects into a type the variously expressed persuasions, found in ordinary as well as in philosophic consciousness, that sense-experience is the sure foundation of true knowledge. Silent sense-experience is invulnerable precisely because the argument for its certitude is not open to debate. What we are called upon to do is to perform the imaginative experiment of interrogating a would-be defender of the claims for immediacy. Only thus may the incongruity of the claims be revealed to rest on the confusion, if I may so put it, between sense-certainty and sense-credulity.

Hardith: Very well! Let us proceed then with the inquiry into such claims as a loquacious adherent might be induced to support. How should the interrogatory experiment begin?

Meredy: Hegel prepares the ground for the experiment by two important considerations. In the first place, we must convince our imaginary interrogatee that sensory awareness, not unlike any other, involves a transaction between the subject of the awareness and its object. No cognition at all without these polar terms in reciprocal relation. The hyphen in the English word 'sense-certainty' graphically illustrates the conjunction of a duality, signifying true apprehension *by* a mind *of* its sensuous deliverances. The very nature of the cognitive situation, no matter how simple, requires that the act of knowing and the knowable datum remain distinct as well as united. Of this truth our interrogatee can be persuaded only if he is unable to exhibit a single case exemplary of the sensuous immediacy he advocates. We thus pass, in the second place, to the evocation of such a case, remembering that the certainty of sense can be genuine solely in a given example, whenever *this* content, and *only* this, manifests its presence to *this* mind, and to this *alone*. Dependence of sense-experience upon particularity would seem ineluctable: whatever object falls within the compass of that experience must possess a specific character in virtue of which it is this object and no other. And here precisely is where our interrogatee will prove vulnerable. If no particular could be indicated, *this* object always turning into *any* object and *this* mind into *any* mind, would there not be lacking a specific datum to contemplate and a specific psyche to enjoy the contemplation? Where the specific is absent, where anybody is aware anywhen and anywhere of anything, we have experience in the abstract, the very opposite of what sense-certainty is presumed to represent. Change of this particular to any particular, whether the particular refer to subject or object, would deprive sense-certainty of sensuousness as well as of certitude. Thus crucial are both considerations: all awareness, sense-certainty not excepted, involves the distinction and relation between subject and object; and sense-certainty stands or falls with the possibility of specifying the particularity pertaining to the apprehending mind and its apprehended data.

Hardith: Differentiation and specification are discursive acts destructive of immediacy, and to ask a champion of sense-certainty to engage in such acts is virtually to call for his self-destruction. Sense-certainty cast in alien form becomes its own other, immediacy and language being mutually exclusive. Why condemn sense-certainty to self-alienation, seeing that it need not be betrayed into utterance. If its ineffable nature be granted, if sense-certainty be held impervious to the syntax of diction, whence the contradiction?

Meredy: You anticipate the conclusion—indeed, the climax—of the interrogatory experiment. The dilemma precipitated by the experiment is formidable: sense-certainty must culminate in nonsense or silence. Silence precludes or ends all discussion: in saying nothing, sense-certainty can of course not be gainsaid. But silence is one thing, argument for silence quite another. What you contend for, foreseeing the outcome of the experiment, is not speechlessness but the rationale of its necessity. This rationale our interrogatee must ultimately adopt, but only after exhausting the resources of discourse to render sense-certainty articulate.

Hardith: I am sorry to move towards the conclusion by skipping the intermediary steps leading to it. We must now consider these steps in detail. And since the structure of this section so notably resembles the structure of a dialogue, let me undertake to play the part of spokesman for sense-certainty. I shall attempt to be faithful to the text in answering the questions you choose to put forward.

Meredy: Your action as interlocutor in a sort of dialogue within a dialogue will obviate the necessity of constant reference to an imaginary interrogatee, a word I have no particular liking for. Before broaching the question of whether an example of sense-certainty is producible, I must remind you of the reflective distinctions presupposed for it. We can of course not specify a case of immediacy unless we first separate its essential aspect from its nonessential. Since all awareness

29

involves the *inter*play of subject and object—and how pregnant is here the prefix!—immediacy of sensory awareness can inhere in only one of the two terms. But where should it be looked for? Should we deem immediate the content of awareness or the state of being aware? Open to choice is either alternative. Which do you prefer to try first?

Hardith: I am inclined to invest with primary immediacy an ostensive object, one palpably and unequivocally here and now, the subject having a derivative status in the cognitive situation. The state of being aware would seem to be secondary to what occasions or conditions it. No sense-certainty in the absence of a specific datum generating its proper sensation. The occurrence of the sensation is contingent upon some prior object serving as stimulus; the object itself simply *is,* and its *being* is independent of the sensation it arouses. The certainty is *of* something rather than *by* someone; the accent should thus fall on that which appears and not on the psyche affected by it. Such a position, to give it a name, is that of a naïve realism, the adjective to be construed in a literal sense.

Meredy: The name does not matter but the position does. To be tenable, the position must be made to rest on verifiable evidence. A sensuous immediacy not leaning on introspection invites public proof. He who argues for sense-certainty, not because he enjoys intimate sensations, but because he contemplates external objects, must be able to indicate their presence, so that another individual possessed of the same organs and perspective would find what he finds. Now sense-certainty has to be 'asked', insists Hegel, to reveal what it endows with objective immediacy and I am asking you, acting as its mouthpiece, to meet the issue. What object do you take to be directly given? What particular is fixed as this and no other? What specifically appears to you as here and now?

Hardith: These are loaded questions worded to make a foregone conclusion inevitable. But no matter, I shall answer in conformity with my chosen role. Assuming that what is objectively immediate must always appear here and now, you demand that I exhibit data to which these two tags may significantly be affixed. Well, let me attend to the temporal label first. To the question, 'what is now?', I simply reply, in the naïve spirit of natural consciousness, that 'now is nighttime', since you chance to interrogate me at this moment. Of course, the answer would differ in accordance with the time of the interrogation. To your question, therefore, *whenever* you choose to raise it, I shall always have a response in terms of an immediate apprehension.

Meredy: Ah, but here's precisely the rub. The word 'now' obviously loses fixity of meaning if it can occur in different contexts and in different relations. To prove the catholicity of application the term enjoys, Hegel resorts to a curious stratagem. Of the statement that 'now is nighttime', a written record can be made for the retention of its truth. (Hegel plays upon the words *wahr* and *aufbewahren,* implying that the true does not forfeit its truth by being preserved.) But another statement, likewise recorded, namely, that 'now is noontime', renders the previous one obsolete. And this statement too becomes out of date at a different hour. The list of statements thus treasured up in written form discloses a striking fact: the same term qualifying so generously a multiplicity of data is too general in scope to denote the object of sense-certainty. If the only expression of immediacy is an abstract universal, how comic the result. The intention clearly is to utter something single and singular, *such* datum and *only* such, but what is actually voiced is something indeterminate and epicene, suited to anything and everything, this as well as that, and exclusively neither this nor that. Surely not by a vocable such as 'now' can the datum of immediacy be designated. There is here the incongruity of not meaning what one *says* (a universal) and not saying what one *means* (a particular).

Hardith: The conclusion hardly comes as a surprise. Nor can the local identification escape revealing itself as untenable. If interrogated concerning what I find to be 'here' I indicate a tree, how easily you could confound me by drawing my attention to another object. The new object—for example, a house—displacing the old, has equal title to the spatial epithet. A succession of different data each in turn undeniably here, proves the universality of the local label, belonging as it does to everything brought into focus. That label likewise fails to qualify as a specific hallmark. How abortive must seem the attempt to denote a particular datum by the aid of a universal token!

Meredy: You are stealing my thunder, you know. This is what I should have said in refutation of the claim that the local epithet is less universal than the temporal. But you are wise in refusing to continue the argument for objective immediacy. Whatever data be vouched for as present, the terms descriptive of their presence, such as here and now, belie the particular and exclusive nature they are held to possess. The consequence derived by Hegel from the situation so far depicted is simply this, that claims for immediacy cannot be satisfied by the capacious modes of discourse. Since attribution of immediacy to the objects of sensory experience is precluded, seeing that their immediacy is contradicted in specifying them, the position of sense-certainty must be shifted to other grounds. The experiment must now be made with the alternative of endowing the subject with paramountcy and of discovering the roots of sense-experience in the privacy of awareness instead of in the publicity of the objects. So the defense of sense-certainty devolves upon you again. What argument may be advanced in favor of a subjective form of it?

Hardith: This is a form susceptible of a more tenable defense. The subjectivist is after all in preemptive possession of the contents of his consciousness. Suiting the words to his persuasion, let me speak on his behalf as follows: I know nothing except what my senses assure me of. The certainty I claim belongs to my senses and not to the objects affecting them. Not inappropriate, therefore, is the name 'sense-certainty' I give to my immediate experience. How can I possibly attach meaning to any experience not my own? When I speak of objects I mean only such as fall within the range of my present awareness. I *mean* nothing but what is *mine.* This wordplay, the equivalent in English for *Meinen,* epitomizes my version of immediacy. Thus, if I am asked to state what I find here and now, I unhesitatingly report that here is a tree and that now is noontime. You may if you wish record the fact. At a later hour and in the presence of a different object I should with equal assurance mean what then and there would be mine. How could I ever be discomfited by conflicting memoranda of my awareness? I am not bound to institute comparisons between my various experiences; to do so would indeed be to betray the immediacy I rejoice in. Every apprehension is a law unto itself; it is irrefutably true; it possesses unassailable certitude. What I recognize as existent or real is but the content of my present consciousness. The scruples of thought are powerless to disturb the sense-certainty I actually enjoy from moment to moment. And should a tag for this position be called for, let it be spoken of as naïve idealism, 'naïve' in the sense of being altogether without any admixture of sophistry or sophistication.

Meredy: Your impersonation of a subjectivist or a naïve idealist is impressive. You have said—and said well—all that could possibly be urged in his behalf. But the diction employed is rather that of a solipsist, and as such Hegel actually represents him, the expression *Meinen,* so admirably rendered by you, being a pun which has here the force of an argument radically egocentric. Here, too, alas! the punctilios of discourse remain to undermine the argument. For the comedy of solipsism lies precisely in the incongruous use of the term 'I'. Of course I can express what I mean by objects whenever I am present to claim them as mine, if to such claim alone do they owe their existence, but how valid is the presumption that the personal pronoun denotes my particular person? The pronoun does not designate a specific entity; the same vocable may be preempted by different subjects, and each may push egotism to the limits of solipsism. But, as the saying goes, there is safety in numbers. The soliloquy of one cannot silence the soliloquy of another. If I consign all would-be solipsists to the limbo of my consciousness, might not each of them dispose of me in like manner? Yes, the pronoun, which grammarians call personal to distinguish it from other pronouns, is one of which no particular individual has a monopoly. It is a universal not available for attribution of uniqueness to any particular. Here again, as in the case of objective sense-certainty, it is impossible to utter the particular meant or to mean the universal expressed. Subjective sense-certainty, too, goes by the board. The personal pronoun here so essential, being a synonym for every subject, cannot serve to individuate a specific subject.

Hardith: The failure of sense-certainty, in both its forms, was of course predetermined by the conditions of the experiment. The demand for a sample condemns it at the outset. Choice and discrimination, which sampling entails, are not open to a mind conceived as pure sentience. To select a particular specimen is to invite comparison with another, a process fatal to immediacy, its differentia thus becoming the abstract quality common to all the specimens, the quality of being *this*. And how great is the deviation from verisimilitude when a naïve consciousness is induced to fall back upon the dichotomy between the essential and the unessential to specify further the immediacy it enjoys! The stage is now set for a comic dilemma: does the essence of immediacy inhere in the object or the subject? The absurdity of either alternative lies in the attempt to render the immediate amenable to discourse. Is not the beginning of speech the end of immediacy? Yes, language, which is alien to sense-certainty, must perforce bring about its self-alienation.

Meredy: What you say expresses accurately Hegel's reduction to silence of the ultimate position of sense-certainty. Since no words are available for its defense, the vaunted certainty of sense now becomes the irrefutable certainty of ineffable intuition. The intuition of the present moment comprises the whole of immediacy, excluding as such memory and expectation—everything indeed not falling within the compass of an instantaneous vision. Pure intuition, Hegel rightly asserts, does not compare or contrast. It is not concerned with the intuitions that preceded it or with those simultaneously enjoyed by other minds. No dichotomy there of subject and object, one more essential than the other. A consciousness dominated by an intense sensation completely withdraws from all distinctions and all relations. While the sensation lasts, the content present and the self aware of it constitute a miniature world; nothing seems real except this content, and in seeing or hearing it this ego is absolute. If a mind succeeds in retreating into the stronghold of a present intuition, refusing to be dislodged from it, what could possibly disturb the solitary enjoyment of a solitary datum? Clearly not a different intuition, for the whole mind is now wholly absorbed in this object: if a tree it is just this and no other tree. Concentration on a single experience, its singleness being perfectly monadic, provides an escape from the intrusive complications of thought: the sole content of sensuous awareness constitutes the unique appearance uniquely here and uniquely now. This of course is solipsism with a vengeance. Unlike, however, a halfhearted solipsism which abolishes everything but the ego, endowing the latter with permanence and continuity, radical immediacy is no respecter of persons. Self-awareness, too, is but temporary. This position, the last refuge of immediate experience, Santayana, no stranger to Hegel's *Phenomenology,* aptly called "solipsism of the present moment."

Hardith: It is useless to assail such solipsism by the method of interrogation. A faithful adherent to its truth will not permit himself to be entangled in verbal arguments. He will boldly declare that his experience simply beggars all description. Indeed, how contradict an intuition conceded to be beneath or beyond the level of discourse? Why not leave the silent solipsist to his silence? What is to be gained from impugning further a certainty certain of nothing but the ineffable?

Meredy: Ah, but impugn it we must if the argument of the *Phenomenology* is to proceed. How could sense-certainty escape from its predicament by escaping into silence without forfeiting the alleged claim to exemplify an experience purely immediate and thus uniquely indubitable? This is a claim variously and repeatedly made by different minds both ordinary and learned. From the present examination of this claim ensues the insight, not that sense-certainty can be abolished, but only that it must be removed from the jurisdiction of discourse. The conclusion that sense-certainty is ineffable merely serves as transition to an experiment with a form of immediacy construed as expressible by a mode of procedure more direct and more efficacious than linguistic.

Hardith: But what can be meant by an experiment with an experience of certainty admittedly inarticulate? How impersonate a mind for whose sensory awareness there are no audible vehicles of expression?

3. Gesticulatory Immediacy

Meredy: We must now dwell on such expressions as are inaudible but not invisible. Hegel impersonates a 'solipsist of the present moment' who, though remaining silent, is nonetheless able to specify the datum of his intuition by pointing. In order to understand what the solipsist means we need only to look in the direction of his gesture. If the datum is there, how can we fail to share his intuition? The new experiment must now be tried. Let us step into the solipsist's shoes, as it were, and see whether the intuited datum can coalesce with the datum indicated. Instead of vocal identification of the immediate, we now embark upon the kind describable as gesticulative.

Hardith: Ingenious, very ingenious! Hegel's triumph over immediacy conveyed by gesture is of course an easy one. The rub lies in the phrase 'the present moment' by which solipsism is here distinguished, a phrase having meaning not 'for it' but only 'for us'. This difference on which Hegel sets so much store becomes decisive. The actual immediacy pointed to and the vicarious immediacy spoken for can obviously not center in the same datum. And the reason seems quite simple; the hand that points is the solipsist's but the voice that speaks is ours, and we thus commit the fallacy of equating the expressiveness of the former medium with that of the latter. Is it possible to experiment with the data of gesticulation without forcing them into the alien mold of discourse? Great indeed is the gulf between objects directly denoted and those verbally communicated.

Meredy: On the difference between what a thing is 'for us' and what it is 'for itself' Hegel does indeed lay here the utmost stress. To us the final phase of immediacy is no more communicable by gesture than by speech. No object of sense-certainty—as *this* and *only* this, having its location and duration absolutely *here* and *now*—can ever be revealed by gesticulation. Consider the temporal situation first; an instant intuition simply does not endure long enough to permit its datum to be directly indicated: the datum indicated is but a datum of another intuition. How point to an intuited datum without freezing the intuition entertaining it? The present datum pointed to is a datum present no longer. Every genuine present is but speciously present; its true essence is to be and not to be. With his characteristic tendency to pun Hegel looks for the *Wesen* of the present in being *gewesen*. Accordingly, if the truth of immediacy is in the intuition now enjoyed, it inevitably turns into a truth that has ceased to be true. Since no datum *as* intuited can be exhibited without arrest of the flux of time, the datum actually displayed must be given to a different intuition occurring at another vanishing instant. The object *meant* at one specious present simply cannot be *shown* at another. For a consciousness depending entirely on gesticulative means of communication there can be no identity between the thing now being denoted and the thing intended to be denoted a moment ago. How indeed could such identity be established by a solipsism which sinks all certainty of experience into a single moment?

35

Hardith: All this is admittedly but for us and undeniably of considerable importance. But how can the position of the kind of solipsism we are talking about be affected or altered thereby? The anomalies you note are hardly such of which awareness is possible at the level of immediacy. The gesture in the direction of a present datum does not fail of its aim just because speech may render it awry.

Meredy: Remember the conditions under which the experiment is to be conducted; we are to impersonate a would-be defender of sense-certainty whose defense is to be gestural rather than discursive. Could a finger be pointed at an immediate datum of consciousness? Not if an instant is never instantaneous. What Hegel does is to insist on the speciousness of the present moment. With sense-certainty no instant can be made consistent save one which is durationless. But in such an instant no datum can appear to be intuited or indicated. The certainty of sense thus becomes a certainty of nothing sensible. For Hegel, too, anticipating William James, in spirit though scarcely in letter, the present is a "duration-block," composed of "succeeding" parts. The term present or 'now' is essentially anomalous: if viewed as a discrete *element* of time, contrasted with past and future, such an element is never experienced; what we do experience is, so to speak a *tract* of time, fading at one extreme and budding at the other. We have no awareness of a period of time not instinct with receding and advancing moments. Whatever span of time we choose to describe as present, an adjective singularly relative and elastic, includes within its compass a plurality of moments of which some have elapsed and others are to come. Is this not true when we speak of the present hour or the present week or the present year? Any unit of duration we characterize as present—a minute or a millenium—always contains two nonpresent ingredients. What then does the present signify? If the present is inevitably a moving present, the course it leaves behind and the course towards which it advances being both intrinsic to its nature, then a present conceived as immobile or without duration may be justly deemed illusory. And if such a present is spurious, the solipsism of the present moment is equally spurious.

Hardith: What is the inference? That the immediate remains incommunicable? Granted. But let me repeat: enjoyment of sense-certainty is one thing, expression of it is quite another. Neither intuition nor datum can be saddled with the paradoxes inherent in the so-called specious present. Incidentally, is it not anomalous to designate as specious the present of actual experience? Let that pass. In the immediate presence of the datum there may be no awareness of one moment succeeding and thus supplanting a different moment; consequently, the datum indicated may appear to be the same as if the intuition were timeless or instantaneous.

Meredy: The issue you raise is important but not relevant. The assumption of an intuition as if it were durationless is clearly a hypothesis contrary to fact. And were all expression abandoned, the gestural not excepted, sense-certainty would naturally cease to be a bone of contention. Yet, there is nothing secret about sense-certainty, the allegation having often been made that it constitutes a unique certainty warranted by the data present to direct awareness. Unless such certainty be rejected outright as nonsense, the data invoked in its corroboration should somehow be intimated. Speech being impotent to reveal them, the resort is to gesture. But gesture, too, made in the specious present fails to identify the immediate.

Hardith: We must not forget the datum's local habitation. Its spatial position denoted by gesture seems unaffected by the specious present during which gesticulation occurs.

Meredy: Hegel has no difficulty in reducing to like speciousness the spatial counterpart of the present, thus reinforcing the paradox of solipsism. If temporal solipsism, so to speak, consists in confining all certainty to what 'now' appears, the view that the object of immediate awareness must be exclusively 'here', may be called local solipsism. The spatial vocable is no less anomalous than the temporal. Nothing can be situated in a 'here' conceived as a point without extension; if anything is to fill it, the smallest bit of space must be conceived as composed of smaller parts. To the duration-block of every 'now' corresponds the extension-block of every 'here', its distinguishable facets being before and behind, above and below, right and left, etc. Accordingly, the spot at which any datum appears, be it ever so constricted, is always distended; the word 'here' by which the datum's position is denoted, represents one extent made up of several extents. And like the duration of the 'now', the extent of the 'here' has stretchable boundaries, the word being applicable to any area of localization, such as a room or a country, a continent or a planet. A unit of space absolutely simple, without divisions or directions, would of course be punctiform, but nothing could appear there to produce the intuition our supposed solipsist relies upon as ground of his certainty. The specious present thus has its spatial analogue. A punctiform here is as illusory as an immobile now. And the elasticity of the here is fatal to local solipsism in the same way in which the flux of the now is destructive of temporal solipsism.

Hardith: If you are not reading into the text your own predilection, the comedy of sense-certainty would seem rather obvious, scarcely in need of such a finespun analysis to show the incongruity between its covert meaning and overt expression. The immediate is simply not communicable either by speech or gesture. The sensuously palpable transferred to the level of discourse ceases to be both sensuous and palpable. And if, abandoning words, the attempt is made to indicate the sensuously given by pointing, the result is no less ineffable: anything thus identified can have no other locus than one which is punctiform as well as instantaneous. But I must repeat my caveat against the conclusion that reduction of sense-certainty to the ineffable is the same as reduction of it to the absurd. And why do you think it necessary to dilate at such length on the speciousness of the here and the now in order to clinch the argument against sense-certainty? On this theme Hegel's treatment is brief and compact, and hardly so clear-cut as you interpret it.

Meredy: To read Hegel is to read between the lines, his thought and diction being what they are. Who can pretend to read him aright? His interpreters, to quote one of them, "have contradicted each other, almost as variously, as the several commentators on the Bible." This did not deter William Wallace, the author of the remark, from proffering *his* key to the secret of Hegel. Any departure from strict adherence to the language of the text runs the risk of possible misunderstanding. Yes, my interpretation of Hegel's concise treatment of the 'now' in terms of the specious present (and extended by analogy to that of the 'here') is perhaps too prolix. The sole justification lies in the light it throws on the twofold meaning of the universal latent in the dialectic of sense-certainty. The distinction is between the universal as abstract and the universal as concrete. Depicted in this section in miniature, as it were, the distinction grows in crucial importance throughout the course of the *Phenomenology*. Consider the here and the now once more; serving as terms germane to whatever we chance to encounter, they are suited to anything and everything. How identify the singular data of sense by affixing to them terms of such vague generality? All intimate experience disappears, as it were, in the abstract universals through which we express them. When gesture supplants speech as vehicle of communication, the universals become reinstated but in a form to be regarded as incipiently concrete. For the experienced data identified by pointing must occupy spatial and temporal loci, each, however contracted, revealing itself as an identical complex composed of different parts. The universal is inescapable—of this the dialectic of immediacy is supposed to furnish the initial proof. In the process of experimenting with it, we discover that it has turned into its opposite. The analysis of sense-certainty, the supreme example of cognitive im-

mediacy, is simply the 'story', as Hegel calls it, of its own inner development or of the implications of its experience made articulate.

Hardith: It is, of course, nothing of the sort. The story is, not of
sense-certainty itself, but of sense-certainty as deliberately feigned, and
the dialectic cannot occur except in the mind simulating it in the manner prescribed by Hegel. What genuine adherent would accept Hegel's
impersonation or take seriously his animadversion? The proof that
sense-certainty is inexpressible proves only the inadequacy of our modes
of expression. Why disparage sense-experience? Why not challenge
instead the hegemony of thought? He who silently enjoys the sensible
qualities of things cannot be charged with contradiction unless he stoops
to argue. And if induced to argue, and to argue absurdly, he may refuse
to graft upon his intuition the equivocations attending his words. The
immediate and its utterance being at loggerheads, what Hegel demands
is sacrifice of experienced intimacy to descriptive propriety. Because
the immediate, admittedly ineffable, turns into its opposite as soon as
we open our mouths, we are required to hold that it is other than itself
on its own plane of being. What a *non sequitur!* The contradiction is
not *in* sense-certainty but only *between* it and speech. The comedy lies
in our attempt to force it into a ludicrous position. Is not the laugh,
so to speak, ultimately on us? The dialectic has its inception in the
false hypothesis that the incommunicable can be represented as if it
were communicable. But for that hypothesis there would be no story.
Hegel undoubtedly succeeds in contriving a dialectical situation but
it is one of his own making, existing only in his own mind and in the
minds of those disposed to deal with sense-certainty in precisely the
way in which the *Phenomenology* directs.

Meredy: Your charge is impressive and may always be brought
against Hegel's cavalier treatment of the claims for sense-certainty. But
withdrawal of the immediate from the domain of discourse would at
the very outset stop the dialectic in its tracks. There is of course no
necessity for Hegel's phenomenology or for the method of its construction. But if we concede the possibility of his undertaking and of the
process guiding it, we must proceed on the postulate that language and
experience are not mutually exclusive. Precluded by the nature of
Hegel's experiment are the alternatives of saying nothing or of courting
contradiction. The unspoken has no meaning and speech is the medium
of the universal; this being so, objects of sense are either nonsensical or
nonsensuous, the former if actually unutterable, the latter if embodied
in words. Nonsense or nonsensuousness—this is the drastic dilemma in
which Hegel's story of sense-certainty culminates. The first alternative
may be safely disregarded: what is unmeaning has no claim on our

attention. The ineffable occupies an invincible position simply because it is unfathomable; an *in*expressible argument is too preposterous to be taken seriously. The second is the only possible alternative: sense-certainty, rendered articulate, issues in the insight, dilated on in the sequel, that experience is amenable to description. What hereafter becomes crucial is experience, not as enjoyed in privacy or secrecy, but as open to discernment and valuation. Raised to the level of discourse, experience, though losing its alleged certainty, retains its true sense. Foreshadowed here is the triple import of one of Hegel's famous keywords, the word *aufheben,* signifying at once to annul, to preserve, to elevate. The claim for sense-certainty, in the extreme form in which it first appears, becomes cancelled, since it proves to be a claim for something on the nether side of meaning. But, in accordance with Hegel's positive use of the principle of negativity, the claim as modified remains conserved on a higher plane; its application has validity solely as relating to an ingredient in the more complex consciousness of perception. The object of sense, if and when described, turns out to be a co-presence—a *Zusammen*—of universal qualities and relations. And to regard it as such is once and for all to escape the pitfalls of immediacy. The way is thus clear for the transition from sensory awareness to perceptual cognition; for to perceive an object is to take cognizance of the attributes to which it owes determinateness. *Wahrnehmen,* another of Hegel's puns, intimates that to perceive is to take truly the sensuously given. And what is it truly? To perception, as distinguished from intuition, a thing must needs appear as an identical congeries of different properties. And so it must now be treated. The comedy of sense-certainty has served as steppingstone to a wider vision. And this too will be seen to entail its own dialectic. Our next task is to examine the incongruities latent in the perceptual situation, the comedy of which will prescribe the reflective experiment to follow.

Perception

1. *The Thing and its Properties*

Hardith: *C'est le premier pas qui coûte,* some witty person is said to have remarked when told of the famous walk through the streets of Paris by the decapitated Saint Denis. Hegel's dialectical march becomes equally plausible if we allow him to take *his* first step. Once we offer no resistance to the manner in which he deals with sense-certainty, both its defeat and triumph are inevitable, Hegel's expression for an outcome so ambivalent being *aufgehoben.* Defunct in the form in which it is made to appear initially, sense-certainty survives as an indispensable element in a more complex way of knowing—namely, in that of perception. There can obviously be no perception in the absence of sensory awareness; but related as it is to specific and specifiable things, perception includes and transcends such awareness. Perceptual experience, since it is amenable to discourse, ceases to be immediate experience; the percipient of describable objects is no mere recipient of ineffable impressions. In perception, therefore we come to accept the truth the dialectic of immediacy was designed to make manifest, this being the sense of Hegel's play upon the word *Wahrnehmen.* Is this a fair way of stating the transition to the next experiment?

Meredy: Before we embark upon a discussion of the new experiment, of the transition to which your statement is admirably succinct, something must still be said regarding the proper approach to the *Phenomenology.* Some strictures voiced by you in connection with the first experiment make it necessary that the purpose of our conversations be briefly reiterated. What are we aiming at? One thing is exegesis, few philosophic texts being so baffling as Hegel's; quite another is criticism of the arguments embodied therein once we understand them. An altogether different thing is concentration upon the method. A systematic commentary on the work must indeed cover all the aspects relevant to

41

it. We have agreed, however, to eschew technical or polemical themes, our task consisting in gaining from the treatise such insight as it affords into some of the recurrent issues with which as reflective men we are perenially concerned. Let us bear this in mind throughout but especially now as we enter upon a scrutiny of the problem of perception which involves paradoxes more formidable than those implicit in sense-certainty.

Hardith: My knowledge of the text is too slight to enable me to speak of matters preempted by the specialists. Who am I to pose as exegete or critic of the *Phenomenology*? But even one sympathetic to Hegel can hardly fail to indulge in occasional caviling when suddenly thrust into the tortuous mazes of the dialectic. I shall accordingly consider the logic of perception in the same captious manner in which I sought to grasp that of sense-certainty. I can be initiated into Hegel's way of thinking only by raising objections to such of his contentions as must at first sight seem so bewildering. Thus you speak of perception as a problem involving formidable paradoxes. Whence the problem and what are the paradoxes? Nothing is more universal than perceptual experience. It is the daily bread, so to speak, on which all cognition must subsist. In perceiving a tree, for example, everyone can convey to everyone else its shape or color or verdure or other discernible qualities, with no consciousness whatever of the anomalies his experience reveals to the philosopher. Why be astonished that the world of perception, which is the world of common sense, should appear so natural and so stable to those familiar with it!

Meredy: It is certainly true that perception does not seem problematic to common sense, with which in fact Hegel ultimately identifies it. The difficulties involved *in* perception cannot be grasped *by* perception. This is the sum and substance of the dialectic. But it is a long and intricate story running more or less parallel with that of sense-certainty. We shall follow the story in some detail. We cannot do so, however, without first dwelling on the relation of perception to sense-certainty. For it is in resolving the issues generated by the diagnosis of immediacy that the perceptive view acquires the significance which the text accords it. Perception, growing out of sense-certainty, escapes indeed the pitfalls of immediacy only to be entrapped in a hornet's nest of its own.

Hardith: Very well! Let us treat perception, not on its merits, but merely as the climax, so to speak, in the story of sense-certainty. There could emerge no consideration of perception, by the method and in the idiom in which Hegel presents it, if the impersonation of immediacy had not precipitated an incongruous situation. Viewed as corrective of the anomalies inherent in the claims for indubitable credibility of intuitive awareness, the perceptual way of knowing is obviously one not precluding 'mediation': its objects are things communicable to the public in terms of the congeries of their given properties. The principle of universality, incompatible with the privacy of ineffable intuition, becomes the soul and leaven of perceptual experience, percipient as well as percept enjoying not only specific but also generic import. *Ich ein allgemeines und der Gegenstand ein allgemeiner*—such in Hegel's words is the outcome of the previous dialectic. Things are what they are in the virtue of the determinate qualities vouched for by everyone's sensible apprehension. What is the matter with this?

Meredy: Nothing of course until the implications of perceptual experience are brought to light. For this experience, too, rests on the duality of subject and object, giving rise again to the question of priority. Should we look for the essence of perception in the act of perceiving or in the thing perceived? Should we regard the percipient as playing a major or minor part in the perceptual situation? In other words, should we conceive of the perceived object as depending for its being on consciousness or as existing apart from it? It matters greatly which line of inquiry we view as the more fundamental.

Hardith: It would seem more in accord with the position of common sense to look upon the object of perception as a 'realistic' entity, in the sense of existing in independence of consciousness. As such it must appear as a thing with qualities determinately its own. How indeed could one thing be distinguished from any and every other thing save by the properties exclusively belonging to it?

Meredy: To be sure, nothing could be a percept without having a 'qualitied' nature. Consider, however, what the term 'property' connotes. In Hegel's use of it, the term must initially be understood in two ways: (a) a property is a quality proper to the percept, and (b) a property is a quality which appropriates the percept. To be perceived in 'realistic' fashion, the object must have qualities of its own, and such as also own the object. And in this, as we shall see, lies one of the paradoxes of perception.

Hardith: You have felicitously rendered into English Hegel's deliberate play upon *Eigenschaft*. Of its sensible qualities, unless we abandon the posture of realism, the perceived object must indeed have indisputable ownership; but it is only by a sort of verbal ruse that the principle of ownership may be extended likewise to the qualities in relation to their object. Assuming, however, that a thing can have no qualities unless it owns and is in turn owned by them, the manner of possessing and the manner of being possessed seem here to be bound by mutual implication. Whence the paradox?

Meredy: The paradox becomes obvious as soon as we observe that the way in which the object possesses its qualities cannot be the same way in which the qualities possess their object. This salt (the illustration is Hegel's) is *here* before me with all its qualities: it is white, pungent, cubical in shape, of a certain weight, etc. They are the salt's own, and in possessing them as *its* properties, not separately but conjointly, consists the object's individual nature. Yet each of these qualities appears to own the object in monopolistic fashion. None of them, as Hegel puts it, has a different extent from the others: each is everywhere in the same place where the others are. And though present in the same locus, for otherwise the salt's qualities could not be spoken of as equally *here,* such presence does not mutually affect them .The quality of being white does not modify the cubical shape, and neither quality touches the pungent taste. Each property, enjoying an inalienable identity and atomicity, appropriates the salt in a proprietary manner, as it were, undisturbed by the fact that all the others do this too. What we thus perceive is simply that one quality is present, also another, also another, and so on. Hegel avails himself of the word 'also', as symbol of loose togetherness (*Zusammen*), to epitomize the absurdity of viewing the percept as being merely a collection of independent and immiscible qualities. And this is the crux of the paradox: unless considered interdependent, qualities can never function as properties, in the sense of belonging to a unitary object perceivable as such. Ownership of qualities *by* an object is inseparable from the notion of its specific thinghood. A thing is specific, not because this quality appropriates it and also that, but because it possesses in concatenation such qualities as compose its proper being. How then do universal qualities of which the percept presents a congeries rather than a cohesion become the specific properties assumed to constitute its particular thinghood?

Hardith: Apart from the contrived ambivalences of terminology in which Hegel's text notoriously abounds, the object of ordinary perception seems single and definite, appearing as if it owned its discernible qualities in private or peculiar synthesis. Only thus may independent universals be legitimately spoken of as properties belonging to a unitary thing. Ownership in the other sense, in the sense in which the object is said to be preempted by independent universals, is more an analytical than a perceptual matter. Given to be perceived is something having qualities and not qualities in possession of it. This, at any rate, is a persuasion of common sense with which perception is allied.

Meredy: You forget that, following Hegel's procedure, we must consider perception as containing the 'truth' of sense-certainty. Perceptual qualities are one and all sensible qualities. Although apprehensible singly and separately (such as the salt's white surface or pungent taste) qualities do not acquire the status of properties unless given jointly as pertaining to the object's individual nature. The distinction between the singleness of the object and the diversity of its properties is fundamental to the dialectic of perception as it emerges from the dialectic of sense-certainty. Forsaking the immediacy of sensory awareness, because it is condemned to remain speechless or contradictory, we enter the sphere of perceptual cognition. The domain of perception is a public domain. Unlike sense-data percepts are expressible in terms of observably determinate properties.

Hardith: I am not sure in what sense we are to understand the notion of determinateness. Is an object's *Bestimmung* or *Bestimmtheit* (to use Hegel's expressions) such as it actually does appear to perception or such as it should appear to it in accordance with the requirement of the dialectic? It clearly must be the former if perception is a cognitive phenomenon in affinity with common sense.

Meredy: Your question goes to the heart of the matter. It points to a basic difficulty inherent in the perceptual situation. Before raising the issue, let me first note this. On the possibility of apprehending determinate qualities hinges the difference between a thing given to be perceived and the immediate data of sensory awareness. But how incorrigibly ambiguous is the word determinative—a word here so crucial! Viewed in one way, the properties determinative of a percept's nature are those that it *includes*: salt is determinate owing to the combination of the positive qualities it harbors. Would salt be salt if we imagined it radically altered in color, shape, taste, etc.? Regarded in another way, the percept's determinateness demands the exclusion of qualities not pertaining to it: salt is specific because it is distinguishable from that which is *not* white, *not* cubiform, *not* pungent. To say what a thing is, insists Hegel, implies saying what it is not. Determinateness is thus double-edged. It cuts both ways. It segregates things by properties whose interdependence contradicts their alleged atomicity. What does it mean to maintain that each property is self-identical, white being white and cubiform cubiform, since none could be distinguished as such without relation to its opposite? The self-identical is at the same time different from its contrary or contradictory. A property enjoys not absolute but only relative identity, relative, that is, to whatever it cannot embrace without loss of uniqueness. Inclusion and exclusion are thus, speaking metaphorically, two sides of the same coin; a thing is determined at once by what it exhibits and by what it fails to exhibit— the positive and the negative, though distinguishable, are inseparable. Accordingly, if a percept is said to possess a certain number of qualities,

45

all the qualities incongruous with those asserted constitute a sort of enveloping sphere—a 'medium', as Hegel calls it—affecting its articulation. Such in brief is an object of perception: it owes its specific nature to the possession of determinate properties, and determinate properties, being exclusive, involve reference to their opposites as a condition of their identity.

Hardith: But in thus fixing the notion of an object of perception we perforce go beyond the actual perception of the object. Such a notion has no meaning save 'for us' intent upon understanding how an object must be constituted to be perceived, and to be perceived especially as an object not dependent for its being on being related to the perceiving mind. The object's complex constitution can hardly come within the ken of unsophisticated consciousness. How formidable are the antitheses with which such consciousness would have to cope! The object to be *one* must have *many* qualities, qualities *positive* related to *negative;* these qualities acquire *identity* by means of *differentiation,* and are capable of *interpenetration* without loss of *atomicity.* Could such logical distinctions be grasped by mere perception?

Meredy: The answer is clear: mere perception is blissfully unaware of them. Determinateness of its object, in the pregnant sense, remains unperceivable. The seat of the problem is in the assumption that perception is passive and its object independent. If a percept is to possess in its own right determinate properties—and only in thus possessing them can it enjoy independence—such a percept simply transcends the limits of cognition deemed receptive and acquiescent.

Hardith: With what a tremendous paradox this leaves us! We are informed how the perceivable object is constituted only to be told that it cannot be perceived. How do we know that perception is so ignominiously foredoomed to failure?

2. Perception as Reception

Meredy: We can know this only by the mode of procedure Hegel prescribes, namely, to experiment with the situation thus far developed. And this involves the method of impersonation. We must histrionically identify ourselves with a supposed percipient whose given percept is alleged to be a determinate thing and independently real. The percipient, in short, must be envisaged as if he were but a recipient.

Hardith: Ah, 'the percipient as recipient'—a nice wordplay, aptly suggestive of unsophisticated consciousness! Etymologically, the word *wahrnehmen* signifies taking truly what is given to be perceived, the implication being that the given thus taken must be received without doing anything to it. To do something to the given in the process of

46

taking it, would be, as Hegel ironically remarks, to tamper with the truth. There is nothing strange in the use of perception as synonym of reception, epitomizing as it does a persistent persuasion difficult to gainsay. How is such a persuasion to be effectively challenged?

Meredy: All we have to do is to conceive of a percipient asserting his ability to receive in sheer passivity the given object as a thing endowed with determinate properties. If he can make good his assertion, his position is impregnable; but if he can receive no such thing, or if the thing is one in the production of which he plays an active part, he stands convicted of self-deception. Let us examine the validity of an imaginary percipient's claim to unmitigated recipiency.

Hardith: But by what criterion should we judge your percipient's recipiency? Perception is not amenable to principles imposed upon it from without. Unless it could be shown to be assailable on its own ground or in its own terms, animadversions on perceptual experience are simply impertinent. After all, the deliverances of such experience are what the percipient says they are.

Meredy: How true! No experience, perceptual included, is open to extraneous criticism. Dialectical diagnosis is, so to speak, immanent; judgment of perception can be no other than such as the percipient himself must make with respect to the validity of his assertions. In the congruity between the 'given' and the 'taken' Hegel finds the percipient's standard of truth; if the object apprehended undergoes no change as a result of being apprehended, cognition of it is veridical, lapse from self-sameness (*Sichselbstgleichheit*) on the part of the object serving as warning that it has been *mis*-taken or untruly perceived. Sameness in the object being a sign of truth, and variation in the consciousness of it a source of error, the percipient may be challenged to identify by undeviating apprehension an object claimed to possess properties unequivocally determinate.

Hardith: So it boils down to the question of whether what is given and what is taken are congruous, on the assumption, (a) that the object perceived has determinateness in virtue of its invariable properties, and (b) that in being thus apprehended by a receptive consciousness consists true cognition of it.

Meredy: Precisely. But consider the anomalies which the twofold assumption precipitates. The percipient, when made to submit to interrogation, cannot escape disavowing one view after another, for each appears as mistaking the allegedly given object. The text here is needlessly full of linguistic twists and turns, yet the gist of what Hegel has to say is not at all unclear. Let me condense, with some approximation to his terminology, the various vacillations to which an interrogated percipient is necessarily driven when induced to defend his position.

1. The object perceived is given as single, in the sense of enjoying numerical unity, but the selfsame entity is likewise given as having many qualities to which it owes determinateness. Are the qualities the object's peculiar properties? They can obviously not appear as such in view of the term's incorrigible ambivalence, properties being private qualities (*Eigenschaften*) as well as shared qualities (*Gemeinschaften*). Not unmistakably, therefore, can perceived qualities be taken as properties determinative of the object's singleness.

2. The percipient's original recipiency must therefore be revised, seeing that the properties said to determine the object's unity are so equivocal. For the sake of specifying the object as one and the same, the percipient is forced to ascribe to it preemptive characters. What is given as determinate must be taken as exclusive. How else safeguard the distinction of a specific thing, enabling it to be this rather than that, if not by its 'own' properties? Qualities can function as properties only when perceived as particular without reference to their assertable universality.

3. But if properties be taken as belonging exclusively to a given percept, regardless of the fact that other percepts may preempt them too, what is lost sight of is their necessary interdependence. Does not the individuality of the object lie in a special combination of properties bound each to each by reciprocal determination? But, alas, perceivable is but one quality after another, none needing or affecting its neighbor. And since qualities are not given as organically related, the percipient *mis*-takes his percept in taking it as having them in privileged concatenation: the percept is what its qualities are, and its qualities are atomic universals in fortuitous relation.

4. If qualities appear to be given as separate in adventitious conjunction, how then should the percept be taken? Sensory universals do not as such specify a particular thing. The direction of the percipient's attention thus becomes uncertain and wavering. If he attends to the object's unity, he fails to take in, as it were, its manifold characters; and if he attends to the plurality of its characters, he is apt to miss the presence of a unitary thing. His last resort is to identify the given object as a particular assemblage of sensory qualities which, despite their universality and discreteness, find in such an assemblage a local habitation, the object being a sort of medium in which qualities appear in invariable or persistent clusters. But this view is patently erroneous. For what is given as single entity is no mere medium of co-present universals. Qualities that make their appearance *in* a common medium without being qualities *of* an individual object lose their value as con-

crete determinants. The term 'medium' (or its equivalent) is a mistaken synonym of the term 'thing' which denotes a definite percept having definite properties.

5. What is the result of all this tergiversation? Is it not to abandon altogether the perceptual attitude? The percipient can no longer claim to have before him a concrete object in possession of determinate properties but only a succession of sensible qualities, each inert and self-same, without relation to any other, present to direct apprehension. This position, ultimately forced upon him, is that of sense-certainty already superseded. If he is not to fall back on his ineffable experience, leading to re-enactment of the comedy of immediacy all over again, he can obviously not revert to a preperceptual situation, the very dialectic of which turned him into a percipient. Unable to go backward, he must advance by transcending the anomalous thesis that the percipient is but a recipient.

Hardith: The dilemma that has emerged—return to sense-certainty or revision of receptive perception—can hardly come as a surprise. It is involved in the language requisite for the impersonation of a naïve realism. Nothing but a chosen dialect, if I may say so, produces its dialectic; ways of 'taking' the percept turn into ways of 'mistaking' it. It is as if the diagnostic harvest reaped by Hegel's experiment depended on confining perception to its purely etymological meaning. The whole procedure seems to rest on a pun. Why suffer it gladly? Would not a less verbal sense of 'taking' and 'mistaking' alter the percipient's comedy which, following Hegel, you so adroitly reproduce? Even common sense, assumed to represent the simple realism here depicted, can scarce be charged with a simplicity so egregious.

Meredy: Hegel's vocabulary, often multivalent, seems designed for the purpose of clinching his arguments. The puns, as we may indeed rightly call them, are not without their English equivalents having similar uses. But there is more than mannerism of speech in the paradox here adumbrated. Does the object perceived depend in no sense for its being on a perceiving consciousness? Is the percipient nothing else than a cognitive patient? Should it be said that to perceive is invariably to be acted upon? An affirmative answer entails many difficulties, the chief of which relates to the possibility of error. No deception could ever be involved in any perception on the assumption that its object be always experienced as owing none of its qualities and relations to the mind experiencing it. How about illusions? They too are perceptions. And if a passive percipient must take illusory objects just as given, error concerning them would by hypothesis be precluded. Yes, the realistic dogma of the percipient as recipient would in any idiom appear vulnerable. But the distinction between the veridical and the nonveridical can here not be considered on its merits, belonging as it does to an inquiry at a deeper level. We are still in the domain of common sense, and even in that domain the given cannot be simply taken as given: the knowing mind is agent as well as patient.

Hardith: Of course common sense is far from being completely passive. As regards dreams and other illusory experiences most men naturally attribute their genesis to mind, explicitly differentiating them from veridical perceptions. Between the veridical and the nonveridical the difference is commonly taken for granted (though not the uncommon phraseology in which the philosophers are wont to couch the difference). Normal realism, accepted as commonplace, is not an absolutely fixed creed free from inner instability. Why then entertain a position so lacking in verisimilitude? A mere breath of criticism would seem to shake it.

Meredy: What you say touches the nerve of the method especially employed for shaking positions appearing originally as if unshakable. No theme treated in the *Phenomenology,* to put the method's guiding principle in the proverbial nutshell, can be revealed as relative unless first exhibited as absolute. This is the principle at work in connection with sense-certainty. And we are now observing it in relation to perception. Although its absoluteness proves so specious, sensory awareness finds nevertheless relative justification within the context of perception, to which we must initially impute an absoluteness of its own. We are at present engaged in the experiment of showing that perceptual experience, too, is ultimately relative. But this can only become clearer in what follows.

3. Perception and Reflection

Hardith: The relativity you have in mind depends, I take it, on the necessity which the percipient is under to introduce into his experience a reflective element, otherwise he could scarcely distinguish between perceptions to be trusted and those essentially spurious. But he needs some standard, and one congenial to his common sense, by which to defend, when called upon to do so, a distinction far from facile. What precisely is the standard to which a 'reflective percipient', as we had better call him, may consistently appeal?

Meredy: The word reflective, having regard to its etymology, suggests the answer. The first step in reflection is awareness that the given cannot be taken except as presented to consciousness. Now consciousness, resembling a mirror, does not receive the given object without modifying it in accordance with the nature of the intervening medium;

unlike a mirror, however, mind may also become conscious of the kind of alteration that accrues to the given object's image. To throw back into consciousness some of the object's apparent features, thus restoring the object to its original status by an act of thought, this is what the reflective percipient, to use your apt name, must now undertake, in order to escape from the impasse brought about by his naïve realism. Reflection, meaning, according to Hegel, "a return of consciousness into itself," epitomizes a fresh advance; for through such a 'return', consciousness may be induced to claim as its 'own' certain aspects previously ascribed to the object, and by disengaging them, it will be able to distinguish the truth of perception from its untruth. Reflective liberation of the percept from what it owes to a reflecting medium will thus reveal its veridical nature.

Hardith: What a subtle wordplay the argument is made to rest on! Only by a strange equivocation can 'reflection' be held to signify two different processes: the return of the object's image from something intermediary and mind's return into itself. But let that pass. Having assigned to the percipient a reflective function, Hegel proceeds to a different diagnosis of the perceptual situation. Not in just taking the object consists the percipient's new attitude but in taking upon his own shoulders, as it were, some of the burden alleged to be borne by the object. But what should he take over from the object as falling within his own consciousness? Where should he draw the line between the object's real nature and the changes wrought in it as a result of his cognitive agency? Incumbent now upon the percipient is the task of establishing a clear distinction between what a thing intrinsically *is* and what it *becomes* in relation to a knower. What man of common sense is able to accomplish a task so formidable, assuming his realism originally naïve grown ever so critical?

Meredy: Of course it is a task which exceeds the powers of common sense. Yet only by first supposing it possible can the attempt be proved abortive. We must impersonate a percipient capable of separating 're-flectively' the actual percept from the way consciousness 'reflects' it. And crucial here is the problem of 'the one and the many'. Here is the salt; it is a single object with several properties. What in this case is consciousness to take upon itself? Should the percipient make him-self responsible for the object's unity or for its plurality? One way of answering the question is to cause our percipient to speak thus:

"I am convinced," he will say, "that this salt is a unitary thing. How could it be otherwise without forfeiting its identity? If my perception compels me to disavow the salt's unity by noting the diversity of its characters, the reason for this is not far to seek. It is due to the phenom-

51

enon of 'reflection'. The object I perceive reaches me through the vehicles of many sense organs and each delivers its peculiar message.
The special 'image' which each organ produces my mind throws back
upon the object, installing it there as a 'property'. If the object could
affect but one organ, I should perceive it in its true singleness. The
object cannot but appear as an amalgam of sundry qualities simply
because it is conveyed to me through various channels. The salt for
instance, appears white to my eyes, pungent to my tongue, cubiform
to my touch, and so on. A thousand senses would 'reflect' it in a thousand ways. Accordingly, the plural aspects which I ascribe to the thing
originates in me; they differ because my senses differ. The eye is distinct from the tongue. I am thus the 'medium' where each aspect of a
thing exists by itself divided from the others. It is my mind which is the
differentiating agent. But the 'reflection' upon this fact, in the sense of
'consciousness returning to itself' and thus becoming aware of its own
operations, rehabilitates the truth: the transfer of properties from the
thing to the mind reestablishes the thing's unity and self-sameness."

   Hardith: Very ingenious and not at all implausible. Yes, a percipient open to reflection must in all conscience somehow account for the
relation of the object to the different senses. How could both unity and
multiplicity, though actually *perceived,* actually *belong* to the object,
on the assumption that they be deemed mutually exclusive? How natural to look in consciousness for the source or seat of sensible qualities,
considering that they are but names for experienced sensations! If the
object taken as single is to be distinguished from the diversity of the
sensations it arouses, our critical percipient is surely justified in holding
the latter to be purely subjective. This comports with common sense
as well as with a philosophic tradition that bears a long date. What is
the matter with it?

   Meredy: Only this; if pressed to *specify* the percept, the percipient
cannot but reverse the allocation of unity and multiplicity. Salt simply
cannot be the object it is unless its various qualities are construed as
objective. What is subjective is the act to which they owe their coherence into a single entity. For in the absence of intrinsic qualities all
things would affect us alike. How could salt be seen as white and coal
as black without assuming their actual dissimilarity? It is hardly possible to look for their distinction in the mere fact of their respective
singleness. In being 'one', as Hegel remarks, all entities are equal. Not
in virtue of numerical identity can a thing be perceived as specific. If it
is determinate qualities alone that distinguish one perceived thing from
another, the hypothesis of their subjective origin remains untenable.
They must be taken as given, and given in all their heterogeneity. Salt

is white, also cubiform, also pungent, and so on. In being this and *also* that, salt ceases to be a single entity; it is just a heap of disparate qualities, and when one is focused upon, the others are kept apart, each in turn clamoring for exclusive attention. But for the unifying agency of the mind, the object would disintegrate. It is consciousness that holds together the objective diversity of characters. What the percipient takes as one thing owes its unity to his power of synthesis. In him, then, does a given congeries of atomic universals acquire the structure of a unitary and identical object of perception.

Hardith: The second attempt to inject into perception a subjective agency, though more subtle than the first, is not the less plausible. Common sense could with little effort be brought to look upon it with equal favor. As long as the possibility of perception is held to depend on mind's activity as much as on mind's receptivity, the subjectification of the percept's unity would seem to be on a par with that of its multiplicity. Assuming that common sense can relinquish a congenitally naïve realism, and only thus *can* common sense become reflective, does it matter whether a realism turned critical takes the form of lodging in consciousness the object's numerical identity or its qualitative difference?

Meredy: But it does matter. As regards the percept's 'subjectification', to use your striking term, the percipient must choose between opposed arguments. One argument preserves the unity of the object by saddling consciousness with the plurality of its aspects, the other leaves intact its plural aspects by relegating to consciousness the function of combining them into a single thing. But being of equal plausibility, the two arguments would seem to entail a third, namely, that the operations of the mind achieve divergent results, and that the thing adapts itself to antithetical categories. Affirm that this salt is one, and I shall proceed to separate its many constituents; assert that it is but a heap of qualities, and I shall show its conformity to mind's synthetic activity. The truth is that the thing manifests itself in accordance with the alternative modes of reflective perception which, requiring the percipient to be both patient and agent, rests on the distinction between what in the percept is given *to* consciousness and what is given *by* consciousness. And since the percipient can alternately attribute to himself the object's diversity and unity, by the same token he must alternately view the object as exhibiting two contradictory modes of being. With the insight that the object is given in twofold manner, he must abandon the attempt to make his consciousness the source either of the object's multifariousness or of its individuality.

Hardith: That the object perceived embodies the percipient's agency in ways mutually exclusive is certainly anomalous. The two procedures of injecting the subject into the object thus cancel each other, and the experiment with critical realism proves no less abortive than the experiment with naïve realism. Are we not back where we were before? What different approach to perception is now possible?

Meredy: It is well, I think, before we proceed further, to sum up the two experiments. The first, which consists in impersonating the percipient as purely passive, culminates in an impasse. It generates a series of recantations of which the last reinstates the superseded position of immediacy. If he is not to become enmeshed again in the dialectical net of sense-certainty, the percipient must renounce the thesis that to perceive and to receive are equatable. The second experiment has to do with the percipient's vain endeavor to introduce his reflection as an intervening and supervening force. The thing is what the percipient takes it to be after discounting the effects that ensue from the interference of his cognitive apparatus. But he cannot indicate what it is his consciousness should take upon itself. Rather he must claim as subjective now the object's qualitative diversity and now its numerical unity. What results is the emergence of antithetical phases of experience as equally objective. The second experiment, too, ends in an impasse, leaving the percipient in the absurd position of allocating to his mind contradictory functions and to the object contradictory attributes. How is he to extricate himself from a situation so paradoxical? Hegel embarks on a third experiment in which the percipient is induced to qualify his previous utterances, and these qualifications constitute a new posture.

4. *Perception with Reservations*

Hardith: The new position appears to be one in which the percipient is represented as if he could have it both ways, enjoying the advantages of a naïve realism from one point of view and those of a critical realism from another. We are bidden, it seems, to take his former theses with more than one grain of salt. Yet, the possibility of reservations supervening upon categorical beliefs is always open, and common sense can and often does yield to their force. What is wrong with this? Qualification is a process that enters deeply into the normal course of reflection, tending to mitigate the validity of persuasions originally contended for with complete assurance. But what Hegel is intent upon, I suspect, is to expose as flimsy and deceptive distinctions to which common sense has recourse in meeting the issues beyond its analytic powers. So in becoming increasingly sophisticated, common sense is prone to grow more and more sophistical. And in this, I surmise, the dialectic of perception culminates.

Meredy: Your surmise is correct. In the new experiment Hegel portrays a percipient at the mercy of a sophistry betraying itself in his constant reiteration of the qualifying term 'insofar'. The object perceived seems to lie in such a tangled context that its veridical experience now hinges on shifting points of view. The object *is* whatever it *becomes* in virtue of its various and variable relations. This may be true enough when fully grasped. But confronting us is not painstaking discrimination but improvised opinion. Repeated use of a jejune phrase here takes the place of genuine understanding. 'Insofar as' a thing is taken by itself, it will manifest characteristics differing from those it seems to have in conjunction with other things. 'It all depends'—how often one hears *this* fatuous qualification! A thing has no fixed status. What it is perceived as being is ever relative to different contexts and different perspectives.

Hardith: Yet, 'insofar', an expression too evasive not to be exploited by common sense, embodies nevertheless the spirit of a principle not alien to thought. What the 'qualifying percipient', to call him thus, consistently adheres to is the principle of relativity. Might he not in accordance with it argue as follows?

"Unity and diversity undeniably belong to the thing perceived but in no absolute fashion. A thing is 'one' insofar as I focus attention on it alone, but insofar as I concentrate attention on its 'many' properties, I must alter my perspective and view it as a medium of universals shared by other things. A thing is doubtless identical with itself and 'undivided' perception of it bears this out, but its self-identity is 'disturbed' by other things, causing perception to go beyond it. The contradiction of 'the one and the many' thus becomes quite innocuous; it arises only when perception is divided, when instead of contemplating the 'same' thing, my perspective takes in a wider context in which 'different' things have properties in common."

Meredy: This is indeed the position of a percipient whose alterable perspectives are alleged to govern his qualifications. But the position is so vulnerable. If the 'perspectival percipient'—and I too may give him a name—isolates for exclusive notice a single object, disregarding the context in which it suffers disturbance of identity, how render determinate its perceived unity? For a thing, we must remember, can enjoy distinction only when differentiated from other things. This is here axiomatic. But since no thing can be differentiated except by its properties and since properties are universal, the ignored context of different things reappears to plague the presumption of perceivable identity.

Hardith: Here again the issue can be met with a qualification. Thus, speaking for our supposed percipient, I call a thing 'essentially' determinate only insofar as its own qualities enable me to identify it; that other objects may appropriate the qualities as equally their own is simply 'unessential'. It is indeed true that the manifold qualities by which a thing is determined do not exclusively belong to it, but how can this affect the actual percept here and now? By the very fact of attending to what is essential to it, I distinguish one percept from another. Considerations drawn from what lies beyond a particular field of attention become completely irrelevant.

Meredy: But are such considerations really irrelevant? The attempt to isolate a thing for true apprehension of its essential nature is foredoomed to failure. For a thing is essentially itself only if it can be explicitly distinguished from other things. Distinction is a relation, and relation implies a context in which things lose their separateness. Hence a dilemma: either a thing is unrelated to other things, in which case it cannot be essentially determinate, or else it is essentially determinate by being related to them, in which case its isolation becomes illusory. Determinateness, which relates a thing to everything it is distinguishable from, nullifies its alleged self-dependence. How then can the percipient withdraw within a quasi-monadic perspective in which the percept would appear intrinsically single and singular?

Hardith: The answer is that he can obviously not do so in absolute fashion. An object's essential aspects are not wholly independent of the percipient's particular perspective. If singleness or singularity appears more essential than the opposite, it can appear so only in so far as attention is focused upon this exclusively. It hardly needs saying that one particular perspective can be always exchanged for another.

Meredy: But exclusiveness—and this Hegel constantly reiterates—is entirely at variance with determinateness. Who can perceive as determinate anything without presupposing for its individual otherness objects individually other than it? Is anything open to perception, whatever the perspective, that can be endowed with uniqueness by perception? And how can anything be taken as qualitatively exclusive without taking it also in relation to the qualities it excludes? Implicit in perception are problems transcending perception. They call for understanding. What to the percipient remains unintelligible becomes amenable to explanation by a method adequate for interpreting sensible particulars in terms of general concepts.

Hardith: How adroit a transition! So the percipient retires from the stage making his bow to the approaching conceptualist. But I must still demur. The problem *of* perception, not being a problem *for* perception, leaves untouched the authenticity of perception as a universal mode of experience. The experience here subjected to such a formidable dialectic seems to be enjoyed by everyone without the slightest awareness of the difficulties injected into it by the philosopher. Perceptual knowledge continues to flourish without abatement regardless of all the theoretical reflections on it; and common sense, said to be dominated by such knowledge, is generally not given to self-criticism. Accordingly, the philosophic issues relating to perceptual experience cannot be raised in the course of this experience without destroying the experience it is. To perceptual experience itself discursive arguments are simply foreign, and to import the latter into the former is to impugn not the experience but the arguments expressly designed to render it anomalous.

Meredy: You entered, as I remember, a similar caveat against Hegel's procedure in dealing with sense-certainty. I should only be repeating statements already made were I to meet in like manner your present objection. I will only say just this. To perceive and to understand the perceived are quite different things. There is more in his experience than the percipient can be adequately aware of, and in this 'more' lies the chief interest of Hegel's dialectic. A related interest here involved is the corollary that every theory of perception is awry which isolates perception from the nonperceptual contexts to which it is naturally joined. That the percipient is more than a percipient clearly emerges from the attempt to portray him as if he were nothing but a percipient. The logic comprehended *in* perception cannot be comprehended *by* perception—this, if I may emulate Hegel in verbal license, expresses the heart of the matter. Things seemingly so palpable require for their utterance the most general of concepts. Being and becoming, unity and multiplicity, identity and difference, existence and essence, individuality and universality, these abstractions, and others like them, are all implicit in any percept given as determinate and *taken* as such. The percept belongs, so to speak, to a mixed species, partly 'sensible', partly 'intelligible'. Present to be seen and touched, it is also under the dominance of opposed terms of discourse. The percipient's dilemma is thus ineluctable: either he ignores the logical distinctions requisite for fixing the notion of a determinate thing, in which case the object becomes that of pure sense, and his attitude to it must be intuitive; or else, he takes full cognizance of these distinctions, and in that case, what he perceives becomes indeed intelligible, but only because for the order and connection of things he substitutes the order and connection of concepts. The perceptive view, though avoiding the difficulties latent in sense-certainty, remains a makeshift until the conceptual position is uncompromisingly assumed. Serving two masters, as it were, perception can attain neither certitude nor clearness. Although rooted in sense, pure enjoyment of ineffable immediacy is not the percipient's lot, since what he takes for his object is describable by universal qualities; although talkative, the percipient's assertions are loose and superficial, improvised to ward off criticism rather than to deepen it. His reflections, as well as his utterances, fluctuate between those of the simpleton and the sophist. Not by his halting essays in comprehension can the issues germane to perception be brought to light.

Hardith: And what irony Hegel lavishes on the perceptive consciousness! Identifying perception with common sense, often eulogized as good sense or horse sense, he expatiates on the sophistry and illusion the percipient is heir to. This identification enables him to give short shrift to the conventional distrust of philosophic thought, a distrust usually based on the contrast between concrete facts and abstract ideas. Real for the intellectual philistine are but the outer and solid things perceived; philosophy deals with the impalpable things of the mind— airy nothings the average man may safely hold in contempt. Is this final attack on perception integral or extraneous to the dialectic?

Meredy: Who can completely separate polemic and dialectic? This is a matter we are bound to consider time and again. Here, however, personal bias and detached criticism seem to go hand in hand. Nothing is more obvious than the indefeasible contrast between objects of perception and objects of thought. Yet how comprehend the former without the latter? It is this question to which Hegel's long and intricate analysis boils down. Yes, it is by means of thought's concepts that the philosopher achieves power over the stubborn facts common sense runs up against. How does common sense challenge the encroachment of the abstractions of the intellect upon the empirical nature of things? To philosophic abstractions it opposes abstractions of its own. But it is continually duped by the shaky notions randomly contrived to justify its faith in the reality of things merely perceived. The philosopher, seeing it entangled in lame conclusions, looks on and laughs in his sleeve. "Common sense is always poorest," as Hegel says, "where it means to be richest." The facts to which common sense clings with such tenacity become distorted by the absurd arguments advanced for the belief in them. The deceptiveness of things lies in the illusoriness of perceptions endowed with independently cognitive authenticity. Only when interpreted in ways fashioned by the intellect can things be properly understood.

Understanding

1. *The Concept of Force*

Hardith: Decidedly disconcerting is the halfway position in which Hegel leaves perception, showing that it occupies a region bounded on one side by sense and on the other by thought. And the two sides are diametrically opposed. Accordingly, if pushed in one direction, perception, chained to immediate experience, must fall back on ineffable certainty; if pushed in the other, perception grows reflective, and the distinction between the object as given and mind's gift to it remains incorrigibly ambiguous and unstable. No wonder the situation such as Hegel exhibits it cries out for reconstruction. The transition to understanding thus becomes quite natural. And what is understanding to accomplish? Nothing less, it would seem, than to conceptualize perceptual cognition, if cognition it may be called, seeing that perception is here turned into a source and occasion of endless and insoluble problems. All this I find exceedingly baffling.

Meredy: I need not remind you that Hegel's task is here confined to the diagnosis of a paradox. The paradox is but *latent* in perception, not manifesting itself until perceptual cognition is considered in isolation and treated as if it were, so to say, autonomous. The paradox, once brought to light, conditions and controls the ensuing phase of the dialectic. It must be borne in mind, however, that not the activity of understanding in general is what Hegel here presents but only a special application of it requisite for the resolution of the issues thus far precipitated. What necessitates a new approach to the cognition of things is the singular impasse reached in the analysis of perceptual experience. The claim to truth made for that experience constitutes the crux of the matter. The claim cannot be satisfied unless we go behind perception to direct awareness of sensible data, and thus to all the difficulties attending such awareness, or else move forward to full-fledged concepts needed to render perception expressly intelligible. The sensible and the intelligible, of which perception is all compact, are present in it as strangers.

May I call attention to a word strikingly suggestive of the dialectic under consideration and for which there is no exact equivalent in German? Is not the term 'common sense' an odd combination of opposites? For what is common, being general, transcends sensory awareness; and what is sensuously given, being a datum of immediate apprehension, is not open to public inspection. What an advantage the English expression enjoys in conveying with such accuracy the presence in perceptual experience of aspects literally poles apart! Hence the propriety of speaking of such experience as a sort of halfway house and the necessity of looking either behind or beyond it.

Hardith: Your attempt to surpass Hegel in linguistic legerdemain is certainly arresting. But of course you are not serious. You know as well as I that 'common' and 'sense' are words of differing meanings and varied uses. The dialectic inherent in their juxtaposition hinges on viewing the first as equatable exclusively with universal and the second with sensation. Who would commit the folly of thus equating and hyphening them? Verbal jugglery aside, it would seem inevitable to take a given percept as both sensuously qualitied and conceptually qualifiable. Without the latter condition, no percept, such as Hegel's 'salt', could ever come to bear the name of a determinate thing. The dialectic of perception involves the precarious distinction and relation between its object's qualities and the qualifications attached thereto. Now perceptual truth, assuming this to be the core of the matter, is unmistakably ambivalent, requiring that we fluctuate between intuition and discourse; the former refers to the qualitied nature of the object, the latter to its qualified status. If perceptual truth is of the intuitive kind, nothing but sensory data directly present can vouch for it, necessitating that we revert to the superseded position of sense-certainty, thus starting the dialectic of immediacy all over again, of which the outcome is the very cognition of objects both qualified and qualitied. So there is no alternative save to advance to the view of perception as definitely qualified by conception. Here truth, apposite chiefly to the object's qualifications, ceases to be intuitive and becomes discursive. But advance to this view is difficult. The section devoted to it, so inordinately complex in detail and obscure in expression, leaves me bewildered. What I find particularly recondite is the concept of force as a concept of the understanding.

Meredy: The distinction between the qualitied and the qualified, which is here quite pertinent, shows that your distaste for playing with words can scarce be so strong as you choose to pretend. The paradox it involves stems from the fact that a particular percept, a thing primarily sensuous, appears as if bearing on its face the stamp of non-sensuous forms. That the thing owes its 'thinghood' to universals not sensuously given as such remains completely inexplicable without 'taking thought'. But the thought resorted to must not be confused with the so-called reflection operative at the level of common sense. What is anomalous in perceptual cognition cannot find its corrective except in the modes of explanation peculiar to the understanding. The only way to explain the particular is to subsume it under some general concept. And force is precisely such a concept with the aid of which an object sensuously qualitied (to use this happy locution) may receive qualified intelligibility.

Hardith: But force seems too multivocal a term to play the part here assigned to it. In its strict sense, when described as 'natural', force is said to explain many physical phenomena as well as nonphysical. Although never quite free from anthropomorphic overtones, many natural forces, gravitational among others, appear as if purged of their original anthropomorphism when appearing clothed in mathematical formulas. What have the anomalies of perception to do with the forces of nature? Are the objects perceived to be understood as phenomena comporting with the postulates of philosophic naturalism? This would evidently follow from an exact construction of the concept. But force has many meanings principally metaphorical, and these differ as widely as the contexts in which it figures as a figure of speech. Consider expressions such as 'the striking force of an experience', 'the probative force of an argument', and many another figurative connotation of the word. So even as a trope its use in explaining the perceptual situation can hardly be taken seriously. How then should force be understood as an explanatory concept? Whence the necessity of applying it to the problem of perception?

Meredy: The section we are considering is exceedingly intricate in structure and abstruse in idiom. It covers too much ground. And Hegel's manner of referring but indirectly to certain thinkers or their thoughts is truly vexatious. His method is studiously allusive. Followed with occasional lapses throughout the *Phenomenology,* he employs the method here with complete abandon, making confusion worse confounded. We have nothing but allusions, and we can only guess as best we may the sources of the themes alluded to. Their exact identification is, however, a scholar's business not essential to our purpose. The earlier references are seemingly to ancient speculations as well as to those peculiar to the sciences of Hegel's day; the later ones are

61

clearly to ideas culled from modern philosophy, and especially to ideas loosely attributable to Spinoza, Kant, and Schelling. What Hegel seeks to accomplish in a survey so panoramic, though much of the subject matter may elude us, is a comprehensive diagnosis of a persuasion conceived as deeply rooted in human understanding, all the diagnostic variations being related to the general topic of explanation.

Hardith: Minutiae aside, which may be safely left to the specialists, what I should like to grasp is the transition from perception to understanding. This is here made to hinge on force, a concept explanatory of natural phenomena, and one admittedly primitive or antiquated. How ineluctable is the transition?

Meredy: The transition is of course dialectical rather than actual. In the light of the diagnosis of perception, shown to be big with paradoxes irremediable in perceptual terms, what corrective may be looked for by advancing to a new position? This, so it turns out, lies in construing percepts and concepts as partly homologous, an act necessary only on the assumption that given percepts are more than sensuous. Not unnatural, therefore, at this stage, is the belief that the sensible things perceived are appearances of a supersensible reality. And equally natural is the belief that the reality they manifest is some force in the name of which the appearances may be 'saved' as well as 'understood'. For force proves to be an object amenable to the very forms the percipient seeks in vain to graft upon his percepts.

Hardith: The gist of the matter seems to be this: sensible things, as long as they are held to be *merely* sensible, cannot be understood at all; to understand them, one must look for the reality of which they are the appearances, force being that reality. And why must it be some force which the sensible things make manifest? Because, so the answer runs, force is subject to those forms of cognition which the diagnosis of perception, following upon the dialectic of sense-certainty, disclosed as indispensable. The escape from the dialectic of sense-certainty leads to perception; and the dialectic of perception conditions the transition to understanding. And requisite for the transition are certain distinctions, those between the sensible and the supersensible and the apparent and the real being here fundamental. This much is clear to me. But what except caprice determines choice of force as the *only* supersensible reality capable of explaining the problem of perception?

Meredy: Choice of force as exemplifying initially the partial homology between percepts and concepts seems arbitrary only if phenomenology is confused with history. The passage from perception to conception is not such as can be definitely dated. Historical material often does enter the text but chiefly by way of illustration. The movements of thought on which Hegel dilates enjoy necessity solely in the dialectical context in which they are traced and developed. The relation of phenomenology to history is a crucial matter to which much attention will have to be given later on. What we are now concerned with is the process of thought involved in the sort of knowledge Hegel calls understanding. And this is a process preeminently dialectical. It is precisely the reflective experiment with perception as an isolated and autonomous experience that gives rise to issues requiring for their resolution recourse to nonperceptual modes of cognition. And if force is made to appear as the inchoate concept explanatory of the anomalies inherent in the perceptual situation, one of the reasons for it is dialectically primary. This has to do with the process of development undergone by every persuasion, the career of which, like that of an organism, necessitates continual change from simpler to more complex expressions. Such is the career of sense-certainty and such is the career of perception. Now the career of understanding must progress in similar fashion. How artless is the first form of force as principle of explanation! The form is clearly congenial to common sense. As such Hegel presents it at the beginning, seeing that common sense constitutes the immediate background of the understanding.

Hardith: How ingenious! Conceptual explanation not far from the level of common sense is certainly primitive, and primitive in time and not merely in the context of Hegel's dialectic. Consider the speculations of the pre-Socratics. These speculations, to which you say the text alludes, show that the concepts of the understanding, posited in the *Phenomenology* as inchoate, happen to be historically incipient as well. Derived from common sense with a vengeance, these concepts are but percepts in thin disguise, water, air, and the like. Naïve explanations of the nature of things belong to the childhood of thought. And each kind of common percept transformed into an explanatory concept might be made to serve the purpose of effecting the transition to the understanding as required by the dialectic. Why preempt force for this transitional office? Simplicity or primitiveness can obviously not be regarded as the only ground. What other consideration is here requisite to justify the preference?

Meredy: One further consideration is here decisive. In force as initially conceived the ambivalences of perceptual experience appear *aufgehoben* or, so to speak, sublimated. We need but to attend to its basic meaning. The details Hegel dwells upon, having merely antiquarian importance, we may safely disregard. How in general do the issues to which the analysis of perception gives rise become resolved by the understanding? And why must force appear as the first concept

63

involved in their resolution? Such are the questions with which we must be primarily concerned.

Now, however vague in conception, force exemplifies the instability and relativity perception exhibits when its qualitied object changes in meaning in accordance with mind's shifting qualifications. Here is a notion connoting a reality essentially dynamic, unitary as well as differentiated, and ever outrunning the various forms in which it appears. A power behind its appearances, as it were, force exists always and everywhere; potential when not actual, it is a universal of which the particular expressions are endless, being one of those notions impossible to think of save in terms of opposites: force pushes and force pulls, it attracts and it repels, it lies dormant and it erupts. What perception implies but fails to reveal—namely, an object's unity in multiplicity and identity in difference—the understanding clarifies and brings to fruition in the notion of force. The notion is familiar enough in modern dress. Its first appearance in understanding, having a perceptual origin, is of course a far cry from its use in the fully developed natural sciences.

2. The Play of Forces and the Kindom of Laws

Hardith: Admitting that by the process of conceptualization perception becomes explainable, the contradictory elements do not cease being contradictory when transferred from perception to understanding. We have simply the same issue on another level. Crucial here is the relation between force as generic and its specific expressions. The many ways, for instance, of pushing and pulling, are they ways of one and the same force? The duality of opposed tendencies may be converted into a sharp dualism. Force would seem to forfeit its unity if construed as displayed in separate powers. Are they or are they not mutually exclusive? The question admits of more than one answer. We might contend (a) that there is but one universal force manifest in the play of particular forces, and, though opposed, the particular forces are nevertheless interdependent, seeing that each is the other's correlative and requires reference to the other for its very meaning. But we could maintain also (b) that force is only a name for polar forces, and each in being a determinate force excludes the other in accordance with the notion of determinateness as applied earlier to the perceptual situation. Here again is the problem of 'the one and the many'.

Meredy: You state in admirably terse fashion what in Hegel's text fills many pages of recondite analysis. Yes, the meaning of force turns out to be equivocal. Because self-differentiation belongs to its essence, force must appear in its initial phase as a concept marked by inner tension. Preliminary consideration of the concept shows that force cannot reveal its true nature except in the interplay of contrary forces; each, whenever actual, appears as the negative of its rival: one is what the other is not or is not what the other is. Force as latent or anterior to its expression and force as operative or expressed are ever related by reciprocal negation, typifying a duality verging on dualism. For the determinate character of each kind logically demands the other's exclusion, yet for its own determinateness each kind depends on opposition to and limitation by the other. But we have only begun our exploration of the career of force.

Hardith: The key to the issue seems to lie in the distinction between force as universal and its particular polarization. How valid is the distinction? A universal force, taken in independence of its polar expression, is a sort of subject without predicates and remains as such altogether indescribable. The word 'potential', applied to force in its quiescent form, is simply a cover for our ignorance relating to the existence of force prior to its perceivable manifestations. How are we to understand the status of force as the independently real? Does it perchance resemble a 'thing-in-itself' in infinite remoteness from external appearances?

Meredy: Your mention of the 'thing-in-itself' would be surprising if it were inadvertent. You know of course that Hegel invokes Kant's dualism of the supersensible and the sensible for the purpose of indicating a supposed way of dealing with the impasse reached at this point. Of the ultramundane reality of force the given play of forces is but the denotable appearance, everything perceived having its ground in the imperceptible. It is a propensity of the understanding to move from empirical data to their non-empirical source, and if the data are preempted as the true objects of cognition, the source must needs remain in the limbo of the ultimately unknowable. The given play of forces thus serves as a sort of 'middle term', as Hegel calls it, linking the two extremes, a nonphenomenal region and a conceptualizing intelligence. The understanding, starting indeed with the overt behavior of force, discerns behind such behavior the covert or supersensible condition explaining it.

Hardith: Apart from the allusion to the dualism in the Kantian form, what the dialectic is here made to hinge on, it seems to me, is the distinction between appearance and reality, and one which turns out to be either too stark or too tenuous. In a pejorative sense, appearance is synonymous with illusion (*Schein*) or with any other term antithetical to reality. Appearance as a nondepreciatory word signifies rather the aspect or aspects in which the real must become manifest (*Erscheinung*). Is the phenomenal simply the nonreal or the real

65

necessarily embodied in it? Must the relation between appearance and reality be construed as disjunctive? It is this irremediable ambivalence of appearance which precipitates the dilemma involved in the given play of forces. If the play is but an outward show, the being claimed for it can be no less specious than that possessed by all things sensible; but if the play is an authentic revelation of a supersensible force, its being becomes as genuine as the being which thus appears revealed. This I take to be the main issue, the animadversion upon Kant being but a side issue.

Meredy: Yes, the word appearance, owing to the inevitable ambiguity you note, seems as if made to order for Hegel's purpose. But the allusion to Kant is here not the side issue you take it to be. The critique of reason's purity, as well as the justification of the role assigned to the faculty of the understanding, rests fundamentally on the notion of appearance, so much so that Hegel could scarce have refrained from dwelling on its notorious difficulty. If the real is inaccessibly behind or beyond the world of appearance, the only world comprising the objects of knowledge, the real thus conceived is too transcendent to satisfy the needs of explanation; but if the supersensible appears and must appear *in* the sensible, the things knowable are so intimately linked with their transcendent source that the distinction between appearance and reality would seem to leave little room for difference. Not by a deeper or higher unknowable force can the given play of forces be explained; here literally 'the play's the thing'.

Hardith: To abandon the embarrassing dichotomy of appearance and reality is of course not to surrender the attempt to explain the given play of forces. The understanding, true to its vocation, must find some other way to conceptualize the perceptible. And now Hegel introduces into the discussion the mode of explanation by law such as the sciences are said to be engaged in. From the supersensible nature of force to a general law of force the transition is quite precipitate. Whence its necessity?

Meredy: The necessity, as observed before, is but dialectical, the necessity every persuasion is under to yield the palm of truth to a logical successor in which it becomes transfigured (*aufgehoben*). Such indeed is the passage from the belief in a 'supersensible world' to the belief in 'the Kingdom of Laws', the expressions being Hegel's. Laws, too, are supersensible but not powers hidden in a region beyond the reach of mind; creatures of the intellect, they are framed to serve the very purpose of explanation. Determinate forces, no longer the appearances of a universal but unknowable force, appear rather in accordance with some definite law determining their nature and behavior. This constitutes a natural advance on a position requiring for its basis the indefensible bifurcation of appearance and reality.

Hardith: The supersensible making way for the 'legal'—what a strange and dramatic development! The temptation is irresistible to conceive of it in historical terms. That scientific laws actually came to replace philosophic speculations in explaining the nature of things is an indisputable fact. I cannot help looking upon this part of the discussion as an anticipation in some measure of Auguste Comte's theory of the stages of human thought. Explanation by scientific laws, growing out of and supplanting explanation by divine volitions or occult causes, reflects the most mature phase in man's intellectual evolution. If force is a summary concept suggesting the era called metaphysical, law is one which typifies the age of scientific progress. Science thus belongs to a higher order than metaphysics. What irony to find this view confirmed in the *Phenomenology!*

Meredy: While the dialectic is not primarily a dialectic of history, historical examples are always available to show that Hegel's diagnosis of human persuasions is not without empirical support. Your allusion to Comte is thus not irrelevant. We must remember, however, that neither science nor metaphysics can enter full-fledged in the present context. Explanation as here treated, being an activity of the understanding, depends on the consciousness of objects presumed to exist in quasi-realistic fashion. Although intent upon transcending perception, the understanding has no data save such as perception alone can vouch for. Reason, presupposing the dialectic of self-consciousness as well as that of the understanding, will in the sequel appear as source of scientific and metaphysical conceptions more complex and less jejune. Here, however, and this implies no irony, scientific belief in natural laws outranks in importance belief in a supersensible realm, 'metaphysical' having precisely the Comtean connotation you so ingeniously attribute to it.

Hardith: You have failed to mention an aspect of the situation on which Hegel, perhaps but parenthetically, lays some stress. What I have in mind is the invariant nature of law assumed to govern the ever-shifting play of forces. If that which explains change is held to be immune from change, what can vie with a law of nature in freedom from mutability? Does the triumph of the understanding lie in the capacity to envisage the flux of things as obeying a permanent order determined by its own conceptual effort?

Meredy: Ah, if thought could only fasten upon a single law by which to explain all the given appearances! But, alas, of laws there is a great variety, each, so to speak, a law unto itself, just as either of two polar forces exerts all the force there is. The kingdom of laws is not so stable as originally conceived; the tensions latent in it exemplify a situation cognate with that inherent in force. Not in law as such can the principle of explanation be vested but only in the determinate laws whose meaning and relevance depend on the contexts to which they apply, and their determinateness is a function of their interdependence; each law differs from all the others, and this difference is part and parcel of its identity. Interdependence of identity and difference is a theme on which Hegel rings numerous changes. As expatiated on in this section, determinateness, whether of forces or of laws, rests on negative no less than on positive grounds, and thus precipitates anew the problem of the 'one and the many'. Is the conception of a law of laws more tenable than the conception of a single force present in all its expressions? Universal law, like universal force, lacks the determinateness that belongs to its particular forms. In other words, law as genus is not law in the same sense in which any of its species is a law, a law relative to the appearances it purports to explain. All important here is the analogy between law and force.

Hardith: The equivocations adhering to the concept of law are seemingly ineradicable. From one point of view, law is a name for various types of order, each independent within its own sphere of phenomena, yet related to the others as required by the principle of determinateness. From a different point of view, law is synonymous with the notion of order itself, having as such the meaning of an abstract universal transcending the particular embodiments it is susceptible of. The analogy of force and law you note is certainly striking. But if the analogy is as close as you suggest, whence the advantage of law over force? For in the dialectic of the understanding, law occupies a more advanced position.

3. The Locus of Necessity

Meredy: But for one consideration the distinction between force and law would indeed remain tenuous. It is the idea of necessity which establishes their difference. Law and necessity are so bound each to each by mutual implication that they are virtually interchangeable. Whatever is subject to law thought takes to be necessary; conversely, whatever thought deems necessary must conform to law. The play of forces ceases to be fortuitous if, as in a game, it can be shown to proceed in accordance with invariant rules. Force thus becomes transformed from an appearance of a supersensible reality into a process necessitated by fixed laws.

Hardith: What a provocative pun! If the play of forces resembles a game determined by conventional rules, what a reflection on nature as well as on science! Is nature nothing more than the source of volatile processes amenable to mind's conceptual ingenuities? And is science nothing else than skill in inventing ways of playing the game of explanation? Surely, this cannot be all that understanding is able to accomplish.

Meredy: Considered isolate and, as it were, autonomous, the understanding can do nothing but display continually its explanatory powers. This will shortly appear as the outcome of its dialectic towards which some further steps must still be taken. Hegel enriches the diagnosis by speaking allusively of certain explanatory efforts of his scientific contemporaries. We must leave it to the cognoscenti to gather from the text the relevant references to the luminaries of his day. Details apart, we must briefly note what, within the general framework of the concepts of force and law, he says of gravitation and electricity.

Hardith: Hegel's excursion into the field of physics—his allusion to Newton is unmistakable—is rather unfortunate. His authority for passing judgment on scientific theories is certainly open to doubt. If the problems pertaining to universal gravitation, for instance, are here incorporated for discussion on their merits, Hegel may justly be charged with supererogation. I assume, however, that they are merely dealt with by way of illustration. If so, matters relating to gravitation, as well as those having to do with electricity, throw an oblique light on the dialectic thus far developed. For gravitation and electricity exemplify forces too subtle for perception; their behavior is subject to laws expressible ultimately in mathematical form. And electricity in particular, distinguishable as positive and negative, reveals polarization on a new level. Here we have again the play of forces, with the attending difficulty of explaining by law its necessity, leading thought to become once more entangled in a net of untenable distinctions.

Meredy: It is always tempting but hazardous to attribute to the author ideas subject to analysis in this treatise. The *Phenomenology* is not autobiography; the mind depicted is not Hegel's own. The section on understanding, concerned as it is with a recurrent paradox of consciousness, is no index to Hegel's philosophic commitments. To construe it as such is to mistake both the aim and method of its diagnostic task. The criticism of science which the section contains is but criticism of the explanatory habit of mind, congenial to thought in one of its dimensions, in the exercise of which, to use your felicitous phrase, it "becomes entangled in a net of untenable distinctions." To be sure, not wanting in this section (nor in subsequent ones as well) are utterances matching those which Hegel expressed elsewhere and which embody

69

his own convictions. Such parallelism has misled many a scholar. The criticism of Newton, touched on in the diagnosis of the understanding, is indeed one Hegel developed along the same lines much earlier and more fully. But the dramatis persona here is the understanding and not Newton. The dialectic is independent of any personage, historical or contemporary, alluded to for purposes of illustration. This is a point important enough to merit constant reiteration.

So let us not be distracted by extraneous considerations. The chief issue here precipitated centers in the validity of the distinctions requisite for the activity of explanation understanding is intent upon. And Hegel shows that the untenability of the distinctions made in explaining the cruder notions of force applies equally to the more refined variants involved in gravitation and electricity. Confining ourselves to the latter, which lends itself more readily to summary statement, the gist of the argument seems to be this. Division into positive and negative electricity is simply a recrudescence of the polar forces whose necessary interplay some law is required to account for. Now one thing is necessity assumed to belong to matters of fact, quite another is necessity ascribable to the laws descriptive of them. No law, however, can endow with necessity the existence or behavior of anything. Electricity is what it is, and no description can prescribe its ways of operation. The notions of law and necessity thus continue to plague explanatory understanding. The relation between the law of things and the necessity of their being remains anomalous.

Hardith: It would be unprofitable to carry the discussion into greater detail. Hegel is dealing with scientific themes, and adequate treatment of them calls for special knowledge. Despite his cavalier approach to them, at which one might feel inclined to take umbrage, the effectiveness of the diagnosis is quite impressive. The conclusion reached is drastic: whatever is, is, and the distinctions made to explain it are distinctions without differences. Explanation proceeds throughout on a verbal plane, explaining nothing simply because the process here relied upon is incorrigibly tautological. And yet, the process is far from futile; it actually yields momentous consequences. How very curious that tautology should come to be charged with so much importance.

Meredy: The denouement of the tautological process inherent in understanding is no surprise, seeing that it accords with the dramatic intent of the dialectical method. Necessity, which is here the central concept, delusory though it be when applied to knowledge or existence, is real and compelling in relation to the activity of explanation. The necessity thought succeeds in revealing is but the necessity of its incessant operations. How can thought avoid the necessity of creating and

70

annuling concepts if its explanations are based on distinctions with vanishing lines between them? Thus force is explained by differentiating it from the law descriptive of its necessary expressions, polarity being then understood as inherent in it. Yet the difference between force and law is specious, since their difference is not one of content. The law of force *is* force viewed under the aspect of necessity. This is typical of the understanding: it always moves from tautology to tautology, each serving as explanation of a reality that in its proper domain enjoys an intrinsic nature untouched by conceptual fluctuations. The world of understanding is thus no other than a world of distinctions it must perforce make and unmake, the supersensible world, the object of its explanatory zeal, remaining meanwhile whatever in its own fixed sphere it happens to be. And as a result of further diagnosis, each becomes what Hegel speaks of as the 'inverted world'. But the topic, growing here more and more recondite, belongs to the province of the meticulous exegete.

Hardith: Understanding must indeed come to grief on the assumption that it can impose upon matters of fact distinctions so rashly bred in the mind. Reducible to tautology or contradiction, they are wholly inadequate for the task of explanation. The root of the difficulty seems to be twofold. (1) The objects to be explained, whose content is inherently sensible, the understanding *must* trace to a supersensible source, unless the conceptual and perceptual positions be regarded as one and indivisible. But the concepts of the understanding are ill equipped for invading the supersensible realm, supersensible signifying in this context the same as the transcendent or the independently real. (2) Yet the concepts here relevant refuse to be isolated and kept apart: the sensible and the supersensible, mutually exclusive at first, end by becoming mutually inclusive: identity always appears burdened with difference and difference with identity: unity and plurality have no meaning except as inseverable correlatives. And so too as regards the other concepts which the understanding must heavily lean upon. From this impasse escape is not possible without radical correction of the understanding. And the correction would seem to require complete withdrawal from the supersensible world and explicit acquiescence in the necessity of contradiction. Is this what the diagnosis of the understanding logically points to?

Meredy: You indicate succinctly the two ways in which the understanding must come to 'understand' itself before finding fulfillment in a more tenable persuasion concerning the relation of thought and being. But this persuasion lies far ahead, and leading to it are several intermediary steps, of which the most important obviously is, in your

71

apt phrase, "complete withdrawal from the supersensible world." Until it abandons the attempt to explain the inexplicable, understanding is precluded from becoming fully self-conscious.

Hardith: In forsaking the supersensible world, is the understanding intent upon merely ignoring or outright denying its existence? In other words, does the inexplicable signify *something* that for the present cannot be explained or just plain *nothing* and thus demanding no explanation? The first meaning, which is quite compatible with scientific procedure, sounds less extreme than the second. I wonder which we should emphasize in connection with an understanding becoming aware of its limitation.

Meredy: An understanding but aware of its limitation would of course not deny the existence of that which remains unexplained, the inexplicable connoting whatever literally transcends its grasp. But the kind of understanding Hegel examines becomes increasingly aware of power rather than limitation, and is thus prone to negate everything resisting it. And this awareness of power is one transition to self-consciousness. Hegel depicts the emergence of this phase in the satisfaction, not to say exuberance, with which thought enjoys the exercise of explanatory activity, an exercise bringing thought, as Hegel says, "in direct communion with itself." The career of understanding thus culminates in self-communion. The curtain alleged to hide the supersensible world ceases to be impervious. If understanding could step behind the curtain, the supersensible world would appear as myth of its own making, created to serve the very purpose of explanation. But the same power that created the myth to explain the world of appearances can also explain it away. All explanatory concepts presuppose mind engaged in their formation, and in growing conscious of its own operation in forming them, consciousness turns into self-consciousness.

Hardith: The portrayal of conceptualism reaching its climax in self-communion is certainly singular. If the career of understanding consists in moving from extrospection to introspection, what ultimately remains to be explained? We seem to have ended with a type of consciousness endowed with an infinite capacity for explaining but without objects on which to exercise it. Why must such a type be exhibited as passing, if I may say so, from phenomenalism to subjectivism, and not vice versa? The outcome of this passage, rendering untenable the notion of appearances deriving from a reality external to them, leaves mind undisturbed blithely to indulge in tautologies and contradictions. This strikes me as a caricature of the work of the understanding.

Meredy: Yes, a caricature, but only when understanding becomes engrossed primarily in the task of conceptualizing the perceptual situation. The development of its career makes then inevitable its last recourse to introspection. Unable to explain things perceived, understanding discovers merely itself in the process of explaining them. This is the gist of the matter, and your choice of the terms phenomenalism and subjectivism is here particularly apposite. For the issue confronting understanding consists in the necessity of distinguishing between sensible appearances and a supersensible reality, but this is a distinction it is unable to maintain. Hegel's allusion to the issue as present in Kant can hardly be disregarded. The objects of perception would have to be considered purely subjective in origin, in precisely the sense in which Berkeley so considered them, but for the things-in-themselves Kant conceived of as their realistic underpinning, and only by contrast with their transcendent source could our percepts acquire the status of phenomena. With the removal of the underpinning by Kant's successors, subjectivism comes to assert its sovereignty again, the phenomenalism by which Kant is alleged to have curtailed its legitimacy becoming obsolescent. For illustration of the conversion of the phenomenal into the subjective, Hegel scarcely needed to go far afield. Yet the caricature, if we choose so to call it, performs for Hegel a dual role: it affords the necessary transition to self-consciousness and it serves to anticipate the profound difference between understanding and reason. When appearing on the scene, following the diagnosis of self-consciousness, reason will contend for a more adequate relation of thought and being, finding in the ubiquity of contradiction, so baffling to understanding, the very basis of that relation. But this is a long and intricate story.

Hardith: If understanding must find its corrective in reason and if it is by reason that contradiction becomes vindicated, why the intermediary elaborate diagnosis of self-consciousness? Why not pass directly to a rational conception of things? Why is self-consciousness needed as passageway into reason's territory?

Meredy: Self-consciousness is indeed the road leading to what you speak of as 'reason's territory'. The term is perhaps misleading since it is not topography we are here concerned with. Each type of persuasion treated in the *Phenomenology* is revealed as having a career. And the career is dialectical rather than temporal (though, as remarked before, not without historical illustrations), running its course from self-assertion to self-alienation. And each contains the seed of another in which it survives in sublated form. The dialectic of sense-certainty, we recall, generates that of perception in which alone its 'truth' remains preserved. And now we have traced the same dialectical evolution in understanding: it proceeds from perception and culminates in introspection. This general pattern recurs in the development of every persuasion; in bringing to fruition what is but implicit in what preceded, it raises the issues of the persuasion to follow. Understanding grown introspective—and this marks the incongruous termination of its career—appears as the new persuasion in embryo incorporating its supposititious 'truth'. For introspection, undeniably intent upon cognition, depends on the very tautologies and contradictions that plague the understanding in its attempts at explanation. To be introspective is to be self-conscious, and to be self-conscious is to be involved in a situation patently anomalous. How avoid redundancy and equivocation in expressing it? The division of the self into subject and object is an act of self-division by one and the same self: here identity turns into difference and difference reverts to identity. It is as if an internal play of forces were taking place when understanding reaches the level of introspection. Polar opposites *within* a unitary being—of this, transcending the explanatory efforts of the understanding, every consciousness knows with complete assurance when it knows itself.

Hardith: What a *tour de force!* This self-knowledge, an expression not quite synonymous with self-consciousness, the understanding, I take it, is prophetic of. Will the promise of such prophecy then become prophetic of reason?

Meredy: Exactly. It is thus not at all strange that Hegel should now address himself to a painstaking diagnosis of self-consciousness. To this diagnosis we must give close attention, for on its outcome hinges the ambivalent position of reason in the context of the *Phenomenology.*

PART II

SELF-CONSCIOUSNESS

Self-Certainty

Hardith: For argument's sake I will not quarrel with the hypothesis that the *Phenomenology* exemplifies a biography of mind on a large scale, with the reservation, however, that the term be taken figuratively, containing but loosely an account of human experience in the order of time. The first appearance of sense-certainty, for instance, may imply but does not denote chronological priority; Hegel presents it as a typical aspect of cognition which, appearing always and everywhere, is assignable to no particular date. Its dialectical rather than historical development leads to perception. That for this aspect of cognition exclusive claims to primacy recur in one form or another, would seem to justify Hegel's treatment of it as involving a fundamental bias. The transition from perception to understanding may likewise be spoken of as dateless; the evolution of one into the other is under the premise stated a logical conclusion. Is self-certainty analogous to sense-certainty? May it be said of the various forms of such certainty that their dialectical sequence need not parallel the sequence of their temporal manifestations?

Meredy: To avoid confusion it may not be amiss to reiterate tersely the sense in which one may view Hegel's treatise as embodying an idealized portrayal of a dialectical movement from one phase of experience to another; the phases depicted are universal, and their verisimilitude is symbolic rather than literal. Their relation to actual experience simply lies in the illustrations to which they are amenable. Although abundantly exemplifiable, the universal phases are not always modeled on the particular examples Hegel chooses to make use of. The experiment with them might conceivably be adapted to different illustrations or, as often happens in the text, to none at all. Each phase has its own internal career, the postlude of which serves as prelude to the phase to come. Self-consciousness is no exception; it too is a name for

76

a universal phase of experience comprising a variety of forms, and each form grows logically out of the preceding one. As we shall presently note, self-consciousness constitutes a major chapter in the life of mind.

Hardith: As subject of Hegel's imaginative biography, mind thus begins with a new certainty, comparable in immediacy with sense-certainty. But the certainty is here on a higher plane, higher, I surmise, because mind requires nothing outside it to be aware of. On the assumption that awareness necessarily involves the duality of subject and object, the latter being the 'other', by becoming, as in self-consciousness, at once subject and object, mind finds the other's locus within itself. The duality, which is here immanent, ceases to be the inevitable dualism such as it appears in the previous persuasions. Is this a fair way of stating the matter?

Meredy: The contrast between consciousness and self-consciousness could hardly be expressed more succinctly—yes, what for the former remains an irreducible dualism has for the latter merely the status of an indispensable duality. What the diagnosis of consciousness culminates in is a *reductio ad absurdum* of the absolute otherness or total independence of its objects. Whatever the objects, whether of sense or perception or understanding, cognition of them depends on a reflective process such as introspection can vouch for. With introspection thus emerges a new kind of cognition entailing a different relation of subject and object. For in introspective cognition alone do subject and object appear both in opposition and unison, thus satisfying the demand that the object, though the other, enjoy the highest degree of intimacy with the subject. And than identity nothing more intimate would seem possible. This then is the new certainty, the certainty that the self introspecting and the self introspected are differentiable *within* and *by* one and the same self. Here is a case of differentiation becoming literally self-differentiation. Hence Hegel's dictum that with self-consciousness we enter the local habitation of truth.

Hardith: In speaking of self-consciousness as truth's native soil, whose conception of truth does Hegel here voice? Is the conception his own or that of the supposed subject of his biography? What is true can have no home outside the subject's experience *at every stage of its development,* and must consequently exchange as experience changes one domicile for another. This, if I mistake not, belongs to the very essence of the dialectical method. Why then the emphasis on self-consciousness? Is it not a phase of experience destined like every other to be superseded?

Meredy: The point you raise is important, drawing attention to a distinction we discussed before. It is the distinction, which Hegel constantly reiterates, between what experience is for us and what it is for itself. The native land of truth, an expression obviously metaphorical, occurs but in the introduction to the section on self-consciousness, and here, as in the introductions to later sections, Hegel speaks in his own character and not in that of his subject. Every type of experience—and self-consciousness is no exception—must inevitably appear to the subject as if all truth resided in it. That this is due to an illusion of perspective, apparent 'to us', the subject, in accordance with the rules governing the dialectic, must come in the end to recognize 'for itself'. But for Hegel, the author of mind's biography, self-consciousness occupies a privileged position. The vision of mind, guiding the biography, is one which Hegel, in the preface to the work, explicitly opposed to that of Spinoza. Everything depends, as you will recall the statement, on grasping and expressing that which is ultimately true not simply in terms of substance but in those of subject as well. In a sense, to be brought out in the sequel, the *Phenomenology* reaches its climax in a glorification of the subject such as only self-consciousness can reveal. In saying then that truth has its indigenous roots in self-consciousness Hegel is simply expressing in terse fashion his fundamental insight.

Hardith: Very well. Let us then approach the theme under the conditions Hegel laid down, one condition being that we consider self-consciousness as logically emerging from the dialectic of consciousness, outranking the latter by including and transcending it. Although it is thus a higher phase of experience, consciousness of self has lower forms of its own, the lowest always appearing as immediate. Of the immediacy of *self*-certainty, corresponding to that of *sense*-certainty, the proposition 'I am I' is alleged to be the embodiment. But the proposition, asserting simultaneously the difference and identity of subject and predicate, is clearly tautological or contradictory. Yet tautology and contradiction, to which understanding gives rise, are here essential for the definition of self-consciousness in abstract terms. Self-consciousness, irreducible to a formula so barren, must therefore be found in assertions more complex or more subtle. All this is plain sailing and presents little difficulty. But instead of proceeding to more adequate expressions of self-consciousness, Hegel passes to a discussion of the notions of life and desire as if it were a necessary interlude. I frankly fail to see its relevance.

Meredy: The interlude, I admit, complicates matters but is nevertheless not superfluous. To show this, however, would involve us in technical details we have agreed to eschew. Speaking generally, the bearing here of life and desire seems to be this. Consciousness of self, as distinguished from consciousness of things, is essentially dynamic.

Even the statement 'I am I', presupposing as it does identity breaking out into difference and difference revolving back to identity, is intrinsically a movement congealed in a tautology. The act of moving to and fro between subject and predicate (or between subject and object) constitutes the very differentia of self-consciousness. Not of a thing lifeless is the consciousness of self, and the inward seesaw between difference and identity is not a lifeless process. The category of life is here so indispensable that in its absence 'self-certainty' would be an expression signifying nothing at all.

Hardith: But without that category all consciousness, whether of self or of things, would be precluded, seeing that none but the living can play the part of subject. What, for instance, is sense-certainty if not the certainty felt by mind reduced to a vital sensorium for receiving immediate impressions? There is in Hegel's text no support for the assumption that physical phenomena such as rocks are capable of sense-experience! And can the consciousness requisite for perception and understanding be other than the consciousness of a living self? Why then the special emphasis on life in connection with self-consciousness?

Meredy: To this the first answer is quite simple. One thing is the contention that every form of consciousness entails a living *subject,* quite another is the attribution of life to the *object.* Now self-awareness and awareness of life are virtually equatable: here the evidence has the force of self-evidence; for self-consciousness constitutes the medium for the living subject's immediate recognition of itself in the very object's otherness. More important, however, is the second answer. This has to do with Hegel's conception of life as cognate in dialectical structure with that of self-consciousness. But first a comment on the notion of desire as a self-conscious posture below the cognitive level.

Hardith: I must interrupt you to raise a point calling for elucidation. It is of course obvious that the subject's awareness of itself in the awareness of the object belongs to the very essence of self-consciousness: the other, in Hegel's quaint phrase, is its own other. But the object of consciousness, as in perception, has a different status, awareness of its otherness being tantamount to awareness of its independence. And let the independence appear ever so mitigated, as in understanding, consciousness of things and consciousness of self cannot be made to coalesce without doing away with things altogether. We are here confronted by two different dimensions of experience and the relation between them must not be allowed to obliterate their distinction.

Meredy: This is a theme that cannot be touched upon here, the issue it involves being central in Hegel's philosophy. No issue is more momentous in it than the distinction and relation between subjectivity and objectivity. These opposites, put into the crucible of the dialectic throughout the *Phenomenology*, emerge in the end as equatable, and to that final equation self-consciousness serves as but a clue. Paradigmatic as self-consciousness is of the primacy of the subject in interaction with its own other, the primacy proves to be replete with anomalies, owing to a preoccupation exclusively introversive. On the levels beyond self-consciousness, on those of reason and spirit, the initial contrast between consciousness of things and consciousness of self becomes progressively attenuated. All this, however, still lies far, far ahead.

Meanwhile we must consider desire but only as prerational experience, its expressions based upon reason being treated in a later context. Now desire, implying the category of life, clearly manifests the subject's predominance over the object, a predominance rather of enjoyment than contemplation. The subject's primitive supremacy derives from the tacit postulate that whatever is and lives, is and lives for the gratification of desire. It is the moment of gratification which effectively marks the loss of the object's alleged independence; long before he acquires self-certainty as a reflective being, man in search of satisfaction of his ego-centric desire is a practical or rather a practicing subjectivist.

Hardith: But Hegel maintains this also, namely, that in annulling the desired object by absorbing it, the subject cannot but indirectly affirm the object's independence. For objects are always needed to make possible their continual absorption. In other words, satisfaction of desire depends on a nonsubjective world in which alone it can be realized. The very subjective need for them invests the objects of desire with a substance of their own, so to speak, and thus with an existence on their own account.

Meredy: How true! Being the prototype of self-consciousness, desire exemplifies the same dependence of difference upon identity and identity upon difference. In desire, too, subject and object are mutually implicative, the distinction between them refusing to remain unalterably fixed. Between the subject of desire and the object upon which, so to say, it feeds, the difference vanishes with the desire's gratification; but prior to being desired, the object must have a determinate nature for desire to feed upon, thus appearing to enjoy an independent existence, different from the subject's. Between these 'moments', as Hegel calls them, the relation is essentially unstable: it is a relation disjunctive as well as conjunctive.

Hardith: Differentiation and identification of subject and object would seem to be processes related in circular fashion. Neither process, outrunning the other and being outrun by it, can ever attain completion. Only the initially self-identical can here differentiate itself, and the

80

differentiated aspects call in their turn for reinstatement within the self-identical. Of this seesaw Hegel's text abounds in various reiterations. The priority of one process thus entails the priority of the rival process. Does this not exemplify a vicious circle? And is there no escape from it?

Meredy: The situation must indeed remain anomalous until the self, ceasing to be merely a subject, moves to a higher plane of experience where thinghood and selfhood appear in forms more concrete, that is, in forms fuller and richer in content. The circularity you speak of, far from being vicious, is a principle inexpungible from dialectical discourse. What elsewhere seems logically offensive has here the function of revealing the mutability and relativity of abstract concepts. Thus the relation of the abstract concepts of subject and object is inevitably circular because it is essentially mobile. It is the aim of the *Phenomenology* to exhibit the succession of the typical 'circles' in their order and development. And these, as internally related, constitute Hegel's notion of holistic truth. This, however, is but anticipation.

Let us now return to the dialectic of self-consciousness involving an 'ego' considered at first merely living and desiring. Hegel makes the ingenius point that life, too, is a concept exemplifying an immanent circularity. Like time which is the Platonic image of eternity, life is the Hegelian image of self-consciousness. For life is process and life is form. As universal flux, life flows, as it were, through all its particular products, yet none can be called living except as differentiated in determinate ways. So here we have again the dialectical alternation of universal and particular, of unity and multiplicity, of identity and difference, of discreteness and continuity, and so on. The notion of life as embodied in discrete forms is not identical in meaning with the notion of life as a process continuing beyond any and every one of its present embodiments. The same process, manifest in the various forms among which it is, so to speak, broken up and divided, must be viewed as reappearing in forms yet to be generated. It is the nature of life to renew itself in countless generations destined to be destroyed by the same process to which they owe their birth. The alternate sides of life in its dynamic integrity are represented by the multiplicity of individuals and species and the generic unity in which they are embraced and transcended. Such alternate sides, akin to those inherent in self-consciousness, epitomize the basic condition for the possibility of self-conscious existence, seeing that all consciousness is a product and function of life.

Hardith: The passage to and fro between self-consciousness and life plainly resists assimilation with a process strictly evolutionary as the term figures in biology. It is quite confusing to encounter in unscientific discourse concepts preempted by a special discipline. The generic view of life as cognate with self-consciousness is too speculative to be convincingly entertained on the basis of scientifically ascertainable facts.

Meredy: We must of course remember that what Hegel here says merely hints at the dialectic to emerge. Scientific attitudes to nature, including phenomena both physical and biological, receive detailed treatment in later contexts. The concepts here employed in the analogy between life and self-consciousness are not meant to be taken as scientific; species and genus, for instance, have admittedly broader connotations. What Hegel attempts in the introduction is cursorily to anticipate the distinction between abstract and concrete universality. Is life a mere universal process to be considered by contrast with the individual or specific forms that exemplify it, or is life universal in a higher sense, in the sense of being the synthesis of the abstract opposition between a general process and the particular forms? It is the idea of life in the latter sense which suggests in the most elementary fashion the idea of a concrete universal. Life as genus resembles self-consciousness in exemplifying a whole that comprehends in interdependence the unstable elements constituting it. The discrete forms in which life becomes crystallized are one and all generable and corruptible but not the genus of life which is continuous and the same in all its individual and specific manifestations. And the genus, strange to say, is itself a crystallization but one of another order, having no existence save as product of reason.

Hardith: I naturally realize that remarks but adumbrative of what is to come defy adequate analysis. Nevertheless, Hegel's use in this context of the idea of genus strikes me as disconcertingly cryptic. What does it mean? The distinction you suggest, one still awaiting elucidation, between abstract and concrete universality, throws but a dim light on this part of the text. That self-consciousness is itself a genus, indeed the only true genus—how baffling an utterance! No less baffling is the statement that only in another self-consciousness can self-consciousness find satisfaction.

Meredy: I am not sure that I can remove the difficulty you voice. The idea of genus, broached so suddenly, does here smack somewhat of the occult. I can only understand it by analogy with the later notion of a concrete universal. If the generic universal represents the union of different but interdependent species what less strange than the conception of self-consciousness as genus and as the only authentic one? For it is self-consciousness in which are united distinguishable but inseparable correlatives, as, for instance, subject and object, identity and difference, continuity and discreteness. And it is self-consciousness which serves as model for the generic ideas of life and desire. Implicit in the dialectic of desire, to which Hegel returns in the end, is the ultimate need for self-consciousness to find satisfaction in another. We have already noted the anomaly inherent in desire touching the relation between consciousness and the other; the subject's independence of the object cannot be asserted without making the object ancillary to the subject's demands, the former always remaining in a state of otherness until satisfaction supervenes to cancel it. But the cancellation is illusory in view of the fact that consciousness of satisfaction is ever conditioned by some independent object. It is otherwise in self-consciousness conceived as solitary; here subject and object are coequal in selfhood, and the object, strictly speaking, is no other at all. When consciousness, ceasing to be solitary, confronts another consciousness, a situation ensues differing from that of mere desire. Upon the next chapter devolves the task of tracing the extreme ways in which one self-consciousness comes to be related to another. The statement that 'self-consciousness attains satisfaction only in another self-consciousness' simply foreshadows the outcome of the entire process. Hegel envisages it as the realization of a concrete universal on a social scale, the 'I' and the 'We' becoming interdependent on the higher levels of experience.

Hardith: I am beginning to see the drift of the experiment to come: it is to discover an incipient social consciousness within the very bosom of self-consciousness. A paradox, a most ingenious paradox!

Meredy: Does it greatly matter whether or not we are dealing with a paradox? We are merely concerned with a study of a significant chapter in the life of mind. The study is difficult. Let us approach it with patience and without bias.

Independence and Freedom of Self-Consciousness

1. Self-Consciousness and Solipsism

Hardith: The intent of Hegel's preliminary remarks is, I take it, to initiate the diagnosis of consciousness *in relation* to another consciousness. The relation appears from the outset as peculiar, requiring that the concepts of identity and difference be regarded as mutually exclusive as well as mutually inclusive. For self-consciousness involves a being recognized as self by another self, divided from and yet united with it. Differentiable selves are thus bound each to each by reciprocal recognition of their essential otherness and essential affinity. The necessity of such recognition inherent in a consciousness at once subject and object represents, as it were, the 'play of forces' internalized: the act of recognizing entails the state of being recognized, and vice versa. All this I find intelligible only when I think of self-consciousness as that of a supposed solipsist. To find the consciousness of one's self in another and of the consciousness of another in one's self, when the 'self' and the 'other' are by definition or hypothesis one and the same, is hardly a momentous discovery. But as soon as we pass from the solipsistic to the social sphere, the difficulty grows apace. That separate selves could not become truly self-conscious except through conscious acknowledgment of each other's selfhood is a debatable matter. Hegel seems to argue as if the dialectic implicit in intrasubjective experience could be simply transferred to types of experiences explicitly intersubjective.

Meredy: It is not a question of transference but one of equivalence. The dialectic of self-consciousness is the same regardless of the context in which it appears; awareness of self on either level, personal or interpersonal, is always awareness of opposites in dynamic relation. To be self-conscious, even for an assumed monad, is to undergo the process of interior duplication and interior reunion. In self-criticism, for example, the subject as critic and the object criticized are virtually divided, their felt identity ensuing from the acknowledgment by each of the other's spurious otherness. Since self-consciousness depends upon mutual recognition on the part of subject and object that each is, so to say, the other's double, it matters little whether the dialectic is exhibited as applicable to solitary or social experience. The peculiar interplay of subject and object inherent in self-consciousness might indeed be exemplified without assuming more than one self. Hegel's treatment of it in social terms reveals self-consciousness as an experience deeper and more intense than could ever be found in solitude.

Hardith: But the process of duplication necessitating recognition by each 'double' of its unity with the other can only be conceived as a goal to be reached when the inward 'play' of forces actually becomes a social 'game'. Separate selves do not originally recognize themselves as mutually recognizing one another. On the contrary, in the immediate or primitive phase of their active interplay, each demands more recognition than it accords. And the other, being literally other, comes to be looked upon as alien. Self-consciousness thus appears at first self-centered and suffers from the illusion of being self-sufficient. If the material Hegel here draws upon is, as it seems to be, anthropological, dialectical immediacy and chronological primitiveness clearly coincide.

Meredy: There is no confusion here between logical and temporal incipiency. Supposed events merely aid in illustrating a recurrent form of experience. Hegel's diagnosis of self-consciousness, though supported by such illustrations as he happens to suggest, is not dependent *on* them. And he obviously does have in mind historically primitive conditions under which separate selves are alleged to have asserted their separateness in the so-called war of all against all. But merely assuming the self-sufficiency *of* each and every individual as a universal principle *for* each and every other, no matter whether or not it ever served as a mainspring of human action, and what must follow, were such a principle consistently acted upon, could be nothing else than a Hobbesian state of nature in which every man was making war against every other man: a never-ending internecine strife is *logically* demanded in a supposititious world of egocentric individuals all equally bent upon proving the validity of the principle. None can make good the claim to be the center of true selfhood without challenging the same claim on the part of would-be rivals, destruction of whose selfhood is here the most effective way of demonstrating the claim's falsity. Mutual carnage of one another thus becomes a law of life, and this for Hegel is not a factual

85

description of a primitive state of nature but a dialectical analysis of an imaginative conception of it.

Hardith: The conception of a state of nature here intimated as but imaginative if not imaginary entails a serious consequence not to be ignored. What in such a conception precludes the final triumph of universal death? One self, and one only, might possibly survive. Having met and overcome all would-be selves, the survivor's solipsism would remain irrefragable with a vengeance. Imagination can do wonders. Let us suppose a society made up of members engaged in mutual headhunting. If each is both hunter and hunted, sooner or later no heads would be left save one, the head of a solitary victor in possession of all the available trophies. Why is this not a necessary outcome of the dialectic? What is the logical transition from mutual destruction to mutual recognition?

Meredy: Quite simple is one transition to a form of self-consciousness supervening upon the fanciful version of a state of nature assumed to issue in universal death. Death in destroying life destroys consciousness. Mutual extermination, as you rightly insist, would leave behind none of the warring selves or but one in triumphant isolation. But the self-consciousness of a solipsist, though possible, provides too limited a scope for action. More important is the other transition which consists in explaining that internecine strife is itself a social process. This the sport of headhunting strikingly illustrates. The illustration, used, as you well know, not by Hegel but by one of his commentators, shows that the very purpose of the game requires that men be brought into active relation without which the eventual distinction between slayer and slain would be precluded. "Headhunting," says Josiah Royce, "implies dependence upon one's neighbor who is good enough to furnish one more head for the hunter." The victor in this sport, in order to prove his prowess, always needs another victim, the sport ceasing altogether with the acquisition of the final trophy. In the absence of the hunted, no hunting, and for the sake of the latter, the life of the former becomes a major desideratum. At any rate, requisite for the war of all against all, whatever be the form it takes, is the existence of interactive individuals. But this interactive kind, culminating as it must in the death of all, calls for transformation into another to which life is indispensable. The individuals conceived as interacting hereafter achieve true self-consciousness only by gradually coming to recognize their essential interdependence.

2. Master and Slave

Hardith: So in the midst of death we are in life, and in killing one another men carry on a social activity! How arresting a thesis! To life obviously belongs priority, temporal as well as logical, if none but the living can die; and every action, even that of mutual slaughter, may be called social if involved in it are individuals in interaction. What is the lesson to be drawn from all this? It seems to be the insight that only in explicit relation to life can social consciousness come to fruition. There are other ways of exercising domination without resorting to mortal combat. The life of the conquered self may be saved and put to work; subordinated as instrument to another's will, a living individual remains to enhance continually the conqueror's self-consciousness. The situation here depicted is one represented by the master and his slave. It is a situation historically primitive, open to study by diverse disciplines. The dialectic of lordship and servitude Hegel develops with unusual clarity. I have read the section without feeling unduly baffled. The issues broached in it seem to me concrete and simple.

Meredy: The situation is more complex than appears on the surface. The relation between master and slave is here treated as a general theme of which there are many variations. Subordination of one individual to another is a recurrent phenomenon in human history and one capable of assuming different shapes. Here again it is incumbent upon us to distinguish between the topic's universality and the particular expressions exemplifying it. But confining ourselves to a primitive type of society here intimated, the relation of master and slave initially appears as a relation which logicians describe as asymmetrical, the dependence of the slave being the measure of the master's independence. The master, in having a slave, is, so to speak, the true master of the situation, for the slave's person and service are under his complete control. The more arbitrary the control, the stronger the feeling of dependence on the slave's part and the feeling of independence on the master's. And enhancement of his consciousness of independence requires that the master be constantly tempted to look upon the dependent self as mere chattel, claiming absolute power over the things produced by the other's labor. Since the slave is but an instrument of the master's will, all the slave's accomplishments become vicariously the master's own. It is thus that the master's self-consciousness finds recognition in another through the asymmetry of the relations of dependence and independence.

Hardith: It is not difficult to perceive that the master, though independent in one sense, is quite dependent in another. There is a type of person whom I venture to call *The Fettered Master*. The distinction between titular and real mastery is not unfamiliar. It often happens in the social world that the nominal is not always the true master, the power behind the throne being one of the stock phrases we accept as proverbial. A throne which is the screen of power, not the essence of it, is an object striking enough for the comic spirit to light upon, but nothing so obvious seems to be Hegel's theme. What he finds paradoxical, if I read him aright, is the very idea of lordship. For the lord who loves power, vainly imagining that power is a guarantee of independence, is apt to discover how much he is at the mercy of those who serve him. The relation between the lord and the persons subservient to his will is essentially unstable. Whether a primitive slave driver or a civilized monarch, the lord depends upon those who acknowledge his power; and this need for recognition, not hidden from his serfs or subjects, is inimical to his self-sufficiency. The more imperious his nature, the greater his demand for submission, and the passionate will to rule and be obeyed conceals from him his real dependence upon the persons over whom he nominally wields his scepter. For he who craves dominion over other men is not free from them; he needs them to satisfy his ruling passion. And they subject to a will that exacts stark obedience soon learn the subtle art of shaping and bending it in accordance with their own desires. In obeying their master they are obeying a will they have cunningly contrived to direct and control. They acclaim him Caesar and render him obeisance, conscious all the while of their own strength and influence. What a comic situation! The lord in his folly thinks he is the master, but in truth he is bound hand and foot by his lust for power and by the arrant ways of those who know how to use this passion for the promotion of their own ends. If this is what Hegel seeks to convey in his cryptic manner, who can fail to appreciate it? History is replete with instances of titular masters becoming actual bondsmen if mastery is their supreme concern and if they are lacking in comic intelligence to perceive their own deluded natures.

Meredy: How refreshingly unlike Hegel's is your locution! In your description of *The Fettered Master,* as you felicitously name him, your accent is on a more advanced social situation than depicted in the text. Of the gist of the dialectic, however, your statement is remarkably accurate. Crucial here is the contention that neither dependence nor independence can ever significantly appear as a relation altogether one-sided. The discovery that for the consciousness of independence the master is dependent on a slave renders abortive the attempt to defend without qualification the alleged asymmetry of either of the two relations. The more the master's sense of dependence increases, the more his feeling of mastery must suffer attenuation. Lordship and bondage are thus shown to be mutually inclusive: the most despotic master, recognizing the inevitable ties that bind him to another, comes in the end to be haunted by a consciousness of dependence not dissimilar to that of the slave; and the slave, be he ever so submissive, in becoming gradually aware of the prowess his work exemplifies, develops a stubborn mind of his own and with it a degree of independence cognate in principle with the master's.

Hardith: In their external transactions, however, master and slave remain in their respective positions; the independence the master enjoys and the dependence suffered by the slave retain their relative asymmetry. Subordination of one self to another here constitutes a phenomenon subject to logical analysis, the analysis being of course powerless to modify the actual state of affairs. If master and slave could exchange places, each turning into the other, would not the asymmetry of the relation be the same regardless of their inverted status? Slavery, as the term is here employed, can never be abolished, if the slave's emancipation takes the form of making him the master's master. Such is the irony of the situation.

Meredy: The irony is of course not lost on Hegel. Nothing, it is true, would in principle be altered if master and slave could conceivably exchange their respective positions. Lordship and servitude, connoting the distinction between individuals regarding their external status and comportment, would continue unabated as if the supposed exchange had not taken place. The asymmetry of the relation between the actual master and his slave is always such that if independence is the differentia of the one, dependence is necessarily that of the other. The issue here broached has to do principally with self-conscious processes. What each thinks of himself and of the other determines the degree of approximation of the master's self-consciousness to the slave's and of the slave's to the master's. Both, explicitly cognizant of each other, come to assume different attitudes towards their dependence and independence. By the fruits of his labor, which the master needs, the slave measures his own power, and the greater the need of the one, the greater the other's feeling of power. Thus the master's putative independence, undermined by dependence on another's achievements, tends to become more and more nominal, while the slave's fortuitous dependence, mitigated by his self-directed work, turns progressively into a posture of self-dependence. In the realm of thought lordship and servitude accordingly acquire a meaning totally different from the meaning they have in the domain of matters of fact.

Hardith: I wonder whether the text bears out all that you read into it. Self-consciousness, even on a level so naïve, turns out to be quite complex. The division of self-consciousness, within the master's as well as within the slave's, seems to result from the ambivalence of lordship and bondage. While in their external relations master and slave acknowledge the objectivity of their respective positions, the acknowledgment requires to be withdrawn in internal reflection. The lord, though conscious of his power over his slave, is conscious also of the indispensability of the slave's services, and this second consciousness contravenes the first. And the bondsman, while ever conscious of fear of the lord, is conscious too of the importance of his work, and this consciousness when in the ascendant renders him invulnerable. Who then is here the master, and who the slave?

Meredy: How sure is anyone whether he has recaptured the spirit of the dialectic in words other than Hegel's? Primitive though the relation of lordship and bondage is here assumed to be, the implications brought out in the text are much subtler than I could indicate. For the paradox Hegel chiefly dwells upon is a psychological one: master and slave *must* think of each other in the twofold manner you express with such admirable succinctness. To the question, 'Who is the real master, and who the slave?' the answer cannot be unequivocal. If dependence defines bondage, the master here considered is so constantly in need of another's ministrations that awareness of this must militate against his feeling of independence; and if independence defines lordship, the slave here depicted is not without the enjoyment of a modicum of it. Neither master nor slave can be identified exclusively with either relational attribute, both having claim on both. Without ceasing to be asymmetrical, independence and dependence are a pair of relations requisite for the self-consciousness of master and slave alike. And this so far is the anomalous outcome of the analysis.

Hardith: In speaking of the slave, Hegel seems to endow him with a self-consciousness deeper than that experienced by the master. Why? Is its depth real or only assumed for purposes of transition to the next phase?

Meredy: If the slave of the sort Hegel has in mind develops a more profound self-consciousness it is because the psychology involved seems more complex. Of the facts dilated on in the text, applicable only to the particular situation here analyzed, are principally these two, to wit, fear of death and enjoyment of formative activity. Both affect the slave's twofold relation to his master. One gives rise to a state of constant anxiety, the other to a growing sense of security. Although his life is always at the mercy of the lord, the slave remains relatively free from jeopardy by the master's dependence on him. The insight that ensues marks the birth of the slave's true self-consciousness, following as it does upon explicit differentiation within himself between his dependent self and his independent self. Such self-consciousness, still infantile, as it were, consists initially in nothing more than discovery on the part of the slave that, regardless of his actual bondage, his mind is his own. But the mind he calls his own (*der eigene Sinn*) must advance beyond a slave's mere stubbornness (*Eigensinn*). By means of a pun, which Hegel evidently could not resist, the transition is made to a higher phase of self-consciousness. This will show how independence and freedom may be envisaged as going together.

3. *The Stoic*

Hardith: I am beginning to see the difficulty of establishing an exact parallelism between phenomenology and history. In the development of self-consciousness we seem to have a signal illustration of a process purely dialectical. Stoic self-sufficiency follows but logically upon the relation of master and slave. The sequence can hardly be called chronological. What a far cry philosophic stoicism is from the primitivism of lordship and bondage! The phase of consciousness alleged to supervene directly upon consciousness peculiar to the slave cannot be described as stoicism except by courtesy or analogy. Am I right in holding that whenever any slave anywhere becomes aware of possessing an independent nature free from his master's control, he virtually becomes a stoic? And becomes a stoic, curiously enough, in the sense that the word figures in a certain historical context?

Meredy: You are right but only partly. The transition from slave to stoic is indeed but dialectical, and the word stoic obviously derives from a phase of human civilization remote from savage society. What Hegel here so briefly considers is not the social structure of a dated culture. His sole preoccupation is with the inward attitude of the individual to whom nothing ultimately matters save his freedom of thought. *To think is to be free; to be free is to be independent; to be independent is to be master.* These are quasi-identical propositions definitive of this new type of self-consciousness. No man need call himself slave as long as he can repair to the sanctuary of his mind; his private thoughts are absolutely his own over which another's will has no authority.

Hardith: But the identity of the propositions mentioned seems to rest on the assumption that thought is arbitrary. Can anyone really think as he pleases? Are there no limits to his liberty?

Meredy: The liberty of thought here made central is not license but autonomy. Note the distinction between perception and conception. The object of the former, called percept, appears as if external to the percipient, whereas the object of the latter, being a concept, cannot be separated from the act of conceiving it. Thought as process and thought as product, though distinguishable, are indissolubly united.

Of this intimate union of process and product, Hegel's term *Begriff*, which he employs in various ways, is typical. The activity of thinking and the result of thinking, like subject and object in self-consciousness, are mutually implicative. In thought, therefore, the self comes to acquire the autonomy conditioning the enjoyment of his inward freedom and independence, for the other of thought, to use Hegel's idiom, is thought's own other. This, however, can only be recognized within thought and by thought.

Hardith: This, I gather, is the sort of freedom serving as preface to the portrayal of the slave turned into a stoic. For the stoic is here presented as owing fidelity to no other principle than the principle of thought's autonomy. The values that have their seat in thought remain entirely insulated from those situate in circumstance. He alone is unbound, regardless of fortune's chains, who remains master of his soul. Yet, the bonds wrought by circumstance, the stoic can never lose sight of. For freedom *of* thought seems to depend on freedom *from* whatever falls outside thought's control. His vaunted independence, like that of any and every master, is fettered to what he boasts to be independent of. How does the dialectic of stoicism differ from the dialectic of the primitive consciousness it is designed to replace?

Meredy: You anticipate a criticism the relevance of which hinges on the stoic's alleged independence of circumstance. The independence takes the form of transcending circumstance by deliberate indifference or deliberate acquiescence, postures related by mutual implication. Declaring that nothing can have a claim on goodness or truth unless thought acknowledges the claim, the stoic may think of everything that happens as subject to rational necessity; confronting chance by denying that it is chance, he is able to face the world with apathy or resignation. From 'every clutch of circumstance', accepted as inevitable, the stoic can always withdraw within his free and unconquerable soul.

Hardith: But withdrawal is so ambivalent. That *from* which and that *to* which the stoic withdraws are unlike in connotation. And this is not merely a verbal matter. Crucial here once again is the question of determinateness. In what particular respect does the nature of stoic self-consciousness differ from the nature of any other? What kind of self, to put the issue bluntly, is the stoic conscious of when conscious of himself *as* stoic?

Meredy: This Hegel answers, though too briefly, by way of animadversion. *Stoic freedom of thought is nothing but the thought of freedom* —such is the sum and substance of Hegel's verdict. Irreconcilable is the contrast between contemplation and action; one thing is a self meditating on abstract freedom, quite another is a self involved in the concrete life of freedom. Freedom from the world's concerns and freedom to participate in them are indeed poles apart. Is it any wonder then that the stoic's indifference to a world containing masters and slaves should be matched by the indifference the world metes out to the stoic? The world in which a Marcus Aurelius and an Epictetus are alleged to be co-equal in the enjoyment of abstract freedom is a world running its course heedless of such innocuous equality. Here indifference becomes a relation completely symmetrical. What then of the stoic's boast of independence? Just as he depends on a determinate world for his indifference, so does he depend on it for his independence. What he is consciously independent of is precisely life's vicissitudes of fortune. The world, alas, is always too much with him.

Hardith: What irony! Stoic resignation goes hand in hand with moral bankruptcy, for the logic of it entails moral apathy or moral scepticism. Only he is his own master who suffers no blow of circumstance to trouble his inner life. The integrity of his soul rests on the judgment that the turmoils of life are either extraneous or unreal. Be his spiritual tranquillity a consequence of indifference or negation, escape from action becomes a moral desideratum. Action involves choice and preference, and choice and preference are incompatible with freedom from the unprofitable strife of restless men. Because complete detachment paralyzes action, pure stoicism is tantamount to moral abdication, refusing as it must to pass judgments of value on competing modes of human conduct. An ethical persuasion conceived as self-sufficient ends in an egregious paradox. And so, as Hegel contends, the stoic must perforce come to doubt the adequacy of his stoicism.

Meredy: The stoic's position appears anomalous only in the terms in which Hegel chooses to exhibit it. If the stoic fails to win the independence he sets his heart upon, it is because his notion of independence is not radical enough. What the stoic is in search of none but the sceptic can attain. This is Hegel's surprising conclusion. And thus we pass to a brief consideration of scepticism said by him to represent the realization of what stoicism aspires to—namely, to give to freedom of thought unlimited scope.

4. *The Sceptic*

Hardith: What are we to understand by Hegel's view of scepticism as the 'realization' of stoicism? Does it mean that the stoic is, so to speak, father of the sceptic in the sense that the child is father of the man? But, speaking facetiously, are all stoics but immature sceptics and all sceptics the full-fledged stoics? Such a notion of their relationship, though arresting, seems quite arbitrary. Stoicism does not generally grow into scepticism nor scepticism grow out of stoicism. They appear in history to have been entertained separately. Whence the necessary connection between them?

Meredy: Your question is pertinent, confirming anew the point repeatedly made that between historical and logical sequences of human persuasions there is in the *Phenomenology* no uniform parallelism. The stoic's fatherhood in the sceptic, a dubious metaphor in the order of time, is fit and apposite in the order of the dialectic. Just as the slave in discovering a mind of his own is a potential stoic, so the stoic is a sceptic in the making when extolling freedom of thought as the highest good. Complete freedom in which alone the stoic seeks assurance of his soul's independence cannot be realized except by the complete sceptic. The world to which the stoic reacts with apathy or resignation does not lose its hold upon the mind until rejected outright by doubt. Freedom to doubt, in short, is freedom of thought par excellence. Accordingly, rational self-consciousness asserts its full independence only when engaged in questioning the truth of whatever seems alien to it: for example, cognition as grounded in sense-certainty and perception, or conduct as based on dogma and convention. There is indeed nothing a free mind could not subject to radical doubt, and in the continual exercise of it, the nisus towards inward lordship latent in stoicism comes to fruition.

Hardith: Am I right in saying that by turning from an apathetic to a corrosive attitude, the stoic becomes a sceptic? The liberty to destroy, all for the sake of according to consciousness a lordly independence of the external world, is certainly a curious notion of freedom. The destruction, however, is but in thought and by thought. If the primitive slave inevitably grows into a stoic, the stoic as sceptic reverts, it seems to me, to the position of the original master. But it is a master whose power is limited solely to the power of intellectual subversion. Understood explicitly both as 'his' and as 'sceptical', the master's consciousness now comes to serve as the ultimate measure of things. Among the things that come and go, the sceptical consciousness retains its undeviating posture. In the universal flux, it feels its own stability. The restlessness or uncertainty everywhere present reflects the disintegrative might of consciousness. Scepticism, in short, succeeds in dissolving everything but itself: the doubting mind remains changeless amid all things dubitable.

Meredy: There is a suggestion in what you say which I find most illuminating. It is that the claim to absolute independence by the sceptic resembles the claim made by the primitive master. Yes, mind engaged in the process of universal negation is magisterial indeed. From the consciousness of the slave to the consciousness of the sceptic the development appears to be essentially cyclic; the slave achieves no true independence until as stoic he emancipates himself in thought from the power of the master, but the thought of the stoic which takes the form of indifference to the world must become transformed into the critical thought of the sceptic, the sceptic thus resuming the place of master who, by his annihilative intellect, can subjugate everything to his imperious will to disbelieve. This will if successfully exercised would constitute an impressive example of assertible independence.

Hardith: The word assertable, qualifying the sceptic's independence, indicates the limits of his power. Independence merely asserted is of course not the same as independence actually enjoyed. Thought and experience are again at loggerheads. There are empirical facts which, like the nonsceptic, the sceptic constantly runs up against and cannot run away from, and these are precisely such as require to be negated. Since the process of negation serves as sole criterion of intellectual freedom, their acceptance inevitably invalidates the criterion. Practical commerce with the external world, essential for sustaining the existence of his empirical self-consciousness, daily contradicts the sceptic's theoretical pose. He acknowledges in action what in thought he feels free to disavow. How pathetic is the incongruity between the mordant posture of his mind and the irrepressible conditions governing his conduct!

Meredy: What is here involved is a pathos deeper than the pathos of distance between theory and practice. The tendency to negate in action negations maintained in thought is universal, and of this tendency scepticism is a striking though not a singular expression. To deny just for the sake of being free to deny—this, having the force of an axiom, is the difficulty inherent in the kind of scepticism here under discussion. Hence a glaring paradox. The development of the paradox culminates in a new situation; the transition to it is the painful recognition by the sceptic of the latent tension between the subject and object of his sceptical consciousness. The subject is the self as changeless, the object is the self as empirical mind in restless motion, an instance of the class of phenomena to be disbelieved. The sceptic thus comes to realize the 'piteous predicament' of being doubter and the doubt, author and product of nugatory thought, contradictor hoist on his own petard. Here as elsewhere, but here in a more radical sense, the differentiated terms end in confusion, each, in Hegel's diction, becoming its own other.

Hardith: Does not all this simply render explicit the insight that freedom of thought cannot be vindicated in terms of unlimited scepticism? Universal doubt is self-contradictory in theory and impossible in practice. Nothing more is here proved than the sceptic's impotence to maintain with consistency his posture of absolute negation. Why not leave the matter thus?

Meredy: But this is not merely a matter of insight for *us*. What we are bidden by Hegel to delve into is the sceptic's self-consciousness when the insight becomes *his*. The sceptic here depicted involves a consciousness exemplifying not merely the logical duality of subject and object. What it entails rather is a psychological dualism so extreme that the self-consciousness of the sceptic turns into profound self-division. And of this inner process Hegel traces the career in the following section which he significantly names *The Unhappy Consciousness.*

The Unhappy Consciousness

1. The Schizophrenic

Hardith: As we approach a discussion of the new and last phase of self-consciousness I am moved to make two observations. (a) The portrayal of the sceptic as an unhappy individual can hardly be called typical. That despair must inevitably follow in the wake of doubt is an assumption not borne out by human experience. The blithe sceptic is no anomaly; he is not absent from the pages of history and literature. Why must a spirit that ever denies be a spirit ever touched with despondency? (b) The sort of experience here depicted, as Hegel's allusion amply attests, seems to be drawn chiefly from the religious life of the Middle Ages. The diagnosis of this phenomenon of religious consciousness is unquestionably profound. But being unduly Christianized, it cannot be considered wholly representative. The dialectic of self-consciousness thus becomes reduced to that of a single illustration to the great detriment of its supposed universality.

Meredy: Both points are well taken. Not every kind of scepticism is attended by unhappiness; cheerful scepticism is certainly not uncommon. The kind Hegel is here concerned with must be understood in relation to the context in which it appears. None but the scepticism dialectically derivable from stoicism is impregnated with melancholy. Unhappiness is a concomitant of the self-alienation that ensues from the process of equating freedom of thought with absolute doubt. The sceptic's affliction is the result of a split personality; painful awareness of inner bifurcation between his two selves, the true and the false, constitutes the essence of what Hegel here calls the unhappy consciousness.

Now as a personal experience, schizophrenia, to use a modern term, need not at all be expressed in an idiom peculiarly religious, and Hegel's allusive language is thus quite misleading, especially since the subject of religion proper does not make its appearance until the end of the *Phenomenology,* religion being genuine for Hegel not in individual but in social forms. For this reason, secular examples of the unhappy consciousness would be more representative as well as more consonant with Hegel's intent. Identification of a typical phenomenon with an illustration so singular and so dated involves a serious misconception of the dialectical procedure. And yet there is a tendency among some scholars who, seduced by Hegel's metaphorical diction, see in the unhappy consciousness nothing more or nothing else than a state of mind influenced by certain aspects characteristic of a certain religion. And some there are who, lifting the diagnosis out of its dialectical framework, look in it for clues to Hegel's spiritual autobiography.

Hardith: Schizophrenia, I suppose, belongs to the vocabulary of abnormal psychology, but the divided self is in Hegel an expression synonymous with self-consciousness, the division being of different types, and an unhappy consciousness need be no more morbid than a happy one. The reflexive statement that, for example, one is ashamed or proud of one's self, embodies a fundamental duality; the self aware of shame or pride and the self as object of the awareness, though inseparable, are clearly distinguishable. All self-consciousness exemplifies an inevitable split of subject and object; unless self-consciousness as such be consigned to the limbo of the abnormal, does it not sound strange to speak of it as schizophrenia?

Meredy: Ah, who can draw an indelible line between the normal and the abnormal? Certainly not Hegel unless we confuse phenomenology with psychology. The phenomenon of self-conscious experience, no matter in what manner it receives treatment elsewhere, does not resist diagnosis by the dialectical method. Since it is an experience characterized by an essential duality of subject and object immanent within the one and the same individual, the relation of these two distinct terms becomes for Hegel a crucial problem and primarily logical. Schizophrenia would seem to be germane only to Hegel's portrait of an individual who suffers acutely from extreme self-estrangement. The plight of the sceptic which his absolute negation must bring in its train could hardly be conveyed except by a word laden with 'clinical' connotations. The duality peculiar to every self-consciousness becomes here a profound dualism. The unhappy self here considered is one tormented by an inescapable awareness of the dichotomous split within him.

Hardith: I should not object to the description of the unhappy consciousness as schizophrenic were it not for the word's special and pejorative meaning. After all, the word does have reference to a pathological state of mind. Does it not seem perverse to apply the epithet to an experience Hegel regards as typical?

Meredy: Not at all. It is characteristic of the dialectical method to reveal the pathology, so to speak, of every persuasion when driven to excess by the illusion of perspective inherent in it. This we have sufficiently noted in connection with the forms of consciousness as well as with those of self-consciousness. In the theme of the unhappy consciousness the pathology of an extremely isolated perspective comes to a climax. Until 'happiness' supervenes—and the search for it signifies the process of uniting in organic wholeness the individual's differentiable aspects—the self-consciousness in which subject and object appear not only divided but completely estranged, agrees perfectly with William James's description of "the sick soul."

Hardith: It would shock a serious Hegel scholar not a little to hear the dialectical method compared to a diagnosis of sick souls. For you do not confine the medical label to the unhappy consciousness. Pathological is, as you say, "every persuasion driven to excess by the illusion of perspective inherent in it." What persuasion examined in the *Phenomenology* is not depicted as going to absurd lengths? In what sense is the unhappy consciousness exceptionally irrational? Are there degrees of irrationality which the various persuasions analyzed may be said to exemplify?

Meredy: If not pressed too hard, medical metaphors, though risky, are not misleading in relation to Hegel's diagnostic method. 'The truth is the whole'—this is the Hegelian thesis as announced in the preface; and the text demonstrates it by showing that every partial truth is infested with falsehood when assumed to be wholly true. Yet, this very assumption is needed for the process of generating the progressive series of truth-claims in which each both loses and retains truth-value, loses it in an absolute but retains it in a relative sense. Nothing but the whole truth, comprising in synthesis all the incongruous truth-claims, can be self-consistent or completely rational. And the paradox is this, that necessary for the rationality of the all-embracing truth is the assertion of irrational claims on the part of the partial truths. Since these claims form a hierarchy in which the later appear less irrational or (if you will forgive the pun) more wholesome than the earlier, their irrationality must of course differ in degree. Medical locution, provided it be kept within strictly metaphorical bounds, is accordingly apposite to all the degrees of irrationality. For the irrationality involved in the unhappy consciousness, however, such locution is peculiarly pat. The sort of unhappiness here brought to light is strikingly pathological,

99

arising as it does from a fissure deep within self-consciousness, and for this the exact modern equivalent is schizophrenia.

Hardith: I am naturally aware that much latitude is required for translating into intelligible prose Hegel's esoteric idiom. This, alas, may easily prove distortive. Since my familiarity with the text does not equal yours, I can hardly accuse you of having taken too great a liberty with it. So I will not quarrel with you further. I note, however, Hegel's own way of expressing the division within the self that sets initially the stage for the dialectic of the unhappy consciousness, and this has to do with the contrast between the notions of the changeless and the changeable. Why precisely these notions? And what bearing have they on the 'fissure' you speak of—'deep within self-consciousness'?

Meredy: We must remember that the unhappy consciousness is latent in the sceptic's conception of freedom of thought. To be free to think is to be free to doubt, and in being free to doubt *anything* and *everything,* consciousness comes at long last to enjoy absolute independence. But if there is to be no restraint on the freedom to doubt, what could escape the touch of corrosive thought? The sceptic himself, steeped as he daily is in the flux of his perceptions, is not immune from scepticism. So here is an unhappy bifurcation within self-consciousness between a doubting self and a self doubted—one self a permanent judge of all that solicits credibility and the other a restless wanderer in his inner world of transient experience. Of this bifurcation the development of the unhappy consciousness is a development in depth. We are dealing here with a consciousness wherein the two selves meet as strangers, the true self being identified with a mind ever the same, the false with a nature ever mutable.

Hardith: By linking them with scepticism you throw considerable light on the meaning of the changeless and the changeable, notions Hegel sets so much store on, but I am still unable to grasp their relevance to the unhappy consciousness. Why should consequences so disastrous follow from failure to transform one's actual nature into a nature conceived as ideal? And why should a consciousness conscious of its mutability be looked upon as a source of misery?

2. *The Mystic*

Meredy: The process of self-alienation, here depicted as ensuing from one's vain search for true selfhood, is long and laborious, and our discussion has done but scant justice to it. We must develop more fully the implications involved in the contrast between the changeless and the changeable as it relates to the unhappy consciousness. And the illustration I have in mind, one Hegel might have made use of, seems to me quite illuminating. Consider mysticism as a phenomenon recurring always and everywhere in many forms and in different idioms, consider it, that is, as a universal theme with specific variations; and consider it chiefly as bearing upon the very problem we are here concerned with—namely, the bifurcation within consciousness between the changeless and the changeable self. There is hardly a version of mysticism that fails to dilate on the unhappiness, in Hegel's sense of the word, attending the quest for one's identity in a shifting consciousness instead of in a consciousness said to be supratemporal. May I quote from a short poem that seems to me to express the essence of the matter? I happened to come upon it in *The Oxford Book of English Mystical Verse.* The piece, by Edmond Holmes, has the significant title *"La Vie Profonde,"* and runs as follows:

> Hemmed in by petty thoughts and petty things,
>   Intent on toys and trifles all my years,
> Pleased by life's gaudes, pained by its pricks and stings,
>   Swayed by ignoble hopes, ignoble fears;
> Threading life's tangled maze without life's clue,
>   Busy with means, yet heedless of their ends,
> Lost to all sense of what is real and true,
>   Blind to the goal to which all Nature tends:—
> Such is my surface self: but deep beneath,
>   A mighty actor on a world-wide stage,
> Crowned with all knowledge, lord of life and death,
>   Sure of my aim, sure of my heritage,—
> I—the true self—live on, in self's despite,
> that 'life profound' whose darkness is God's light.

"The true self in self's despite"—how neatly this epitomizes the ambivalence of selfhood voiced by mystics generally! The true self, having overcome the false, receives in mystic literature many strange expressions, all converging upon a single thesis: *the true self is one with the One.* And what is the One? Variously described as simple, undifferentiated, without form, not in space or time, ineffable, pure being, Nirvana, etc., it might also be called changeless, hardly a misnomer, in view of its obvious resemblance in connotation to the other descriptive terms. Not in the changeless One can the mystic live or move. He can only have his being there when at the end of an elaborate preparation he is in immediate union with it.

But observe the irony. Prior to his absorption in the changeless One, the 'surface self' alone can experience the unhappiness attending the

101

consciousness of separation from his true identity; but 'deep beneath', where darkness and light are the same, the true self does not find but loses his identity. Absorption in the changeless One and sacrifice of self-consciousness are here mutually implicative. This ironical result seems inevitable in connection with a consciousness whose divided selves are kept so absolutely asunder.

Hardith: Poor unhappy consciousness! How perplexing the desire for a self one is not and for not being the self one is! With the fulfillment of the desire, it is assumed, unhappiness will cease. But if the desire's gratification lies in winning the true and losing the false self, is it not doomed to frustration, seeing that both selves have their being in one and the same individual? Whichever self the individual is conscious of cannot be separated from the other, each depending upon each for determinateness, be the determinateness specified as changeless or changeable. The two kinds of selfhood must coexist in the same mind if one is to be sought and the other shunned. The polar opposites here discerned, like those dealt with before, will have to be somehow united in accordance with the method governing the dialectic. Self-estrangement must accordingly be followed by self-reconciliation, entailing abandonment of the absolute dichotomy generative of the unhappy consciousness.

If this be the outcome foreshadowed, how inept is your illustration! The would-be mystic and the mystic can scarce be said to constitute a single individual; the 'surface self' is a particular being, open to sundry ways of experience, under the dominance of volatile thought or desire; the 'deep' self ultimately disappears in the bosom of the changeless. The twain literally never can meet, choice of one implying rejection of the other, and not only rejection but downright denial. Between the nonmystic and the mystic, even within the compass of an identical consciousness, no communication seems possible. Mutually estranged, their union remains precluded.

Meredy: Your comment is singularly pertinent. Yes, between mystic and nonmystic (if the mystic is one who has finally shed his surface self by becoming fused with a changeless and ineffable being) the breach is complete. And their contrast has little bearing on the diagnosis of the unhappy consciousness. For this is a consciousness with which not every nonmystic is burdened and from its burden every mystic is free only because he surrenders *all* consciousness. Of special importance, however, is your admirable distinction between the mystic and the would-be mystic. It is but the latter who is tormented by the division within himself between the actual self he is aware of being and the inverted image of the same with which he would fain be identified.

As long as he is only a mystic in the making, he must remain, as it were, suspended in midair, conscious at once of being and of not being self-estranged. The illustration seems particularly relevant since it shows how intimate is the relation of scepticism and the unhappy consciousness. For the would-be mystic is nothing if not a sceptic. Before he enters his Nirvana—the profound abode which goes under many aliases—he must uncompromisingly tread the *via negativa,* a path cognate more generally with the sceptical. Requisite for the purpose of purging himself of himself as nonmystic, the negative method must be applied universally, otherwise the unhappy consciousness will continue unabated and the way will be barred to the ultimate vision of pure being by which the would-be mystic reaches his promised land. Accordingly, until he becomes a full-fledged mystic, he who is still a tyro resembles the distraught sceptic in search of changeless being impervious to doubt, and if complete absorption in such being ends all doubt and all misery, this is scarcely odd, seeing that it brings about total extinction of consciousness.

Hardith: By adopting the distinction I have ventured to make, you manage quite plausibly to relate mysticism and the unhappy consciousness. But it is only the would-be mystic, as you acknowledge, to whom such consciousness could properly be attributed. The would-be mystic thus occupies a middle zone between the mystic and the nonmystic, sharing the former's spiritual ambition and the latter's everyday experience. Now, according to Hegel's dialectic, the unhappy consciousness is a prelude to reason which alone can unite the opposition inherent in it. But neither you nor Hegel can cast the mystic in the role of reason's avowed champion. The half-mystic impugns and the whole-mystic abandons all rational discourse. This is an issue in which the half-mystic alone is implicated. By transcending his unhappy state in pure mysticism, he disappears from the scene, and the dialectic, as far as he is concerned, comes to an ignominious end; if, on the other hand, his unhappy condition is to be reversed by reason, he must become his own other, the dialectic requiring the conversion of the half-mystic into a nonmystic. I hazard to generalize the dilemma thus: either mysticism is the final answer to all dialectic or else dialectic is the reduction to the absurd of all mysticism.

Meredy: How ingenious! The dilemma touches the nerve of the matter. Mysticism and dialectic are indeed mutually incompatible. This is implicit in Hegel's treatment of self-consciousness—here the principal theme. Consciousness of self, as we have seen, advances in dialectical progression, deepening from phase to phase. Thus the relation of master and slave is such that each tends to become conscious of dependence on as well as independence of the other. The stoic, disregarding the actual difference between lordship and bondage, finds in the freedom of his thought the measure of true independence. The sceptic, going beyond the stoic's posture, identifies freedom of thought with absolute freedom to doubt, thus precipitating the grave division within his consciousness between his invariantly sceptical and his empirically variable self. The unhappy consciousness grows out of the sceptic's inner division acutely felt, the profound self cherished and the surface self contemned remaining poles apart. And if the would-be mystic adequately exemplifies the plight of the divided self, what ensues is a paradox resembling in form the dilemma you mention. For the would-be mystic, since his is a halfway position, can neither forgo his ineffable aspiration without turning renegade nor satisfy it without loss of personal identity. Union with absolute or pure being is ultimately sacrificial, all existence ceasing to be differentiable or seperable. What a climax! What begins as a search for the true self ends in finding no self at all.

But with this we need not be concerned at this juncture of our discussion. My chief purpose in alluding to mysticism was to illustrate an extreme case of the unhappy consciousness. I recall a pithy remark by Georg Simmel which is here germane. Speaking somewhere of the German mystics, he says, *"sie können es nicht ertragen nicht Gott zu sein."* Precisely! Those aspiring to be God must find it utterly unendurable to be men. Here in brief is Hegel's notion of the unhappy consciousness.

3. The Adolescent

Hardith: I am beginning to doubt the wisdom of introducing mysticism into our discussion. The unhappy consciousness is a phenomenon too normal to require explanation by an illustration so singular. The very experience of self-consciousness, hardly an esoteric one, involves an essential duality which on occasion comes to be felt as a grievous dualism. Who can often fail to draw a line between his constant and his fickle self, now one in the ascendant, now the other? Or who can long remain unaware of the struggle between savage passions and humane sentiments, at one time the brute in him and another the man gaining victory? No need to mystify an experience so familiar by resorting to the locution of religion or the newfangled vocabulary of psychology. We encounter the divided self in virtually all literature. How tragedy or comedy would languish without the protagonist's self-estrangement as central theme! Hegel's analysis has the merit of making the subject recognizably universal. Its universality is attested,

I venture to assert, by the adolescent consciousness which is marked by the same tormenting dualism exemplified by mysticism. But whereas mystic phenomena are admittedly uncommon, those of adolescence are open to verification by anyone able to recall this unhappy period of his life. I know all this will displease those for whom Hegelian obscurities are indexes to Hegelian profundities. Yet typical of adolescence is precisely the cleavage between the image of an ideal self in which one's true identity is to be found and the humdrum self of transitory experience. 'Who am I'—a poignant question, this, and excessive preoccupation with it by the young suggests considerations remarkably like those that enter into Hegel's diagnosis of the unhappy consciousness.

Meredy: What temerity! The adolescent consciousness would seem to many interpreters too commonplace an illustration of what purports to be a high and subtle theme. But never mind. Our conversations about Hegel are free of commentarial pretensions. Up to a point your illustration is quite apt. The bifurcated selves within the unhappy consciousness are readily translatable into adolescent terms. To the adolescent, as to the would-be mystic, there is ever present the image of a self more authentic and more cherishable than the person his daily life is bound up with. Initially, it is nothing more than a sort of inverted picture of himself invented by his fancy. The self of his heart's desire is simply other than and remote from the restless and discontented being with which he is for the nonce identified. Unlike the would-be mystic, however, the adolescent gradually comes to give definite form to the distant self he longs for, fixing his mind on some hero, actual or conceivable, who might serve as model for his personality. The desired self thus becomes a determinate being with the attributes of a sharply defined character. The distance between the model personage and the imitative youth remains unbridgeable until the latter makes the discovery that he and his ideal are not strangers, the ideal being his own self purged of present imperfection and cured of juvenile grief, thus passing from adolescence to maturity.

There is unmistakably some parallelism between the unhappy consciousness and the consciousness of adolescence. Even the Hegelian terminology is not inapplicable. What the adolescent aspires to be must appear stable or changeless, contrasted with his unsettled and changeable nature. And his transition to maturity must be passage from attachment to a fixed or changeless paradigm to recognition of individuality as dynamic, since rational self-consciousness depends on the process of self-unification supervening upon self-differentiation. But the analogy must not be pressed. Hegel's treatment of the unhappy consciousness

105

brings to light many features not easily assimilable with the adolescent mind.

Hardith: I am glad you are not averse to the possibility of seeing in adolescence, "up to a point," as you say, a manifestation of the unhappy consciousness. The analogy, assuming it to be nothing more, does prevent the theme from becoming too closely identified with a particular form of religious experience. His metaphors to the contrary notwithstanding, Hegel undoubtedly conceived of the unhappy consciousness as no less universal than the sceptical consciousness from which he derived it. I am aware of course that the analogy tends to oversimplify a complex subject but I happen to be among those who prefer a modicum of clarity to muddy depths. Be that as it may, and disregarding the analogy, let us consider the development of the long and weary process whereby the unhappy consciousness, prey to self-alienation, seeks to win union with its own true but remote self. The text mentions three stages of that process. Each unfortunately is couched in a bewildering vernacular; the figures of speech employed disconcertingly suggests special ideas and beliefs uniquely conditioned. Here if anywhere it is difficult not to confuse the typical phenomena Hegel is intent upon with their local and dated instances. Devotion, aspiration, resignation—these being the stages—would seem to forfeit their putative generality by being wrapped up in a diction so evidently sectarian.

4. *The Monastic*

Meredy: How right you are! Yet, it is doubtful whether Hegel could have phrased the three stages in a wholly secular manner, nor whether he would have required them at all, and in just that order, if he himself had not confused the general with the particular. This lends some color to the possibility of evoking the mediaeval monastery as exclusive setting for their analysis.

Consider devotion as the first stage in the process of bridging the gap between the changeless self and the changeable. For a consciousness merely devout there is no escape from the pathos of distance. The remote does not become present by thinking of it as present, be the sentiments inspiring the thinking ever so pious. Playing upon the word, Hegel speaks of devotion as *Andacht,* signifying adoration touched with thought. This indeed is no longer the abstract thought of stoicism or the negative thought of scepticism; here thought has for its object an individual being dimly appearing identical with the adoring self. Hegel's vocabulary, redolent of the cloister, plainly suggests the dialectic of the religious consciousness. Venerative thinking, if thinking it be called, associated, for instance, with the clang of ringing bells or the drift of aromatic clouds of incense, is essentially formless; at best, it is 'thinking in music', but such thinking can never reach determinate concepts to which alone inner objectivity belongs. The adored object, being an object of thought saturated with feelings, is ultimately incomprehensible and unutterable. Viewed as a vocation, to speak of it thus, devotion is condemned to failure, involving as it does ceaseless longing for a mysterious 'beyond' that remains forever unapproachable.

Hardith: There is of course no necessity for the reduction of the devout consciousness to such a plight. Hegel's language, in spite of its mystic overtones, or perhaps because of them, seems to prejudge the outcome. Why should longing for the unattained lead to despair? The would-be mystic, for example, may feel in the very process of longing some proximity to the object he longs for, his devotion serving to attenuate the painful awareness of remoteness from the ideal. Temporary separation from what his heart desires need not turn devotion into sorrow, as if he were in the presence of 'the sepulchre of his true life'. Such locution is hardly the locution of the mystic. Hegel's image of the 'tomb' is not pertinent except in relation to that consciousness whose yearning is explicitly for a vanished object of love. To the mystic the same image would seem appropriate in precisely the opposite sense. His is the attempt to dig a grave for the false self whose burial is the condition precedent to the discovery of the true self.

Besides, there is another version of longing on which Hegel's analysis has no bearing. I have in mind romantic longing of the kind with which Hegel was only too familiar. This longing culminates in irony rather than grief. Mere allusion to the theme suffices to show the ineptitude of applying to it the language of piety. Devotion to longing conceived as infinite is obviously devotion to a universal ideal too deep for particular utterance or embodiment. Although always pining for what is not, one must nevertheless look before and after for transitory tokens of the unattainable. Romantic self-consciousness is deliberate self-estrangement, the self as subject fastidiously refusing to be completely identified with the self as object. Between the two—between the I and the Me in James's phraseology—the relation is singularly subtle; the former, impetuous and uncontrollable, moves everywhere in search of what by definition can be found nowhere, the latter, at once eclectic and fickle, tests and shuns all things and all forms of beauty, all objects of passion and of love. Irony, consisting of the power to repudiate the self's (the Me's) attachments and commitments, redounds to the glory of the self's (the I's) infinite longing or, in Schlegel's paraphrase, "longing for longing." Here is, in Hegel's terms, the self's division be-

107

tween the changeless and the changeable aspects of his nature; the self remains always the same in his capacity for unceasing yearning, but the self is also protean in his experiments with everything thinkable and imaginable. The tension between devotion to the changeless and engulfment in the changeable, which irony is designed to relieve, does not seem to entail the pathos Hegel reads into the devout consciousness.

Meredy: I am not disposed to quarrel with what you say. I only question its relevance. Romanticism is not so homogeneous as you choose to intimate. Concerning its very definition there is, as you well know, no unanimity among the cognoscenti. And many a romantic poet, unacquainted with the grace of irony, has expressed with the poignancy of despair the melancholy aspect of the gulf between the ideal and the actual. Yes, the unhappy consciousness, in the precise form in which Hegel depicts it, finds repeated utterance in romantic literature. But let that pass. The thoughts and the emotions described as romantic are too sophisticated for our purpose. We encounter them much later in the text in connection with more advanced types of experience. The devout consciousness, an episodic theme in the dialectic of the unhappy consciousness, is relatively simple and artless, Hegel portraying it as if by adoration, a species of thought mixed with emotion, the separation between one's changeless and one's changeable self could be overcome. But it cannot be thus overcome. Devout yearning is not for an abstract universal but for a determinate individual in intimate union with the yearning consciousness. In so far as devout yearning appears infinite, the object of it must needs recede further and further into the distance, proving mere adoration to be futile and empty. A consciousness including but transcending the devout becomes dialectically necessary. Can service bring the unhappy consciousness closer to the ideal it feels estranged from? To this new theme we must now turn.

Hardith: Service, I take it, as distinguished from adoration, is a positive link with an ideal still remote. But the consciousness engaged in service is susceptible of two views regarding the origin of the will to serve. Either the actual self initiates specific acts such as are calculated to reach thereby the transcendent ideal or they are acts appearing as if commanded from afar and appearing thus with an air of sanctity. Much of course depends on which source the acts are derived from. And the issue does not require to be couched in Hegelian terms. 'Let me serve you!' so anyone might be imagined addressing the impalpable entity to which he feels spiritually related—his god, his soul, his superego, his star. Is this the ambivalence to which service is open? Are the acts intended to serve the private affairs of the individual, in which case they are no less vain than sentiments of piety, or are they impelled by a higher or deeper being to be performed for its exclusive advantage?

Meredy: As usual you manage in a phrase or two to go to the core of the matter. Yes, service suffers from the equivocation you indicate. It is not by service that the unhappy consciousness can be relieved of inner division. The division, indeed, becomes deepened with the discovery that serving the ideal is no more effective than adoring it; the ideal remains as unapproachable as ever or else it sinks to the level of the actual individual the unhappy consciousness desires to escape from. Let us but ask for whose benefit the good deeds of the unhappy self are to be done and we have on our hands a formidable dilemma: either the deeds redound to the profit of the ideal or they contribute to the enjoyment of him who performs them. If the ideal is in need of them, its fortunes, so to speak, hinging on the adequacy of their execution, the ideal ceases to be ideal and becomes instead the very replica of the individual serving it. If, on the other hand, the self derives satisfaction from his deeds, the satisfaction rather than the ideal served assumes primary importance, the ideal being the means whereby the self seeks to develop his talents and virtues. In other words, ultimately the unhappy consciousness serves not the ideal but itself.

Such is the dialectic of good works supervening upon pious meditations. To set out, for example, to labor for the good of one's soul, is to embark on a hopeless enterprise. If the soul's interests are intimately bound up with the self's activities, the soul is manifestly not independent of the self; if the soul is completely unaffected by the tasks undertaken for its sake, the self and his soul are strangers as much as the self and his star.

Hardith: In terms of your example, the predicament of the poor unhappy self seems to be this: if, in doing his good works, he finds his self, he loses his soul; to reach his soul, he must, abandoning the notion of service, renounce his self. The predicament would of course retain its force if for soul we substituted any other term exemplifying Hegel's conception of the changeless. Since loss of the soul is an alternative not open to choice without bringing the dialectic to an abrupt halt, self-abnegation appears as the only possible alternative. And yet, self-abnegation turns out to be the process requisite for recognition of the self's integrity!

Meredy: But self-abnegation must not be a pose hidden under the cloak of hypocrisy. Service, because of its inherent ambiguity, lends itself to an attitude of self-assertion masquerading as self-surrender. Not until the corruptive tendencies latent in service are seen in their true light can the unhappy consciousness become purged of false resignation and false humility. Of the spiritual pride and selfish satisfaction to which a supposed servant of the ideal is subject Hegel's analysis is very elaborate. Awareness of merit in one's work and the feeling of gratitude for one's ability to do it are shown by him to entail a self-consciousness not easily severable from self-complacency. Recognition by the unhappy consciousness of the complacency which service is apt to breed has the effect of intensifying its anguish. The dialectical process minutely traced in the text is thus from self-complacency to self-abasement and from self-abasement to self-chastisement. The unhappy man now embarks upon his last effort to approach his ideal. Looking upon his very individuality as basis of his misery, he seeks forcibly to crush it, the method chosen being that of asceticism, on the assumption that consciousness of individuality is the same as consciousness of the animal functions of the body. Consequently, mortification of the flesh comes to assume the dignity of a spiritual career, and the irony is this, that what should be deemed contemptible and of no moment—namely, everything pertaining to the body—turns into an object of earnest concern and assiduous thought. We therefore witness, as Hegel concludes, merely a brooding and wretched personality occupied exclusively with its little self and its little tasks.

5. Transition to Reason

Hardith: Curiously enough, this last phase of the unhappy consciousness, in which rationality seems reduced to its lowest ebb, is to provide the transition to reason. A paradox, of course! Hegel speaks obscurely of a middle term, present in the unhappy consciousness, linking its two extremes, as if the issue could be resolved by an Aristotelian syllogism. And even more enigmatic is his personification of this third element as mediator (*Vermittler*) between the ascetic's paltry deeds and the spiritual needs they dimly but perversely reflect. The conception of a middleman introduced within the heart of the unhappy consciousness for the purpose of healing its broken spirit, necessary though it may appear as a turning point of the dialectic, leaves me, I must confess, quite bewildered.

Meredy: The finale of the unhappy consciousness, intended to serve as prelude to reason, contains indeed much that is cryptic or nebulous. But much also, in spite of the opaque diction in which it is embedded, stands out quite clearly. Two points are of special importance in their bearing on the notion of individuality condemned to destruction by the votary of asceticism. What must be mentioned first is the insight, indirectly attested by the unhappy consciousness even at its unhappiest, that deeds done deliberately are impossible unless done by some individual. The sacrifice of individuality attempted by the ascetic would obviously preclude the very activity by which the attempt is made. This the ascetic can only see as if through a glass darkly. The self, in short, is what the self does. Next in order is the related insight that the self, being fundamentally active, must possess an organic consciousness for the achievement of rational individuality. Such language is of course redundant, organic and rational being for Hegel predicates essentially synonymous. It is thus not surprising that the types of self-consciousness so far examined, owing to the deep imbalance latent in excessive self-differentiation, should each and all appear as out of joint. The proper balance between differentiation and unification is precisely what reason aims at when reason is conceived as dialectical. What reason puts asunder reason can join together. No rational self-consciousness is accordingly possible, seeing that it is amenable to processes so diametrically opposed, those of division and conjugation, unless some agency within it performs the function of mediating between them. What Hegel calls the mediator is simply an agency hypostatized into an agent. I do not think it necessary to read into Hegel's utterances, abstruse though they are, the theological implications which certain of his commentators have read into them. The only implications they seem to warrant are these: self-consciousness remains irrational as long as it is considered but structurally in terms of the abstract dichotomy between subject and object. In a rational or organic conception of it, structure makes way for function and dichotomy for trichotomy, the trichotomy which is the very soul of the dialectical method. To attain the level of rationality, it is therefore incumbent upon self-consciousness to act, so to speak, as its own middleman or middle term between the opposed aspects or strains of its nature. Until it does so there can be no relief for a self-alienation that results from a discriminable duality appearing as an absolute dualism. At the transitional stage, the unhappy consciousness has but the assurance, given by the mediator within it, that all will be ultimately well. This mediator, not fully recognized as such, gradually implants in consciousness the conviction that in its organic individuality it is the embodiment of reason and thus the very paradigm of all reality.

PART III

REASON

Reason's Certainty and Truth

Hardith: The transition to the new chapter in Hegel's biography of mind hinges on the discovery by the unhappy consciousness of an agency relieving it of the misery arising from the feeling of self-estrangement. This agency turns out to be reason. The development of reason must thus advance further the dialectic of self-consciousness. Although distinct from self-consciousness, reason, I assume, is not discontinuous with it: reason *is* self-consciousness on a higher or organized level. I ventured earlier to illustrate the unhappy consciousness by comparing it to the consciousness of the adolescent. May I recall the illustration merely to suggest that a rational consciousness is that of an adolescent having arrived at maturity? Whereas the adolescent mind is painfully aware of the gulf that separates the actual from the ideal self, the mature mind seeks actively to bridge the gulf. By means of a distinction such as this much of what Hegel comprehends under reason becomes intelligible. Does this mode of approach to the text strike you as too naïve? The ingress provided through the introduction I find very difficult.

Meredy: As in the introduction to self-consciousness, so in that to reason (and so, in fact, in the introductions to later divisions of the text), Hegel speaks in his own name before proceeding to a new stage of the dialectic. The introductions enable him to look both behind and ahead, summing up results attained and foreshadowing the tasks to follow. His statements made *ex cathedra* are indeed difficult; they are full of allusions, some annoyingly elusive, and often contain animadversions on views differing from his. In the introduction to reason the tone is markedly magisterial. But the identity of the men alluded to is happily not doubtful, and the reflection on their ideas brings into focus Hegel's conception of rationality as contrasted with conceptions he deems one-sided or otherwise inadequate.

114

Before considering some of the details, let me comment first on the appositeness of the distinction between adolescent and mature self-consciousness. The distinction would be unexceptionable if it could be employed without prejudice. Does not adolescence often carry a pejorative and maturity a laudatory sense? To the unhappy consciousness, it is true, belongs in the *Phenomenology* a dialectical priority over reason comparable to the way in which in the life of the individual adolescence is chronologically prior to maturity. There is no scandal in the comparison. If the measure of a man's mature life is prevalence in it of reason's imperatives, dialectical progress of rational consciousness may not inaptly be spoken of as progress towards ever greater maturity. But we are here deliberately dealing with tropes.

Hardith: I am continually impressed by the tropes upon which Hegel himself constantly relies for conveying his thoughts, and if by changing tropes we can express the thoughts in simpler or clearer fashion, we are less likely to go astray than by parroting his forbidding vocabulary. May I take this as a position on which we fully agree?

One of the things I find puzzling in the introduction is Hegel's use of the term 'idealism'. He applies it to the view that rational self-consciousness is aware of constituting the source of all reality, this being, as the very title of the introduction proclaims, reason's certainty and reason's truth. At first sight there seems no necessary connection between the contention that reality is derivable from the nature of self-consciousness and the contention that reality is in accord with principles of reason. The first contention alone may be subsumed under idealism, the second has its appropriate affiliation with rationalism. And this is not merely a matter of terminology. Should it be asserted of all idealism that a cardinal article of its faith is acknowledgment of reason's hegemony, conceptions of reality rooted in mind's nonrational or irrational elements being dogmatically ruled out of court? On the other hand, is it not possible to adhere to some variant of rationalism whose principal thesis simply affirms the structural harmony of reason and reality, the assumption of self-consciousness as the measure of the nature of things being extraneous or impertinent? Why, in a word, should an idealist be committed to rationalism or a rationalist to idealism?

Meredy: This is a crucial question. If we were to debate the issue on its merits, we should of course have to distinguish between the various species of idealism as well as between those of rationalism, and we could no doubt find species of the one either coinciding with or diverging from species of the other. For Hegel, it is clear, idealism and rationalism are one in principle, in their fully developed or most mature expression, to wit, *his*. His criticism is here directed to such versions

115

as are embodied in imperfect or immature form. The polemic of which the short introduction is largely composed presupposes his own view that the real world is ultimately intelligible precisely because it is the very image of reason. This he expressed in a later epigram containing the famous equation that the rational is the real and the real the rational. This of course is nonsense when the terms equated are allowed to retain their ordinary meaning. The truth is the whole, declares Hegel, and it is on the basis of this declaration alone that thought and being become equatable, when that is, they are grasped as mutually implicated in a dialectical process of development that aims at all-inclusive comprehensiveness. Short of the whole, the real and the rational remain divided and incompatible.

Hardith: In your terse explanation of Hegel's thesis relating to the identity of the real and the rational, you omit reference to self-consciousness. Why the omission? The idealism under consideration, though instinct with reason, is one the basic principles of which derive from the nature of self-consciousness. The formula more apposite here should therefore be expressed thus: the self-conscious is the real and the real the self-conscious. The equation of the real and the rational seems to be but a corollary from an equation more primary.

Meredy: Explicit reference to self-consciousness has seemed to me superfluous because reason is what self-consciousness culminates in. The unhappy consciousness does not cease to be self-conscious when cured of self-estrangement. In reason self-consciousness loses nothing but its immaturity. The dialectic we have followed shows reason to be the fulfillment of self-consciousness in precisely the sense that self-consciousness appeared as the realization of the understanding. Their continuity lies deeper still. Remember that for Hegel the nature of self-consciousness clearly exemplifies the triadic pattern of his logic. Indeed, for a logic, the dynamism of which depends on the repetitive rhythm of dialectical opposition and unison, self-conscious experience provides the very archetype, involving as it does the interplay of identity and difference as if they were internalized polar forces. Of the double mutuality of concepts, being at once mutually exclusive and mutually inclusive, which is the moving principle of Hegel's logic, self-consciousness is the phenomenalistic fount and origin. Reduced to an equational formula, assuming this to be possible or desirable, Hegel's idealism might be thus compressed: the self-conscious=the rational=the real. This idealism, which consists in complete development of all the implications latent in the formula, Hegel uses as standard for judging defective versions of it.

Hardith: Let us not pursue the matter beyond necessity. Discussion of Hegel's idealism is here but ancillary to an understanding of reason conceived as self-consciousness attaining self-possession. We may now proceed with the analysis, having received from the introduction the requisite preparation. But before leaving the introduction, one more topic requires to be touched upon. We can hardly ignore Hegel's polemic directed against that defective kind of idealism which he patently though indirectly attributes to Kant.

Hegel alone—so Hegel avers—can furnish the needed demonstration of a truth which Kant is here alleged to have merely postulated. The postulate of idealism—Hegel speaks of it as bare assurance (*reine Versicherung*)—is nothing without demonstrable proof. And to show that Kant's idealism is deficient in probative force, Hegel centers his attack on what he considers to be its basis. On the one hand, this idealism involves self-consciousness as its sole and primary category, and on the other, a plurality of differentiated but unrelated categories. It is the problem of 'the one and the many', as applied to Kant's categorial idealism, if I may so name it, which seems to constitute the crux of the difficulty. What more precisely is the difficulty?

Meredy: Hegel never misses an opportunity to subject Kant to criticism. The *Phenomenology* is replete with reflections on many aspects of his teaching. In understanding, for instance, it is the conception of a supersensible world which comes in for censure; here it is the doctrine of the categories. And we shall encounter subsequently strictures passed on other of his tenets. A collection of the various attacks on Kant made by Hegel in the course of the *Phenomenology* would look quite impressive. In the present context Hegel's criticism is strictly limited to what you felicitously call Kant's 'categorial idealism'. The criticism makes no sense except on the basis of the standard Hegel brings to it. The standard is embodied in the statement that 'reason is the conscious certainty of being all reality'. This is simply another way of expressing the equation of the rational and the real. In the light of that equation, what is a category? If a category signifies, as Hegel says it must, the unity of thought and being, there is, according to him, but one concept with a claim on categorial universality, the concept of a thinking self (or, in Kant's terminology, the concept of the transcendental unity of apperception). Upon the thinking self alone can devolve the categorial function of uniting thought and being. Whence then other categories exercising the same function, and what is their relation to the unique category of the thinking self? To speak of discovering the plural categories in the given table of judgments is to speak of them as if present in prefabricated patterns, as it were, to be stumbled upon at haphazard. Are we to look upon the categories as a lucky find? Are

117

we just to accept them without proving the necessity of their determinate differences and of their intrinsic interdependence? Such a notion of the categories is nothing less, Hegel harshly observes, than a philosophic scandal. Of what use is understanding, the alleged source of necessary judgments, if it is unable to demonstrate the necessity of its own nature? The necessity Hegel demands, I need hardly mention, is dialectical necessity.

Hardith: Hegel's tart criticism of Kant, if I am not rash in saying so, boils down to the charge that the Analytic is not a Dialectic. Must Kant be reproached for being Kant and not Hegel? The number and nature of basic categories must obviously vary with the method to which they owe their discovery and deduction. But this takes us beyond the purpose to which we have agreed to confine our discussion. Our purpose being to comprehend without bias the comprehensible aspects of the *Phenomenology,* we need no longer delay the approach to the dialectic of reason. To be sure, we must thus neglect the remaining material covered in the introduction which deals, and no less harshly, with the kind of idealism presumably ascribable to Fichte. As far as I can judge, however, its bearing on what follows seems less direct than the attack on Kant.

But before proceeding, there is one point to be clarified. It is this: while reason represents a more mature stage of experience than the unhappy consciousness of which it is, so to speak, the transfiguration, reason, too, typifies a career the dialectic of which requires that it develop by means of relatively naïve or crude expressions. If reason is a stage of experience whose maturity is but that of self-consciousness, is reason not precluded from laying claim to a maturity intrinsic to it? Should we regard the whole career of reason, in the part of the work bearing its name, as inevitably moving in the direction of a stage of experience in which its supersession will be its fulfillment?

Meredy: Yes, reason has the ambivalence you note. Being midway between self-consciousness and the stage called spirit, reason appears essentially Janus-faced. As the nisus of self-consciousness is towards reason, so is that of reason toward spirit. Although bringing to fruition the self's integrity, reason can reach no spiritual depth on its own plane. The persuasion regarding the unity of the rational and the real, when falsely conceived, leads to egregious paradoxes, to the diagnosis of which the sequel is assiduously devoted. And here, too, the dialectic hinges on the experiment with false positions as if they were true, for in such experiment lies the only proof of their falsity. Rational self-consciousness, viewed as consciousness no longer introspective, confidently embarks on the ambitious task of representing the world

118

everywhere in its own image, holding nature up to the mirror of reason. The world thus becomes reason's own other, enjoying but a borrowed objectivity, one imposed upon it by the concepts of thought. Planting the signs of its sovereignty, as Hegel remarks, "on the heights and the depths of reality," reason can afford to leave the world as other, the otherness being there by reason's leave. But the reason to which Hegel gives such excessive attention remains immature; his description of it as *Vernunftinstinkt* is strikingly apposite. The instinct of reason, although sound as instinct, cannot surmount the anomalies it harbors. Reason can indeed cope with them but only when it ceases to be instinctive and becomes full-fledged, when, in other words, the method reason follows becomes explicitly dialectical.

But enough of preliminary consideration.

Rational Observation of Nature

1. Observation as an Activity of Reason

Hardith: The general theme of this lengthy section seems less difficult than its detailed development. Hegel, so I gather, is intent upon
showing what happens when the attempt is made to verify by observation the postulate of a preconceived harmony between the rational and
the real. That the harmony *is* demonstrable, but not by reason in its
role as mere 'observer', is this not the persuasion by which the whole
discussion is guided? And do we not revert to the problem considered
earlier under Consciousness, now raised to a higher plane as a result
of the examination directed at Self-Consciousness? The issue of the
previous analysis centers on the relation of subject and object, the
object being primary for consciousness, the subject for self-consciousness. While the analysis of all cognition requires their differentiation,
that of self-cognition hinges on their self-differentiation. It is this which
Hegel takes to be the crucial point. Cognition of self, though presupposing the homogeneity of subject and object, depends for discovery
of their homogeneous nature on the initial experience of their inward
heterogeneity, an experience turning self-consciousness into self-alienation. Reason it is which restores the balance between subject and object, proving them to be complementary rather than antithetical.

The equation of the rational and the real, the supervening postulate
of a maturing self-consciousness, Hegel expressed by a curious pun
for which there exists no English equivalent. In the word *Bewusstsein*
(consciousness) the syllable *Sein* (being) is a structural component,
having when detached an independent meaning. Of this term he makes
subtle use, expressing thereby reason's postulate (or, as he calls it,
reason's instinct), the postulate that nothing can have *Sein* except as
Sein which is *bewusst*. What this implies, to render it freely, is that
reason is precluded from affirming being of anything unless it conform
to reason's own nature. Am I reading too much in a random wordplay?

120

Yet it does serve to facilitate the transition to reason's career. The transition, to put it graphically, is simply from *Bewusstsein* as univocal to its hyphened form as *Bewusst-Sein*.

Meredy: Hegel's puns are seldom spontaneous; they seem expressly contrived to suit his purpose, the purpose varying with the context in which they occur. The play upon *Bewusstsein* is a case in point, aiding, as you rightly note, in making the transition to the instinctive persuasion in accordance with which reason's observational enterprise is to be launched. Indeed, it provides also a distinct clue to the nature of that persuasion, especially when the syllable *Sein* is seen to have for Hegel the added meaning of a possessive pronoun, his own statement running thus, *"Dieses Bewusstsein, welchem das Sein die Bedeeutung des Seinen hat."* Phrased in English this simply avers that the being now present *to* consciousness has *for* consciousness no significance except to be its *own*.

Apart from such verbal legerdemain, the reintroduction of consciousness has the importance of reviving in a new form the cognitive distinction and relation between subject and object. And the consciousness to which we are bidden to return is chiefly that of perception. The experience of perception reverted to, however, is no longer to be regarded as the experience of being acted upon by stubborn facts. Here perception is not synonymous with reception. Instead of just taking the object as given, the object must now be observed as conforming to rational criteria. In the close cousinship of perception and observation will be found to lie the root of the dialectic of a reason under the dominance of a non-dialectical logic. *Perception with a purpose*—and this is what observation here signifies—constitutes the universal theme the variations of which Hegel draws from diverse sources. We shall not lose ourselves in details if we constantly bear in mind the affinity of observation with perception from which it differs only by being deliberate and controlled. The personage we are now dealing with, if I may say so, is the former wayward percipient transformed into a systematic observer.

Hardith: Observation of nature instituted by reason involves, according to Hegel, various activities which in modern parlance we are accustomed to associate with the scientific method. The sciences generally depend upon such activities as description, inference, induction, experiment, requiring for their relevant exercise reference to data of observation. May we regard the section devoted to observation as containing a comprehensive critique of the method of science? And must it not strike us as curious that a method commonly held to be empirical should here appear under the auspices of reason?

121

Meredy: Yes, Hegel does disclose the difficulties inherent in the scientific method when considered in isolation. His criticism has to do with the neglect of the philosophic ideas and beliefs upon which the method depends for its validity. Unfortunately, the criticism is enmeshed in a net of bewildering references, the sciences mentioned being either obsolete or spurious. When disentangled from contexts of no interest save to the antiquarian and applied to examples drawn from disciplines extant or accredited, Hegel's analysis appears to have singular relevance. Of this we shall take note later. Meanwhile just a word about the legitimacy of affixing the epithet empirical to scientific procedure. In what sense is the epithet appropriate? To be sure, the process of observation, cognate as it is with that of perception, is undeniably empirical if its data are phenomena sensibly present. But their sensible presence, assuming the necessity of such presence, is not sufficient for differentiating objects of scientific observation from objects of mere perception. Requisite for scientific observation are prior distinctions and operations that have their source in reason, and it is these Hegel's analysis is designed to bring to light.

Hardith: With the distinction and relation between sense and thought we are here not concerned. The previous discussions in connection with consciousness proved the futility of attempting to insulate the sensible from the intelligible. Whatever the empirical may be said to connote, it certainly is not synonymous with the sensible. The empirical, though including the sensible, passes beyond it. I am aware, however, that the word means different things to different men. Although the designation of the scientific method as empirical is not without cogent grounds, the issue regarding the proper use of the adjective is so largely semantic that it need not divert our attention from Hegel's text. The chief question at issue here is the extent to which observation may serve as a process capable of revealing the truth that the rational is the real. Reliance upon observation to perform this feat rests on the premise that it is a process of reason. In what sense can it be such a process in view of its similarity to perception?

Meredy: The things which continually impinge on our senses are objects we cannot help perceiving, perception, unlike observation, being as a rule involuntary and aimless. The data of observation, on the other hand, when observation becomes a scientific procedure, are deliberately selected and carefully discriminated in relation to a special subject of inquiry, and it is in this sense that observation, differing from perception, is a rational activity instinct with purpose. But observation is an activity hardly sufficient for the task of proving the truth of the persuasion which is here alleged to induce it. Reason's faith, justification of which is but intuitive or instinctive, defies observational verification. The demonstration that the rational and the real are commensurate transcends the limits of a reason depending exclusively on a process so superficial. The first difficulty the process runs into reveals its gross inadequacy. To what specifically is observation to be directed? As distinguished from perception, observation is not random or indiscriminate, some data being obviously more relevant than others, nor are all the features of those chosen worth noting and recording. A principle of selection is requisite for focusing attention on these objects rather than those, and for distinguishing within the preferred objects the significant from their negligible aspects. Without some principle of selection, it is clear, observation becomes a useless exercise. What is here at stake is the basis of the principle as well as its validity.

Hardith: To be sure, without data, no observation, their priority, quite in keeping with scientific belief, being here explicitly recognized. And data of observation, again in agreement with scientific belief, are assumed to be furnished by nature. But what is nature? Is there any term more open to abuse? In Hegel's text, however, nature is seemingly but a collective name for the things amenable to methods contrived by the inquiring mind, observation being here the supreme methodic activity. In the discussion of the nature to which observation is directed Hegel's approach is certainly not unconventional: his division falls into the accepted rubrics—physics, biology, psychology. The division, representing a division of scientific labor, enables him to follow the various twists and turns of the observational process, one that varies in technique with differences in subject matter. I see nothing so very difficult in all this. In fact, Hegel's analysis of scientific methodology, despite the outmoded illustrations, is surprisingly pertinent. What is observationally veridical and what is not? The relativity of scientific observation, cognate with the relativity of ordinary perception, involves as an incontrovertible postulate the possibility of error. If this is one of Hegel's contentions, who would be disposed to quarrel with it?

2. Observation of Inorganic Nature

Meredy: The problem is not quite so simple. The section does indeed contain a criticism of a quasi-scientific methodology but not without reference to the ontology it entails. Method presupposes relevance to subject matter, and the specific nature of any subject matter depends for its discovery on an appropriate method. This circle, if such it be, is unavoidable so long as method and subject matter remain interdependent. As regards inorganic nature, to which we must turn next, the observable datum and the manner of observing it are clearly bound to each other by mutual implication. But for this mutuality the observing process would go on and on without let or hindrance. Every observer seeking to describe an object's observable features is always faced with a superfluity of them. To catalogue without rhyme or reason any and every feature would be sheer folly. No scientific observer, it is safe to say, can forgo the assumption that some traits are more worth describing than others. The observer's activity must somehow be held in check, and what else could do this if not a defensible principle of selection? But among so many observable traits, which are to be recorded as the 'elect'? Here Hegel introduces the distinction (employed by him on former occasions) between the essential and the nonessential. Only such features or traits as are deemed essential merit cognitive attention and exact description.

Hardith: Ah, the blessed word essential! Essential, by what standard? What is essential from one point of view need not be so from another, and principles prompting selection of the essential may vary with the interests to which they are ancillary. Are such principles then entirely subjective? Yet, although the operations involved in noting and differentiating and recording the essential properties of things have their genesis in mind, to these very operations the things admittedly belonging to physical nature are held to be amenable! What is essential for the physicality of the things, if I may put it thus, is not identical with that which is deemed essential in physics or for physics. The latter is a science that depends on man's and not nature's agency. The issue, I take it, has principally to do with the relation between knowledge based on variable observation and the intrinsic properties of nature. And so, when the concept of the essential is said to guide our cognitive acts, the question arises, essential for what? Essential for the *knowledge* of objects or for the *objects* of knowledge?

Meredy: We must remember that for instinctive reason the harmony between nature and science is a fundamental postulate, so that the essential relative to cognition must as a matter of course be ascribed to its objects. The task devolving upon observation is simply to seek in the external world evidence of the postulate's truth. The conformity of nature to concepts rationally contrived being premised, it follows ineluctably that none but facts regarded as essential in accordance with scientific procedure can enjoy objective authenticity. But here as elsewhere in the *Phenomenology,* the duality of subject and object does not disappear with the surrender of dualism. The duality here is between nature and its antonym. And what is nature's antonym if not an artificial product—*das künstliche System,* as Hegel calls it—which is not unsuitable as a synonym of science? The attempt made solely on the basis of observation to describe the natural order of things as comporting with the artificial order of science can here have no other than intuitive justification. Its failure follows from the propensity of the observing consciousness to neglect recalcitrant or negative instances. Artificial and natural groupings are apt to overlap or to collide. Many borderline cases defy exact classification. The difference between one kind of description and another seems quite arbitrary, the terms chosen being symbolic rather than literal. Marks useful for purposes of identification may prove altogether useless as grounds of evidence. In short, reason in the role of mere observer is unable to bridge the gap between the natural and the artificial. No description of natural traits considered essential can escape the charge of being but factitious unless laws are invoked governing the constitution of their observable appearance and the manner of their behavior. It is thus, and thus alone, that the essential can become converted into the necessary, and reason, instead of only noting and classifying things, now turns to discover their laws.

Hardith: Let us proceed then on the assumption that among the observable features of things such alone are essential that reveal themselves to be necessary. But demonstration of their necessity can obviously not fall within the competence of observation. A law of nature, alleged to necessitate whatever appears essential in the data observed, is itself no observable datum. Evidence attainable by a method having its roots in observation is by common consent adjudged insufficient to support claims to a necessity such as the conception of law is here said to entail. Laws whose validity the natural sciences vouch for are generalizations never transcending the limits of probability, no matter how high the degree to which they may be made to mount. As regards Hegel's criticism of scientific methodology, which I take to be his main concern, the situation appears to be this: if observation is fundamental to scientific knowledge, the generalizations drawn from it fall short of necessity; but if the generalizations attested by the scientific method are endowed with necessity, they forfeit continuity with their observational base. The difficulty of reason at this stage lies in its inability either to renounce or to retain its observational posture.

Meredy: The anomalousness of observation will be seen to grow apace as we pursue the analysis further. The difficulty relating to the conception of law, which you state with such admirable succinctness, is very formidable indeed. For the laws of things, held to express their intrinsic nature, are laws discovered and certified by reason. However sensibly variable all things appear to direct apprehension, they must be regarded as subject to laws descriptive of their underlying uniformity. Uniformity pertains to reason and therefore also to nature. The natural order is uniform because its laws rationally ascertained are constant. Such laws, far from being but probable generalizations, enjoy universality and necessity. This follows from the premise that all the processes associated with the scientific method, including the process of observation, derive their probative force from criteria determined and sanctioned by reason.

It is only in such context of ideas that some of Hegel's contentions, strange though they may sound to a student of modern science, become more or less intelligible. Germane here is the contention that the laws of nature, being the fruits of rational processes, are laws of both the actual and the possible, of what is as well as of what ought to be. The law of gravitation, for example, to which Hegel alludes, applies not merely to the behavior of falling bodies such as are observed and observable, in which case it would indeed be a generalization only, but the true function of the law is to serve as universal norm to which all bodies, whether observable or not, must conform always and everywhere. Every descriptive law, like that of gravitation, is thus prescriptive; in stating how things do act, it dictates, so to speak, the conditions under which they should act. "What is universally valid," as Hegel says, playing on the words *gültig* and *geltend,* "is universally applicable: what ought to be, as a matter of fact, is too; and what merely should be, unrelated to actual being, has no claim on truth." A cryptic utterance, this; the allusion is clearly to Kant and his followers who, in the sphere of practical reason, drew a line almost indelible between the 'is' and the 'ought'. There is, according to Hegel, no warrant for such a line wherever drawn. Law as thus conceived—conceived, that is, as both descriptive and prescriptive—can neither be elicited from nor verified by observation, and to prove this is the purpose of the dialectic.

Hardith: Hegel's animadversions on laws not possessed of complete universality and necessity would strike as bizarre those acquainted with the logic of modern science. Of general statements based on induction and varying in extent of probability Hegel in effect declares that they have no truth at all. For we not only debase but we annul the meaning of truth by thinking of it as qualified and subject to increase or diminution. The qualification of truth as probable, involving also its quantification, since probability differs in degree, Hegel finds to have its source in reasoning by analogy, and to analogical reasoning he gives short shrift. Such reasoning is often so deceptive that, as he says, "the inference to be drawn from analogy itself is rather that analogy permits no inference to be drawn." The epigram is amusing but scarcely relevant to the refined processes of induction and the mathematical judgments of probability characteristic of genuine science. The search for truth which is more probable seems definitely precluded as long as the search is contingent upon data of observation from which it must take its departure and to which it must ever return. And yet, reason, though but instinctive, is not untrue to its vocation in clinging to the observational level. How curious!

Meredy: Curious, indeed, but only because reason as here depicted is made to owe fidelity to two kinds of persuasion that are at loggerheads. The union of the rational and the real, reason's first and more basic persuasion, can be verified by observation, this being the other persuasion, and it is the conflict between them that precipitates an incongruous situation. What Hegel calls reason's instinctive propensity to observe its own nature in nature's phenomena has implications that none but a dialectical logic can fully develop, and such a logic is merely intimated in the career of observation as a tale of vacillating claims. The instinctive reasoning which finds expression in the sciences involves assumptions of which their votaries may not be aware, the term instinctive, in the sense of unconscious, being here particularly pertinent.

Hegel illustrates this by referring to the experimental method as one requisite for investing hypotheses with true universality. What is an experiment and what necessitates it? Hegel's answer, extractable from his forbidding idiom, seems to be this. A law, owing its validity to observations made under natural conditions, can obviously enjoy but a limited generality; always hinging on the actual instances observed, the law is never immune from conceivable failure to apply to data beyond the present range of observation. How then can a general law attain the status of a universal? No general law can attain such status, Hegel contends, unless artificial conditions are contrived for testing it, conditions not duplicated by nature. A law receiving experimental verification receives it in circumstances under which it actually never operates. After all, the experiment is not nature's but the experimenter's, and the latter's observations, allegedly confirming the law's validity, are observations of data not observable except under ideal or laboratory conditions. By means of experiment mind intervenes in nature, translating it, as it were, to the laboratory; as thus translated, the data observed are data artificially produced, the laws of whose behavior, ceasing to be at the mercy of contingency, now become adaptable to reason's demands for universality and necessity. The men of science, creating ingenious ways for the control of their observations, appear oblivious of the fact that what they observe is a nature deliberately altered if not transformed to satisfy their sentiment of rationality. The transition from the natural to the artificial—or, if you like, from nature to science—is quite in keeping with the instinct of reason, an instinct still bound to the superficial plane of observation.

Hardith: Our discussion of reason as observer has so far been couched in terms germane to nature generally, though, judging by the illustrations mentioned, with some emphasis on inorganic or physical phenomena. But whatever the phenomena, they must be observed as subject to deliberate operations designed to make them progressively more pliant to reason. Hegel's view of scientific experiments as elaborate devices for testing natural laws under nonnatural conditions is certainly singular. The experimental procedure, commonly understood as preeminently empirical, here becomes its 'own other', a procedure typically rational. What a tremendous *tour de force!* Although conceived as intent on 'rationalizing' nature, the experimental method has but limited applicability. All the stubborn facts and contingent events and recalcitrant data remain to plague a reason committed to its faith in the possibility of bringing within the observational orbit nature's intelligibility. On the inorganic level, at any rate, observation as a process of reason appears to have met with failure.

Meredy: Inability to observe inorganic nature as according with rational norms does not militate against the privileged position of an observing reason. Other fields are open to observation requiring more proficient ways. One such field is organic nature. Here observed object and observing subject are bound to each other by natural affinity. They are essentially kindred. Let us follow the development of the new and advanced stage in reason's observational career.

3. Observation of Organic Nature

Hardith: You speak of a new relation between the observed and the observer as one between 'kindreds'. This of course is a figure of speech having more than one meaning. Biological phenomena, being living organisms, clearly include their scientific observers. Subject matter and the subject may here indeed be said to exemplify generic cousinship. But this is obviously not what Hegel has in mind. If organic nature comprehends the biologist's particular organism, so does inorganic nature contain the individual body of the physicist. Generic connections are not necessarily preferential. The union of the rational and the organic must be of singular intimacy to enable reason to advance to a fresh and more subtle kind of observation.

Meredy: The section on organic nature is exceedingly complex, almost esoteric, burdened as it is with allusions to ideas distinctly archaic. Whether they have more than historical interest need not concern us. Hegel's speculations on biology we must reduce to skeletal form, disregarding the illustrative material that gives them flesh and blood. To the speculation relating to the close kinship of the rational and the organic, closer, at any rate, than the affinity between the rational and the inorganic, certainly belongs primacy, and you are right in raising the issue at the outset. Hegel looks upon the organic and the conceptual as if they were adjectives almost synonymous, descriptive alike of such natural phenomena and rational products as exemplify configurations of diverse but interdependent components. The likeness between a product of reason (the concept) and a natural phenomenon (the organism) being premised, the task of observation has for its focus not the inner nature of the organic object but rather its outer comportment. Reason can thus dispense with further evidence for what it intuitively knows to be cognate with its own products. How may the organism's behavior, which alone is strictly observable, reveal an intrinsic nature antecedently acknowledged by reason to resemble reason's own? This is the question we are now required to examine.

Hardith: But this way of stating the matter omits all reference to the inorganic as if it had no influence on the being and conduct of the organism. Besides, not all concepts are organic in structure, and even those so describable may have for their content material drawn from the physical world. I am out of my depth here, I know, but I detect some flaw in the unqualified comparison between the conceptual and the organic.

Meredy: What you say anticipates what lies much further ahead. The difference in concepts you vaguely intimate Hegel dilates on at great length in later contexts. It appears as a difference in universals, one kind abstract, the other concrete. It is the concrete type of universal, here but foreshadowed, which, in being a whole of mutually implicated parts, has a structure resembling that of an organism. But universality called concrete, the nisus, as it were, of abstract reason, is not an observable datum, though all observation, as Hegel contends, must instinctively be guided by it. This, awaiting subsequent discussion, may throw some light, as yet obliquely, on observation of the organic as distinguishable from observation of the inorganic. To the question, why is reason on a more intimate footing with phenomena biological than physical? the answer is simply this: the unity of the rational and the real sought appears more manifest in organic form, a form homologous with that of concrete universality to which reason's abstractions are progressively leading.

Hardith: The paradox here involved seems to lie in the necessity which reason is under to uncover by direct observation the covert life of the organism. But if observation is confined to the organism's overt behavior, among the observable data the organism's responses to stimuli

129

from inorganic nature must of course be included. The relation between the organic and the inorganic being so obvious, how can physical phenomena be ignored in any serious study of biology? Hegel, it is true, speaks of some link between them but in too parenthetical a fashion.

Meredy: It is manifestly unfair to demand of a pre-Darwinian writer that he concern himself with matters pertaining to the origin or development of species. Yet, there is a hint of some evolutionary process in Hegel's allusion to the 'great influence' of the environment on the organism. Of the inorganic conditions influencing the development of organic nature he mentions air, water, earth, zones, and climate. Do these constitute the observable conditions accounting for organic differentiation? No, says Hegel. A causal explanation in such terms is too simple, too superficial, too arbitrary. The explanation cannot do justice to the manifold variety of organic nature; it precludes adequate generalization, there being too many observable exceptions, such, for instance, as sea-animals having characteristics of land-animals; and it lacks logical necessity, for nothing in the nature of a specific environment can justify the deduction of a specific organism. To an observing consciousness, in short, the connection between the conditions and the conditioned can appear neither universal nor necessary. This is of course another variation on a familiar theme. Ultimately, as Hegel remarks, it is the organism itself which is the object of direct observation, and the explanation of its action as purposive would seem to be a nearer approximation to the truth.

Hardith: The organism's behavior alone being observable, it follows that explanatory laws whether mechanical or teleological are as such not open to direct observation. Yet, the concept of purpose is here made to afford a more adequate clue to the nature of organic phenomena than the concept of the environment. Why? Although all nonobservational factors are equally inferential, explanation of the organism in terms drawn from the external environment would seem to have an advantage over explanation in terms derived from the organism's inner life, an advantage, that is, for a consciousness reluctant to stray too far from the level of observation. Definitely arising within biological theory are the questions, how extensive is the environment's influence on the organism? and how sufficient is such influence as principle of explanation? They are questions based on different but relatable observational data, data of organismal action, on the one hand, and data of inorganic processes, on the other. But consider a biological theory intent upon accounting for organismal action as essentially purposive. The only directly observable data being the behavioral ways of the organism, the purpose alleged to explain them is

130

simply and purely conjectural. The evidence for it is completely lacking. Why then must the dialectic proceed as if the teleological approach to organic nature constituted an advance in the development of reason's career as observer?

Meredy: Here (as so often in the *Phenomenology*) Hegel interrupts the thread of the argument by prophecy of its supposed outcome. The outcome, in a word, will be explicit recognition that the purposive and the rational are equivalent. At this stage, however, reason but instinctively stumbles upon the notion of purpose without being aware that what it has thus stumbled upon is actually itself. That the logic of purpose—namely, the logic of self-differentiation—is the same as the logic of self-consciousness, is obviously not a matter that can be settled by observation. The meaning of teleology, as Hegel cursorily indicates, depends on a duality that refuses to be frozen into a dualism. The initially envisaged end and the finally realized end, though distinguishable, cannot be separated: the initial phase of purposive action presupposes the final and the final constitutes the fulfillment of the initial. Purpose thus involves a process of self-differentiation in which the formal cause and the final cause are interdependent moments, each distinct from yet in need of the other, the whole process being the unity of their differences. Does not this follow the pattern of self-consciousness whose differentiable moments come to be internally related when self-consciousness reaches the level of reason? In seeking by means of teleology to find itself in the organism, observing reason, alas, fails to know itself in what it finds.

Hardith: Failure to recognize it for what Hegel says it is renders purpose altogether otiose as a descriptive or explanatory category, indirectly justifying the abandonment of final causes by modern science. But this could scarce have been Hegel's intention. Be that as it may, as here stumbled upon, the concept serves to hide but thinly a gross tautology. For merely to assert that purpose explains the organism's behavior—its responses to stimuli, the coordination of its functions, the complexity and range of its adjustments to the environment—is simply to subsume under its name all the organism's self-preservative activities. It matters little whether we speak of the activities requisite for self-preservation as expressing the nature or the purpose of the organism; the substitution of one term for the other is purely verbal and adds nothing to our knowledge. If the 'teleological relation', as Hegel calls it, is to have a meaning not reducible to sheer tautology, how conceive of it otherwise than as a relation of external origin? So to conceive of it is to regard the organism's actions and reactions as determined by final causes not inferable from its specific nature. At any rate, the teleological relation as intrinsic to the organism, one resulting from its self-determination, must perforce remain hidden from a science that depends on observation for its basic data—data needed for launching as well as for sustaining its explanatory theories of organic nature.

Meredy: We have, closely following the text, expatiated now on organic nature and now on the organism as if the terms were interchangeable, and this inevitably produced much confusion, especially in connection with the teleological issue. Could the confusion have been deliberate on Hegel's part? To speak of the organic generally or of the organism generically is to speak of no observable entity capable of behaving in mechanical or purposive fashion. Nature at large does not act, nor can one of its genera be said to seek a previsioned end. About nature *en masse,* which is obviously not a perceptual datum, speculations are clearly preclusive of empirical proof. As long as the method of observation is held to enjoy primacy in scientific inquiry, the only sort of object to which inquiry can initially address itself must be particular and static. If this is the gist of the dialectic so far pursued, the process of observation must now be focused on the single organism, the individual function of which plays the role of middle term, as it were, between two extremes, one being the organism's hidden purpose and the other its visible structure. Of this new phase Hegel carries his analysis to excessive and tedious lengths, showing in varying ways that concentration on a single organism sharpens rathen than mitigates the familiar paradox. Observation being always limited to *ein Seiendes und Bleibendes,* a thing overt and fixed, what is open to extrospection is but an organism's structure, its function, which is no less dynamic and inward than its putative purpose, remains to be inferred from its perceived structure, an inference warranted solely on the basis of a general law that the outer structure is the expression of the inner function. In what sense can it be called a law and whence its validity? Is it here more than an instinctive dogma? If the outer is believed to express the inner, and so believed by merely observing the outer, the whole distinction between them becomes virtually abandoned. There is but the outer. That alone is accessible to observation. The rest is shrouded in mystery.

Hardith: Many of the details, so needless and so boring, seem altogether out of harmony with the ostensible intent of the work. Its subject matter, not being primarily historical, since it consists of mind's *recurrent* persuasions, does not require extensive analysis of particular illustrations, unless they happen to be singularly pertinent. Now observation of nature is a process admittedly typical of the scientific

132

method, and the paradoxes Hegel discerns to be latent in the extravagant claims made for its supremacy, are certainly chronic. The fallacy of confusing a pervasive theme with but one of its variations is notorious. Of such fallacy Hegel is clearly guilty; he identifies the credulities of the observing consciousness especially in relation to organic nature too intimately with examples drawn from current science, with the result that a type of persuasion supposed to be expressible in different forms appears to coincide completely with certain local and dated versions of it. The polemic against ideas so endemic woven into the dialectic of an attitude presumably pandemic strikes me as gratuitous. This is a pity. For Hegel's criticism of a universal bias is not impertinent, uncovering as it does what happens when the method of observation is allowed to run wild. What is to be gained from ferreting out theses buried in oblivion as the exclusive objects of dialectical manipulation?

Meredy: Your strictures are not unjust. Hegel's view of the episodic as if it were typical must indeed seem perverse. In the present context, however, the view is not without justification. What science not prevalent in his day should Hegel have availed himself of? Not a little influence on Hegel's analysis may be traced to philosophic speculations on nature then very much in vogue. Preoccupation with nature on the part of his contemporaries must have seemed to him as exemplicative of tendencies indigenous to the human mind. Although we may safely ignore the forgotten theses on which his diagnostic labors are so lavishly spent, no account of organic nature can readily dispense with certain distinctions dilated on in the text, chief of these being the distinction between structure and function, one especially crucial if knowledge by observation is to be invested with such decisive importance.

We may smile at the old-fashioned way of correlating an animal organism's threefold structure with its threefold function—the nervous system with sensibility, the muscular with irritability, the intestinal with reproduction—but time was when the subject was taken seriously. Which in this correlation is inner and which outer? Hegel's answer that each is both, a dialectical *tour de force,* may likewise provoke mirth. Nevertheless, on any view, structural forms and functional properties, whatever they are described as being, condition in their interdependence the life of an organism; but if the former are data observed and the latter data inferred from them, the issue raised by Hegel throughout his analysis is inescapable; structural forms, since they alone are open to observation, must be held to enjoy cognitive priority, yet it is in virtue of functional properties derived by inference that organic nature owes its basic differentiation from inorganic. This, it seems to me, is here the rub.

133

Hardith: What is the matter with inference? How reject it without rejecting the possibility of scientific knowledge? Is reason in science but engaged in a 'futile play of laws' (*leeres Spiel des Gesetzgebens*) comparable to the preoccupation on the part of the understanding with the 'play of forces'? The sense Hegel gives to the word 'play' is here as there patently pejorative. Yet the play of hypotheses is an integral part of the method of science, some attaining the status of laws in accordance with the empirico-logical evidence deemed necessary and sufficient in support of their induction or probable validity. But why cavil at a word? The truth is that Hegel condemns all science, and not just biology, because the method employed is not dialectical. His attack is not limited to observation as an isolated process; it extends to all disciplines to which the process is fundamental. And since biology operates, as does every empirical science, by 'linear inference' from basal observations to summital generalizations, its claims must be disdainfully repudiated. How preposterous a conclusion!

Meredy: You would of course find me on your side if we debated the theme on its merits. You seem to forget that as detached students of the text our task is neither to defend nor to refute its contentions. You read, I think, too much into Hegel's criticism of a biology said to rest on an observational base. What is here at stake is the very possibility of justifying the ultimate difference between the organic and the inorganic. On the supposition guiding the dialectic that only the static or the inert can come within the observer's apprehension, the dynamism or purposiveness that might be concealed therein must fall outside his direct range. Obviously inference must follow in the wake of observation. But if the inside of the outside, so to speak, can only be inferred, what prevents the supervening inference from explaining biological phenomena in terms of mechanical processes, epitomized previously under the 'play of forces'? Hegel shows the ease with which reason's categories may come to be exchanged for those of the understanding. Biology as a branch of physics, intent upon reducing the animal to a machine—what a startling outcome! Yet, it is an outcome not incompatible with the logic of observation.

Hardith: Nor does the logic of observation preclude going to the other extreme. Could not the biological idiom be grafted upon physical phenomena with equal propriety? Speculation is free to assimilate the inorganic with the organic. The antidote to universal mechanism is universal vitalism, and from its coign of vantage, the molecule may be observed as exhibiting a structure comparable to that of the amoeba. No observation of any given entity, simple or complex, forbids the inference that the contrast between the nonliving and the living is one

134

which a hylozoic conception of nature may overcome and render *aufgehoben*. Since Hegel, indeed, the ancient doctrine of hylozoism, renamed vitalism, has had a remarkable rebirth, a doctrine not inferior in plausibility to that of mechanism. I don't see why one should seem more surprising than the other. It is obvious, however, that Hegel seeks to retain the dichotomy between the organic and the inorganic lest mechanism achieve their assimilation. Would he, I wonder, have been equally adamant against their assimilation by vitalism?

Meredy: The point you raise touches the nerve of Hegel's own philosophy of nature of which only hints appear in the present context. What Hegel relentlessly pursues here is solely a conception of nature such as ensues when its basis constitutes observation prompted by the belief that between the matter observed and the observer's reason there is a predetermined affinity. In observing nature, therefore, reason seeks nothing but its own image, reflecting chiefly its formal and abstract features. It is this which lies at the root of the story Hegel traces, a story of a tremendous failure. The issue comes to a head in the possibility of reducing organic nature to its opposite, biological phenomena appearing as if they could be subsumed under the descriptive laws governing the physical. Such a reduction Hegel considers a reduction to the absurd. For the separation of the organic from the inorganic is simply inexpugnable. Why so? Because, Hegel maintains, certain indispensable categories germane to organic nature are not applicable to inorganic, the most fundamental being genus, species, and individual. Products of reason, these categories are distinct universals, not to be confused with the general concepts of the understanding. They represent rather differentiable wholes of varying scope. Organic categories such as these are intimations of the concrete universals which reason, ceasing to be mere instinct, will find embodied in human life beyond the biological level. The discussion of this lies far ahead. Meanwhile the dialectic of observation must be allowed to run its course. Having for its object human nature, the ensuing kind of observation will reveal anomalies even more egregious. But to the analysis of observational psychology, to speak of it thus, we must give special attention.

Rational Observation of Human Nature

1. Logical Laws and the Logic of Observation

Hardith: How appropriate is the title of the remaining text devoted to the dialectic of observation? The one chosen, which is not Hegel's, seems too comprehensive a designation of the well-defined subject matter treated. The author's own headings are so specific and so descriptive. Why change them?

Meredy: I have a distinct preference on grounds both heuristic and æsthetic for short and general titles designed to intimate instead of denoting the subject matter. Why reveal too much of it in a summary phrase? Hegel's own titles are certainly clear but redundant. Thus of the introduction to the new section the descriptive name reads, "Observation of Self-consciousness in its Pure Aspect and in its Relation to the External World—Logical and Psychological Laws"; and of the main section the name is, "Observation of the Relation of Self-consciousness to its Immediate Actuality—Physiognomy and Phrenology." But choice of a name relating to a particular theme of discourse is a matter of literary taste, and one would be foolish to make an issue of it. Apart from considerations of taste, it happens that the title I give to what we are about to discuss is eminently appropriate. What could be more pertinent to human as distinguished from organic nature than logical and psychological processes? And observability of such processes in their outer expressions is precisely the basic issue before us.

Hardith: Hegel's comments on the laws of thought, contained in the introductory part, seem strangely out of place in connection with observation. Can reason observe its inner operations and the principles governing them? Is logic open to introspection, and does introspective observation enjoy the same validity as extrospective? If so, there is here a radical shift of ground on Hegel's part, and the antithesis between the inner and the outer on which the dialectic depends thus goes by the board. For no longer can a paradox be said to inhere in the assumption that the outer alone is observed and the inner but inferred in accordance with the dogma of their essential congruity. Accessibility of the inner to direct observation would seem to destroy the basis on which the preceding criticism was made to rest. If the laws of thought may be observed, why not the laws of inorganic or those of organic nature?

Meredy: The change in diction and accent is here undeniable. With respect to formal logic, at which Hegel hurls with such vehemence the shafts of his polemic, a broader notion of observation appears implied. Subsuming under it whatever is simply accepted as found, he considers the laws of thought as having been traditionally thus accepted. To speak of these laws as requiring no demonstration is to speak of them *as if* they were open to observation. This inevitably endows observation with a new sense, involving serious attenuation of the difference between the inner and the outer. I do not see how such a lapse from consistency can at first sight be mitigated except by construing the prefatory remarks as forming no integral part of the argument which is to follow.

Hardith: I do see why Hegel should think it necessary to enlarge the process of observation when he reaches the diagnosis of the psyche. For the psyche is explorable from within as well as from without, its experience being open to introspective and its behavior to extrospective observation. Recognition of two species of observation seems to reinforce rather than weaken the issue inherent in observational biology. The same issue arises in connection with observational psychology, and may be stated in this fashion. To what extent does the individual's overt behavior observable by extrospection reveal the individual's covert experience not observable save by introspection? Here too we retain the contrast of inner and outer as well as the dogma that the latter is an expression of the former. What I fail to understand is the injection here of the laws of thought. Why assume an observational logic differing in kind from an observational psychology?

Meredy: Not extraneous is the attack launched by Hegel on formal logic. The logic of observation and formal logic are bound each to each by natural affinity. This, in a word, is the gist of the matter. His criticism is thus double-barreled. The method of observation and the laws of thought are equally grounded in the notion of fixity—the method is inoperative except in relation to arrested particulars, and the laws are applicable only in the shape of frozen universals. But static entities, whether things or thoughts, are abstractions from their dynamic contexts and organic relations, and it is in such abstractions that at this stage reason is shown to be constantly floundering. How inert are the forms of logic—and how ambiguous? Emptied of all content, they are nevertheless alleged to be relevant to any content, thus having claims on universality. But the kind of universality attributed to pure forms— forms purged of intrinsic content—appears purely supposititious. Formal logic, alleged to have the status of a branch of knowledge, can scarce be conceived without reference to its preemptive subject matter. And what could serve as content of this special discipline if not its own vacant forms? These forms, to which the laws of thought are fundamental, must needs seem as if they were individual objects, each a law unto itself, as it were, thus bearing a striking resemblance to objects of observation in separateness and immobility. This, at any rate, though *mit ein bischen anderen Worten,* is the sum and substance of Hegel's contention.

Hardith: I appreciate your way of paraphrasing Hegel in a diction so happily remote from his. I confess that I could never have gleaned from an unaided reading of the text that his criticism of formal logic was in effect a criticism of the logic of observation. Yet the sense in which the laws of thought are themselves observable still escapes me. If these laws are rendered amenable to observation, assuming introspection to be a species of it, does not logic come thereby under the jurisdiction of psychology? Are logical laws in the end indistinguishable from psychological laws?

Meredy: This is precisely Hegel's point. The formal logician when called upon to indicate the locus of his laws is bound to turn into an introspective psychologist. Where indeed is he to situate them? They can obviously not be sought in the nature of things, seeing that the principles of identity and contradiction and excluded middle enjoy but formal universality, their existential exemplifiability being irrelevant. The laws of thought can be found only in thought. By looking within, mind, so it is alleged, may observe directly the abstract laws of the thinking process, in abstraction, that is, from all possible objects of application. This is a strange way of safeguarding the contentlessness of logical laws. But what consummate irony! To escape the Scylla of ontology, logic must be made to seek safety in the Charybdis of psychology. Such a foundation of logic is of course but a quicksand. Introspection resembling extrospection in revealing merely the stable and the detached, the laws of thought can thus not be found except separately, without internal relation to each other, and especially without necessary connection with the unity of self-consciousness, within the matrix of which alone they appear distinguishable and interlinked. Like observational physics and observational biology, observational logic, too, is faced, but at a deeper level, with the problem of the one and the many. How account by the introspective method for the self's unity and continuity present in the plural laws of thought and the discrete acts of thought?

Hardith: It was of course to be expected that failure of the observational method should here as elsewhere—and particularly here—prove so decisive. The task of revealing thought's dynamism and organicity devolves upon the dialectical method which is the method of speculative and not of abstract reason. But the logic based upon that method lies beyond phenomenology. Here we must perforce merely note reason's struggle with the anomalies inherent in its abstract conceptions and formal concepts. Paradoxical though it be to seek psychological sanction for logical laws, why is it necessary to impugn the validity of psychological laws, laws applicable to states and acts of mind not exclusively noetic?

2. Observational Psychology and its Issues

Meredy: If it seems absurd to subordinate logic to psychology, it is equally absurd to conceive of psychology as preoccupied principally with introspective observation of the inner life. For such observation can find nothing but a profusion of mental facts as if they were external to or independent of the observing consciousness. Such an approach to the sundry phenomena of mind, alleged to be 'empirical', Hegel regards as exceedingly paradoxical. The paradox lies in the contradiction between the empirical inventory of mind's miscellaneous furniture and the unity of consciousness which, not being observable, cannot be inventoried. The inevitable failure to recognize mind's integrity in the variety of its manifestations must give rise to excessive wonder at the appearance of data so heterogeneous, as if the mind were a 'bag'—the image is Hegel's—somehow containing in loose fashion a congeries of objects. The problem of the one and many emerges anew; the psyche as matrix of multifarious states and acts is at the opposite pole from the concrete and self-conscious individual. It is the existing individual, functioning as one and whole, that must come to serve as the given subject of psychology, one demanding a less anomalous kind of observation.

Hardith: But does not the shift in subject matter involve a return to the method of extrospection? The human individual, like the animal organism, is indeed a single observational datum, but one whose movements and comportment can only be perceived from without, observational psychology thus seemingly coinciding in principle with observational biology. Yet Hegel notes a radical difference in the aim and technique of the observational process in connection with the two disciplines. How amusing is his way of expressing the difference! Procedures such as statistical and taxonomic, to modernize his vocabulary, he considers to have no merit in the field of psychology, where indeed they are downright senseless (*begrifflos*). Human beings are not insects. These lowly creatures are readily amenable to numerical and classificatory treatment, belonging as they do, so Hegel disdainfully disposes of them, "to the province of fortuitous particulars." The conscious individual is an instance of mind, and mind is essentially rational. The purpose of psychology, distinguishable from that of biology, is to formulate on the basis of external observation the laws to which the conscious individual owes his idiosyncrasy. An ambitious program, this!

Meredy: What is and what is not common to psychology and biology is certainly important. The reduction of the former to the latter Hegel regards just as absurd as the reduction of biology to physics. What unites the threefold nature examined—inorganic, organic, human —is but the observational method of examining it, a method considered fundamental when guided by the instinct of reason. Psychology defined as *observational*—and the adjective must be underlined—thus joins in methodology the same group of sciences to which biology and physics belong, joining the group only if, as you rightly insist, its procedure becomes strictly extrospective.

Between observational biology and observational psychology there is also the parallelism in dialectical development; both proceed from the general to the particular, that is to say, from organic nature to the organism and from human nature to the individual. And in observing the individuality of the individual, comparable to the observation of the organicity of the organism, reason looks at first to the environment as principle of explanation, utilizing here too the concept of influence. Man's environment, however, is wider than the animal's, comprising as it does not only the physical factors but social and religious, as well as many others. The explanation of the individual is thus to be found in his total milieu; he is what he is in virtue of all the circumstances affecting him. All we need to do then is to seek in the environmental influences for clues to the individual's mentality as expressed in his external behavior, both the influencing conditions and the resultant behavior coming within the range of observation.

3. The Individual and the Environment

Hardith: But environmental influences so inclusive are too indeterminate to have any explanatory value. The individual's *entourage* may thus be held to coincide with the whole world, and to say that his individuality is the product of its varied and variable cross-currents is to utter a tautology. The individual's idiosyncrasy is what it is, reference to everything under the sun influencing it simply becomes otiose. Have we not here a reiteration of the same paradox encountered earlier in connection with observational biology?

Meredy: Not exactly. You overlook one basic difference between the human and the nonhuman organism. Unlike other animals, man is aware of his environment and capable of interfering with it in certain determinate ways, fostering its influences here and frustrating them there. In the manner in which he chooses to react to stimuli, the individual not seldom succeeds in determining the kind of influence they are to exert. To admit this is to weaken the force of explanation by the concept of influence. The premise that the individual is inconceivable save as subject to environmental conditions does not militate against his capability of modifying his environment or of exchanging one environment for another. On the human level, at any rate, in contradistinction to the animal level, the relation between the organism and the environment is not strictly asymmetrical. Man, though always affected in his individuality by external influences, is not in his turn without power to affect them.

Hardith: But lack of strict asymmetry renders the concept of influence even more futile. If influence were a symmetrical relation between the individual and his environment, should we not be able to infer one from the other? Such putative symmetry would clearly make it possible to deduce from a given state of the world the kind of the individual capable of flourishing thereunder and from a certain type of individual the condition of the world requisite for its existence and behavior. Were the world and the individual thus reciprocally related, either would be comprehensible from the nature of the other. We should have, to speak in Hegel's metaphors, a double gallery of pictures, each the reflection of each. One gallery would represent the world of outer and pervasive circumstances, the other gallery would be a translation of the same circumstances in the form in which they appear in the conscious individual, the former the spherical surface, the latter the center mirroring the surface within it. These tropes are striking, suggesting the absurdity of conceiving influence as a symmetrical relation between the global environment and the self-centered individual. The two galleries exemplify a distinction of which the difference becomes ultimately tenuous.

Meredy: This is indeed the inevitable outcome, ending one phase of observational psychology. The dialectic is implicit in the attempt to relate exclusively in terms of influence the state of the world and the conscious individual. From such an attempt nothing else can ensue save the empty proposition that the world is what the individual is or vice versa.

Hardith: It would seem as if Hegel had proved but little in proving the uselessness of influence as an explanatory concept. Yet the proof is not without importance, and I wish he could have condescended to indicate how widespread is its actual use. I am thinking particularly of the fallacious procedure prevalent among writers of literary history or literary biography. To hunt for the influences exerted on a given poet is a favorite sport. And when the influences have all been enumerated and classified, what remains is still the unexplained and inexplicable uniqueness of the poet's consciousness. Never can the secret of his life and art be deduced from the outer conditions that happened to impinge upon it. Hegel's 'double gallery of pictures', to mention it again, does here retain its irreducible doubleness and asymmetry. Mere allusion to this theme shows that the text is here concerned with a fairly common practice, and Hegel's strictures on it should serve as a salutary corrective. But this is said in passing and so let it pass. The transition to the individual himself as revealed in his observable appearance and action now becomes almost compelling.

4. *Mind's Perceptible Traits*

Meredy: Yes, driven back to the concrete individual, reason is under dialectical necessity to enter a new field of observation. The difference between the inner and outer exhibited by each and every organism—denotable as difference of function and structure—becomes once more focal, but no longer purely biological. Man, being a psycho-physical organism, exemplifies, in ways comporting with his specific nature, a deeper duality of inner function and outer structure. It is, in short, the relation of an individual's mind to his body which is now singled out as a special problem for detailed consideration. But the problem is strictly psychological, falling here completely outside the purview of metaphysics. Reason, not having done with psychology, is still in mid-career, engaged in progressively narrowing the range of observation. The inner and outer now become concepts applicable to the individual as a separate entity both conscious and perceptible.

Hardith: The postulate that the inner must find expression in the outer is thus to be operative with even greater force than heretofore. Although the body is manifestly external and publicly observable, its connection with the mind seems more intimate than all the facts in the environment said to exert their influence on the individual's hidden psyche. But the body has a complex structure, and its parts are not

142

coequal in serving as intimations of a man's distinctive mind. Of his inner nature only certain of his bodily aspects or organs may be found to be expressive. The mouth that speaks and the hand that works, adding perhaps the legs too, are vehicles of conscious action. Why should not an individual's language and labor be held to convey his true individuality? Words and deeds are commonly assumed to indicate traits of character.

Meredy: It is indeed a common assumption that a man's character is reflected in what he says or does, an assumption betraying an instinctual faith in reason. This obviously accounts for Hegel's interest in so many strange opinions about the connection of inner and outer. Being in accord with reason's demand for them, they are not irrational but only logically defective, exemplifying the predicament of observational psychology.

As regards the expression of the inner by means of one bodily organ or another, consider the difficulty it involves. Conscious action performed by hand or mouth is essentially ambivalent, its roots lying in inner intention and its flowering in some outer fact. The intention is clearly other than the organ supposed to do its bidding; and the *fait accompli,* too, differs from the intention behind it. If an organ acts at the behest of a mind to produce a certain result, the organ in so acting becomes, as it were, the mind's deputy. How far does it express what is inner? Too much or too little? Too much, says Hegel, because, if it completely does express the inner, the inner is nothing but what the outer expresses, and the distinction between them tends to vanish altogether. And too little, because what *is* expressed, the spoken word or the accomplished deed, in emerging as an independent fact and left at the mercy of misconstruction or transformation, may be always disavowed by the individual as contrary to his original intent. The organs of the body, the products of whose action make their appearance as detached objects of the external world and hence as open to observation, are unable save fortuitously to express what their action reflects, namely the non-observable inwardness of a man's character.

Hardith: The connection of the inner and outer, the dialectic being what it is, must now assume a systematic and thus a more plausible form. As a matter of fact, certain so-called sciences, by concentrating attention on the human countenance and skull, sought at one time to show that traits of character reveal themselves in facial and cranial configurations. Hence Hegel's lengthy discussion of physiognomy and phrenology, the bearing of their hypotheses on the subject of observational psychology being particularly pertinent. His too elaborate treatment of them is nevertheless surprising. Why such minute analysis of

143

beliefs so clearly vulnerable? Surely, *we* need not go into matters that have no claim on serious consideration.

Meredy: Detailed discussion of beliefs now dear only to the antiquarian must here of course be forgone. But they cannot be ignored entirely. For they are beliefs that seem as if made to order to illustrate the necessity of the course of the dialectic. Had there actually been no zealous advocates of them, Hegel would have been driven to invent hypotheses not unlike those of physiognomy and phrenology for the purpose of binding more closely the relation of mental life to its visible expressions.

Consider physiognomy. What Hegel is chiefly interested in is the principle underlying this pseudoscience, being the principle of any and every observational attempt to find in the marks or traits of a man's physical appearance the mirror of his distinctive mind. Physiognomy is simply a rationalization of a general tendency to look a man in the face for evidence of his character. The features of a countenance are said to betray true individuality more intimately than language or handiwork. This, according to Hegel, constitutes an advance in the progress of the dialectic.

Hardith: The face does have the advantage over the organs in being observable without relation to anything produced by it. Smiles or frowns are not agents of words or deeds that enjoy separate being as soon as uttered or done. They but reflect or mask such moods or feelings as prompt their appearance. And this holds of the gamut of sentiments and passions which the human visage is capable of registering. Such 'natural physiognomy', as Hegel calls it, is not irrational; it simply seeks, as does observational psychology generally, a law connecting the inner and the outer. If the invisible is somehow embodied in visible shape, should we not be able to know a man's mind by noting his facial form and expression? Here literally the play's the thing—the play of the features. The pathetic fallacy this involves is patent. For the visible alone is observable, and to speak of a face as betraying benevolence or cruelty—or any virtue or vice—is to ascribe traits of mind to a physical object. How does this differ in principle from speaking of a smiling sky, a pitiless storm, a passionate rose, a chaste moon, a brooding mountain, a weeping willow, and so on? If to attribute consciousness to nature is to commit a fallacy, is it less fallacious to attribute it to a man's face? Not by a would-be science such as physiognomy can a necessary relation be established between physical traits and mental traits. There remain a man's volition and a man's action to which his facial expressions lend no countenance.

Meredy: What a clever pun! And how admirable a gist of Hegel's

144

technical argument! Yes, to volition and action, in which alone true individuality must ultimately be sought, the face is a deceptive and capricious index. Physiognomic principles and laws have no firmer foundation than the random generalizations in which the vulgar indulge. They rest on flatulent opinions that can never approximate the level of knowledge. Between the physical and the mental the relation is deeper than the process of observation can ever fathom, no matter what form it may take. Yet physiognomic conjectures do not cease with the impasse so far reached. Observational psychology must proceed until stifled with unmitigated folly, a climacteric reserved for phrenology. The physiognomist might still make a last attempt to find on the human countenance the stamp of mind by inserting it, like a middle term, between the extremes of willing and doing. It takes little astuteness to concede that behavior may often conceal the real motives actuating it. And if greater store is set on the motives than the acts, how gain access to them by observation? There would seem to be no other clue to an agent's true intentions than the visage that indelibly reveals them. If this is so, a man's distinctive individuality, regardless of what he may say or do, becomes an open secret, imprinted as it is on his outward aspect. To drive home the ludicrousness of this position Hegel quotes from a writer he condescends to mention by name. If, according to Lichtenberg, "a physiognomist were to say to anyone, 'You certainly act like an honest man, but I can see from your face that you are forcing yourself to do so, and are a scoundrel at heart,' every manly person thus insulted would to the end of time retort with a box on the ear." Unable to resist a pun, Hegel characterizes the retort as striking (*treffend*), simply because it exhibits contempt for the face and because it demonstrates the truth that man's real individuality expresses itself in action.

5. *The Physical Seat of Mind*

Hardith: Physiognomy thus amusingly disposed of, we must now, I suppose, turn to phrenology. This pseudoscience, having paved the way for the accredited doctrine of cerebral localization, may lay claim to some historical importance. And since it is also more difficult, a detailed examination is naturally precluded. We may safely leave this to the exegete. What chiefly interests me is the dialectical transition from physiognomy to phrenology. Am I right in thinking that the latter's conjectures are in greater accord with the logic of observation than the former's, phrenology appearing as if it were the fulfillment of physiognomy? For the logic of observation requires the invisible to become visible and the visible fixed, requirements bound up with the postulate of reason that the outer, which alone is observable, be always taken as expression of the inner. The absurdities of physiognomy arise, as we have seen, from the attempted reduction of man's inward life to his external appearance. Physiognomic reduction must inevitably prove abortive for lack of adequate or sufficient data. The face, though denotable, is too variable in its expressions, hence not subject to arrest to be strictly observable. The failure of physiognomy, in short, is the failure of the face to lend itself as basis for the objectification of mind. It is otherwise with the skull; cranial data are certainly, to describe them in the terms Hegel used earlier, *seiend und bleibend,* and none but the existent and the persistent can serve as objects of observation and inference. Does this explain the transition to the new theme and the lavish attention Hegel devotes to it?

Meredy: The transition is not quite so simple or so direct as you indicate. The belief in the necessary connection between the mind and the cranium involves some intermediary considerations. But of the logic of the method that makes such belief unavoidable your statement is indeed clear and succinct. Yes, an inescapable dilemma lies at the root of the observational procedure in relation to mind: either mind is not open to observation at all or else it can be observed only in physical shape. This is the theme with which the entire section is variously preoccupied, the variations being so related that the later always appears as the fufillment of the earlier. The last variation is now before us, consisting in the attempt to seize upon the data most intimately and causally connected with the individual's mind, those of his brain and skull. The range observation thus becomes narrowed down to objective or physical facts, enjoying the forms of real thinghood. I fear that we must dwell on a few details to bring out the significance of Hegel's discussion.

Hardith: Very well. I doubt, however, that we need go into Hegel's reflections on the neural conditions of consciousness. These are scarcely worth our attention. His chief emphasis falls on the head, commonly held to be the seat of mind, and it is precisely the head, a solid and stable thing, upon which phrenology concentrates its observational labors.

Meredy: But the head, the putative locus of the mind, is an ambivalent concept, belonging to physiology, on the one hand, and to anatomy, on the other. It is related to the brain as well as to the cranium. We are once more confronted, but on the highest level, with the distinction between function and structure. Directly observable is but the structure of the skull; the functioning of the brain, its pulsating life, cannot become perceptible except as externalized. Are mind and brain identical

146

or different? Observational psychology requires that they be identified on the basis of the causal principle here explicitly invoked, namely, that "the individual psyche if it is to have an effect on the body must as cause be itself corporeal." The identification in question is of course but methodological or 'scientific'; the brain serves as a sort of middle term between pure consciousness and cranial formation, being both inner and outer, inner in relation to the skull and outer in relation to mind. It is thus that we reach the ultimate object of psychological observation. This is not the brain itself, which is mind existing in physical but generally invisible form, but the other extreme from mind, the shape of the skull, a shape fixed and perceptible.

Hardith: Cerebral functions, here considered equatable with mental, thus become visible in the structure of the head, the assumption being that what happens in the living head, must conform to the shape of the skull, a *caput mortuum,* as Hegel calls it, an object inert and ossified. But the play upon the word, though humorous, does not militate against the serious attempts made to localize mental functions in the cerebral hemispheres, and for the success of such attempts the empirical evidence is quite impressive. For the brain too has a known structure causally related to its functions. And between the anatomy of the brain and the anatomy of the cranium there must surely be some causal connection. It was the merit of phrenology, ludicrous though its tenets now appear, to have done pioneer work in cerebral localization of mental traits. Its basic error simply was to seek access to the brain exclusively through the skull.

Meredy: The contentions of phrenology, as Hegel treats them, are in principle like those of any psychology intent upon deriving the individual's inner life from external data open to direct observation. Indeed, the emergence of phrenology as an observational 'science' Hegel regards as dialectically inevitable at the stage of reason he is examining. If observation must necessarily be observation of the directly observable, if, that is, it presupposes objects present to perception, then search for mental characteristics in the features of the skull, far from being a mere vagary, has its very rationale in the logic of observation. The absurdities in which phrenology abounds are perfectly consistent with the postulates guiding its methodology—namely, that the outer always expresses the inner, that such expression is causally determined, that the objective nature of the outer—and it must be objective to be observable —guarantees the objectivity of the inner. There is nothing wrong with the postulates but only with their application by a reason still instinctual. Applied in uncritical fashion, the generalization of phrenology boils down to the statement, as Hegel sardonically remarks, that "the objective existence of man is his skull-bone," a reduction to the absurd of a psychology required by its logic to emulate the method upon which the physical sciences depend.

Hardith: The wild surmises Hegel attributes to phrenology, wilder than in fact they were, must indeed culminate in nonsense. How can cranial localization of processes and attitudes of mind by a method so crudely employed avoid being reducible to the absurd? And the height of absurdity seems to be reached in the conflict between the possible and the actual which phrenology is here made to precipitate. As in physiognomy, so here, external observation of the concrete individual may justify ascribing to him latent dispositions not borne out or even contradicted by his overt behavior. Judged by his cranial shape, its bumps or hollows, the concrete individual ought to be what in fact he is not, a theme on which Hegel expatiates with particular relish. I am nevertheless moved to ask whether a modern type of observational psychology, such as behaviorism, may not succeed in evading the difficulties Hegel finds insuperable in the studies of mind now definitely obsolete. Would not the dialectic suffer loss of generality if a new psychology could be shown to contravene it?

Meredy: I am glad you mention behaviorism. This theory, alleged to be in conformity with the canons of the scientific method, illustrates rather than disproves the Hegelian dialectic. As the name implies, the theory is not of mind or consciousness but of phenomena of behavior which, like those of any natural science, are open to direct and public extrospection. Behaviorism points up the dilemma in which, according to Hegel, psychology is of necessity involved: either a scientific psychology is precluded for lack of observable data or else it must be made to rest on external data which as such can never be observed as conscious or mental. It is the second horn on which behaviorism chooses to be impaled. Although in scientific credibility poles apart from phrenology, in fidelity to the logic of observation behaviorism is even more radical. Claiming to belong to the family of scientific doctrines, behaviorism eschews reference to mind or consciousness as much, for instance, as chemistry or bacteriology; and the language it uses descriptive or explanatory of its specific phenomena must accordingly be purged of all subjective connotation. It is a strange psychology that so deliberately ignores the psyche. Yet no other seems compatible with the method of strict observation. Such a psychology and phrenology are thus clearly of a cousinship in their consistent effort to externalize man's conscious life.

Hardith: The positive result of Hegel's long disquisition seems to be the lesson that outer existence as such, which alone can provide

148

data of observation, is unable to reveal the truth about mind. The last stage of reason's observing activity is thus the worst, and on that ground its complete reversal now becomes imperative. But the reversal takes a strange form; the objectification of mind culminating in phrenology does not make way for its subjectification. This is what we should expect in accordance with the dialectic of one extreme passing into its opposite. On the contrary, the outcome of phrenology is twisted into a sort of embryonic truth. Instead of being prepared to revert to mind's inwardness, we are bidden to anticipate, in Hegel's final survey of the observational process, more adequate expressions of mind's objectivity. Phrenological objectification becomes defensible simply because it serves, as it were, 'to point a moral'. This, I confess, sounds to me too much like sophistry.

Meredy: Irony rather than sophistry is what I find in Hegel's summary statement, though it would be difficult to draw too sharp a line between them. Be that as it may, however, the career of observation resembles a wheel that has come full circle: beginning with external facts under the auspices of mind, it ends by observing mind in the shape of an outer thing. Yet the foolish search for mind in a bone is not without significance. The dialectic of observation, despite the anomalies it brings to light, reveals also, albeit vaguely, the truth regarding the unity of thought and being, a truth awaiting demonstration at a level of speculation transcending the limits of phenomenology. Here to be noted is just this, that the things identified with mind must partake of its rational nature, identity being a symmetrical relation. The end of the observational process, culminating in a proposition seemingly meaningless, vindicates the assurance—and mere assurance it must here remain—that reason's categories imply, even at this stage of the dialectic, the union of the rational and the real. The assertion that mind is a thing has for its correlate the counterassertion that the thing is mind. The assertion affirms, though in absurd fashion, mind's objectivity. Paltry indeed is the objectivity of a bone, still it does have objectivity. The attribution to mind of perceptual objectivity has its source in the perversity of the observational method according to which 'object' signifies 'percept'. To objectivity other than external and visible that method is clearly not conducive. But the proposition that mind exists and is real becomes indefeasible in the light of the very paradoxes which strict pursuit of the observational procedure engenders. Reason must advance beyond observation if it is to discover that 'objectivity' and 'thingness' are not synonymous or synonymous only in nonobservational form. It follows that reason must abandon the observational posture and look for more sufficient ways through which to exhibit mind's true objectivity.

Reason and Individual Aspiration

1. Preliminary Remarks on Individualism

Hardith: It is natural that Hegel's criticism of theoretical reason should be followed by a criticism of practical reason. Our task ahead, it appears, is to discern in the sphere of conation the same abstract rationalism dominant in the sphere of cognition. Hegel's insight that scientific observation is guided by tacit assurance of harmony between thought and being cannot be lightly dismissed. In looking at the world the observing mind may for all we know be simply looking for evidence of its own processes and categories. Such a view, though open to challenge, is not indefensible. But how can this be made to apply to the aspiring mind? What bearing has the assumed affinity between thought and being on the nature of human volition and action?

Meredy: The dialectical story of the observing reason shows with increasing force the impossibility of verifying on the observational level the postulated congruity of the rational and the real. Yet from the futile attempts to achieve this impossible feat the dialectic draws its ultimate support. Every asserted persuasion portrayed in the *Phenomenology,* as we now know, must be acted upon for the very purpose of proving it untenable. Nevertheless, the career of the observational consciousness does not end in failure, seeing that it succeeds in exhibiting mind's undeniable objectivity. That mind's objectivity is other than what mere observation is capable of affirming represents the new insight now definitely won. And it is this insight which the ensuing analysis is designed to clarify and to deepen. Before proceeding, however, Hegel, in a short introduction, pauses to relate the argument thus far advanced to what preceded as well as to what is to succeed it. A cursory discussion of his preliminary remarks is necessary, in the course of which the question you raise will find its appropriate answer.

Hardith: You called attention earlier to the significance of Hegel's introductory utterances in which, dropping the histrionic mask, he offers personal comments on the particular persuasions impersonated. Not forming part of the dialectic, the comments constitute a summary and appraisal of the diagnostic results attained. The relation of the introduction to every new stage in the dialectic is not unlike that of Shaw's prefaces to his plays. Although the playwright speaks through his dramatis personæ, the prefaces explain why and how he does so. Hegel's preface to the new play of ideas relating to practical reason seems eminently suited to justify the analogy. For here he initiates the reader more freely than elsewhere into the purpose and structure of the impersonations to follow.

Meredy: The suggestion regarding the similarity in function between Hegel's introductions and Shaw's prefaces is ingenious, all the more so because there can here be of course no question of 'influence'. You are quite right in singling out the present introduction as exemplary.

Looking back, what Hegel notes is a certain parallelism between the lower planes of experience and the stages of reason. Thus observation of inorganic nature corresponds to sense-certainty, exemplifying reason's own credulous attachment to the visibly given. Observation of organic nature is similar to perception and that of human nature to understanding. The difficulties involved in observing the unitary organism in the variety of its vital forms and functions are cognate with those of finding the unity of the perceived object in its many and heterogeneous properties. And the antinomies confronting reason in the duality of the inner and outer sides of the conscious mind are analogous to those with which the understanding grapples in explaining the law governing the interplay of polar forces.

The same correlation, looking forward, will appear in the dialectic of the persuasions to come. Before reaching its goal of genuine objectivity, reason must repeat in the sphere of practice the anomalies of self-consciousness. This means that reason has to incorporate in its nature the pathos of acting as if the world's rationality consisted in conforming to the self-centered aspirations of different individualists. In the dialectical evolution of reason individualism serves as necessary transition to a collective life. Implicit in all subjective aspirations is an inevitable trend or nisus towards the community in which alone true individuality can find fulfillment and expression.

Hardith: What is here at stake, if I am not mistaken, is the distinction and relation between two kinds of individualism, the community being equally essential to them. But on this matter Hegel's language is not free from ambiguity. It is one thing to speak of the social order as the needed background (*Grund*) for the expression of self-assertive individuals. It is quite another thing to conceive of the social order as the goal (*Ziel*) that cannot be attained unless differing individuals seek its attainment by conscious interaction and cooperation. Using the Hegelian terms, am I right in thinking of one kind of individualism as 'abstract' and of the other as 'concrete'? Abstract are individuals when acting as if the social order were but a foreign substance, separate from and external to them. And they apparently must so act if they are to discover the community to be their own selves writ large, the source and fruition of their concrete and interdependent lives.

Meredy: Hegel's language is here clearly equivocal but, as we shall see, deliberately so. It is true that his initial emphasis is on the goal of individual endeavor. This he depicts as an ethical order composed of determinate individuals, each acknowledging the others and being in turn acknowledged by them. Such an order, which is the very opposite of an abstract universal, a conceptual entity or law (*ein gedachtes Gesetz*), constitutes a living community, the embodiment of a united people. Here is a concrete universal in social form. It may also be called a spiritual substance, in the sense of being the enduring and stable reality underlying all dispersed subjective aspirations. But the prototype of a commonwealth is the organism whose existence exemplifies the synthesis of unity and multiplicity, identity and difference, persistence and change, structure and function, etc. Remarkable indeed, to mention it in passing, is Hegel's eulogy of a commonwealth as a sort of divinity on earth—and this before 1807! Mutually exclusive elsewhere, abstract opposites are inseparable complementaries in an organic whole of interdependent parts. Of such an organic whole or concrete universal, expressed in social terms, we have in Hegel's text the first explicit intimation.

Hardith: The spiritual substance, which organized society exemplifies, appears as if endowed with the character of an objective mind universal to and immanent in the subjective minds of each and all. Is this what the ensuing discussion is headed for? And does mind thus objectified serve, if I may say so, to refute in practice a theoretically possible posture of solipsism? Such objective mind Hegel looks upon as being an ideal which individual 'subjects' must bring into existence or an original state from which they have broken away. Which is the more tenable alternative?

Meredy: It matters little for the present whether the social order is conceived as a reality still to be won or a reality that has been lost. In either case society depends for its being on intersubjective activity. To assume the priority of separate 'subjects', the community existing to

serve their private interests, is to be face to face with the incessant conflict of individuals in pursuit of incompatible ends. This involves the
logic of self-consciousness, each center of which, suffering from the
illusion of perspective, comes to regard itself self-confidently as self-
sufficient. The dialectic of such illusion, when allowed to run its course,
necessitates the transition to reason. The same illusion reappears on a
higher level. Self-centered individuals, though perforce participating in
a collective life, are prevented by their illusory perspectives from
grasping the full significance of their actual participation. Blindness
to the profound import of the social order is precisely what appears to
be requisite for bringing individuals in conflict with one another and
with their spiritual substance. For upon this very conflict hinges the
ultimate realization of the true community. But all this lies ahead.

Hardith: Pardon me for harping again on the relation between the
objective mind of society and the subjective minds constituting it. Mere
individuals, so Hegel implies throughout the discussion, are fictions.
Who can define or find them apart from some social context? Are not
their social bonds as primordial as their physical? Can an individual's
aspiration be conceived in abstraction from its relations to other individuals? This being so, the assumption of priority on the part of independent individuals, as if they were separate atoms moving in the void,
is the very model of an assumption contrary to fact. Of the existence
of individuals prior to their association we have no evidence; both
science and logic unite in discrediting the hypothesis of an original state
during which men lived solitary lives. The very birth of an individual
depends upon prior association of the parents, and his earliest experience is conditioned by membership in that group we designate as
the family. Does not all this militate against the tenets of abstract individualism?

Meredy: What you say is important but not quite relevant. Here
much depends on the sense given to priority. Temporal priority is one
thing, dialectical priority is another. Some social life must have obviously preceded in time the emergence and the development of self-
conscious entities unless we suppose their existence reducible to
that of physical corpuscles subject to mechanical attraction and re-
pulsion. But precedence in phenomenology is not the same as precedence in time, a matter already dwelt upon which we must not lose
sight of. To repeat: phenomenology is not history and thus not bound
by chronology. There is in the text we are considering a statement,
appearing as mere parenthesis, which throws much light on this point.
"Every moment, being a moment of the essential process of reality,"
asserts Hegel in his characteristic diction, "must [logically] arrive at

153

the stage where it comes to look upon itself as the sole representative of the essential process." This contains in the proverbial nutshell the supreme principle of the Hegelian dialectic. It is inevitable that the particular or the individual should claim exclusive exemplification of the whole before finding in the whole its appropriate place and function. The logic is thus the same whether we view society as background or goal of individuality. In the former case, society must loom as the oppressive power to be opposed for the sake of vindicating the individual's claim to be solely essential; in the latter case, the individual, when becoming aware of his specious independence, discovers that genuine individuality requires a community brought into existence through the activity of its interlinked members.

Hardith: If you are right in maintaining that chronological sequence is not relevant to phenomenology, Hegel should have begun with the putative priority of individuals, showing society to be an emergent reality, so to speak, one emerging from the abortive struggle for supremacy among equally self-centered men. The dialectical method would seem to require a social organism to evolve from the internecine wars in a so-called state of nature. Why in the name of consistency is this not Hegel's procedure?

Meredy: There is one reason why Hegel's starting point could not have been an alleged natural condition of unrestrained individualism. Such a starting place would have entailed the notion of the community as an artificial product, a product generated by a fictitious covenant or contract made by fictitious aboriginals to escape from a fictitious state of universal warfare. Hegel assumes that the social organism is coeval with individual organisms; to proceed on the contrary assumption, though feasible dialectically, is to sacrifice verisimilitude to human nature. It thus seems to Hegel more normal to exhibit the dialectic against a social environment. For it is in relation to such environment that men's varied idiosyncrasies can find expression, in the process of which the substantiality of a social order receives recognition and demonstration. But enough of introductory generalities. Returning to the main line of the dialectic, let us consider the first type of individualism. This type, which is that of hedonism, presupposes a whole system of laws and customs, representing the 'lost' substance underlying the possibility of individual self-expression.

2. *Pleasure and Necessity*

Hardith: The hints contained in the introduction enable the reader to see the parallelism between the cognitive and the noncognitive functions of reason. These functions are united by the common belief in the harmony of the rational and the real. Just as the observing consciousness expects nature to accord with its methodology, so the conative consciousness expects the world to conform to its desiderata. It is the instinctual basis of the belief to which Hegel ascribes the paradoxes revealed by the dialectic; in the sphere of theory as well as in that of practice, the real is misconceived as amenable to a logic formal rather than organic, fixed instead of dynamic, abstract and not concrete. Observationalism and individualism thus appear tarred with the same distortive brush. Is this a fair statement of the transition to the business of pleasure-seeking which Hegel treats as if it were a rational enterprise?

Meredy: Hedonism may indeed be assumed as rational until the assumption of its rationality proves untenable. He who no longer prizes or is still to achieve the individuality that comes from participation in the life of the community will be naturally inclined to endow the vocation of pleasure-seeking with supreme importance. The hedonist here depicted is a civilized being, the rebellious product of a social order that has shrunk in meaning and value. The self, breaking away from moral and intellectual attachments, in order to embark on a hedonistic career, is deeper and more subtle than the self whose hedonism is more spontaneous or less deliberate. What Hegel dwells upon is the posture of an individual for whom the search for pleasure is the search for a good rationally superior to any other.

Hardith: Yet the social order cannot be forsaken. Its instrumental worth remains indefeasible. Is not a community needed to render refined pleasure-seeking possible? Can a civilized hedonist repudiate civilization in which the pleasures he is intent upon are deeply rooted? Casting consistency to the winds, he is here portrayed as turning his back on knowledge and action: he finds them simply barren and futile. What more rational, he is made to aver, than denial of the value of everything but gratification of desire? What more commensurate with the search for individuality than search for pleasure? The words he is here induced to utter are faint echoes of Goethe's *Faust*. From that poem—and he knew it only in fragmentary form—Hegel draws a singular illustration of a phase of human experience supposed to be universal and necessary. How strange that he should have gone to a special product of the imagination for a representative expression of the hedonistic position!

Meredy: Why strange? It is characteristic of Hegel to discern in imaginative dress typical examples of human comportment possessing greater authenticity than those present in the episodes of history or in the disquisitions of the learned. The *Phenomenology* abounds in allu-

155

sions to literary works of art. And so, with unmistakable reference to the early version of Goethe's poem, the hedonist is made to speak somewhat as follows: "The world is mine to enjoy. In the process of enjoying it, I discover my own vital nature as well as the world's instrumental value. Indeed, where should I look for an adequate principle of individuation if not in pleasure, and where for a better measure of the world's significance than in its capacity to satisfy desire? Let me then plunge into life and pluck the ripe fruits it so generously offers. The growth in enhancement of self-awareness requires a never-ending succession of fair moments for me to revel in."

Hardith: It would of course be easy to challenge the hedonist's position if forced into language so essentially equivocal. Consider but the one statement you attribute to him: 'The world is mine to enjoy'. It is obvious that he cannot enjoy a world assumed to be merely his; and as far as he does enjoy it, the world cannot be his exclusively. This is so because civilized desire differs in kind from uncivilized, the latter involving a negative relation to its objects. On the primitive level, as noted earlier, desire has for its sole aim destruction or consumption of the objects desired. In the present context, desire and its objects seem from the outset to be linked by rational ties: the world can be the hedonist's to enjoy only if the world is an external and stable order capable of producing by its intrinsic ways of operation the objects requisite for civilized desire. And when you speak of the fair moments the hedonist is ever in search of, the predicament of his career Goethe epitomized once and for all. Faust is in pursuit of a moment to which he could say, "Stay, thou art so fair," but when the moment comes neither is it fair nor will it stay. Is this the necessity which Hegel says the hedonist is up against?

Meredy: Without considering whether or not any moment can ever be fair enough to be bidden to tarry, the fact remains that no moment could actually heed the invitation. The hedonist's predicament lies in the necessity which time is under to admit no arrest of its flux. But the necessity confronting the pleasure seeker is ultimately dialectical. Search for civilized pleasures presupposes for their gratification the prior existence of a flourishing civilization. The world's delights can be pursued only because the world is objectively constituted to render their pursuit possible. But the demand for an objective world into which the hedonist may rush to gather its rich fruits contravenes the assumed rationality of pleasure-seeking, seeing that these fruits, to speak metaphorically, have a way of growing and ripening in accordance with a necessity of their own, regardless of the hedonist's private desires. Must this not lead to the insight that the world's constitution or

156

destiny cannot be squared with subjective aspirations? Having forsaken the gray fields of learning and endeavor for the sake of returning to the ever-green pastures of hedonic experience, our blithe individualist cannot escape encountering at every turn a world strange and obdurate. The nature of things appears to be subject to a necessity at variance with the business of pleasure-seeking. Explicit awareness of this proves fatal to an enterprise involving the belief in the rational claims of individualism. The hedonist assumed a world responsive to his desires only to discover a world alien and hostile.

Hardith: I am still not clear about the notion of necessity on which so much here depends. It is a notion lamentably ambivalent. Is necessity a synonym of fate concerning which, Hegel declares, nothing can be said, its laws of operation remaining incomprehensible? Or is necessity that of ascertainable laws, descriptive or explanatory, to which the nature of things must conform, in which case it is the very antonym of fate? The necessity to which the disillusioned or thwarted hedonist is here alleged to succumb is a necessity that passes his understanding; the things, which he seeks to enjoy but cannot grasp, appear to have a nature, in Hegel's words, "impervious and irresistible, operating to reduce to nothing the existence of the individual." Whence the necessity, if I may say so, of turning the hedonist into a fatalist rather than a legalist?

Meredy: The necessity, I repeat, is dialectical. Hegel is dealing with a certain type of individualism and not with a specific version of it. He shows that search for nothing else than pleasure—and 'nothing else' are the operative words—is search for a phantom. For pursuit of any sequestered ideal as absolute condemns to death every other ideal. The hedonist's plight lies in his singular devotion to the task of 'taking life', an ambiguous expression of which Hegel makes adroit use. Aspiring to take possession of life through incessant enjoyment of satisfying moments of experience, he only succeeds in taking life away from all the values to which he is beholden for his civilized selfhood. From his ivory tower he thus descends into a whited sepulcher. No wonder that the things outside should appear to him as sinister agents ruled by a mysterious fate. From this predicament he can only escape by turning, to borrow your felicitous distinction, from fatalism to legalism. When he becomes a legalist, one acknowledging the necessity of laws, the hedonist moves to a higher plane of aspiration. He still remains a hedonist but so reformed that his ambition may not inaptly be described as that of a hedonistic reformer. To this new type of individualism, inspired by what Hegel calls "the law of the heart," we must now give our attention.

157

3. The Law of the Heart

Hardith: The title chosen by Hegel for this section certainly affords an easy transition to a new type of individualism. It is a type in which the opposites of desire and necessity, so fatal to hedonism, become mutually reconciled. Not the experience *in* society but sentimental concern *for* society constitutes here the central theme. What society chiefly needs, the ardent reformer is made to asseverate, is to embrace and cherish *his* aspiration. His mission consists in persuading society to conform to whatever plan his love for the good of mankind dictates. 'The Law of the Heart', a felicitous name for the passion by which the reformer is inspired, denotes a necessity in social form; and this necessity, far from appearing, as it does in hedonism, synonymous with fate, has its very fount and origin in self-consciousness. Here then is law the necessity of which is impregnated with the fervor of desire. And of this strange conception—the conception of desired law—we are, I take it, to follow Hegel's diagnosis.

Meredy: Yes, the union of desire and necessity is just what the law of the heart implies. And this union marks the advance of the reformer's position over the hedonist's. But since the reformer too is here depicted as an individualist, the universal law he desires is ultimately the law of a single desiring heart. And herein, as will presently appear, lies the paradox.

Hardith: The romantic reformer, such as Hegel portrays him, strikes me as a contrived caricature. Hegel no doubt has in mind the sentimental literature of his time. Unmistakable, for example, are the allusions to Goethe's *Werther* and Schiller's *Robbers*. And it is difficult not to think of Rousseau in connection with Hegel's general attack on sentimentalism. Here again he lays himself open to the charge of confusing a universal type with the dated exemplifications of it he inveighs against. It is only as related to the latter that Hegel's animus seems pertinent—or impertinent. Great indeed is the folly of the caricatured reformer who impetuously starts on his career to remake the world in accordance with his heart's desire. Consider the excessive pessimism by which he must be guided in condemnation of the things that call for change. How preposterous the supposition that the world would go to wrack and ruin unless speedily saved by *him*. Yet this is precisely what he is here made to announce. He proclaims that the world is ailing and dying and can be restored to health only by submitting to a special sort of cure. Where indeed would the reformer be without an evil world waiting for *his* panacea? This initial pessimism necessary for the reformer's vocation is matched only by the equally inordinate optimism that inspires the reformer's belief in the world's recovery under his infallible treatment. What incredible simplicity! The world, alas, suffers from many strange ailments; but they are not so incurable without the reformer's officiousness, as he would have us believe, nor are they so easily remedied by it. The reformer's pessimism and optimism, at loggerheads in his own mind, are both childish. And does such a childish being, drawn with such consummate ruthlessness, have any existence outside Hegel's text?

Meredy: With that text you have certainly taken many liberties. Are you, if I may ask, entirely free from animus in reducing to such absurdity Hegel's diagnosis of a not unfamiliar human aspiration? Your comment on his manner of dealing with it is not altogether irrelevant in relation particularly to the literary expressions alluded to. Hegel's polemic against romantic sentimentalism is equal only to his polemic against formal rationalism. But the attitude of the reformer here presented need not be stated in the terms of the special illustrations he considered representative. The attitude is of course impossible except on the assumption that there is a world calling for reform and that numerous persons in it are eager to trust in the zeal of some prophet to deliver them from evil. And it is often the individual weary of a disillusioning life of pleasure who becomes an active crusader with a mission. And as such Hegel exhibits him. Judging the world to be evil because, in the first place, its objective necessity is not one to which the heart can give assent, and because in the second, a necessity not sanctioned by the heart is bound to seem cruel and oppressive, the crusader sets out to inspire the world to believe in the altruistic laws he has at heart for the salvation of the suffering hearts of mankind.

Hardith: But the crusader's avowed altruism hides but thinly an incorrigible egoism. This becomes manifest when the reformer succeeds, as not infrequently happens, in accomplishing his purpose. The victorious reformer is here envisaged as cutting a figure egregiously comic. How he exults in his pet plan! How he rejoices that the law of his humanitarian heart is at length the stern law of the land! Upon his impassioned faith now depends the hope of the world. So let no man dare interpret the meaning of *his* dream. And when others, whose hearts too throb for the good of mankind, feel prone to assimilate his cause with theirs, watch the great reformer rise to fight for the pristine purity of his ideal. No dross must be suffered to impair the glory of his vision. Improvements in accordance with dreams having their genesis in alien bosoms become intolerable. There must be no concessions and no compromises. His reform or none. For it is his reform, and his alone, the world needs, and he in his egoism verily believes it. Such is Hegel's harsh picture of his imaginary reformer.

159

Meredy: Once more you are inclined to be unjust to Hegel. The propensity he depicts is redolent of actuality and strikingly authentic. What reformer has failed to encounter the difference between a law bred in his mind and the same law embodied in statutes and ordinances? And what reformer is eager to abandon his crusade once the law of his heart has become judicial law? The distance between the reformer's dream and its reality is here shown to be full of pathos. And Hegel shows it with impressive acuity. What more pathetic than the demand that a particular and private ideal, the reformer's very own, should become universal and incarnate? When realized and released from its author's control, the ideal tends to follow a course often contrary to its original intent. Is it consistent with the character of a passionate reformer that he acquiesce in any debasement of his inspired vision? Can he refrain from reminding the world of the contrast between the law of *his* heart and its corrupt versions? Yes, to prevent other reformers from perverting his pure ideal now becomes the aim of his new crusading zeal, all in the ardent belief that mankind's salvation depends on the promise of his singular prophecy.

Hardith: But what monumental egoism is the reformer's! He is shown to care for his utopian dream more than for the world waiting to be regenerated. He is of course never without rivals; and he soon discovers that mending the broken world is an activity in the exercise of which many may lay claim to competence. Numerous are the doctors intent upon healing the sick world—and they disagree. The collision of ardent reformers, each using solicitude for mankind as a form of self-assertion—what a delectable spectacle for the comic spirit! 'What the world needs above all else'—a favorite phrase of the inveterate crusader's—is always the inimitable way of salvation dear to a particular heart; and he must indeed be possessed of unconscionable arrogance who thinks that to him alone is vouchsafed the knowledge of what an ill-contrived world requires for its repair. But all this applies to none but the romantic reformer, representing a special type, whose mainspring of action is warm sentimentality and not sober thought. No wonder he is impatient of restraint. A fervid heart, not a clear head, is the pilot of his soul. And in all his concern for the world he never forgets himself. Accordingly, it is humanity he charges with perversity, not his sentimental heart, if his utopian plans are ignored by the world. That in the end he loses faith not in his dreams but in the world, is this not proof of boundless egoism?

Meredy: You state after your own fashion the core of the difficulty which lies in the failure of individualism to provide a basis for social reform. As long as the would-be reformer, like the would-be hedonist,

160

is an individual detached from his social moorings, it matters little by what epithet he is described. Not every reformer who follows the dictates of his heart need adapt himself to the language Hegel adopts under the influence of the examples he deems typical. But what is here all-important is the image of the 'heart'; it fittingly invites attention to the subjective derivation of the reformer's professed altruism. His inner oracle infallibly tells him what must be devised 'for the relief of man's estate'. We thus reach the climax of the dialectic: it is the discovery that there are others likewise imbued with the passion for reform, and everyone, heeding the voice of his own oracle, declares his particular nostrum to be the universal hope of mankind. What other result is possible on the assumption that no law is a true law unless it springs from the heart? For a law from which the heart recoils represents the very evil from which mankind must be delivered. Accordingly, the law of the heart tends to become the law of each and every heart, and the world the scene of strife among many and different special pleaders. With obvious allusion to a fictitious 'state of nature', Hegel views the situation as involving on a higher plane a recrudescence of the warfare of all against all.

Hardith: The outcome of this imaginary 'warfare' is rather curious. I should have expected the would-be reformer to retire from the scene turning away from his folly instead of turning against the world. But no! Failing to perceive his own perverted nature, he accuses of perversion those who refuse to acknowledge that his panacea ought to be also theirs. Worthy are they of their chains who choose to remain deluded. Mankind, whose plight kindled his passion for reform, now becomes an object of contempt. The pity he feels is for his own heart so deeply injured by a cruel world. And so "the heart-throb for the welfare of humanity," says Hegel, with evident allusion to Schiller's early drama, "passes into the rage of frantic self-conceit." Unaware of thus betraying his egoism and vanity, he continues to cherish his ideal for a world not deserving it. Whence the necessity for such a conclusion? Hegel seems to have allowed an individual example drawn from fiction to prescribe the development of a situation alleged to be typical. Would the dialectic have here taken this particular turn if it had not been modeled on a single literary product? One wonders.

Meredy: The language here is clearly that used in a speech by the hero of Schiller's *Robbers,* but the 'self-conceit' it expresses Hegel regards as following inevitably upon public rebuff of a policy dear to a particular individual. A literary utterance of a mood or an idea often serves in the *Phenomenology* to clinch a dialectical argument. The present instance is a case in point. Apart from the borrowed locution,

161

what Hegel so forcibly sketches is the natural comportment of a mind conscious of the hurt of rejection. The heart scorned, whether in love or aspiration, does not as a rule swallow its resentment. The reformer spurned remains a reformer embittered. Far from forgoing his mission, he vehemently defends the merit of his cause, lost though it be for the present. He continues to look with pride upon an ideal scheme which, but for the stubbornness of those it is intended to redeem, would not be disparaged as chimerical. What a noble scheme! But what a blind world! That the future will vindicate him is the consoling hope to which he clings. Such is the logic of a singular altruism rooted in self-conceit.

Hardith: But what about the world in which individuals carry on the struggle for utopian reforms? No such struggle is of course possible in a social vacuum. A social background is requisite for every kind of individual aspiration. We have noted its necessity in relation to the career of the hedonist; it is no less necessary in connection with the vocation of the reformer. How then can it be asserted, as Hegel does, that the world too suffers from perversion? It can obviously not match the distorted perspectives peculiar to self-absorbed beings.

Meredy: Yes, the world does seem perverted but only if taken as nothing else than the scene of the war among individual souls and their separate passions. And even as such it enjoys the status of universality, though not in concrete or organic form, transcending the votaries of mutually exclusive interests such as those centered in pleasures or crusades. At this stage, however, the universal is but the unstable equilibrium of restless and willful selves in essential opposition, each finding all the others united against him. Such is the course of the world in which, after attempting in vain to change its direction at the bidding of his subjective temper, the individual experiences continual challenge to his individuality. The world marches on heedless of his idiosyncratic crusades. Thereupon a new type of consciousness emerges which, under the guise of virtue, is driven to renounce the claims of individualism.

4. Virtue and the Course of the World

Hardith: The dialectic requires of course that the transition to the new type of consciousness be a transition from one extreme to another. The sentimental reformer comes to grief because he seeks to alter the world's course in conformity to his heart's desire. The conflict he inevitably becomes engulfed in is that between the universal and the individual. It is a conflict that cannot but culminate in surrender and sacrifice of individuality. Now the progress of the dialectic, though demanding the triumph of the universal, must perforce develop implications bound to turn victory into defeat. Initially, however, the disaster suffered by individuality sets the stage for the appearance of a new point of view. It is exemplified by a reformed reformer, as it were, transmogrified into a preacher. But a reformer he remains nevertheless; his mission, too, consists in influencing the direction of the world, his aim being to induce mankind to abandon the path of vice and to take the high road of virtue. But what is vice and what is virtue? This, I surmise, will prove to be our hero's heel of Achilles.

Meredy: I like your description of our hero as a reformed reformer. Yes, the transition here is from reformer to preacher, and to a preacher imbued with a reformer's zeal. The new reformer both rebukes and transfigures the old; in becoming *aufgehoben,* the reformer simply sheds his covert egoism and reappears as apostle of true altruism. Strikingly different, however, are the issues and the methods of meeting them. Here exhortation becomes a rational vocation. The world is base; its course is determined by evil men; its apparent cohesion is the result of a precarious balance of contending self-seekers; it must be taught to conform to the moralistic precepts of the virtuous soul. Attack on the wickedness of selfish individuals and praise of nobility inherent in universal virtue—upon these mutually implicative tasks the preacher lavishes his rhetoric. It is this sermonic approach to the actual world which we are called upon to examine. Basic to the examination is a twofold question. Is it true that the social order represents but an unstable equilibrium of competing egoists, an 'invisible hand', as it were, keeping its course on a relatively even keel? And is it true that the principle of individuality is as such a principle of evil to be turned into the major theme of expostulation?

Hardith: In exhorting the individual to revert to the universal by inverting his relation to it, the preacher must be possessed of considerable arrogance to assume the role of mouthpiece of virtue. He is here made to speak as if he were the chosen instrument for delivering the world from the evil bred in the consciousness of private individuality, a consciousness assumed by him to be the source of all vice. Preachment has but a single aim. It is nothing less than mankind's conversion from baseness to goodness. What presumption! And what irony! Is this not the claim of the law of the heart all over again disguised as counsel of perfection?

Meredy: Are you not too hard on the 'knight of virtue'? Under this name Hegel conceives of him as seriously believing in the hope of man's conversion such as he underwent in his own soul. For he too, blind before, now sees. The world remains ignoble only because the

163

hope of universal salvation is condemned to be infinitely deferred if not frustrated. But the universal good, though a goal still distant, is destined to be realized by the contagion of virtue. If asked, "What is the universal good to be achieved by the spread of virtue?" the preacher's answer is surprisingly simple. The good is virtue itself. Disposition to do good is the only good there is. Nobility of character is everything. Man's righteous will can rededicate gifts and powers now, alas, in the service of vice. Without reference to the ends to which they may become ancillary, human talents and capacities are not amenable to judgments of value. They can be called evil only when degraded to further selfish aims. For—and this is the burden of the preacher's song—vice resides in individuality asserted, virtue in individuality laid aside.

Hardith: But in all this we never seem to leave the verbal level. Apart from the tautologies involved in the reiterated equations of virtue and the good, certain assumptions requisite for the preacher's position render it singularly vulnerable. What *is* ultimately the preacher's chief desideratum, since man's personal gifts and powers have but instrumental value, depending upon their use; and since the specific ends they subserve are not here under consideration, the spirit guiding their employment being all that matters? What can it be if not to effect by his discourse a change of heart in each and every individual? He who preaches virtue must assume that his hortatory eloquence will move men to will the good of all. And what is here the good if not the universal disposition to prefer virtue to vice? This is, if I may say so, just phrasemongery. One must have incredible faith in the efficacy of edifying words to take the preacher's zeal seriously. Besides, how can he pursue his vocation without addressing his sermons to particular individuals? For it is in their souls that the seeds of a conversive disposition must first be planted. There can of course be no collective good unless virtue becomes universally distributed. Ironically, the verbal attack on individuality presupposes the reality of detached individuals. Upon them alone and not upon society can virtue be inculcated.

Meredy: In condensed and rather cavalier fashion you partly anticipate Hegel's elaborate diagnosis of what ails his imaginary knight of virtue. The diagnosis seems a satire but is no caricature. Hegel regards the preacher's career as an inevitable phase in the 'story' of individualism. The didactic assault on individuality is bootless, the very assault entailing a vindication of it. And the appeal to virtue as a subjective bridge to the universal cannot be made or sustained save on the plane of verbal edification. This is the sum and substance of the dialectic, growing out of the analysis of the contrast between virtue

164

and the course of the world, a contrast on which the argument against the principle of individuality is here shown to hinge. It is in the world that vice is said to have its habitat, the principle of individuality being in the ascendant there; but in the privacy of the soul the selfish ways of the worldlings can be renounced and virtue become the governing spiritual disposition. In the process of converting the world to the ideal of self-surrender, the knight of virtue thus enters into warfare with men addicted to self-assertion. But, alas, the struggle can here be nothing less than a matter of words and only a sham fight (*Spiegelfechterei*). Has virtue but a subjective source and does it merely represent a meritorious quality of character? If so no man can say of his neighbor that he is without virtue. What prevents anyone from asseverating that he is disposed to promote the very end the knight of virtue is intent upon? Who is debarred from laying claim to the possession of a will to act for the universal good? Verbal allegiance to the universal good is within everyone's reach and competence as long as the nature of the universal good remains indeterminate. Accordingly, the world is full of knights of virtue, each professing to champion the universal good, and each assailing the others with the same high-sounding phrases as the only weapons.

Hardith: And is this not the very course of the world against which the knight of virtue is engaged in verbal warfare? The war of words, seemingly about nothing, clearly reveals that what the noble warrior is fighting for is already here, to wit, the universal good in the shape of different talents and capacities which their possessors assert are exercised for the purpose of advancing the cause of social well-being. Let none dare deprecate the assertion as mere lip service. This is a compliment which is here ever returnable. The actual world may thus be regarded as if it were the preacher's ideal incarnate, containing as it does apparent self-seekers of whom each is able to proclaim without fear of contradiction that he is the very model of virtue. The alleged enemy is thus no real enemy; the battle is between self-styled virtuous souls, a maneuver to flaunt individuality in the very act of verbally repudiating it. What is the upshot of all this?

Meredy: The caustic exposure to ridicule of a type of consciousness essentially quixotic serves an important aim. It demonstrates the fact that the world's process is one in which individuality is indispensable—not, however, in radical opposition to the universal. The universal, which is supreme over the individual and includes him, is omnipresent, ever dependent on as well as ever independent of its particular spokesmen and agents. The sense in which this is true can be revealed only in the attempt to assert or to assail the individual's individuality. The present attempt is to denounce it by pious utterances issuing from the lips of a well-marked personality. A preacher who lives in phrases confirms the individualism he rejects. He remains the dupe of his own declamations until he recognizes that in fighting the alleged giants of wickedness he is but fighting windmills. The distinctions on which his position rests are specious if deemed absolute. There can be no absolute antithesis between the individual and the universal, seeing that the universal good is the work of individuals that in one sense expresses and in another transcends their individuality. Nor can the contrast between what is and what ought to be, constituting the preacher's didactic pabulum, apply validly to the real world; of the common good that should be brought about by individual effort and skill actual society is a living witness. Such and similar oppositions are purely verbal, and verbal accordingly is the original opposition between virtue and the world. The world's process is not perverted because absent from it is the form of universality cherished by the individual, perverse is the individual who demands that the world march in tune with the kind of universality dear to his heart. The world thus easily triumphs over virtue. But the virtue defeated is merely subjective. Hegel differentiates it from objective virtue, anticipating a later theme, such virtue as formed in antiquity the basis of an ethical order. That virtue (*die antike Tugend*) was truly substantial because it governed the entire life of the people and had for its purpose the realization of a concrete good comporting with individual aspiration. The idle activity of preaching, to reproduce the sense of Hegel's wordplay, no doubt edifies but contributes nothing to the social edifice. That only deeds, not words, can build.

Hardith: What a punster Hegel is! A compilation of the wordplays dispersed through the text would prove, serving though they do to drive home a crucial point, that not all are equally felicitous. The juxtaposition of *erbauen* and *aufbauen* belongs to his happier efforts: it succinctly conveys the difference between the edificatory and the edificial as it relates to the nature of virtue. And does not this difference afford the necessary transition to the new type of consciousness?

Meredy: The difference you mention does indeed provide a convenient bridge to the type that follows. Individual aspiration to cultivate virtue, like the aspiration to seek pleasure or the aspiration to reform society, erects a barrier between the self and his world and ultimately leads to their estrangement. Virtue turns into vice when kept imprisoned within the walls of the soul. Virtue is service and service virtue. In active devotion to an objective cause must be found that virtue which signifies the sacrifice as well as the fulfillment of individuality. And to this theme and all that it implies we must now turn.

The Individual and the Universal

1. Pseudo-Objective Individualism

Hardith: The difficulty in connection with the preceding types of individualism has its source in the equivalence of the terms 'individual' and 'subjective'. All those intent upon satisfaction of desire clearly are subjective individualists. Desire, using the word comprehensively, covers a multitude of desiderata: desire for pleasure, desire for reform, desire for virtue. Whatever the objects, desire presupposes a private psyche *in* which the issue chiefly matters. To whom can it matter if not to the person involved whether his pleasures are denied or gone sour, whether the law of his heart is repelled or distorted, whether his sense of virtue is inhibited or outraged? And the individualists here portrayed are conceived as civilized beings, depending on an objective world for supplying desired stimuli and the means of possible gratification. But the objective world needed, which is determined by a necessity of its own, foredooms to frustration attempts to bend its course in harmony with personal aspiration. The sophisticated hedonist, the utopian dreamer, the preacher of the selfless life—they all run afoul of the inexorable nature of things. The individualist soon learns that the world is not his oyster: it refuses to be opened by the sword of his subjective reason or will, passion or purpose. Does this not sum up, though in words not exactly Hegel's, the predestined collapse of the three versions of individualism?

But now a new version, definitely understood as objective, is about to enter upon the stage. No longer will the individual appear sundered from the universal. Work will replace desire, and service aspiration. The true principle of individuation will be found in the world and not in opposition to it. Are we to assume that in the ensuing discussion the truth about the individual will be finally revealed?

Meredy: Not exactly. The section before us serves as a sort of introduction to the notion of real individuality. What it depicts at first is a type of individual deceptively united with the universal. To unmask the deception is the aim of the analysis that follows. The universal and the individual can come together by reciprocal dependence only when they assume a form Hegel calls 'concrete'. Such a form, however, of which we have already had some hints, awaits explicit treatment, at a later stage. The organized community, holding in solution the two extremes, will not emerge until completion of the diagnosis of a type of subjectivism so subtle that the unwary might be easily misled by its pseudo-objective posture and language.

The champions of such subjectivism, to anticipate the examples Hegel has in mind, are those learned worthies who profess disinterested devotion to an objective task, yet all the while hiding under a cloak of false humility the passions of greedy creatures avid of honor and adulation. Of covert subjectivism disingenuous scholars are not the sole representatives. The noble cause of art, too, has among its devotees not a few whose feigned self-surrender betrays only too clearly the never-ceasing hunger for personal glory. "The kingdom of the spiritual animals," as Hegel partly entitles the section, exhibits when viewed at close range unrivalled opportunities for comic laughter. What a wealth of incongruities! Here we see humility hand in hand with conceit, self-surrender in alliance with vanity, lifelong devotion in company with envy, manly service in union with self-glorification. Such incongruities are not confined to the tribe of sequestered scholars or artists; they are discernible in the wider world of society. But what renders them more comical when perceived in the vineyards of the erudite animals is their refinement and luxuriance.

2. *Animal Behavior in the Realm of Reason*

Hardith: Hegel's title given to this section is complex, implying an ironic and biased judgment. It is thus more than a mere heading. The original runs: *Das geistige Tierreich und der Betrug oder die Sache selbst.* What a provocative challenge to the translator! It cannot be said of the English translator that he succeeded in meeting the challenge. He entitled the section as follows: "Self-conscious Individuals Associated as a Community of Animals and the Deception Thence Arising: The Real Fact," replacing his earlier and shorter title, namely, "Society as a Herd of Individuals: Deceit: Actual Fact." What a curious example of humorless adherence to supposed literal accuracy! A free and witty translation is Royce's, "The Intellectual Animals and their Humbug; or the Service of the Cause." Yours is freer and briefer, suggesting none the less and rather slyly what the original tends to convey, with a little, perhaps too little, of its sardonic quality. After all, it is in the life of reason that the subjectivism under consideration occurs, and the animus peculiar to the conduct among its different exemplars often does manifest animalistic truculence. Am I too punctilious about a small point? But Hegel's titles interest me. Some are so maliciously phrased as if designed to prejudice the matters at issue. Is Hegel's own animus entirely free of animalism?

Meredy: Hegel's titles often do appear prejudicial. The one you speak of is certainly not without pejorative overtones. Yes, Hegel himself definitely belongs to the class of 'animals' he castigates, and thus incurs the risk of being tarred with his own brush. But all this is neither here nor there. His diagnosis of a prevalent type of consciousness would under any heading be deemed arresting. We have here the emergence of a novel conception of individuality, one permeated by the universal, differing markedly from the conceptions that involve the synonymy of individualism and subjectivism. The bond binding the individual and the universal comes to be regarded here as having its basis in service; the universal becomes concrete in virtue of those serving it, and its servants achieve distinction in virtue of some objective task defining and determining their individuality. Granted. But if service is to function as principle of concretion as well as of individuation, what meaning should be attached to it? That is here the crucial question.

Hardith: Service as such—Hegel calls it action—can hardly be said to qualify as principle or criterion of anything. Not all individuals have the capacity to serve all universal causes. Are they equally endowed for the pursuit of even the same end? Service would appear to be a word signifying nothing until the ability of those serving and the determinateness of what is to be served receive adequate consideration.

Meredy: This is precisely what Hegel insists upon—but at great length and with technical severity. So circuitous is his method and so tortuous his prose that I am not sure whether I follow the analysis sufficiently to epitomize it in plain English. But let me try.

The possibility of service clearly presupposes individuals differently endowed, each possessing, says Hegel, an "original nature." As thus differentiated by nature, the individual sets out to engage in voluntary action. Little astuteness is needed to see that action essentially deliberate depends upon certain conditions in the absence of which it would simply be random. The agent must be conscious at once of the purpose impelling the action, of the means requisite for performing the action, of the goal to which the action is directed. And of these conditions determining the action the agent must be aware as being both distinct and inseparable. Hegel has no difficulty in showing the circularity of their relationship: no action without a will to achieve a certain end;

169

no attainable end except by certain means; no choice of means save as necessitated by the purposes guiding and the end justifying the choice. It is thus that action, involving in circular relation purpose and means and end, makes its appearance as principle of individuation. Or hence it is, as Hegel declares, "that an individual can never know what he is until he makes himself real by action."

Hardith: So man is what he does and *what* he does serves to make real both the universal end *by* which activity is inspired and the particular individuality *in* which activity must originate. What an ingenious way of uniting the universal and the particular! But it is the self-importance of the particular lurking in the background Hegel is here mainly concerned with. May I dilate on this—in the spirit but hardly in the letter of the text—by reverting to the example you have briefly touched upon?

Consider those we call scholars. They are apt to think of themselves as servants of a great ideal: what can compare in value and dignity with the cause of learning and truth? How devoid of significance must all else seem when the work to be done it to advance the boundaries of knowledge? Here if anywhere is a cause sublime enough to lift its votaries above the paltry interests of the common herd. Yet though many profess to serve it whole-heartedly without a thought of personal ambition or glory, the professions can hardly be accepted at their face value. Hegel's 'intellectual animals' are indeed concerned with the extension of human knowledge but they will not let one forget that it is *they* who extend it. They will avow with false modesty that their contribution is only a small offering on the altar of learning but how querulous and vindictive they appear if, challenging their feigned humility, the critic agrees with the avowal. Let some erudite sensible of his own eminence find his work ignored in a treatise written on his specialty, and the notorious jealousy of a jilted beauty is as nothing compared with the emotion roused in the breast of the proud pedant. Or if one pundit's claim to originality be disputed by another, the vanity displayed in the vehement defense of the claim is scarcely well-concealed. The universal element lending grandeur to the pursuit of knowledge becomes adulterated with the contentiousness and coxcombery of those who are subjective individualists at heart. Such is the animal behavior of reason's champions and the deception it entails. Is this not essentially the pith of Hegel's animadversion?

Meredy: What you say, and you say it vividly, is partly pertinent in pointing up the tenuousness of the bond binding here the particular to the universal. The tenuousness is involved in the very concept of work, a concept both distinguished from and related to the concept of activity, their distinction as well as relation becoming dialectically crucial. The ambiguity inherent in the concept is notorious, work denoting either antecedent effort or the finished article in which its exercise is embodied. Of this ambiguity the expression 'work of art' affords a striking illustration. What is it if not labor objectified? Does it not signify process as well as result, neither intelligible without the other? But mutually implicative though they are, either may be viewed as enjoying prior importance. If work is primarily conceived as activity, the inward purpose inducing it, whereof the individual artist alone can have authentic knowledge, is obviously not on public exhibition. An artistic work is open to general contemplation and judgment only when supremacy is accorded not to the labor of creation but to the incarnation of it, an object external and extant, independent as such of the mind that willed and realized it. One thing, in short, is identification of work with the activity of production, quite another is its equation with the resulting product. And it is the implications of a concept so incorrigibly ambivalent that the dialectic now centers in.

Hardith: But this applies with singular force to the difference between the process of production and the ensuing product in the realm of the intellect. "My work," contends the scholar, "is exalted above all else as long as the advancement of learning remains a universal ideal of undisputed worth." The disingenuousness of the contention lies in its ambiguity. For what does he mean by 'his work'? Is it his *work* that is exalted or *his* work? The unworldly ideal of scholarship exacting labor of love and love of labor, without personal bias or gain, is one thing; the particular achievement of a particular individual, bent on honor and adulation, is quite another. The scholar's deception lies in the arrogant substitution, hidden or overt, of the particular for the universal, as if his contribution to learning, precisely because it was *his,* were coequal with the ideal cause of truth.

Meredy: You have hit on a happy way of epitomizing the dialectic by resorting to a subtle change of inflection. There is indeed all the difference in the world between saying *my* work and saying my *work.* If the emphasis falls on the possessive pronoun, my work, expressing as it does my original nature, admits no comparison, save, so to speak, with itself. How compare it with anything else? Comparisons of differing achievements amount to comparisons of personalities. Such comparisons are of course odious. Since everyone simply is what he does in accordance with his endowed gifts, all criticism becomes sheer impertinence.

Hardith: No, if I may interrupt you, not *all* criticism. Need every critical standard be based on comparison between works of sundry individuals? A distinction might well be drawn between a given product and the producer's original nature embodied therein. The result of his productive labor may appear altogether incommensurate with the capacity for production he is believed to have. "Even good Homer sometimes nods," you know. Such internal criticism simply consists in judging a man's work in relation to what he is capable of doing.

Meredy: How true! And is this not the basis of all self-criticism? Who, measuring his actual against his possible achievements, could not regard them, honestly or not, as inadequate if not untrue to his original nature? Between purpose and fulfillment there is not seldom a yawning abyss. Few scholars and artists are strangers to the experience of self-disapprobation. So when *my* work turns into my *work,* when, that is, the product of my individual labor comes to exist on its own account, it hardly ever remains anonymous, for the activity (*Tun*), to which it owes the status of an independent object (*Sache*), marks the product inexpungibly as mine, no matter whether I secretly disparage or extol the quality of the performance. All this may sound like an idle play with noun and pronoun, yet the inflective seesaw between them graphically tells a dialectical story.

Hardith: But this seesaw cannot go on indefinitely. The *act* of production and the *being* of the product, opposites involved in the ambivalent notion of work, must somehow come together within a wider idea, and this appears to be what Hegel calls *die Sache,* a term on which he rings numerous changes. Has the term a central meaning? And what is its exact English equivalent?

Meredy: Ah, *Sache!* What does it mean and what does it not mean? Here translators are apt to go sadly astray by equating it with but one or two English words. Very different are the senses in which Hegel employs it, depending upon the context in which the term occurs. Thus its connotation is obviously similar to that of object or fact or thing which the product of a production—the finished work of artist or scholar—may be said to exemplify. But *Sache* has another and a more comprehensive connotation, the emphasis falling on the internal relation of product and production. Semantic scruples aside, the term, in its more catholic sense, has many English cousins, such as cause, ideal, end. For example, the cause for the sake of which work is done, art for art's sake, let us say, or learning for learning's sake, represents, at least superficially, a synthesis of self-assertion and self-surrender. One's individual activity is an earnest of devotion to an objective task, and the outcome of such activity constitutes but a particular contribution to a universal end. Acknowledged explicitly as universal, the cause unifies all particular efforts and all particular achievements. Here we

172

have, as Hegel puts it, "the interpenetration of individuality and objectivity." This view of the matter leaves room for all ways of production and all kinds of products.

Hardith: So constructed, however, the cause or ideal or end (or whatever be the equivalent of *Sache*) is too indeterminate, and "the interpenetration of individuality and objectivity" is apparent rather than real. For service of the cause may assume so many variable expressions that almost everything may be justified in its behalf. "They also serve who only stand and wait." The abstract ideal to which one professes devotion does not predetermine the manner in which it is to be served. What lover of an ideal sufficiently vague (patriotism, for instance) is precluded from invoking its sanction for any deed of his? Here is an opportunity always open to champion in the name of a cause modes of conduct mutually destructive. What happens (to allude to the earlier illustration) when an artist creates an original work designed to promote the cause of art, and the critic, no less intent upon furthering it, treats the creation with undisguised contempt? To ask the question is to answer it. Artist and critic, averring fidelity to the same noble ideal in the same lofty spirit, are bound to become deeply estranged; each will throw aspersion on the other's competence, and each will look upon the other's conception of the ideal as a travesty. Men's declaration of allegiance to a common end does not prevent them from comporting themselves as bitter if not savage rivals in relation to their individual achievements. The vehemence in attacking or defending such achievements simply proves that the humble appeal to the supreme ideal (*die Sache selbst*) is nothing but deceit and subterfuge. Professions of self-surrender to an objective calling turns unashamedly when challenged into naked confessions of passionate self-assertion. The frauds perpetrated under the aegis of art or science or any other abstract cause are only too familiar, and Hegel's diagnosis of them though ruthless must give us pause.

Meredy: Hegel's indictment of a subjectivism that exemplifies but speciously the relation between the universal and the particular is perhaps unduly harsh. Some of its aspects are grossly overdrawn. Not all scholars or artists or critics are guilty of hypocrisy and vanity. Yet the animus with which he exposes the foibles and pretensions rampant in the life of reason is dialectically called for. For the subjectivism here exhibited, following upon that of hedonist and reformer and preacher, is more adroitly disguised and thus more apt to deceive, seeing that 'the interpenetration of individuality and objectivity' appears as if actually attainable. Such interpenetration, however, since it presupposes the acknowledged supremacy of the universal, reveals itself as mere appearance. The universal is but a shadow and disinterested devotion to it a sham. The universal, but in concrete form, will indeed be the reality in which alone selves can thrive, in which alone, that is, they can find and express their true individuality. The argument for this lies directly ahead. But the subjectivism just considered, culminating in the fustian game of individual wits (*ein Spiel der Individulitäten*), must needs remain triumphant until the universal becomes both substance and subject—the former as the reality supporting the claims of individuals to uniqueness, the latter as the reality which only the action of uniquely conscious individuals can uphold. So the appeal to the universal by the hounds and foxes of the intellect becomes simply ludicrous. Yet the emphasis on the universal is misplaced only because the universal meant is abstract. This I take to be the purport of Hegel's remarkable satire.

3. Reason as Lawgiver

Hardith: The two short sections concluding the third part of the *Phenomenology* strike me as an anticlimax. They read as if intended to serve as mere appendices. Yet they constitute the culmination of reason's career. Although insufficiently developed, they contain a final attempt to vindicate the harmony of the individual and the universal. The harmony—and this will appear crucial—is one which every individual has the power to establish. But this power can only be demonstrated by deriving the principle of individuation from the very nature of reason, with the result that the equality of individuals rather than their difference becomes the focus of attention. A theme so important certainly deserves a discussion less cavalier.

Meredy: The allusion throughout the last sections is chiefly to an aspect of Kant's moral teaching which Hegel could safely assume as familiar. This may account for his reluctance to expatiate on the matter at great length. With references to Kant Hegel's work is replete, and a collection of them would be quite impressive. Kant's ideas loom very large in the *Phenomenology,* and we shall encounter in a later context a detailed polemic against his ethics. Here the categorical imperative alone, supposedly unifying the individual and the universal, fits so organically into the dialectic that more than summary treatment of it must have seemed to Hegel scarcely necessary. I agree, however, that the topic should have received fuller consideration.

Hardith: Individualism, but now resting on a collective principle of individuation, is thus once more in the saddle. This results, it would seem, from the equation of individualism, not only with subjectivism, but also with rationalism. When grounded in reason, the principle of individuation turns into a principle relevant to the human species and not merely to a single specimen. For reason is the common possession of all mankind in virtue of which the race is distinguishable as human. It is accordingly their universal reason that defines men as men and that has the power to liberate them from the sway of goading desires and passions by which alone they are set in mutual opposition. To enter the realm of reason—and nowhere else can they enjoy a commensurable nature—men must forgo acting in accordance with inclinations and impulses which, while differentiating them from one another, assimilate them with the animal kingdom. Here is a type of pure individualism in which all individuals may share and share alike. In submitting to his reason every individual is not only under the governance of the universal—he is the universal. What a daring position! How is this kind of universality related to that of the various 'causes' examined in the previous section?

Meredy: There is but one absolute cause (*die absolute Sache*) to which the individual owes allegiance, this being the moral law, and this alone, since it is definable by a homogeneous reason, unites him with all other individuals. This interindividual union exemplifies here what Hegel calls the ethical reality (*die sittliche Substanz*) and ethical is every individual who is conscious of it. There thus appears on this level a new variant of the identity of thought and being, for the moral law of which the individual becomes aware (his 'thought' of it) is the selfsame moral law present in the thought of each and every individual (such presence denoting its 'being'). Hence the contention that the plurality of individuals, which is so axiomatic a premise of other types of individualism, can be transcended in a moral individualism the foundation of which is reason universal *in* and universal *to* every constituent of that plurality. All must act alike when acting in conformity with the moral law that issues from and appeals to the same consciousness of rationality. Causes other than that of the uniquely universal moral law can have but a subordinate or relative universality. It is a universality that accrues to them from individual action conceived as morally—that is, rationally—defensible. Such, phrased abstractly, is the gist of Hegel's view of the categorical imperative; its universality is absolute and its function legislative.

Hardith: All's well as long as we remain on the verbal plane. Separate selves, heretofore professing to serve causes that enable them to outshine or outdistance one another in glory or gain, are made *pro forma* to lose their animal competitiveness in a rational humanity on whose behalf each may act as moral legislator for all. Reason as lawgiver thus emerges to resolve—but only by definition—the anomalies inherent in subjectivism. Yet the law of which reason is the giver is a moral law, that is, a law of action, in accordance with which choice becomes possible between conflicting courses of conduct. And the choice is at once free and determined. For reason is the source of law as well as the source of its necessity. And of its certitude too there can be no doubt. For each individual, possessed of what Hegel calls sound reason (*gesunde Vernunft*), knows the law immediately and thus knows intuitively what is right and good. And nothing in all this is more bewildering than reliance on immediacy. Is it here more justified than elsewhere? Is there a difference in principle between sense-certainty and moral certainty? And is the formulation of a law so broadly conceived more than a counsel of perfection?

Meredy: You have put your finger on a crucial point. The claim to immediate certainty entails the same paradox whatever be the context in which it appears. Such certainty becomes everywhere reducible to that of an abstract universal lacking in determinate content. Hegel shows the futility of appealing to immediacy in the moral sphere by commenting on two maxims assumed to involve duties intuitively recognized as universally valid.

The first is that 'everyone ought to speak the truth'. This command, though expressed unconditionally, actually rests on the tacit condition that the truth be first known. With this condition, however, the maxim is at the mercy of shifting senses. The moral certainty enjoyed by so-called healthy reason is no less contradictory than the certainty of sense-experience. Both are kinds of certainty the meaning of which is at loggerheads with their assertion. The maxim that 'everybody should speak the truth' must initially be taken as a command unqualifiedly universal but when it appears in qualified form, namely, that 'everybody should speak the truth in accordance with his knowledge of the truth', the maxim forfeits the universality claimed for it. A necessity is turned into a contingency: the maxim is made to vary with different claims to knowledge. No wonder that one man's truth often seems another's falsehood. But when the maxim is transformed into the imperative that everybody must *know* the truth, the issue becomes transferred to the plane of reflection transcending the subjective limits of immediacy.

Hardith: The example simply shows that moral maxims have but a specious claim to absoluteness; the conditions requisite for their application, whether tacit or expressed, always reduce if they do not contradict the universal validity ascribed to them. Is Hegel's example a fair one? The duty to speak the truth, while admittedly general, is admittedly also subject to qualification, and a duty, too, that has built into it, as it were, the necessity of its very violation when the so-called white lie becomes imperative on strictly moral grounds. Can a maxim so vulnerable serve as basis for Hegel's sweeping animadversion on reason as lawgiver? And in what consists its resemblance to Kant's conception of the moral law Hegel is here bent on satirizing?

Meredy: I wonder whether you will find the second example more palatable. 'Love thy neighbor as thyself'—this is another celebrated duty that proves anomalous. The command that a particular individual extend to another particular individual the love he feels for himself reduces the relation between them to a relation of sentiment. Does the maxim permit the inference that in the sentimental relation between particular 'neighbors' is to be found the essence of morality? It would seem so if we take the words at their face value. The love commanded, if a literal inference is to be eschewed, must cease to remain mere feeling and become a principle of action; for only through a love which is active as well as discriminate can we relieve a man of evil and bring him good. A love not ruled by intelligence may easily turn into evil the good it unknowingly seeks to accomplish. Unintelligent love, as Hegel shrewdly observes, may do harm perhaps even more than hatred. But organized society, too, is engaged in the process of promoting the good of its members, a process compared with which the sporadic actions of particular individuals are relatively insignificant. Hopeless is a solitary person's struggle with society over his neighbor's good! All effort entirely and solely particular must needs be momentary and fortuitous as contrasted with public policy and concerted operation. Thus a duty, assumed as if having the force of a law, is consigned to chance. It is accidental whether action induced by love will or will not benefit one's neighbor. The famous maxim simply *commands*; it is not a law descriptive of things as they are or prescriptive of values capable of realization. Like the duty to speak the truth, the duty to love one's neighbor remains a duty that never could but only should be performed.

Hardith: The second example seems more relevant to Hegel's dialectical design. It enables him to draw certain distinctions basic to his polemic against pure formalism in ethics which he regards as serving essentially to justify the claims of subjective individualism. For the universal, the supremacy of which is here postulated, coincides with reason conceived as a distinct 'faculty', and in relation to this faculty alone does any and every individual acquire membership in the human race. Hence the possibility of any individual legislating for every other if and when the principles governing his conduct enjoy the sanction of *his* reason. Has Hegel's dialectic of this legislative power more than tangential bearing on Kant's moral philosophy? And does he not offer a mere parody of the categorical imperative by likening it to maxims and commands so obviously open to logical attack?

Meredy: I repeat that Kant's moral philosophy is here not under consideration, its full discussion being reserved for another occasion. And the categorical imperative is but alluded to as illustrating a law applicable to no determinate content. Like the maxims mentioned, the categorical imperative simply commands that it ought to be the law of moral action but can prescribe no concrete mode of behavior comporting with it. Formally, everything may become one's duty; materially, nothing appears to be one's duty. This epitomizes the crucial difficulty involved in assigning to reason a legislative function. Reason's laws, assuming reason to be the lawgiving agency, are without efficacy in resolving the conflict of specific duties. Reason must be looked upon not as creator but as critic of human duties. And as such it now emerges. Or, in words more consonant with Hegel's locution, reason's function is judicial rather than legislative, supplying criteria for testing the validity of laws of action already laid down. Abandoning the role of legislator, reason now assumes the office of judge. Let us briefly follow the dialectic of reason's last posture.

4. *Reason as Judge*

Hardith: The change in reason's office from giving to testing laws inevitably follows of course from two considerations. The first has to do with the rift between an abstract principle of conduct and its concrete application, the second with the necessity of introducing into human affairs some rational order. The single and formal command to act so that one can will the maxim of one's action to become universal (which is in essence Kant's categorical imperative) would clearly be universally applicable if one were never confronted by alternative courses of action. In the face of conflicting laws to which the moral agent is subject, and laws 'empirical' in origin, his reason can do no more than adjudge their differences. Would not one law be just as good or right as another in the absence of a rational standard for measuring their claims to moral validity? It is not reason that exacts conformity to opposed laws; reason can only bring to the opposition a universal law of valuation. This, I take it, is the sense in which reason turns judge, and the sense too, unless I am mistaken, which Kant gives to his categorical imperative. What is the matter with it?

Meredy: The basic trouble lies in what is here conceived to be the sole rational criterion in terms of which the conflict of rival laws may indeed be resolved but resolved, alas, in favor of either or both. The criterion, regarded as a law of moral valuation, is nothing else than the law of contradiction, involving the postulate that, because no rational being can *think* a contradiction, no rational being can *will* a contradiction. The postulate, though not unexceptionable, need not here be questioned. The chief problem relates to the possibility of invoking in any specific situation the law of contradiction as a test both necessary and sufficient. What particular mode of action can that law, and that law alone, prescribe a priori or proscribe a priori?

Hardith: Since we are not debating the issue on its merits, I will not point out the fallacy of confusing discourse and conduct. A logical statement which, if the will is not directly involved must obviously come under the jurisdiction of the law of contradiction, is one thing; quite another is a moral decision which, principally engaging the will, need not in the same sense be judged by that law. It is only when the decision is cast in the form of a proposition that the question of its self-consistency becomes relevant. Does not the dialectic here mainly revolve around the assumption that a product of thought and an act of will are amenable to the same criterion of rationality?

Meredy: Precisely! The special union by the law of contradiction of thought and will illustrates not only the alleged autonomy of abstract or formal rationalism; it illustrates also the inescapable tautology in which reason is involved when attempting to test the moral validity of particular laws divorced from their determinate content. This, in brief, is the gist of Hegel's argument. Without reference to the content of a law, what remains to be tested except the congruity of its formulation with reason's a priori form? Alternative laws mutually exclusive with respect to content may thus be exhibited as enjoying equal freedom from formal contradiction. Conformity to reason's one and only law here constitutes the sole test of any other law's claim to validity. Can reason's moral valuation be anything else than discursive valuation? The question goes to the heart of the matter.

Hardith: But volition which must be somehow differentiated from thought can scarcely ignore the specifically moral values embodied in particular laws competing for preferential status. From the point of view of the moral agent, called upon to exercise his will, reason is merely ancillary, having but the judicial function of determining which among the opposed laws should be followed in accordance with the principle that it alone deserves to become universal. Surely, the will may be rationally incited to act on this rather than that law on the ground that in acting upon it something of greater universal value would be established.

Meredy: Yet, if the will to act is to be guided by reason, reason's sole criterion being the law of contradiction, then any set of values could be squared with any principle of action. Reason's criterion is adaptable, as Hegel says, "to one content as readily as to the opposite." Suppose, following Hegel, we ask, "Should there not be a law guaranteeing the existence of property?" Now the concept of property does not contradict itself and repels no qualification. Property may be possessed, or not possessed, and if owned, the ownership could be private or public. There is nothing in the abstract notion of property to render it inconsistent with any economic system. If a law is to exist safeguarding property for man's benefit, should the law be in favor of protecting it for individual enjoyment or collective use? And can reason, applying its a priori criterion, pass judgment on the superior merit of a particular law?

Hardith: Of course, *if* a system of economics could be modeled on that of geometry—and not a few scholars in that field conceive of their subject matter as if it were the subject matter of an exact discipline though perhaps not so rigorous as mathematics—a law of property might indeed be judged on a formal basis, on the basis, that is, of whether or not it were consistently deducible from the postulates of that system. But a law of property not entirely isolable from other laws governing human relations can have no such logically provable necessity. It denotes a special relation affected by needs and interests both individual and social, the relevant test of its validity thus involving essentially material criteria. In respect of such a law, at any rate, the role of reason as formal judge would seem a rather awkward one.

Meredy: Yes, awkward, but only because of the impartial attitude alleged to belong to the nature of judgeship. True it is that reason—as reason is here exhibited—is precluded from exercising its judicial power with reference to the question of the material adequacy pertaining to property laws. Related to various nonideational ends at once personal and interpersonal, these laws are prone to precipitate violent conflicts and to yield to modification under pressure of untoward circumstances. Neither their conditions nor their operations, not coming within the purview of abstract reason, are subject to its canons. Yet there remains a formal subject to which a disinterested judge may properly address himself. To what extent are given property laws consistent with the social structure in which they are embedded? Is there or is there not a contradiction between the professed polity of a community and its economic practices? For example, how compatible with democracy is nationalization of industry, and how reconcilable with communism (*Gütergemeinschaft*) is unequal division of goods? Property laws may thus be tested by reason's law of contradiction, not as regards their

180

intrinsic rationality, but only as regards their congruity with the context of values within which they operate.

Hardith: I will not pause to comment on the supposed disinterestedness or impartiality of human reason in fields in which complete abstraction is possible from all matters of fact as well as from all matters of value. Can human reason be implicitly trusted to remain unbiased in fields precluding such abstraction? Whose reason, in particular, can be trusted to test without prejudice the laws of property as they happen to flourish in a given social order? Learned economists are not wanting who can demonstrate that in *their* society there is no contradiction between its property laws and the system of values it embodies. And the same demonstration is presumably achieved by the same human reason in societies as opposed as capitalist and communist. Even apparent lack of consistency seems open to 'rationalization'. One looks in vain for the judicial temper in disquisitions devoted to the defense of property laws as operative in a preferred kind of economy. But all this is beside the point. Relevant here is but the question of applying a rational test to the individual's behavior in the face of existing laws concerning property taken in isolation. To violate or not to violate them under certain conditions? That is the question his will is called upon to resolve on the assumption that the principle acted upon be conceived as if acquiring through the action a universal status. What his resolution ultimately entails is whether he can consistently will a world in which such a principle should have that status. We must return to the principal issue, the issue of the efficacy of the categorical imperative to serve as guide to moral action.

Meredy: This *is* the crucial issue, Hegel's remarks on property having no other purpose than to bring the issue into clear focus. For property is a concept of so many qualifications that every possible attitude to it may be defended on the authority of the categorical imperative. Here is an authority which, though absolute, tends to justify divergent ways of behavior, resulting—and this is the irony—in leaving morality at the mercy of total relativity. This Hegel shows by considering a putative case of embezzlement. Suppose, he says, I receive in trust a certain deposit. It is manifestly the property of another. Recognition of it as such defines and determines my relation to it. Suppose, however, I decide to keep the deposit for myself. In that case the property simply ceases to be another's and becomes mine. Whence the inconsistency in keeping what I no longer regard as belonging to someone else? The notion of property does not prohibit me from altering my relation to it. Just as I may give a present to somebody, thus relinquishing possession of what is mine, so too, I can reverse the process and take what is another's. The point is that property *as* property remains unchanged whoever happens to own it. How futile here is the appeal to abstract reason! Not by the law of contradiction can embezzlement be proscribed. There is nothing, property not excepted, in relation to which I could not change my point of view, and as long as the one chosen is consistent with itself, reason's formal criterion would seem to have suffered no infringement.

Hardith: But this can hardly be said to justify theft in conformity with the categorical imperative. For that command relates to the will inciting the act. The question is ultimately this. Can one actually will without contradiction to live in a society where the act of embezzling should become universal, where, in other words, breach of trust should become the rule governing human relations?

Meredy: Yes and no. In the act of committing a breach of trust in connection with a deposit, this being the only act here envisaged, who could not consistently desire that the practice should become common? A man of communist persuasion, for example, whose desideratum is a society where the rights of private property will be abolished, obviously can without self-contradiction will that the act of embezzlement be followed universally. Nay, in harmony with the categorical imperative, he may even prescribe it as a positive duty, for the more generally the act is done, the nearer the advent of the cherished millennium. Rights of property, not unlike other rights, may be violated with logical impunity, on the assumption, of course, that the test of their validity depends entirely on a formal criterion drawn from abstract reason. The reluctance to subvert them is not logical but moral; the basis of the reluctance lies in the determinate structure of values to whose allegiance a community of individuals owes its coherence as an individual community.

Hardith: Hegel's criticism of the categorical imperative seems especially designed to afford a transition to a new chapter of the *Phenomenology*. The union of the individual and the universal, situated by Kant in conscience, must thus be looked for elsewhere. If it is a pathetic fallacy to assume that the burden of the universal could be borne by a solitary conscience, Kant must evidently be charged with it, but only when the issue is formulated in Hegelian terms. This fallacy, of which the text offers many variants, forms the background, as it were, for the discovery of an ethical order which only a living community can concretely realize through the devoted efforts of its self-conscious members. Is it fair to maintain that Hegel is now directing the course of the dialectic from the pathos of the individual to the ethos of a community construed as a concrete universal?

Meredy: The terms pathos and ethos are here admirably apposite; in a broader sense they will later prove useful in marking the passage from the lower to the higher types of the concrete universal, for the ethos of every type generates the pathos germane to it. Hegel intimates this by choosing as the first version of the concrete universal a community such as Sophocles depicts in the *Antigone*. The laws that constitute the ethos of that community determine the pathos of the tragic heroine. Neither their origin nor their validity is open to demonstration. Of these laws Hegel simply says: *they are.* Antigone's moral code is unwritten and unchangeable, of which she avers, Hegel echoing her famous words,

> This is not of today and yesterday,
> But lives forever, having origin
> Whence no man knows. . . .[1]

It is thus that we now pass to a consideration of laws of conduct operative at different levels.

---

[1] Sir George Young's translation.

PART IV

SPIRIT

The Ethical World
and the Rule of Custom

1. Transition to Spirit

Hardith: As we approach the fourth major division of the book we face a difficulty inherent in its very title. What is *Geist*? Its ambiguity is notorious. The translator's lot is here not a happy one. The word completely blurs the distinction, however tenuous it may often appear, between mind and spirit, *Geist* doing service for both. Which of the English equivalents is the more comprehensive noun? Is spirit a species of mind or vice versa? Fortunately, this is a linguistic point of but minor importance which only the punctilious are apt to raise.

Meredy: There is a certain advantage in the ambiguity attaching to the original. The word seems as if made to order for Hegel's purpose, ambivalence being what his dialectic thrives on. For *Geist* is synonymous with mind as well as with spirit, yet these its synonyms, though the same in one sense, are not the same in another. And mind becoming progressively conscious of itself as spirit—this in a word is the subject of Hegel's diagnostic inquiry. More specifically, the inquiry is into man's typical persuasions for the purpose of discovering their dialectical order and connection. Although all persuasions have their source in mind (and in what else than mind can they originate?), the series they exhibit is one which is marked by increasing growth in spirituality, a quality characteristic of the concrete universal. Varying in their objects, the persuasions so far examined, from sense-certainty on, fail to grasp and enunciate the particular focus of their awareness or aspiration, and thus find themselves in the end enmeshed in abstract universals. If the previous stages of mind presuppose or imply a concrete content from which they are abstractions, the stages subsumed under spirit reverse the process and move towards their ultimate and

186

explicit concretion. Yes, the movement from abstraction to concretion is the movement of the dialectic throughout the *Phenomenology*. Transition to spirit is simply transition to mind comprehending as internally related the aspects of mind that hitherto appeared as if separable. Let us agree then to speak of mind as the generic subject the *Phenomenology* purports to be the biography of, spirit being the name of mind's culminating phase.

Hardith: Mind or spirit would seem equally appropriate by which to designate the generic subject of the 'biography', provided only that the noun be qualified by the adjective indicative of the subject's course of development. There must be adjectives other than those you mention capable of performing the office of qualification. Abstract and concrete, though technically unexceptionable, have too special a meaning to be intelligible to the lay student, assuming as they do full grasp of Hegel's systematic doctrine into which the *Phenomenology* is to furnish the initiation. They who are still in the middle stream of the dialectic can hardly be expected to derive much enlightenment from the brief and cryptic transition to spirit. How could the transition be stated in a form comporting with our nonprofessional approach to the matter?

Meredy: The notion of individuality is perhaps best suited to answer the purpose of a more exoteric approach. Individuality is one of the major themes of the book, and in the previous stages of mind, the individual appears rather single than singular, granting that this verbal distinction connotes a real difference. To be *one* instance of a type is not the same as exercising a *unique* function in the life of the community. The claim to individuality on the part of *any* single self is a claim which *every* single self can make, individuality thus sinking to the level of a general quality, not differing in principle from redness or any other property common to many particular specimens. Every self enjoys in isolation the same numerical singleness and thus the same individuality as every other self. The beliefs and aspirations treated previously require mind to entertain them but mind as represented by any single individual. It is the single individual who bears witness to the certainty of his sense-experience and it is the single individual whose duty is dictated by his reason's categorical commands. Between these extremes appear the varieties of persuasion all having their origin and inspiration in the bosom of the single individual. The transition to spirit is transition to singular or unique individuality which no man can achieve apart from active relation to others in a common life. The pregnant principle of individuation, in short, lies not without but within a social context. In such a context alone can a self's distinctive selfhood come to spiritual fruition. Spiritual existence can pertain neither to the world nor to the individual unless the bonds binding each to each are of the organic kind, and it is through the intimacy of their linkage that the uniqueness of the one entails the uniqueness of the other. The metaphor of 'the body and its members', derived from biology, affords a significant clue to the meaning Hegel accords to spirit. What now emerges is a new variation of individualism, germane to the 'body' as well as to the 'members', in which the former unreal forms survive as transfigured or *aufgehoben*.

Hardith: Although you so studiously avoid the distinction of abstract and concrete, that between the single and the singular seems hardly more illuminating at the present juncture of our discussion. The accent on individualism, 'transfigured' beyond recognition, is here also misplaced. Hegel's introductory statements, on which our attention should be principally focused, lay greater stress on the body than the members, to use the felicitous metaphor, describing it as substance become spirit. Spirit alone he declares to be self-sufficient and self-supporting—the basis and reason (*Grund*) of individual activity. If it is on a spiritual substance that individuals depend for their individuality, dependence is here clearly an asymmetrical relation.

Meredy: If the relation appears unsymmetrical from the perspective of each, does it not acquire symmetry from the perspective of all? The world is obviously everyone's substance, in the literal sense of being the underlying reality of everyone's separate mode of existence. But there can be no spirituality in the world save as product of collective effort, and on such effort the world must depend for the kind of ethos it comes to possess. How great is the difference between a world accepted on sufferance merely to serve as medium or condition for the interplay of self-centered individualities and a world in whose life, while retaining their idiosyncrasies, individuals find a common meaning and a common purpose! The distinction hereafter to be encountered is that between individual 'world-forms' (*Gestalten einer Welt*), each a spiritual order in which different selves seek the identity of their ideals and values. With the utmost brevity Hegel hints at the succession of such individual forms of a world with whose death and transfiguration, so to speak, the ensuing dialectic will be occupied. Thus the world order under the governance of custom grows unstable and passes into a world of legally defined rights. This leads to the discrepancy between the actual and the juristic person, culminating in the separate worlds of culture and faith. Both become confused and shattered by rebellion. Rebellion brings in its wake the kind of enlightenment and insight that produces a deep chasm between *this* world and a world *beyond*. This is followed by morality, then religion in intimate union with art, and finally philosophy proper (identified by Hegel with absolute knowledge). Such is the sweeping program that lies ahead.

Hardith: Consonant with Hegel's procedure the beginning must of course be made with the life of spirit at its simplest level. Spirit, too, has an initial phase grounded on absolute certitude, corresponding to that of consciousness, self-consciousness, and reason. Is it a certitude open to immediate apprehension? More specifically is it possible to speak of the immediate certitude of social experience as comparable to the immediate certitude of sense-experience?

Meredy: This is an important point to be borne in mind. To render the two kinds of experience comparable, we had better speak of them as equally ingenuous. Lack of sophistication or subtlety is characteristic of all incipient persuasions. The first appearance of spirit will accordingly be exemplified by a society where its members are conscious not of individual rights but rather of individual duties, to be performed in accordance with determinate laws the certainty of which seems no less compelling than the certainty of sense-impressions. It is the ethos of a commonwealth ingenuously acknowledged we are bidden to consider first.

2. *The Ingenuous Society and the Two Laws*

Hardith: Your rendition of Hegel's *sittliche Welt* as the ingenuous society is quite ingenius. "The Ethical World," the literal English translation, does not offhand suggest an order based on customary laws spontaneously or naïvely accepted. Before we proceed, however, to the analysis of the first appearance of spirit, we should clarify further the bearing on it of certainty and immediacy, terms here regarded as if interchangeable. There seems at first but little analogy between matters cognitive and social. It is one thing to argue for the certainty, let us say, of a color patch given here and now, and it is quite another to contend for the certainty of a given law determining such or such conduct in a given situation. The word 'certainty' can obviously not mean in the sphere of action what it is alleged to signify in the sphere of cognition. Are sensory experience and ethical experience strictly comparable?

Meredy: There is of course no resemblance but only parallelism between them, each having for its starting point unreflective acquiescence in the given. Indeed, at each and every level of experience such acquiescence is the initial posture which precipitates the difficulties requisite for the dialectical process. Thus the ingenuous society, directly impinging on the consciousness of its members as an uncomplicated and indubitable fact, turns into a 'body politic' of considerable complexity, analogous to a thing possessed of perceivable qualities and relations, analogous to it chiefly in being fundamentally unstable. It is naïve acceptance of the given which here constitutes the sole basis of comparison between sense-certainty and social certainty, a comparison important only in foreshadowing a parallel development.

Hardith: The development of the ingenuous society appears predetermined by the structure peculiar to it, its ingenuousness, like that of sense-certainty, being at once ineluctable and untenable. Such a society must thus come to exemplify the dialectical necessity, which every type of consciousness is under, to move from initial self-sufficiency to ultimate self-alienation: its very ethos contains the seed of its subsequent pathos. Consideration of the former must obviously precede that of the latter. Of primary importance, therefore, is the morphology of the society destined to come to grief by the action of its members. Strange that for the study of the form characteristic of a commonwealth ruled by custom, Hegel does not depend on material furnished by history or anthropology. It is the ethos of a social order created or re-created by the poetic imagination which Hegel here subjects to minute analysis. What he describes is not an actual state but one required for the occurrence of the pathetic events depicted in Greek and especially Sophoclean tragedy. How typical of the ingenuous society is the structure of an ethical order demanded for the portrayal of the dramatic conflict in which an Antigone becomes involved? Whence the universal significance of the duality of laws which, inspired by Sophocles, Hegel treats as corresponding to the two sexes?

Meredy: It cannot be reiterated too often that persuasions or attitudes expressed in imaginative form seem to Hegel not seldom to excel in verisimilitude those open to 'empirical' verification. Only those intent on interpreting the *Phenomenology* as a chronicle of actual experience will be baffled by his lavish use of literary subject matter. But the bafflement has its basis solely in attempts to read into the text an historical design. I have said this before and will probably say it again. Thus the structural details of the ethical order here examined are unmistakably derived from Sophocles. The two laws on which Hegel lays his chief stress are precisely those that govern Antigone's society. Each law, having a different source, appears just as authoritative as the other. One, which Hegel calls the Human Law, is overt, being ever present in the prescribed customs to which the city owes its status as an organized community; the other, which he describes as the Divine Law, is hidden in shadowy tradition, no man knowing its origin, defying formal codification, and addressing itself

190

exclusively to individual conscience. The human law is the law of the day, visible as it is in the familiar and prevailing customs; the other is the law of the night, deeply rooted in the dim and immemorial past. These two laws appear as powers determining the nature of Antigone's conduct; one resides in the legally constituted government of the state, the other emanates from the inner recesses of consciousness dominated by the unwritten precepts of family piety. Being the structural components of the ingenuous society, the two powers, political and familial, can be distinguished but not separated. The moment of universality, in Hegel's idiom, is represented by the state, the moment of particularity by the family, both together belonging to the ethos of Antigone's world. The distinction between the claims of the community and the claims of the family (which is a community within the community) is obviously not without general significance.

Hardith: How unequal are the roles assigned to the two powers! Envisaging the social structure as essentially Sophoclean, Hegel preempts for the state all the functions distinctly ethical, leaving to the family the task of preserving intact the individual's individuality. The individuality which the individual enjoys in the family is markedly different from that which he attains in the larger community. In the latter he is a citizen, being spokesman or agent for the universal, and only in specific relation to it does his individuality become determinate. This relation, strictly functional, serves to differentiate the various members of the community. To the family, however, the relation of the individual has for its basis consanguinity or love, involving an emotive rather than an operative principle of individuation. With the line between the functional and the sentimental so sharply drawn, what ethical process vis-à-vis the individual could possibly devolve upon the family? Is it not the process of safeguarding the individual's enduring and inalienable individuality? If so, what actual self could be amenable to that process? No man can be separated from the community in which alone he can live and act. Accordingly, not as living but as dead does the individual wholly belong to the family, and the family in turn is distinguished from the state by its exclusive claim to complete possession of its defunct members. As Hegel phrases the matter, "Because it is as citizen that he is real and substantial, the individual belongs to the family only when, ceasing to be a citizen, he becomes an unreal and ineffectual shadow." The only true member of the family is thus a dead member! What an egregious paradox!

Meredy: Yes, a paradox. And is it not one that lies at the root of Antigone's tragic dilemma in connection with a slain member of her family? Apart from this for the present, and apart too from any principle of individuation, the really crucial issue turns on the manner in which the individual *can* belong to such distinct groups as the state and the family. Although he does belong to both, his ways of belonging to them are clearly not the same. Parenthetically, the contentions advanced earlier that the self belongs principally to himself have become obsolete, the experiment with subjective individualism having been tried and abandoned. We are now in the realm of spirit, a realm of 'world-forms', of which the ingenuous society is the first manifestation. And the world-form whose ethos we are considering derives its very significance from the two powers inherent in it, its inevitable pathos ensuing from their ultimate collision. But confining ourselves meanwhile to a description of its ethos, what we find is that the self, far from being, speaking mathematically, an 'independent variable', is intimately fused with the values and fortunes of the two powers that constitute his ethical sphere. Each power represents a distinct group subject to its own laws, the interests of which are not extraneous but essential to those of its members. The two groups being noninterchangeable and noncompetitive, the individual who belongs to both can obviously not belong to them in identical fashion. Membership in one entails duties not commensurable with the duties which memberships in the other calls for. And by contrast with the ethical claims of citizenship, what familial claims not proceeding from sentiment remain to be based on a sense of moral obligation? It is this general question to which Hegel's analysis gives rise, and from the analysis it would seem to follow ineluctably that the family has preemptive right solely to its dead members whose decease terminates their active membership in the community.

Hardith: The conclusion would indeed appear inevitable if the analysis were concerned merely with the implications of a particular work of dramatic art. But Hegel alleges to be portraying a universal form of spirit. The delineation of the two powers, for example, depends entirely on the special and local situation in which an Antigone is involved, without relevance save to her own predicament. Imagine a tragic dilemma caused by an unburied corpse! A vengeful king, obedient to political custom, forbids the burial, while the sister of the slain is moved to defiance by scruples of religious piety. How representative are the characters and how typical the circumstances? One wonders whether, without the tragedy of Sophocles, it would ever have occurred to Hegel to see in burial an act of supremely ethical importance. This act, ordained by divine law, is here depicted as if it constituted a spiritual challenge to death. Death, so Hegel argues, has the peculiar effect of uniting the individual with universal matter. The living individual is a particular person, once dead, however, he becomes, through bodily corruption, indistinguishable from abstract being. Hence a twofold duty of the bereaved family to the deceased members: it must not surrender completely their last phase of being to nature alone but should in relation to that phase assert by some prescribed deed the right of consciousness; and then, too, it must rescue the dead from oblivion by providing suitable mementos of their continuing association with the Penates of the family. No wonder that burial, which adds to death a moral dimension, should appear as a positive ethical act towards the individual, being indeed the only act consonant with the divine law, for every other ethical relation pertains to the human law through the operation of which the individual is lifted above the confinement within the family circle. All this must strike the critical reader as speculation without much pertinency beyond the compass of a Greek literary product.

Meredy: Your criticism is not unjust and may be fortified by Hegel's further discussion of the two laws with particular reference to the sexes. How great is his dependence on the ancient tragedy for a paradigmatic structure of the ingenuous society! The details he dwells upon are excessive and tedious, some appearing quite forced and others downright trivial. Nevertheless the general theme treated is of perennial importance. The corpse, whose burial becomes such a bone of contention, does not much matter; it is but a symbolic occasion for the contrast between the two kinds of law—governmental and familial—controlling human conduct. The social order, requiring both, cannot be realized without their undisturbed interaction, one sex safeguarding one kind of law, the other sex the other kind. When both are in accord, as they often appear to be, all's well; but grave are the consequences when convictions rooted in conscience are forced to remain unheeded at the bidding of the state. The incidents and ways of behavior involved in the *Antigone* are indeed remote, and Hegel's interpretation of them is certainly labored. But in spite of this, the issues he raises are not headed for obsolescence, the issue, in particular, relating to woman's place in the world as contrasted with man's. What society, be it ever so modern, is not concerned with it?

Hardith: Yes, Hegel extracts from Sophocles's play an attitude to the female of the species far from archaic. 'Woman's place is confined to the home'—this is the insight, hardly original or profound, which the author of the *Phenomenology* gains from a meticulous study of the *Antigone!* The division of labor prescribed by the two laws is a division strictly sexual. The division is embedded in the very culture of which Hegel himself is the product. His interpretation of the tragedy

193

is accordingly not free from bias. Man is here depicted not merely as the other sex. His is the primary sex. It is he who rules and commands, plays in society the sovereign part, decides the issues of life and death. What Hegel calls the human law is but half human, law made and executed exclusively by the human male. Woman, being the secondary sex, thus comes to occupy a subordinate position; her principal domain is the household, her chief concern is the family, her sole power is love. And the love that moves her differs in kind, depending upon whether she is wife or mother, daughter or sister. With but one exception, woman's varied relationship is essentially emotive and not, in Hegel's use of the term, purely ethical. It is the relationship between brother and sister he considers unique; they meet as free and equal individualities, not governed by desire as are husband and wife, nor depending on each other as are parents and children. Woman's supreme fulfillment, viewed in its ethical significance, ultimately lies in her relation as sister. No wonder Hegel can declare that "the loss of a brother is thus irreparable to the sister, and her duty towards him is the highest." This, but for the influence of Sophocles, Hegel could have hardly proclaimed as universal. For none but a particular woman related to a particular brother feels in the *Antigone* impelled to perform a particular duty believed to be ordained by a law not of today and not of human—that is, of male origin. But, alas, not every woman is blessed with a brother. And if towards a brother alone is her duty paramount, does it not follow that towards any other member of her family woman's duty must remain morally impure and incomplete? A curious conclusion, indeed, and more curious still is the implication that woman's office as guardian of the divine law must undergo, if she happens to be brotherless, a radical diminution in ethical stature.

Meredy: Hegel's attempt to graft on the basic structure of ancient society details chiefly drawn from a work of art does lay him open to the charge of confusing a typical theme with but a single variation of it. His emphasis on the ethical purity of woman's duty towards a brother is a case in point. Whence the necessity of a sense of obligation so high and so noble? One thing is *dramatic* necessity conditioning the plot and action within a particular tragedy, quite another is the *social* necessity germane to a commonwealth under the governance of laws which, though differing in origin, are equal in authoritativeness. Of such a commonwealth there might conceivably be versions not involving in their structure the peculiar relationship between brother and sister, Hegel here treats as if it were universal. Not misplaced therefore is the irony prompting your comment on the ethical plight of woman born brotherless. What then is the symbolic meaning of the

Antigone? Of what spiritual ethos entailing its appropriate pathos is the tragedy a typical expression? Is it not the ethos of a community subject to two kinds of law containing seeds of divided loyalty? The state and the family constitute spheres of interest that are indeed concentric but each is ruled by fundamental imperatives of its own, and neither can surrender its claim to autonomy. In the claim to autonomy on the part of these spheres lies the universal significance of Sophocles's tragedy, everything else being secondary, requisite only for its dramatic construction. Hegel's detailed analysis of the play, seeking to incorporate all of its aspects into the structure of a bifurcated order, tends to defeat the very purpose of the *Phenomenology,* a work concerned with the general or recurrent forms of consciousness. But thus far our discussion has centered mainly on the morphology of a commonwealth whose two major structural components appear coequal but not coeval. It is a commonwealth destined to decline and to fall: its two-pronged ethos leads through action to an inevitable pathos.

3. *The Tragedy of Conflicting Imperatives*

Hardith: The two laws so deeply embedded in the structure of ancient society would seem to collide only when crises arise that require action at the bidding of the one or of the other. Such laws are distinguishable but inseparable components of its ethical substance. Descriptive merely of the ethos to which they are fundamental, the laws emanate from powers upon whose stable equilibrium the life of the community depends. All's well and all's serene as long as the functions belonging to the state and those preempted by the family are free from mutual encroachment. It is as if such a happy society once existed, held in balance by complementary powers, as complementary as the sexes between which they are divided, each dominant in a different sphere of vital interest and purpose. In what eulogistic fashion Hegel describes this idyllic condition! Here the whole is the harmony of all its parts, and every part derives satisfaction from being an integral part of the whole. It is thus, and only thus, that the ethical order can appear as a world without taint or guilt, untroubled by internal strife. Passage from one power to the other is a process free from friction, each needing and sustaining the other. Their division, being one of function, can in principle not lead to opposition. The rules of life are laid down by custom and tradition, and everyone knows immediately what is prescribed and what prohibited. That man should turn from the distaff side to take his place in the world, while woman remains bound by the bonds of the household, comes to be accepted without question, the ethical role of each sex being assigned by nature and fixed by convention. Of this established order Antigone is the product, an order not revealing its latent instability until she, as well as the existing ruler of the state, is called upon to act. The necessity of overt action involves her in a desperate dilemma, forced as she is to choose between irreconcilable imperatives: to act in obedience to the demands of piety is to defy the will of the state; to act in obedience to the government is to violate the rights of the family. In this tragic conflict of imperatives Hegel sees the inevitable dissolution of society in this form. Here again Hegel depends for his generalization solely on what he gleans from or reads into Greek tragedy.

Meredy: Of the abstract features belonging to the ingenuous society your epitome is admirably luminous. A social structure separated from individual action must perforce appear abstract, in any sense of the term, and especially in the Hegelian. Apart from individual action, mere morphology, whether of the self or the community, is the morphology of shadows. The dynamic individual alone can aspire to true individuality. The self is what the self does. And the community, too, lives in and through the deeds of its members. This being so, an individual's duty can thus not be made amenable to principles purely formal. Once again Hegel seizes the opportunity of attacking Kant. The imperative to do one's duty must indeed be deemed categorical. But whence its categorical validity? Not by individual conscience is duty decided in ancient society. No struggle there between passion and duty or collision between duty and duty. This Hegel dismisses as 'comical'. In the ingenuous society duty appears single and, so to speak, impassioned, known immediately to everyone, and the attempt to define or justify it by a universal formula would simply seem downright preposterous. The social order prescribes what is to be done. That and nothing else is the individual's duty. Nature, Hegel insists, and not fortuitousness of circumstance or caprice of choice, assigns one sex to one law, the other to the other law. It is through the two sexes that the powers of state and family find their natural expression and ethical significance. And the duty of individuals consists in unquestioning conformity to the laws governing their action, laws explicit and current or embodied in immemorial custom.

Hardith: But these laws, as observed earlier, though structurally complementary, come to function as rival guides to action. The *Antigone* would have been written in vain, forfeiting all claim to verisimilitude, if the mounting tension between two irreconcilable powers did not constitute the heart of the matter. In spite of Hegel's argument to the contrary, the martyrdom of the heroine follows inevitably from the fatal collision of duties. This collision, deprecated by him as comic when criticizing Kant, becomes in the *Antigone* deeply tragic, for the duties colliding, again Hegel notwithstanding, appear undeniably absolute. The ethical persuasions of both major characters are of like imperiousness. Creon can act in accordance with nothing but the demand for the safety of the government; Antigone can act in accordance with nothing but the dictates of piety. The whole tragedy hinges on the fact that neither character is able to contravene an ethical persuasion felt with elemental passion to involve a categorical imperative. Yet the claim to paramountcy for but one of the contending persuasions cannot be renounced. No wonder then that the defenders of one law should ever accuse of perfidy the defenders of the other law. Action by the state must thus appear cruel to those invoking imperatives more authoritative than political, while action by those in support of extra-political commands must seem to the agents of the state perverse or corrosive. The duality of laws turns through action into a dualism of allegiances; the duality, being one of complementaries, belongs to the ethos of the ancient world as here envisaged, the dualism of absolute warring claims engenders its ultimate pathos. Is this not the gist of the dialectic in the present section?

Meredy: It is not necessary to debate the issue you raise concerning the collision of duties; that Kant and Sophocles are not so far apart as Hegel contends, and contends with not too convincing a cogency, can certainly be maintained. But this is a digressive matter and hardly essential to the course of the dialectic. Hegel finds it apparently irresistible to engage whenever possible in polemic against Kant. More to the point is your felicitous distinction between the duality of laws and the dualism of allegiances. How clearly it illuminates Hegel's preoccupation with the *Antigone!* For he sees in the tragedy an authentic expression of a universal theme. To his dramatic vision society appears as if continually shaped and transformed by ever-recurring Antigones. Are not the Antigones of the world the impassioned champions of ideals running afoul of the established order? Such individuals are not rebels who take the law into their own hands. They are the very models of loyalty. But their loyalty is either to traditions from which the present rules have swerved or to values of the future which those in power abhor. The ethical persuasions of the Antigones are as compelling as those actuating the Creons, the defenders of the existing state of affairs who regard as subversive all opposition to things as they are.

Hardith: I will refrain from urging in rebuttal that your recurrent Creons and Antigones are scarcely as pronounced as the actual characters of the tragedy. Granting, however, the sweeping generalization you read into or extract from the text, for Hegel the characters simply

197

represent powers equal in moral autonomy but not equal in coercive force. Within the ethical substance, the state alone is fully conscious of real power, conscious, that is, of being in possession of physical means to enforce its decrees; the power of the family is on a relatively unconscious level, a power but vaguely felt, being without any but spiritual force by which to exercise its authority. To the division of the ethical *substance* into conscious and unconscious powers corresponds the division within the ethical *subject* of knowledge and ignorance. On the latter division Hegel lays great stress: the individual's guilt and pathos are bound up with it. In being exclusively loyal to one of the powers, the individual is apt to take little cognizance of the claims of the other. Although the ethical substance is embodied in both powers together, to the partisan it appears as if it were wholly present in but one. In such unwitting guilt lies the individual's pathos; he defends the ethical order against what he falsely supposes to be violence or caprice but in so doing he precipitates warfare between powers equally objective and equally indefeasible. Does guilt consist in action by those unknowingly challenging the rights of one of the powers? How then should Antigone's action be explained? She clearly knows that by keeping faith with the sacred obligation to the family she must act in opposition to the laws of the state.

Meredy: Let us attend first to the notion of guilt which action in the ingenuous society necessarily entails, postponing for the moment reference to Antigone's special case. It is Hegel's contention that in such a society no act can escape turning into guilt; unaware of the ineradicable doubleness of the social order, the individual must offend one power whenever he acts in obedience to the other. Failure to recognize at this stage the nature of society as bipartite is to do violence to its peculiar ethos. The deeds of the individual, if related to but one of the dual powers, are thus inescapably tainted with guilt and not infrequently with crime. In conforming to but one ethical law, consciousness affronts the other; the irony being that in a society as thus constituted, every law-abiding person inevitably becomes at the same time a lawbreaker. Hence innocence—and this is the crowning paradox —belongs solely to inaction, comparable, as Hegel so drastically phrases it, to the mere being of a stone, a state which is not even true of a child.

Hardith: The fact that guilt inheres in the nature of action would seem to absolve the individual from all personal responsibility for his conduct. It is as if his behavior had been preordained to reveal itself always as incorrigibly wrong. Yet upon no particular individual can the burden of wrongdoing be laid, as if by free volition he could have chosen to act in a different manner. No longer consulting the oracle of his private conscience, the individual can here not act as he pleases. He is but a shadow apart from the social order in which alone he finds his concrete reality, and it is the social order which prescribes what should be done or not done. But consider how striking is the ambivalence of individual action! Primarily, guilt adheres to action and not to the actor. And it adheres to action simply because the ethical substance is of two powers all compact and permits the existence within it of an ultimate dualism of imperatives. The logic of the situation requires that the individual, though bearing no personal responsibility for deeds he is called upon to perform as agent of the community, is nevertheless fated to perform them by defying one imperative in obeying the other. Is it fatalism in which at this stage the dialectic of action culminates?

Meredy: Yes, over the ancient world, as Hegel interprets it, following closely the dramatization of life in Greek tragedy, hovers an inexorable destiny. Whichever law, human or divine, individual action is in harmony with, the action cannot avoid being culpable and thus inviting disaster. The law violated by exclusive fidelity to its rival reveals itself as hostile and revengeful. The offended power, ever covertly present, comes out of concealment and shows its wrath directly the irrevocable deed is done. This is the hopeless situation depicted in the Oedipus trilogy of Sophocles. Destiny, which here operates as if it were the chief dramatis persona, predetermines the crime and its guilt. In developing further the dialectical relation of guilt to action, Hegel makes copious references to the trilogy, showing the contrast between the unwitting conduct of Oedipus and the deliberate one of Antigone, and showing, too, that in the catastrophic behavior of each an omnipotent fate makes its appearance.

Hardith: How different is the use which Hegel makes of Sophocles! From the *Antigone* he derives the duality of laws and the notion of inevitable guilt attaching to action at the command of one law deemed of superior authority; from the *Oedipus* he infers more the fatalism than the culpability of action, the contrast between the two laws remaining rather obscure or attenuated, with the result that the action is so unpremeditated as to seem almost innocent. Oedipus is clearly less responsible for his behavior than Antigone and his tragedy is accordingly a greater manifestation of Fate. Is the tragedy of the one more tragic than that of the other? Why?

Meredy: There is for Hegel no difference in principle whether the violated law is or is not present to the doer's consciousness. He holds, however, the ethical consciousness to be more complete and the guilt

199

purer if the doer knows beforehand the law and the power to be opposed and, defying them as wanton and arbitrary, openly and dauntlessly, like Antigone, commits the crime. But the essence of tragedy is here not the issue. Hegel returns to this important theme at a later stage of the *Phenomenology* in connection with the dialectic of religion. The works of Sophocles, though differing in many respects, have in this context a common significance. It is this. Acknowledgment of guilt, whether by an Antigone or an Oedipus, is acknowledgment that the law violated is no less real or no less necessary than the law from obedience to which guilt ensues. But to acknowledge that the law opposed and flouted enjoys the same right as the law followed and defended is to pass beyond an ethical community subject to customary powers sanctioning conflicting imperatives. In the new order growing out of the old the concept of right supplants the concept of custom. If the ingenuous society is one the laws of which are reducible to rules of conduct having their source in convention and tradition, a society governed by laws based on human rights, might well be called the ingenious society.

Hardith: What a felicitous name you choose for the order into which the ingenuous society makes its transition! Much ingenuity indeed must be involved in making socially basic or central a concept so notorious for its ambiguity. What is right? Is it to be understood in a moral or a juristic sense? Should its application be confined to the sphere of individual behavior? Or is the domain of its relevance much wider?

Meredy: Your questions are premature. They do, however, justify my description of the society to which a concept so rich in connotation will be found so essential. But before proceeding let me indicate by way of summary the dialectical advance. The two powers in control of the ingenuous society become transformed in the process of recognizing the fateful consequences which obedience to them entails. For neither power has any advantage over its rival: the victory of one is the other's defeat; nor can either afford to be victorious without mortally injuring the ethical substance. Dissolution of the ethical substance in this form is thus latent in the contradiction of the laws emanating from the two powers that constitute its intrinsic nature. The power of the state in suppressing the power of the family suppresses what it cannot dispense with. The family thus remains to mock at the state's pretension to absoluteness. Woman, whom Hegel describes as "the everlasting irony in the life of the community," changes by various devices the universal aims of the state into individual ends and transforms its public undertakings into private activities of such or such specific men.

200

Every high achievement of the community woman is prone to look upon as redounding to the glory of some person dear to her. The accomplishment is not the government's but that of father or husband, son or brother. Nothing indeed that takes place in the world beyond the distaff side fails to be drawn within the range of feminine wiles. Woman has the knack of reducing everything to a level purely personal. And she not seldom stoops to conquer by intrigue or chicanery. This recrudescence of individualism, which Hegel's indictment of womanhood is intended to point up, the state cannot tolerate. How should the community preserve itself without uprooting its spirit? Even war, one way in which the community asserts the right of the whole over the individual, cannot suppress the rights of the family, rights ultimately those of its constituent members. It is thus that the old order changes making way for the new, the new designed to resolve the contradictions inherent in the old.

Condition of Right and Legal Personality

Hardith: This brief section is altogether too brief. The material, drawn from the history of Roman Law, would seem to merit treatment no less detailed than the treatment accorded to the material derived from Greek tragedy. Hegel speaks in almost cavalier fashion of what he simply calls *Rechtszustand,* a theme intrinsically complex and undeniably momentous in the life of the human spirit. Why such slight consideration of a subject so important?

Meredy: Here again it is not irrelevant to enter a caveat against the historical fallacy which may be easily committed in connection with the *Phenomenology.* The relation Hegel here seeks to establish between the Greek city state and the Roman empire can hardly be regarded as causal. To account for the decline of Athens and the rise of Rome, requiring reference to determinate events subject to the principle of explanation by cause and effect, is a task devolving upon the historian rather than the dialectician. With local and dated phenomena the author of this treatise is not concerned; his themes are generic ideas freely extracted from specific contexts in which they may or may not appear completely embedded or embodied. Thus Hegel refers not to the literal history of the city state but to a literary idealization of it, and even its dramatized form in tragedy serves but to illustrate a typically human situation. The reference to a social order based on a system of jurisprudence, such as the Roman, is likewise studiously allusive, intended, if I may say so, merely to point a dialectical moral. From a simple commonwealth held together by custom and tradition to an imperial state involving rights maintained by the rule of law the transition need not be conceived in terms exclusively temporal. Dialectical necessity alone here determines the passage from one to the other. Given a community resting on a duality of powers, the division of whose authority is such that active fidelity to one power entails

guilty opposition to the other, given a community inherently so unstable, and its supersedure by a higher type becomes inevitable, higher
because the conflicting powers, together with their equally just claims,
appear capable of regulation and adjustment through a body of laws
applicable alike to rights private and public. The illustration from
Roman history represents a particular variation of a universal theme,
and only such of its aspects Hegel dwells upon as the dialectic at this
stage clearly calls for.

Hardith: Let us assume then that passage from the customary to
the juristic society, though historically exemplifiable, is here to be construed as purely dialectical. But could such passage be made without
reinvesting the individual with an independent status? The two powers
in control of the pre-juristic society leave the individual in a fatally
precarious condition, his doom being sealed whichever power compels
his exclusive obedience. From this hopeless situation the dialectical
escape lies in the conception of a social order organized on a non-
fatalistic or rational foundation, an order, that is, depending upon
legal definition and equitable enforcement of private rights and public
duties, the subjects of rights and duties now coming to be regarded
explicitly as individual persons. With the accent on the individual once
again, does such conception constitute a real advance? Does it not
rather involve a return to an individualistic position abandoned earlier?

Meredy: Yes, we do revert to individualism but to one of an
entirely different kind. The individualism here emerging presupposes
an elaborate social context the ethos of which is no longer determined
by the pathetic interplay of forces directed by custom and tradition.
The new ethos has for its basis juristic principles, and these, embodied
in codes and statutes, prescribe what within the legal system of the
community the individual may claim and what he must forgo. Such
ethos, though generating a pathos of its own, is clearly an improve-
ment on the ethos it supplants. Within the legal framework of society
the individual is released from the bondage to fate, for his, and only
his, is the responsibility for any action deemed judicially transgressive.

Hardith: What sort of individuality can the individual enjoy within
such a social structure? His personality other than legal can receive no
adequate recognition. No personal distinction attaches to any person
entitled in principle to the same treatment to which every other person
is subject: equality before the law is here a cardinal assumption. Upon
atomic units alone, to which the spiritually distinct members of society
must first be reduced, can legal equality be conferred. Inevitably blind
to the countless ways in which individuals differ, the law refines the

notion of a juristic personality, turning it into a universal quality identical in any and every subject of rights and duties. The two so-called laws of the ingenuous society—the human and the divine—now become ingeniously merged into a single abstraction reified as 'The Law'. That which before appeared as the divine law has in fact, so Hegel declares, come out of its dark concealment to the full light of day. Formerly, the individual could not as such be called real save as blood relation, acquiring separate personality only after death; now, however, the living individual receives recognition as a separate person-ality but a personality conceived solely in legal terms. Either form of separateness is of course an abstraction. To be sure, a person living is preferable to a person dead; yet a person *merely* legal is an entity no less abstract: it is his destiny to share with other abstract entities the status of being nothing more than an independent subject of ab-stract rights and duties.

Meredy: How can the realm of law be other than a realm of ab-stractions? The law hypostatized is clearly an abstract universal, for under it are subsumed or comprehended all the diverse codes and statutes; and the legal person, denoting any entity coming under its jurisdiction, is no less universal and no less abstract. There is here a necessary relation, if I may say so, between impersonal legality and legal personality, the first adjective (impersonal) being synonymous with impartial, the second (legal) merely signifies capacity for rights and obligations. If in one sense the law is no respecter of persons, in another, and because of its assumed impartiality, the law must accord equal respect to all persons with claims on justice, the independence of each and every claimant being here a fundamental postulate.

Hegel notes a profound analogy between stoicism and legalism both in origin and result (origin as well as result to be understood of course as dialectical). The thought of stoic independence has its source in the bifurcation that develops within the consciousness of master and slave in the course of their external relations; independence by juristic definition is also the outcome of a prior bifurcation. But what in stoicism is an individual attitude becomes the legal basis of an empire. And the independence alleged to be enjoyed by the members of an imperial society is as remote from their actual and concrete life as the independence merely thought by the stoic; independence is equally abstract and unreal whether confined to the limbo of stoic self-con-sciousness or conserved in the formal locution of the law. Hegel's man-ner of dealing with this theme is cursory, but since what is here epito-mized is but a recapitulation on a social scale of the dialectical process exhibited in connection with the stoic's self-consciousness, more than brief mention of a previous analysis must have seemed to him super-fluous.

Hardith: But stoicism, as we know, is followed by scepticism and scepticism by the unhappy consciousness. Does legalism correspond to stoicism in result as well as origin? May one speak in social terms of a sceptical or unhappy consciousness?

Meredy: The dialectic is parallel rather than repetitive. Carried to extreme lengths, legalism brings in its train doubt or negation of the person's inner personality to which the law is indifferent or in-applicable, and this inevitably culminates in an unhappy estrangement between the individual as a spiritual being and the world subject primarily or principally to standards derived from jurisprudence. For nothing in a legalized society is so fortuitous and expendable as the concrete and nonlegal person. What ultimately matters therein is legality of form and legality of procedure from which no specific content should be exempt. The law must be made to prevail as absolute and universal—at whatever cost to the individual, the individual being but a person involved in the meshes of abstract right. Hence, as Hegel remarks, to designate an individual as mere person is to use a term of contempt, a contempt which even in English may be conveyed through a certain inflection.

Hardith: Whence the power of the law to reduce concrete in-dividuals to the status of abstract persons? What is the source of its authority? How long could a society endure in the absence of a sov-ereign's legitimate authority capable of maintaining and enforcing 'law and order'? And in what is legitimacy grounded?

Meredy: To these questions the text contains the requisite an-swers but couched in Hegel's forbidding idiom. Their gist may be paraphrased as follows: In a world of mere persons it could not but come to pass that a particular person should boldly declare that in his own self lies the source of all power and all authority. Proclaiming himself lord and master of the world, he—the single and solitary in-dividual—becomes transformed into the absolute person. And having challenged and conquered all, he celebrates his triumphant universality by daring to assume the sovereignty of a 'living God', his apotheosis marking the spiritual gulf between the one and the many. But how precarious is the relation of an emperor deified to the persons of lesser breed subject to his will! All is indeed well as long as men submit with-out reluctance to the edicts of a Caesar. But let him beware of the fury when, the glory of his exalted personality gradually fading, the authority of sovereign power to which he lays claim faces effective opposition!

Hardith: The allusion is of course to the long history of the Roman

Empire but simplified and telescoped for the purpose of fitting it into the design of the dialectic. Hegel's highly condensed treatment of so large and complex a segment of human history can hardly be said to be free from distortion. For some readers it may perhaps have the significance of a masterly miniature but to many others it must rather seem like a grotesque caricature.

Meredy: Whether Hegel's sketch of imperial Rome should pass muster as having some verisimilitude or be rejected outright as travesty is beside the point. Remarkable here is simply the portrait of a society drawn chiefly if not exclusively in terms of its jurisprudence. The portrait, though imaginative, dictated solely by the exigencies of the dialectic, is not altogether imaginary, as the historical material exemplifying it abundantly shows. And how adroit is the use which Hegel makes of the material! For what follows from his analysis is the necessary emergence of an ingenious society, as we have agreed to call it, differing from the preceding ingenuous society by the command of rational means for transcending the double powers and the double imperatives characteristic of the city state, the fatal collision of which determines its inevitable decline and supersession.

But in the process of overcoming the difficulties inherent in the ingenuous society, the ingenious society develops difficulties of its own, and these turn out to center in a dualism even more radical. On the one hand, there is the abstract legal person profoundly divided from the individual's concrete personality which exists beyond the reach of the law. On the other hand, there is the legal person as subject of right and the absolute person as sovereign from whose might alone all right derives. The experiment with a society, such as the Roman, but not necessarily or wholly Roman, thus proves abortive—abortive only because the difficulties generated, which are more formidable than those supplanted, involve at a deeper level the individual's unhappy self-alienation. The process of culture, the next theme to be examined, sharpens and intensifies that contrast between the formal and real aspects of human personality which the diagnosis of pure legalism was intended to adumbrate.

Self-Alienation Through Culture

1. Preface to the Cultural Process

Hardith: As Hegel approaches the new theme—his comprehensive designation of it is *Bildung,* denoting a process of formation and transformation—he briefly dwells upon the transition from the preceding analysis to the dialectic to follow. Each of the two social embodiments of spirit so far considered leads inevitably to the individual's pathetic estrangement from a world the ethos of which is marked by a fundamental doubleness. In the city state, the duality of opposed sets of custom is such that allegiance to one set entails violation of the other, a violation tainted with guilt and attended by disaster. In the imperial state, there is the dichotomy, on the one hand, between subject and sovereign, and, on the other, between the individual as legal person and the self-conscious personality with which the law is not concerned. A social order reduced to its legal level must presuppose the existence of individuals as if they were but atomic entities, a presupposition requisite for the application of the universal laws of the land to all alike; and the individuals composing this order, aware of being more than legal persons, must come to apprehend it as if it were an alien reality inimical to their uniquely determinate personalities. The diagnostic outcome of legalism would thus seem even more dispiriting than that of a society divided by custom. And yet Hegel deems the former superior in spiritual meaning and value. How curious!

Meredy: A world dominated by law, in distinction from one ruled by custom, depends for its genesis and development on man's deliberate spiritual effort. Law is spiritual not merely in the sense of owing its creation to mind, it is spiritual in the deeper sense of having been explicitly designed for the purpose of serving as rational basis of a social order. As instrument governing the comportment of men in relation to one another with particular reference to their individual rights and mutual obligations, law is a spiritual achievement par excellence. The individual's failure to recognize the spiritual significance of law as a controlling force in the life of society belongs to the pathos of an ethos still grounded in abstract universals. Small wonder that the solitary individual in whom the authority of sovereign power is vested should at this stage appear as if he were a mere person owing his position to the accidents of birth or circumstance. Accordingly, the rule of law, far from being acknowledged as a positive function of a spiritual process, seems rather as the negation of objectives prized by separate individuals. And this very estrangement between the individual and his world Hegel shows to be dialectically necessary for advancing to more adequate expressions of spirituality.

Hardith: Yet the more adequate versions of spirituality, as Hegel hints in the short preface, will all be found to exemplify ever deeper forms of estrangement. Thus the state of culture, succeeding the state of law, produces conditions similarly disjunctive, adaptation to which requires the individual to live a double life, so to speak, the life of social conformity and a life of inward self-assertion. It is a self-assertion that consists in the freedom to entertain the belief in a world other than the present, prompted by the insight into the futile ends of the established order. But this insight, involving transvaluation of the prevailing values, proves ambivalent. One thing is the insight culminating in faith in a world beyond the spurious standards of civilization, quite another is the insight inducing doubt and rejection of the reigning norms of conduct. The rhythmic alternation of faith and doubt to which insight gives rise calls for clarification, a task destined to be achieved at this stage by enlightenment (if this be an adequate translation of the pregnant term *Aufklärung*). Enlightenment grown pervasive constitutes the very essence of spiritual impoverishment. Of this movement from one form of estrangement to another Hegel promises to trace in detail the dialectical necessity. Culture, it would seem, represents a phase of spirit that reaches through a process of self-alienation its climacteric in complete loss of spirituality. What a paradox!

Meredy: The paradox is ineradicable from the type of consciousness under consideration. Hegel's long chapter on culture is but an interlude in the life of spirit, one marked by progressive diminution of spirituality resulting in progressive intensification of self-alienation experienced by the individual. Thus, the loss of concrete personality in a world of abstractly legal persons has its analogue in a state of culture based on sacrifice of the natural to the artificial individual. The life of man's inward self remains the antipode to the formal and polished ways governing his external behavior. And enlightenment, a necessary

208

phase of culture, intent on clarifying the self's self-division, enhances the felt division still further. For clarification, growing into a cult of the superficial, tends to deny or to distort such concerns of spirit as are still hidden or recalcitrant and thus unclarifiable. Inexpungible from the dialectic of culture is accordingly man's self-alienation it perforce generates. Of this dialectic the final outcome is revolution, signifying both the process of revolving back to the supremacy of the individual and the process of ushering in a reign of terror. Not in the sphere of culture can the individual's aspiration to absolute freedom find expression, culminating as it there does in universal frenzy and destruction. This sphere must be exchanged for that of the inward moral consciousness where alone absolute freedom may be sought and perhaps found.

All this, however, is anticipatory. We must proceed first to a diagnosis of social conduct under conditions of cultural uniformity and conformity. How designate a society held together by ties chiefly cultural? If ingenuous is a social order ruled by custom and ingenious one governed by law, an order subject to forces or powers determinative of the individual's manner and taste may be called artificial.

2. The Artificial Society and the Factitious Individual

Hardith: Since cultural and artificial are here considered synonymous, what precisely are we to understand by *Bildung* which is Hegel's term for the process making for individual as well as social self-alienation? Are *Bildung* and culture words strictly cognate? Like civilization, its closest equivalent, culture is a concept on which anthropology would seem to have a prerogative though not a preemptive claim. Hegel does not employ the concept as a generic name comprehending under it a variety of species. He confines himself to a particular species. The material he depends on for purposes of illustration is drawn entirely from a chosen segment of European history. His references are to modern movements such as the Renaissance, the Reformation, the Enlightenment. The singular civilization analyzed is that of France under the reign of Louis XIV, and the revolution alleged to be its culmination is the French Revolution. Repeated use of Diderot's *Le neveu de Rameau,* a literary creation of the same epoch, emphasizes Hegel's exclusive interest in cultural currents belonging to a definite age. Clearly, the dialectic can hardly be said to have for its object a pervasive process discernible as recurring under different conditions in different periods. Here as elsewhere excessive fidelity to certain dated events and ideas tends to jeopardize the purported generality of the dialectic. What Hegel says seems to apply solely to a unique form of culture. We know, however, that culture is a phenomenon varying with every age and every society, and what holds of one variant need not hold of another. It remains to be shown, and this Hegel fails to do, that alienation is not a particular concomitant of a particular expression of culture but is universally conjoined with every expression of it. Derivation of the dialectic from a specific phenomenon would appear to destroy both its universality and necessity. My difficulty might perhaps be removed or attenuated if *Bildung,* on which Hegel rings numerous changes, could be rendered by a concept less evocative of anthropology than culture.

Meredy: Yet culture is a term remarkably appropriate here—not in spite but because of its association with anthropology. For any state of culture owes its origin and evolution to human effort. Human agency operative in seeking and attaining certain ends distinguishes a state of culture from a state of nature. In this precisely lies the pregnant meaning Hegel ascribes to *Bildung.* It is a term denoting a process creative of norms and codes comporting with conditions of life that are factitious and thus more or less remote from their natural roots. However relative and variable be the remoteness of cultural from natural conditions, every culture, even the most primitive, exemplifies some distance from nature, and hence some degree of alienation from it, in virtue of which a type of culture is the type it is. Consider the word 'artifact': it denotes a fact but one the genesis of which is not natural. And if we enlarge its sense to connote whatever is formed by art, in distinction from that which is made by nature, culture comes to signify the aggregate of artifacts fashioned in a society at a given stage of its development as expression of its peculiar ethos. That man himself appears to resemble an artifact, as it were, a product of civilization trained to speak and to act in ways foreign to his nature, is culture's crowning achievement, and it is this apex of culture's career that Hegel is particularly concerned with.

Hardith: This sounds as if the matter could be reduced to the verbal level. Is but a nominal definition the basis for holding nature and culture to be opposites? If so, every cultural phenomenon becomes *eo ipso* a nonnatural phenomenon. And the individual, shaped by the civilizing forces of an artificial world, must—and again by definition—shed his natural idiosyncrasy and turn into a sort of artifact. But the dialectic is presumed to be more than a dialectic of words. He, for instance, whose status in society is that of an abstract legal person, must actually become spiritually depersonalized; and in developing into a man of culture, his daily behavior must evince the exemplary traits of a denatured *espèce,* a term Hegel borrows from *Rameau's Nephew.* The text illustrates the dialectic by passing directly from the imperialism of the Antonines to the royalism of Louis XIV. The flight from Rome to Versailles is of course purely imaginary, yet Hegel represents it as grounded in logical necessity.

Meredy: Imaginative rather than imaginary is the 'flight' you speak of. The transition from Roman Law to French Culture is here a supposed event with no claim on historicity. The subject matter of the *Phenomenology,* it scarce requires reiteration, consists of ways of experience and conduct conceived as generic, and as thus conceived the question of their chronology becomes totally irrelevant. Datable are not the genera exhibited but the species chosen to exemplify them. The illustrative material culled from such different sources makes abundantly clear that the genera are deliberately distilled from species empirically discoverable. Hegel's procedure, though highly imaginative, is emphatically not fanciful. The verisimilitude he aims at, as I have urged before, is more symbolic than actual. There should thus be no confusion between the conceived genera and their exemplary species. Unfortunately, the text contributes not a little to the confusion when a pervasive or recurrent type appears in form and expression as if it were identical with but a singular instance, with the result that the latter tends to usurp the universality to which only the former may lay claim. Against so deplorably a deceptive tendency we must be on our guard lest we ascribe dialectical necessity not to the universal modes of human thought and behavior but to their particular manifestations.

A case in point is the passage from the ingenious society to the artificial society or, if you prefer, from the jurisprudence of Rome to the culture of Versailles. The passage for Hegel is simply a transition from one form of spiritual depersonalization to another. Speaking generically, any society whose component members are but legal persons inevitably ignores and alienates their extralegal personalities: the individuals must accordingly come to experience increasingly a feeling of self-estrangement, since their legal and extralegal selves are condemned to remain essentially divided. It would seem to matter little whether under Rome's imperial rule spiritual depersonalization actually arose and spread in the manner Hegel depicts. Rome is but a pregnant illustration of consequences ineluctably following from the rampancy in any social order of abstract and formal rights. Yet by his exclusive allusion to but one instance of the predominance of law Hegel is apt to create the confusion between the contingency of an historical phenomenon and the necessity it is alleged to symbolize.

Such confusion is still more conspicuous in connection with culture: a definite species with a local habitation and name is treated as apparently exhaustive of the entire genus. As shown, however, any culture, wherever and whenever it flourishes, being a name for grafting upon nature forms and operations alien to it, must inevitably turn society into an artificial system and the individual into an artificial entity. Here again dialectical necessity belongs to the generic process creative of denatured individuals, a process operative in every culture, not confined to a specific expression typifying it more or less approximately. The historical type which Hegel chooses for detailed examination seems to him to provide an almost perfect example of a cultural process reaching its acme in individual as well as social self-estrangement.

Hardith: Very well. We shall then proceed to a discussion of a species of culture as if it were a faithful image of the genus. And let us admit at the outset that under such a species the individual is bound to live a double life, as it were, the life of social conformity and the life of mental isolation. In outward comportment he complies with the ruling fashion of the day—in speech, manners, dress, taste, opinion, and so on; in the privacy of his mind, to which he can always retire, he may wander as if in a forest free and untamed. The cultured or cultivated person must thus perforce present to the world a self essentially different from the self to whose inward thoughts and feelings he alone has direct access. It is this duality of selfhood which contains the seed of self-estrangement, a duality ultimately generative of an inevitable conflict between his overt and secret personality. And more crucial than the conflict is the individual's growing difficulty of recognizing his true personal identity. Where should he look for it? Should he seek it in his natural consciousness free from artificial influences or in his conscious behavior in behalf of values prevalent in his social system? This appears to be the essence of the matter as developed in what follows. Or am I mistaken?

Meredy: How often you manage to phrase the central issue in simple and concise language! Once again you hit the nail on the head. What is at stake in Hegel's analysis is indeed the kind of selfhood pertaining to those needed to sustain a state of culture. It is a state that can obviously not be realized except by individuals able to transcend a natural selfhood resisting social education and control. Culture and nature are mutually exclusive, and to live in the sphere of one requires withdrawal from the other. Thus none but denatured individuals can carry on the cultural process, and no group becomes the beneficiary of the process unless it exchange a natural for an artificial mode of being. That nature as such is uncivilized is a flagrant truism; her products, including human organisms, are able to persist without benefit of cultural discipline. It follows that moral judgments, with their predicates good and bad, are not pertinent to the behavior of those

212

living in a supposed state of nature. It is the conduct of denatured selves, serving as members of an artificial society, to whom alone moral judgments are here applicable. And the question of the standards that should govern such judgments now becomes the paramount issue.

Hardith: May I interrupt to ask whether your reference to *standards* is deliberate or inadvertent? I gather from the text that there is but a single standard to which cultured demeanor is amenable, and that standard is social conformity. The social code in a cultured society, as here depicted, must be generally uniform, and behavior not conformable to the uniform code thus comes to be looked upon as proceeding from perversity or eccentricity. Individual deviation from the universally accepted norm is deemed incompatible with the acknowledged supremacy of the cultured way of life, and unless complete conformity to it were practised, its supremacy would be exposed to jeopardy. Loss of idiosyncrasy here becomes the chief desideratum: it is an axiom of a cultured society that the conduct of ladies and gentlemen must always and unexceptionally be decorous. The person of distinction, strange to say, is virtually an outcast. What a paradox to view as offensive whatever appears original or unique in personal taste or bearing! Must peculiarity then be thought of as synonymous with uncouthness?

3. The Twin Pillars of Culture

Meredy: Speaking generally, conformity is indeed culture's supreme test, and departure from it by those intent upon acting in peculiar fashion constitutes a breach of etiquette. But there are different concrete applications of it, and its status as unitary criterion can hardly be more than formal or nominal. Consider the two powers which Hegel singles out as major pillars of a cultured society. He speaks of them as the power of the state and the power of wealth. Harmony with them turns out to be relative and variable, now one and now the other appears to have prior claim on individual allegiance. Of the first power Hegel says that it is the pervasive 'substance', the underlying condition as well as the ultimate fruition of spiritual selfhood, wherein the essential reality of individuals is expressed and the universality of their activity reflected. In other words, the power of the political state is the power of the individual writ large, submission to it being simply submission to the mainspring of law and order without which the cultured mode of living would be impossible. Opposed but actually complementary to the power of the state is the power of wealth, a power no less universal, exemplifying as it does the distribution of labor and enjoyment, each in his labor working for all, and all for each. The

213

assumption that economic power is wielded by private individuals engaged in private enterprise is here untenable. While it is true that wealth is the result of individual action and open to individual enjoyment, the entire process productive of enjoyable riches is a process incapable of being carried on by solitary individuals. The illusion of their solitariness tends to be fostered by the fact that consumption is an experience none can enjoy save in *propria persona;* the riches created as if for personal enjoyment owe their accumulation and diffusion to interpersonal endeavor.

Dispersed among sundry individuals though it appear, economic power shares with political power the indispensable function of subserving the ends of culture. What Hegel here inveighs against is the principle of self-interest alleged to lie at the basis of a community's economic life, governing not only the consumption but the production of wealth. The cultured individual, since he depends for his cultural values on forces political as well as economic, must acquiesce in their separate but equal rule. But it is an acquiescence that may be seen to vary greatly in fidelity.

Hardith: Is not the drift of the dialectic just this? Since the ethos of a cultured society requires two different powers to generate and sustain the values characteristic of it, its pathos resides in the necessity which the individual is under to trace those values more to one source than to the other. For whichever power be taken as mainspring or mainstay of culture, the other power would seem to forfeit thereby its claim to the individual's complete adhesion. The following questions are thus apposite. Is the state but ancillary to men's economic interests which constitute the real power behind it? Or is economic power to be regarded as vested in the community, creation of wealth being a function of statecraft? With which power should the individual spiritually identify himself? In the world in which he lives and acts both powers represent values the individual would fain adopt as his own. Yet, if his true self is bound up with the one rather than with the other, self-alienation in relation to the power disparaged appears as a necessary consequence. It thus seems inevitable that in the cultural process as actually carried on one power involved in the process must be adjudged good, the other bad. Which is which?

Meredy: The individual's self-estrangement here fathered upon the cultural process becomes intensified by the individual's quest for his true identity in exclusive attachment to but one sphere of cultural values, with the result that the label 'good' is attributed to the sphere that fosters consciousness of his real self, and the epithet 'bad' to that which frustrates it. Unfortunately, neither the political sphere nor the

214

economic sphere is incompatible with either adjective. And if both spheres are subject to contradictory valuations, the situation is clearly paradoxical.

Hardith: What justifies such contradictory valuations? Precisely what is the individual in search of with which either or neither sphere is held to be consistent?

Meredy: Hegel expresses the standard of valuation called for at this stage in a sentence of the utmost generality and brevity. Any object, to paraphrase the sentence, is inherently good or bad to the extent to which the object does or does not enable self-consciousness to affiliate itself with it. Thus it is the state which at first seems bad because it tends to control if not suppress self-consciousness by exacting submission to overindividual ends. And wealth seems good because it enhances self-consciousness by dispensing enjoyment to all and sundry, involving in fact more than one 'invisible hand' to spread its benefits. (Hegel's expression is *tausendhändiger Geber;* is the notion of a thousand-handed benefactor, one wonders, an allusion to Adam Smith?) Yet this valuation may be reversed. Could not self-consciousness find its elective affinity in the state, the substance from which flow all legal and moral conditions requisite for the pursuit of a life of culture and thus entitled to be called good? And from wealth, the product of restless labor and source of transient enjoyment, self-consciousness might well recoil as being foreign to its essential nature and hence be called bad. The result is a double judgment, the subject of each open to qualification by a pair of contradictory predicates. This would seem to follow from the status of the individual in a cultured society. Everything here hinges on whether the individual as self-conscious is conscious primarily of his natural self or his factitious self. His feeling of kinship with the cultural powers and their ways of operation must accordingly vary with his variable approach to them. The judgments of value passed by his spontaneous and inward self could not but appear poles apart from those made by his artifical and overt self.

Hardith: The experience of self-estrangement undergone by the individual in a state of culture seems to have reached an extreme phase. For two self-consciousnesses now come to dwell in his breast; in one he is acquainted with a peculiar and in the other with a standard self. And in acute awareness of the contrast between them lies the poignancy of his self-alienation. His is a plight from which he cannot escape except by a drastic choice: he must either turn his back upon culture and return to nature, or else he must continue to live a life more or less completely denatured and aspire to become in appearance and behavior a perfect instance of an artificial type.

215

Meredy: It is the relative distinction between nature and culture hardened into an absolute contrast that entails the absurdity Hegel's analysis is designed to show. Not their duality but their dualism is impugnable. Valid indeed is the duality, and its uses are many and variable. The completely denatured individual would be as monstrous as the individual wholly untouched by art however aboriginal. No man, let his transformation by culture be the greatest possible, can actually shed his natural propensities, nor can any man return to nature, as the saying goes, without carrying with him the memory of the culture he seeks to leave behind. The alternatives mentioned are false alternatives. The self-alienation which culture brings in its train signifies for Hegel a spiritual experience serving as necessary transition to values higher or deeper than cultural. The historical culture he has in mind affords ample evidence of the potency possessed by certain influences so to shape the individual that he comes more and more to assume aspects of an artificial product. But let us pursue further the diagnosis of self-alienation characteristic of the fully cultured individual Hegel is portraying.

Hardith: The fully cultured individual—or the individual as product of a fully developed culture—must somehow transcend the antithesis of the power of the state and the power of wealth, each subject to a pair of contradictory judgments. Yet for the possibility of culture each power is as indispensable as the other. How recognize the equal necessity of those powers after the demonstration of their equal goodness and badness?

4. *The Noble and the Base*

Meredy: The solution at this stage simply consists in transferring to individual consciousness the predicates heretofore ascribed to the cultural powers. Neither power is amenable to moral judgments, each, in being necessary, is beyond good and evil. It is the individual's attitude to them which is good or bad—in Hegel's words, noble or base. Nobility belongs to that consciousness which is in accord with the realities requisite for a cultured society. Thus in relation to the state, the noble consciousness bows to political authority because without its exercise all cultural values would remain purely subjective—nonsocial if not antisocial. And as regards its relation to wealth, the noble consciousness looks upon it as a creative force the enjoyment of whose products enters into the very definition of the cultured life. By contrast, baseness is an attribute of that consciousness which is out of harmony with political as well as economic power. The authority of the state, in tending to fetter and suppress individuality, can command neither obedience nor reverence. Indeed, hatred of political rulers becomes almost a virtue. And as for riches, a critical consciousness rejects the supposititious claim made for their universal beneficence, seeing in them rather a manifestation of the power of the few over the many, and contempt for those dedicated to the accumulation of wealth need debar no one from cynically enjoying the fruits of exploitation. Such is the opposition between the noble and base postures in relation to the forces to which a cultured society owes its existence and ethos.

Hardith: When all is said about minds noble and base, does not their difference here reduce to the difference between conformists and nonconformists? The noble acquiesce in the established order, the ignoble rebel against it. What a preposterous antithesis! The dialectic seems to hinge on a word radically ambiguous. What is nobility an attribute of? Does it refer to a person's rank or birth or to his mind or character? Social distinction and moral superiority are not mutually implicative. Not all the villains are among the lowborn. Here again is proof of Hegel's tendency to adapt the dialectical method to the historical material by which it is said to be exemplifiable. In equating conformity with nobility Hegel has in mind a particular class of individuals. The allusion is clearly to the patricians and courtiers forming the *entourage* of the kings of France, and especially of Louis XIV. It is the dialectic involved in the conformity of these nobles which is here treated in great detail.

Meredy: You are always returning to the same attack, forgetting or refusing to heed the distinction often made between two kinds of verisimilitude. The *Phenomenology,* not following the historical method in dealing with past events or ideas, is of course not called upon to discuss the question of their literal or actual verisimilitude. The specific references, whose sole function is to illustrate the dialectical movement of the human ways of knowing and acting conceived as generic, can nevertheless be said to possess verisimilitude in a sense symbolic or ideal. If Hegel models some universal persuasion or behavior on a particular example, as he often does, it is because the chosen example seems especially suited to represent it in a symbolically more verisimilar form.

The equation of nobility and conformity is here a case in point. Hegel's historical references have a wider sweep than you indicate; it is true, however, that his frequent quotations from Diderot's dialogue seem to accentuate unduly matters too intimately related to a specific cultural area and a specific cultural era. But what the references are intended to exemplify may under certain conditions find expression again and again. To the dialectic here delineated every society is subject whose ethos depends on the absolute position of its monarch and a privileged class of peers. And as for the association of the peerage with high standards of comportment, this too is a generic conception embedded in many specific cultures. *Noblesse oblige!* This is more than a cliché. The noble's acceptance of the social order on noble grounds, so to speak, appears in the text initially as a sincere attitude of self-abnegation which only by degrees leads to its very reversal.

Hardith: Is not the self-abnegation but another name for self-alienation exalted into a virtue? The man of noble station cannot express his noble character save by self-sacrifice—sacrifice of the self-assertiveness to which by nature he is always prone. Such self-sacrifice obviously calls for heroic measures. The natural man, ever lurking in the background, is ever ready to assert his claim. He who is truly noble thus comes to be cast in the role of hero, his heroism consisting in deliberate suppression of his natural bent. How much Hegel's argument is here made to depend on the ambivalence—or rather multivalence—of nobility! Distinguished by birth or rank, as well as by all the courtly graces, the noble attain perfect nobility only when voluntary self-estrangement becomes the heroic principle of their conduct. What a *tour de force!*

Meredy: Yes, the self-estrangement, which the cultural process inevitably produces, appears in the course of the dialectic as if deliberately achieved by the noble consciousness. Is this not, one might well ask, a case of making a virtue of necessity? But as Hegel shows, the self to be estranged from remains to turn the virtue back into necessity. The Old Adam never ceases to plague the noble consciousness. This Hegel demonstrates by expatiating on the different 'heroic' attempts made by the higher self to renounce the claims of the lower.

The first of these lies in the effort of the noble self to merge his interests with those of the state, thus relinquishing the subjective purposes the ignoble self is spontaneously intent upon. By serving the state the self serves a power concerned with universal ends, ends cognate with his superior but alien to his inferior nature. This Hegel speaks of as 'the heroism of service': service becomes indeed most heroic if and when its performance requires complete sacrifice of all personal gain or advantage. And the state in its turn must grow in strength and stability in proportion as it can command such service in ever increasing measure by the greatest number. The result of this kind of heroism is twofold: the noble self liberated from the ignoble now becomes truly actual, and truly actual, too, is pervasive acceptance of the state's supreme authority.

But precisely because the state depends for the supremacy of its power on heroic service, the sacrifice or self-abnegation here so essential can never be complete. For consciousness of the *need* of one's service is apt to breed a consciousness of self-importance. Service by the noble may assume the form of imparting counsel of what is to be done conducive to the general welfare, service such as proud vassals are called upon to render. And there is hardly a question more subject to dispute than the question of what is best for all. In the absence of unanimity among counsellors the counsels given tend to generate into rivalry of private opinions, ultimately precipitating the conflict of separate wills in opposition to the power of the state.

Hardith: It takes little astuteness to discern the dialectial somersault which the so-called heroism of service brings about in the noble consciousness. Under the conditions here considered, heroic service, though initially entailing self-sacrifice, must in the end culminate in self-assertion. And the self asserted is the very self to be denied, the noble consciousness thus turning into its opposite. What irony!

Yet there is another kind of heroism whose completeness can be proved beyond a peradventure. It is the heroism of death. To die a hero's death in the service of the state is to sacrifice one's self in a literal and absolute sense. For death, impervious to dialectic, can never become its own other. Here is a form of self-alienation than which none can be more final and irrevocable. And what society fails to honor the heroic dead whose nobility consisted in having chosen to die for it? Hegel, mentioning this theme, dismisses its significance in too cursory a fashion. Yet the heroism of death is a genuine alternative to that of service.

Meredy: In comparison with heroic service, the sacrifice involved in heroic death is indeed complete, reaching, as it were, the point of no return. But it can hardly be said to qualify as a genuine alternative. As here used, the word 'heroic' denotes the act of voluntary withdrawal from the importunities of one's lower self while constantly remaining aware of their goading influence. And precisely in such deliberate withdrawal consists the experience of alienation. To the heroism of death this manner of speaking is inapposite: it is a heroism intent, not on the continuity of self-consciousness ever exemplifying difference and sameness of subject and object, but rather on its ultimate extinction. Alienation, in a word, becomes annihilation. The conscious life that makes the sacrifice of self does not survive the sacrifice made, and disappears irrevocably, as Hegel says, into its unreconciled opposite. Self-alienation, precluded without an inner tension between the agent creating and the patient undergoing it, is a process essentially self-conscious. Cessation of self-consciousness, as in death, leaves behind it neither agent nor patient and thus no concrete individual as a possible victor over himself. And where is nobility to be found if not in the individual's heroic triumph over his subjective or personal interests? That alone is true renunciation of individuality which preserves individuality in the very process of renouncing it. Let us consider a new type of heroism which, though remaining self-conscious as in service, resembles death in completeness.

Hardith: One might have expected that the antithesis of service and death would not remain unresolved. A synthesis, in which the contrasted types of heroism would survive as transfigured, must of course make its appearance. If the dialectic is not to suspend operation, the opposites are now required to pass into a higher unity. But this higher unity, strange to say, turns out to be language. Words alone, it would seem, can accomplish the self-alienation so essential to the noble consciousness. And through words, too, the individual can rise to the supreme plane of service and sacrifice: they are the sole vehicles for conveying repudiation of his false and asseveration of his true self. Clearly, language assumes here tremendous importance. The claim that language is conducive to the emergence of a new kind of heroism seems at first rather extravagant.

Meredy: Hegel dilates on the nature of language more generally before embarking on a discussion of the sort of heroism it affords. Although a universal medium of overindividual origin and significance, speech may be employed by the individual to express his idiosyncrasy. By the language he speaks a man may intend to reveal or to hide his true nature. Words are always subject to disavowal on the ground that, being incorrigibly general, they cannot denote an individual's inner life. Moreover the words through which a particular personality receives utterance in the presence of others belong to two distinct domains of fact: they are vanishing things but they are also relatively enduring. The *spoken* words, once they pass the speaker's lips, lose their actual existence and become part and parcel of the dead past; but as *heard,* and released from the speaker's control, words become the property of every auditor in whose mind they continue to dwell and have their being. Accordingly, words may be said to mediate between two extremes: at one end, they are subjective bearers of variable meanings, and at the other, objective signs open to public interpretation. Language and self-consciousness are of a cousinship in relation to the process of mediation which they must needs carry on between polar opposites. Language thus appears to Hegel as the very image or symbol of spirit. This, a highly condensed translation of Hegel's lengthy and technical analysis, must suffice for our purpose.

Hardith: What Hegel says about language is undeniably important and the language in which he says it illustrates the very point he insists upon—namely, that words more often than not tend to conceal instead of disclosing the speaker's meaning. How great indeed is the gulf that often separates speaker and auditor—or, for that matter, writer and reader! The words used are apt—and not seldom designedly—to widen the gulf rather than to bridge it. Can we actually be sure that elucidations of another's utterances do not in fact distort their inward sense? Hegel's language about language leaves me in a quandary as regards its exact purport, your lucid epitome notwithstanding: it may be profound but it is certainly obscure.

But the language, which forms the subject matter of his analysis, has an intimate bearing on 'noble' self-estrangement, and this the analysis surprisingly illuminates. For it is not language in general with which Hegel is here concerned. The speech examined is principally that of a culture deliberately cultivated by the elite—the speech of a special class. The individual, viewed at first as exemplifying the noble consciousness, appears to be a man of distinction only outside his homogeneous group. Within it, however, his speech-behavior is that of his peers, and strict adherence to it determines and guarantees his social status. The language of culture is thus essentially the language of estrangement, serving as decorous medium of communication of class-conscious individuals in their external relations. It is obviously not the language in which they clothe their private thoughts and sentiments when engaged in self-communion.

5. Heroism of Flattery and the Language of Disintegration

Meredy: How well you have the finger on the main point! Alienation does indeed find its most pregnant expression in language. The more a language departs from its natural or spontaneous base by becoming artificial and staid and fastidious, the deeper the estrangement between the self holding converse with himself and the self involved in overt discourse. And it is the locution exemplified by its higher strata which in every society comes to be looked upon as culturally *comme il faut*. Cultured diction is thus generally dictated by those who rank high in the social scale, and the higher the rank, the greater the distance that separates the cultured few from the uncultured many.

But in the present context Hegel's preoccupation is with self-alienation as a mode of self sacrifice, a process characteristic of the noble consciousness. Sacrifice of self through service proves abortive, and sacrifice through death proves nothing save the end of all conscious-

221

ness. If the heroism of service is too incomplete, that of death is altogether too perfect. It is thus that Hegel introduces us to a new type of heroism by means of which the individual may retain the consciousness of nobility without forfeiting it in dumb service or asserting it once and for all in the act of dying. Language now appears to provide a more nobly heroic way of mediating between the separate individual and the power of the state. And of this heroism Hegel speaks with consummate irony as "the heroism of flattery." A curious juxtaposition of words, indeed! It is through flattery that the individual makes the supreme sacrifice of his own individuality in exalting the will of another individual. But the individual so flattered, since his will is the will of the monarch and hence the will of the state, is of course unique. The very name of monarch distinguishes him from all other individuals. And such an exclusive and solitary individual becomes truly absolute only when acclaimed as absolute by flattery. The language of constant praise performs a double function: it creates in the monarch the consciousness of universal and unlimited power, and in his sycophants it creates the consciousness of alienation from their self-centered and self-assertive individuality. Lip service, if one may say so, now assumes the dignity of a noble profession.

Hardith: The paradox of identifying nobility with sycophancy is egregious enough, attenuated though it appears when nobility is held to be descriptive merely of rank and not of character. To go further and speak of sycophancy as heroic would seem to carry linguistic license beyond permissible limits. But for the historical material on which Hegel leans so heavily, would it have occurred to him, one wonders, to find a place in the dialectic for a conception of heroism so preposterous? This, however, is an old criticism of mine which need not be reiterated. How seriously should the language of flattery be taken as a language requisite for mediating between the individual and the state?

Meredy: It would be quite foolish to approach everything Hegel says in pedantic fashion. His speech suffers from paronomastic excesses not limited to ordinary puns. The incongruous union of flattery and heroism is clearly playful and none but the dullwitted would take it literally. Yet, irrespective of the heroic quality facetiously imputed to it, flattery seems to be an essential concomitant of power in the absence of which *consciousness* of power would remain dormant or but rudimentary. Indeed, power and flattery are conjoined by a process of reciprocal enhancement. The higher a monarch is praised, the stronger his feeling of authority, and panegyrical voices are apt to grow in number and volume with the growth of the monarch's dependence on their continual praise. How mighty and concordant must be the chorus of his flatterers to permit the monarch to believe in the validity of his own claim, *L'état c'est moi!* But for the paeans of praise of his absolute power and personal glory, the famous apothegm often quoted, perhaps too often, would contain nothing more than arrogant boast.

And let it not be said that the flattering function is one confined to the historical context to which Hegel alludes. It is a function which in modified form seems to be exercised elsewhere. In its nonpejorative sense flattery is requisite for the self-confident rule or reign of any chief of state, whatever be the constitution under which he governs, and men are not wanting to perform this service for reasons supposedly patriotic. And is such service entirely unheroic when, as not seldom happens, he on whom praise is bestowed, principally out of loyalty to the nation or the party, proves personally to be unworthy of it? And the irony is this, that many a modern leader, transformed by incessant eulogy into a living myth, develops the will to believe in his false image, created though it was to act upon the credulity of the electors, presumably for the purpose of furthering their general welfare. So even today's political panegyrists are not altogether unlike those Hegel has in mind.

Hardith: How long can the flattering function remain compatible with nobility of character? Depending for the extolling of his image on continuous laudation, the ruler requires the constant presence of eulogists to proclaim that he is in truth the personification of the state. Flattery thus enters into statecraft as one of its ingredients, and with the growing importance of flattery must grow the prestige of the flatterers. Panegyrists, when in the ascendant, come to constitute a special class or estate, distinguished from the other estates of the realm by the duty or privilege of exalting the sovereign's position. Small wonder, then, that a group, whose function is chiefly encomiastic, should in the end aspire to be the power behind the throne, as it were, its members becoming more and more self-assertive with increasing awareness of their political influence. What is particularly significant in all this is the relation of flattery to self-alienation. Hegel assumes that flattery is initially a form of self-sacrifice, the self sacrificed being the natural or separate and hence the base individual. But the process becomes subject to reversal. Knowing his activity to be indispensable and feeling proud delight in its adroit exercise, the flatterer discovers in flattery a source of self-gratification, the self gratified being the very base individual previously repudiated. Laudation, which at the outset seems so ingenuous and selfless, tends to degenerate into cynically self-seeking sycophancy. Not heroism but hypocrisy is the essence of flattery. Is it not absurd to speak of it as sacrificial? If power corrupts, and absolute power is said to corrupt absolutely, the flattery that glorifies power would seem to be corruptive in a more radical sense.

Meredy: Not unlike other forms of obeisance, ritualistic praise of another, be the other a god or a king, is incorrigibly ambivalent, for the feeling of reverence behind it may be genuine as well as counterfeit: outer self-abasement does not preclude inner self-complacency. If flattery is said to induce in the flattering individual a consciousness of self-estrangement, which self becomes estranged from which? The language of culture, of which that of flattery is such a pregnant illustration, is well adapted to hide the truth about the individual's actual personality. Hegel speaks of it as the language of disintegration (*Zerrissenheit*), a language through which the individual appears as if rent asunder, his outer self completely divorced from his inner. It is the idiom of extreme sophistication, equivocal and eloquent, not meant to be taken seriously. Nobody believes anybody's utterances couched in a style deliberately designed at once to deceive and to undeceive. The style, such as that of Rameau in Diderot's dialogue, is a peculiarly fit medium for attacking in oblique fashion the prevailing values. But the attack veiled so adroitly and voiced so facetiously produces no resentment: the venom of its sting is scarcely felt. It comes to be generally regarded more as *jeu d'esprit* than an expression of malice. Such, as Hegel ironically observes, is the language of 'pure culture'. And in a state of culture when it has reached the stage of 'purity', the individual can never say what he truly believes or truly believe what he decorously says. Sincerity belongs to thought and insincerity to speech. Hypocrisy, which is culture's supreme achievement, grows indeed triumphant in the language of flattery.

Hardith: Before leaving the subject of flattery, its relation to the power of wealth deserves a brief comment or two. In flattering that power the so-called noble consciousness turns into its opposite as soon as its pretension to nobility becomes punctured. Whereas political power, when embodied in the person of the monarch, is undivided, and eulogy of its sovereign authority may tend to create in the eulogist's mind the illusion of heroic self-sacrifice, economic power is dispersed among many and different persons, none capable of laying claim to exclusive praise. The encomium lavished upon any 'economic royalist' is not necessarily extensible to every other. Flattery, in short, cannot be addressed to wealth in general so unequally distributed but only to those individuals and groups producing it, provided the activities in which they are variously engaged, whether in competition or in concert, may be alleged to be conducive to universal beneficence. But under the cloak of universal beneficence are concealed but thinly shameless pursuits of self-interest, and laudation of the quasi-benefactors is hardly successful in screening the image of naked individualism. Thus individualism becomes rampant again but under cover of a language celebrating the abstract universal. It is the language of flattery in its most corruptive form: the self-praise of the captains of industry and the lords of commerce finds its sublimation in the praise of their paid sycophants. Hypocrisy, inexpungible from the world of culture and reaching perfection in the language of flattery, is deleterious in every sphere of social intercourse, but strikingly so in the sphere of economic power.

Meredy: What an excellent résumé of a theme of which the treatment in the text is so elaborate and not a little labored. And here if anywhere does the analysis apply with deadly accuracy to the way we live now. Hegel could not have anticipated the culture of our own time. Yet the method of flattery, in the form of commercial advertising, has become an integral part of our economic life, having in fact assumed the status of a separate industry with its own captains in command. What is salesmanship if not a name for the various devices involved in plethoric praise of every product of every industry, not excluding the products of the laudatory enterprise? Yes, salesmanship is marketable and by the same contrived operations of which it is the original matrix. And salesmen are available in profusion whose artificial smiles and artificial voices can be bought to promote the absurdly magnified claims for every possible commodity and every possible nostrum. Hegel's identification of the language of flattery with the language of disintegration should thus cause no surprise. Employed to extol desires rooted in self-interest, speech so manifestly lacking in candor and integrity must loosen and eventually break the bonds that bind the individual to ends social and spiritual. What an affront to reason is the blatant tongue of the commercial advertiser! Not for sale are the things that pertain to the life of mind. The individual must perforce come to look upon his civilized world as one where self-seekers are ever bred anew, the very system of values embedded in culture abetting their ascendancy. A return to a state of nature presumed to be innocent is of course impossible save as a romantic pose, simply because the world is too civilized to revert to actual primitivism. The vanity of life in an artificial society must be more deeply experienced before it can become superseded. And to a discussion of this new theme we may now turn.

Culture and Enlightenment

1. Belief and Insight

Hardith: The transition to a new phase in the dialectic of culture is contained in the highly abstract analysis of the relation between the postures of mind which Hegel calls belief and insight. The section devoted to that analysis I find exceedingly forbidding. The two postures, differentiable at first, become in the end converted into species of one another. And their contents, too, appear now distinct and now fused. The theme here covered suffers from excessive obscurity. Why such elaborate complication?

Meredy: The section is indeed needlessly involved. Yet it provides a suitable bridge leading from the self-estrangement produced by culture to a dialectical attempt to transcend it in a new and universal form of rationalism.

The approach to the heart of the matter may be facilitated by reviewing the corrosive influence of the cultural process on individual personality. The cardinal point to accentuate is this: on the level of culture thought and language are in a state of mutual alienation, with the result that a sort of curtain intervenes between the individual's overt utterances and his inward reflections. From the postulate of incongruity between speech and cogitation follow certain corollaries, to wit—(a) what a man thinks is too private to be disclosed in the idiom subject to cultural approbation; (b) not by his secret ways of thinking but rather by his ways of speaking in accordance with the approved norms can the individual be adjudged cultured; (c) the individual's escape from the factitious life of culture is precluded unless he can find in the privacy or secrecy of his mind an inviolable sanctuary; (d) but his haven of refuge is not yet the domain of pure intellect, for at this stage thought appears as but another name for the inner life contrasted with external comportment. The inner life where thought or belief becomes

226

the individual's retreat remains completely closed to the stereotyped language dominant in an artificial society.

Hardith: The terms in which thought or belief is here couched seem to have a connotation chiefly religious. Should it be asserted generally that disillusionment with the life of culture must perforce drive the individual into the arms of religion?

Meredy: The religious overtones in Hegel's analysis are unmistakable. But the inwardness here considered is not that of religion proper. In its fullest and richest sense religion forms the subject of a later discussion. Before it can emerge as a spiritual force in its own right—emerge, that is, in the context of the *Phenomenology*—aspects or elements of religion enter into prereligious types of consciousness. The unhappy consciousness, for instance, brooding in solitude over separation from a selfhood conceived as immutable, undeniably represents a religious constituent. So, too, in the ethical order, a religious ingredient is present in the claim by the family to a divine mission not subject to the secular authority of the state. Appropriate also to the disillusioning experience undergone in an artificial society is a religious attitude which, growing out of the self-alienation rooted in the cultural process, grows in depth as the divorce between the essential nature of the self and his actual existence becomes a matter of poignant preoccupation. It is the individual's painful awareness of the contrast between his inner being (found in the privacy of his thought) and his outer appearance (exhibited in action and language) which generates the belief that one side of the opposition is true and the other false. But the religiousness of this belief is rudimentary, having its source in a vague conviction touched with emotion.

Hardith: If a self dominated by belief is more genuine than the self molded by culture, his state of mind would appear strictly analogous to the consciousness described as unhappy in a previous section. Both have in common the same sense of isolation and the same feeling of anxiety induced by the division between existential and essential selfhood. And in speaking of belief as engendered by painful awareness of this division, do you not presuppose, though under another name, insight as a necessary condition of belief? Are awareness and insight equivalent? To what extent does belief differ from insight or awareness? Assuming their distinction, what is the nature of their relation?

Meredy: To your first question the answer seems to be this: unhappy indeed is the lot of the cultured individual when his self-consciousness turns into self-estrangement. But the unhappy consciousness is here on a social scale. Not the solitary individual is now a lost soul

227

pining for the blessed state that would be his if he could exchange his present false self for the still remote true self. The individual here considered is one transformed by the ethos of a well-defined community, and it is his social self that appears alien contrasted with a private self always within reach of thought. Everyone must experience the unhappiness that supervenes upon the apprehension that the artificial self displayed in speech and demeanor is poles apart from the inward self disclosed to reflection. In the type of unhappiness depicted earlier, the pathos derives from the psychological distance of the genuine self longed for; here the relation is reversed: the real self introspectively vouched for (to adapt freely Tennyson's familiar line), "closer is he than breathing, and nearer than hands and feet." And on what depends this new phase of the unhappy consciousness? Requisite for it, in answer to your other question, is a subtle relation of belief and insight, one revealing itself as circular and dynamic.

Hardith: There can of course be no relation except as holding between distinguishable terms. Between belief and insight, however, the distinction fails to remain distinct. Belief, the text shows, is the result of insight which in turn rests on prior belief. Because they are thus mutually involved in the same conscious process, belief and insight lapse into tautology and each becomes the other. All this can make little sense to the uninitiated. Relata must somehow be differentiated, not only verbally, but chiefly as regards their contents or objects. How, in short, do belief and insight, distinguishable as well as identifiable, apply to the cultured individual's unhappy state, this after all being here the crucial issue?

Meredy: It is precisely in their bearing on the self-consciousness of the cultured individual that belief and insight come to be related in circular and dynamic fashion. Does not the experience of self-consciousness as such exemplify perfectly the dialectic of identity presupposing difference and difference reverting to identity? For Hegel this experience is the matrix of his logic—the logic, at any rate, applicable in the *Phenomenology* to the order and connection of mind's generic persuasions or perspectives. It is thus not surprising that the terms required for the analysis of the cultured individual's condition should develop relations comporting with the general pattern of a dialectical logic. Thus, belief in the reality of his private self, a self not shackled by conformity to artificial modes of behavior, depends on the insight into the spuriousness of the self living in the genteel world of culture, and this very insight is precipitated by the antecedent belief that in the individual's inner life alone is the true self to be found. This is the 'circle' in which insight and belief are involved: one presupposes the other, and each inevitably turns into each. Insight here coincides with the belief in the deeper self behind or beneath his superficial appearance and belief becomes one with the insight into the falsity of the self decked with the artificial trappings of culture. Of the strange union of difference and identity characteristic of all self-consciousness the union of belief and insight is a signal illustration.

Hardith: The illustration is of course not singular, the dialectical structure of self-consciousness being for Hegel archetypal. Every individual, conscious of the bifurcation of his inner life and his social life, and conscious also of remaining nevertheless the selfsame individual, exemplifies the strange union you speak of. The cultured individual with whom we are here concerned constitutes a special case. His peculiar experience is marked by features deriving from a particular ethos. He is principally conscious of his self as subject to valuation by opposed predicates. As a result of his discontent with the artificial conditions under which he must live in a state of culture, he is driven to look askance at his disingenuous behavior, nor can he refrain from imagining a different sort of world in which his true self would appear uncontaminated with falsehood and hypocrisy. We are here dealing with a variant of self-consciousness the nature of which is determined by a determinate social order. And not only is the cultured individual conscious of his self as existing in a certain kind of society; he is conscious also of his self as criticizing that society and his relation to it. His consciousness is of a self engaged in making judgments the content of which is now the state of civilization and now his individual status therein. This I take to be the gist of the argument. Is the argument incapable of being expressed without recourse to the operations of insight and belief? Or is the dialectic of their mutual involutions an excursus complicating instead of explaining a difficult theme?

Meredy: What you say is but apposite to those disillusioned few whose critical weapons remain to be sharpened for the attack on the spiritually deleterious concomitants of culture. The individuals here depicted occupy a halfway position in transit from culture to enlightenment; adhering though restively to the ideology of culture, their conversion to the ideology of enlightenment is still remote. The dialectic is thus confined to the cultured in the process of becoming enlightened. The idiom proper to this midway posture must thus of necessity suffer from vagueness: hence the accent on such ambiguous terms as belief and insight. Belief, religious in tone, is a faint echo of faith as the substance of things hoped for, the evidence of things not seen; and insight, assumed to be cognitive, lacks conceptual form.

Small wonder that belief and insight should turn out to be mutually implicate as well as mutually assimilative.

It would be tedious to follow in detail Hegel's analysis which is so finespun and not free from bias. What he shows in general is this: if belief is to serve as religious escape from the worldliness of the world of culture, the escape must prove abortive, simply because the reality sought as substitute for the reality of culture is but the domain of culture inverted. It cannot be defined except by contrast with the vain and deceptive standards of the actual world. That world, alas, remains too much with the believing consciousness, must indeed be ever present to it, for without constant awareness of the specious claims of the state and the spurious values of wealth the transcendent reality contemplated by the believer must appear illusory too, a reality destitute of all but negative attributes. This awareness, a synonym of insight, involves more than merely seeing *into* the actual state of affairs for the justification of belief in a paradisiac sphere; it involves also looking *beyond* belief itself to win a clarified view of the world it longs for. This is the object of an insight which Hegel describes as 'pure'.

Hardith: Hegel could obviously not resist the temptation to play on the word insight, and numerous are the changes he rings on it. There are of course different ways of carrying on the process of 'looking into' things, amenable as the process is to sundry qualifications, those here central being pure and impure. No word other than insight, it would seem, which Hegel regards as a species of knowledge, could have served so well his purpose of making the transition to the subject of enlightenment, a term whose literal sense comes under his treatment to have likewise various metaphorical uses. The transition appears to lie in the initial equation of purity with clarity, a pure insight being *eo ipso* a clear insight. But what about belief? Is insight incompatible with belief as such or only with religious belief on the ground that the insight supporting it remains impure or unclarifiable? And is it possible to arrive through pure insight at belief entitled to be adjudged enlightened? Have we not here the crux of the matter?

Meredy: You anticipate. Insight must indeed develop into definite awareness, awareness namely, that the actual world is corrupt and corruptive, and that cultural values are false and subject to supersedure. But the initial appearance of such awareness is of necessity contingent, sporadic, endemic. Hence the resolve of those to whom it is vouchsafed to make this awareness increasingly infectious and so eventually universal. A corrosive influence comes to pervade more and more assiduously the cultural world, insight (*Einsicht*) first taking the form of intention (*Absicht*). (Here is a striking wordplay

230

untranslatable into English.) The intention is simply heuristic; its aim is but to effect in minds everywhere a change of heart in relation to values at present in the ascendant, thus bringing about a more receptive attitude to new sets of belief in place of the old. But insight's final goal is to instill in all minds faith in their essential rationality and doubt of everything not illuminable by the light of reason. This pure insight, pure because reflecting the light of reason, "is the spirit," says Hegel, "that calls to all conscious beings: be *for* yourselves what you are all *in* yourselves—rational." With the response to such call becoming more general, enlightenment proper comes upon the scene.

2. *The Struggle with Alleged Superstition*

Hardith: What a penetrating analysis the text affords of an intellectual movement so momentous! The themes treated are numerous, all derived from European and chiefly French history. And once again ideas conceived as generic are made to depend for their illustrations too exclusively on special and dated expressions, so much so that the illustrations tend to usurp—here as elsewhere—a dialectical necessity attributable not to them but only to the matters they are said to illustrate. This criticism urged before bears constant reiteration. Now insight is not a particular phenomenon subject to causal determination, conditioned though it is by the ideology of culture and conditioning in turn that of the enlightenment. The necessity Hegel ascribes to the emergence and culmination of insight is clearly dialectical and not historical. And the insight he dwells upon enjoys here a peculiar significance, having, as he declares, no content of its own. But a content—or an object—it must perforce possess, even though it be a borrowed one, if insight is to be regarded as a form of cognition, and Hegel evidently so regards it. Where then can its content come from? And how does the insight leading to enlightenment differ from the insight latent in culture?

Meredy: It will serve our purpose best if I draw a distinction sharper than appears in the text between mere insight and pure insight, the latter alone being central in the career of enlightenment. Mere insight, which involves belief and is involved in it, is a placid kind of awareness touched with sentiment. Implicit in the ethos of culture, it is generated by the consciousness of self-estrangement to which that ethos condemns the individual. Who can be true to his inner and deeper self as long as he is made to conform to the artificial code governing life in a cultural society? The more perfect the conformity, the greater the pathos of separation between conventional speech and uninhibited thought, between proper conduct and intel-

231

lectual rebelliousness. Such a pathetic division, experienced by a mind whose self-alienation has for its concomitant no strong feeling of revulsion, must needs breed hypocrisy and cynicism. But how ignominious a conformity radically disavowed by mental reservations! This situation it is which forms the content of an insight arising within a cultured society when here and there some individuals definitely feel the antithesis of outer conformity and inner revolt to be intolerable. But this insight, still inert and personal, does not go beyond intention to clarify and resolve the antithesis by articulate thought. The intention must come to animate an active crusade against all the irrational tendencies overt or dormant in a state of culture. Only when the diffusion of effort to challenge everywhere the presence of the irrational becomes actual and effective, may pure insight be said to have made its appearance. Hegel expresses this by distinguishing *das einzelne Einsehen* and *die allgemeine Einsicht*: the intent of this untranslatable wordplay is to show that pure insight cannot be found in introspective awareness attained by this or that individual but only when such awareness swells into universal vision. With sporadic intention growing into a widespread movement, dynamic enlightenment enters upon its crusading task.

Hardith: But the distinction between two kinds of insight, buttressed by Hegel's pun, only proves that collective vision is a rational force more potent than individual. Does this not reduce the distinction to a numerical difference? The fact that many rather than few may look upon an incongruous situation as amenable to rational elucidation would not seem to throw light on the quality of the requisite vision. But the issue is even more embarrassing. Does not an insight's purity result from its prior purgation? If so, what must insight be purged of to be called pure? As I read the text, the essence of the problem relates to the radical contrast between insight and belief. Seeing is emphatically not believing if seeing is a process having in reason its source and consummation.

Meredy: The standard here invoked, strange to say, is both qualitative and quantitative. Purity of insight does indeed consist in freedom from contamination by irrational belief, no insight being pure unless purged of such belief. Irrational belief thus remains for enlightenment the omnipresent object of ruthless militancy, and its objective lies in extending the exercise of reason from the few to the many until it gains universal supremacy. Pure insight, in the sense noted, is accordingly the moving soul in the dialectic of enlightenment. And enlightenment, whose mission it is to make converts to pure insight, is ever confronted by stout beliefs either resisting conversion or posing as insights with claims to greater significance.

The enlightened consciousness now embarks on incessant struggle with what it comes to view as offenses to reason and truth. But these offenses appear egregiously stubborn and insistent. What is their origin? Whence their delusive power? The answer proffered by enlightenment Hegel speaks of as threefold. Human gullibility and priestly deceit and despotic oppression combine in various ways to create a realm of error at which enlightenment must direct its assault. Intent upon deception and preying on men's credulity, priesthood is said to conspire with despotism to serve the dominant interests and powers of the world. It is all a matter of looking into causes and exposing to the light of reason their baneful effects.

Hardith: The historian of ideas would have little difficulty in detecting in Hegel's allusions echoes of the doctrinary opinions advanced in the eighteenth century in defense of reason as the measure of all things. Nor could the learned fail to verify the references to vile priesthood and cruel despotism as the two dark evils that need to be exposed to the shafts of light. This simply goes to show the extent to which the topic here treated is modeled so faithfully on a determinate rationalistic movement. Accordingly, the dialectic largely derives plausibility from the prominence given, not to all deceptive beliefs and false insights, but only to those rooted in Christian tradition and practice. Would the dialectic, I wonder, have the same direction and emphasis if 'the realm of error' to be invaded by enlightenment were chiefly to involve prepossessions non-Christian or, more generally, nonreligious? And yet, after showing error to flow from a threefold source, Hegel declares that enlightenment does not assail the three causes with equal weight. Priesthood and despotism are not the primary objects of hostile attack. Why not?

Meredy: Although Hegel does depend for illustrations far too much on the peculiar claims for the dominance of reason during a dated period, they nevertheless appear typical of any age or any society in which individuals are deliberately kept in ignorance for the purpose of securing unquestioning adherence to established creeds and established institutions. Ignorance inevitably breeds superstition. And superstition, though not always stemming from religion, is not apt to languish for lack of ecclesiastic support. The destruction of ignorance becomes therefore the primary aim of enlightenment, and with the fading of superstition must wither likewise whatever nourishes it. Hence the derivative importance of everything else enlightenment is bound to struggle with; the attack, for example, on priesthood and despotism,

233

must follow and can obviously not precede the seed to which their influence may be traced. That in ignorance lies the original cause of all error and thus of all evil presupposes the postulate dear to every form of rationalism, the postulate, namely, that knowledge is virtue. Here, however, knowledge is identified with pure insight and its virtue with a determinate panacea. Ignorance, in short, and especially when it assumes the shape of superstition, is the foe enlightenment is ever warring against.

Hardith: But, as Hegel remarks, not by open warfare can enlightenment initially accomplish its task, belief being too solidly entrenched to be easily overcome. There must needs be a preliminary phase during which the work of enlightenment must be done by stealth. Reason's light cannot appear everywhere at the same time, its rays now falling on this obscure region of error, now on that. Varying his metaphors, Hegel likens pure insight to a vapor silently penetrating an unresisting atmosphere or to an infection insinuating its way through an organism's vital parts. This alarming spread of insight passes at first almost unnoticed, and such awareness of it as gradually develops remains but endemic. Sooner or later, however, the pervasive influence of enlightenment becomes generally apparent, foreshadowing the imminence of the struggle to come. And once the strife takes place, the disaster threatening all beliefs can no longer be averted. Forced to be on the defensive, they are called upon to give proof of their credibility. And what credentials can they submit which enlightenment will deem sufficient? If they are cozened to fight with the weapons of the enemy, the battle can only end in their abject surrender. Indeed, admission that rational defense is necessary spells their doom, for the defense must be carried on in hostile territory where beliefs are already captive. But what kind of a struggle is this? It clearly 'isn't cricket'. The contest is a priori so arranged that one party cannot lose and the other cannot win. Would it be too impertinent to speak of it as a sort of confidence game?

Meredy: Your badinage is amusing but not exactly relevant. Initial lack of effective opposition to the contagious spread of rationalism represents but one phase of the dialectic the aim of which is to exhibit the utter defenselessness of beliefs in the face of enlightened criticism. Although couched in Hegel's special idiom, the dialectic is not without general significance. The attempt, for example, to demonstrate the truth of a religious persuasion by the scientific method, illustrates the predicament Hegel has in mind, precipitating an inescapable dilemma. Either the method must be radically modified to include among its objects of application the tenets of religion or else these tenets must be made to undergo complete transformation if they are to lay claim to the same probative force enjoyed by scientific hypotheses. Is it possible to construe the articles of any faith as fruits of inductive inference? Without explicitly raising the question of whether or not religious creeds and scientific opinions are subject to the same standard of credibility, Hegel's analysis touches the nerve of it. On the assumption that all beliefs be adjudged credible solely in accordance with rational criteria of credibility, an assumption basic to enlightenment, justification of some beliefs, notably those held on religious grounds, becomes difficult if not impossible. Religious beliefs are thus called upon to defend themselves against the charge of being rationally indefensible. It is this charge which ushers in a new phase of the dialectic. Rejecting the usurpation of jurisdiction by biased critics over religious beliefs, those committed to them will contend for their credibility on evidence other than rational, the standard invoked having a basis deeper than the basis on which scientific thought is wont to lean. Faith in the sacred represents a faith enlightenment cannot give or take away. Against the overt attack on them by a sacrilegious rationalism, beliefs fighting with their own weapons enter the battle for the preservation of their own autonomous and inalienable rights. Militancy engenders militancy, and belief and insight now become gravely involved in open warfare.

3. *The Distortive Effect of Clarification*

Hardith: The new phase of the dialectic seems to hinge on two distinct ways of approach to belief. May I speak of them as centrifugal and centripetal? The first represents action at a distance, so to speak, since it is not belief which is the proper object of concern but rather its remote and external manifestations. The other has to do with the inward state of belief itself, its peculiar quality and intimate relation to the individual aware of entertaining and cherishing the belief. The distinction between knowledge by description and knowledge by acquaintance is here singularly apposite. Enlightenment, which is by hypothesis purged of belief, can only view it from without. Intent upon explaining it in terms of origin and influence, it affixes to belief pejorative epithets and traces it to the combined chicanery of state and church. But the center of belief lies in the will instigating it, and none can actually know belief from within save those personally familiar with its impelling force. And it is generally conceded that having a belief and believing it true go inseparably together. What a gulf divides the outer view of belief from the inner! Those convinced of the truth of their faith must needs feel appalled at the denigration of it by the enlightened critics. Not by malicious caricatures can a faith be shaken

235

held by its adherents to be invincible. Does not the conflict thus epitomized inhere in the inevitable contrast between experience uniquely enjoyed and its conceptual translations?

Meredy: The contrast you note reappears in different forms throughout the *Phenomenology*. The development of the dialectic is partly determined by the recurrent tension between what seems intrinsic and what extrinsic to the types of experience examined, *seems* because the two crucial terms vary in import from context to context and their relations shift continually in the course of the analysis. Belief, too, exemplifies the tension between what it is intrinsically felt to be and what it is extrinsically described as being. The requisite vocabulary, though flexible, Hegel adapts to the peculiar nature of religious belief at war with its rationalistic detractors. The gravamen of the charge against enlightenment is simply this, that its conceptions of belief are not only extraneous but essentially distortive, striking the confirmed believer as being wanton *mis*conceptions. What, for example, could be more preposterous than inclusive condemnation of belief as superstitious because, forsooth, it does not accord with a standard of credibility germane to abstract logic or exact science? If credible is whatever mind can see itself in, to emulate Hegel in playing upon the word insight, the issue boils down to this: is the notion of mind posited by enlightenment necessary as well as sufficient for the double task devolving upon it? One task, the negative, consists in discrediting belief because rational thought fails to recognize itself in it; the positive task involves the defense of credibility as an attribute belonging solely to everything that proves pervious to the light of reason. But does not the believer likewise find himself in what he believes? He contends that his mind is broader than the rationalistic. Imbued with trust and certitude, his mind is inspired by reasons of which reason is ignorant. The heart has reasons which the 'enlightened' are too purblind to see.

Hardith: You have clarified admirably some difficult passages of the text. Are you sure the clarification involves no distortion? You may, for all I know, have done to Hegel what enlightenment is here accused of doing to belief. Seriously, clarification not seldom turns out to be misrepresentation when what is being clarified relates to the reflective processes of another's mind. The rationalistic explanation of belief as having been fostered by a corrupt and deceiving priesthood the believer must reject as scandalous. How can deception enter a mind whose belief is vouched for by intuitive certainty? No consciousness, unless it be open to outer inspection, may be said to suffer from delusions; accordingly, a believer, deeply convinced of the truth of his belief, would unhesitatingly repulse a charge so outrageous, retorting that the maker of the charge must himself be deluded. With matters affecting a man's inner life no outsider can have direct acquaintance. But belief usually finds expression in denotable and inspectable objects, such as documents, emblems, ceremonials. Here enlightenment seems to be on firmer ground; belief though not directly subject to rationalistic animadversion, may be approached as it appears in forms externally observable.

Meredy: Although the manifestations of belief do come within the compass of external observation, they defy explanation by reason as much as belief itself. Without vicarious participation in their symbolic aura, they are apt to be reduced to mere objects of perceptual experience. And to such, enlightenment does indeed reduce them, thereby missing altogether the spiritual significance they have for the believing consciousness.

The worship of things made with hands—for example, statues and pictures—thus come to be confused with what they symbolize and are easily derided as if the worshiper actually believed works of human contrivance to possess divine attributes. How unjust is the equation of all image-worship with barbaric idolatry! Rationalistic criticism directed at the believer's attitude to the visible objects of his worship sheds more light on the limitation of enlightenment than on the consciousness of belief.

The same may be said as regards rationalistic treatment of the sacred events narrated in sacred books. In vain does the enlightened student look for clear evidence of their alleged historicity. The higher criticism may of course subject them to scrupulous examination, and enlightenment, going further, can point with malicious glee to this or that supposed event as inherently incredible and scientifically discreditable. All this, however, must appear to the convinced believer as sheer impertinence. Sacred books, he might aver, can furnish no support of religious belief such as would commend itself to the scientific historian, insisting that his belief's truth does not depend on the antecedent authenticity of certain documents but rather that certain documents derive their authenticity from the prior truth of belief. What believer worth his salt would suffer a jejune rationalism to usurp ultimate jurisdiction over questions of faith? And whenever a believer does appeal to historical evidence for confirmation of his religious persuasion he simply evinces the corruptive influence of enlightenment and fights a losing battle with weapons borrowed from the enemy's arsenal.

Rituals, too, and sundry practices which belief prescribes, must strike the rationalistic outsider as acts without rhyme or reason, incapable as he is of perceiving the harmony within the devout consciousness between religious faith and religious observance. Judged by the standard of utility, how purposeless, not to say foolish, seems the believer's assiduous concern with matters of so little consequence? Why, for instance, renounce the pleasure of indulging in certain food on certain days? But what the enlightenment may find trivial or meaningless forms part and parcel of the secret of belief; when practised, belief entails sundry postures and exercises the inwardness of which must needs remain a sealed book to the uninitiated.

Such then is the threefold attack on belief's observable expressions: religious worship is but idolatry; religious evidence has no rational basis; religious observance lacks practical usefulness. To such attack the genuine believer remains immune as long as he refuses to submit his faith to any external standard of description and explanation.

4. *The Rise of Enlightened Belief*

Hardith: That belief should ultimately succumb to enlightened criticism was of course dialectically necessary. And the historical references on which Hegel's analysis depends so heavily bear witness to the fact that many a religious tenet gradually became feeble and anaemic under the pervasive influence of reason. The arguments for natural religion, purged of mystery and superstition, mark the entrance of rationalism into the very heart of belief. The conception of enlightened belief is here particularly significant, implying partial surrender of dogmatic faith to critical thought. The war between them appears for the nonce to be over. In terms of the historical material, which again determines the progress of the dialectic, Hegel exhibits the triumph of rationalism on all three fronts.

As regards the object of religious consciousness, the victory seems complete. Ceasing to be literally—or even symbolically—present in sensuous form the object acquires the status of an abstract universal. Of the deity acknowledged by enlightened belief nothing more can be said than that it is a supreme being, an indefinable spirit, a subject to which no positive predicates are attributable. And such a subject Hegel contemptuously speaks of as an 'absolute vacuum'. But in so depreciating it he simply voices his prejudice. What is the alternative to a divine being anthropomorphized by the unenlightened? Is a predicateless subject so absurd? A negative theology may serve as profound basis of a positive religion; adherence to it has been widespread and not exclusively among the mystics. Rationalists, too, can have their supreme reality the supremacy of which would suffer denigration by any attempt to characterize its nature. What Hegel derides is but a special historical conception—to wit, the French *être suprême*.

Evidence for enlightened belief can obviously not be sought in sacred books, seeing that doubt of their historicity forms an integral part of such belief. What supplants them is pure intuition or natural light or immediate certainty. And here, too, the reliance is on human reason, trust in which presupposes a *lumen naturale* as its major endowment. Here also polemic is allowed to intrude itself in the analysis. By drawing too close an analogy between intellectual and sensuous certainty, Hegel betrays a personal bias. Can one properly compare intuitive apprehension of an absolute being to direct experience of a sensory datum? Both kinds of awareness seem to have nothing in common save their immediacy. But of immediacy Hegel himself discerns different forms. I am therefore baffled by the contention that, in claiming to have immediate cognition of an absolute being, the enlightened believer must abandon all experience except the experience afforded by ineffable sensations.

As for action induced by enlightened belief, the principle Hegel selects as paramount is the principle of utility, in accordance with which everything may be invested with usefulness, including the religious way of life. Of all things profitable, as Hegel ironically remarks, none can outrank in profitableness a rational religion. To the supreme being itself, considered as original source or first cause of all that is useful, must thus be accorded supreme utility. In utilitarianism Hegel sees the final catastrophe which enlightenment portends. Of this the analysis represents a curious mixture of acuity and maliciousness. Is the dialectic here inevitable or does it but serve as vehicle for conveying animadversions on a doctrine Hegel contemns?

Meredy: You correctly describe the last stage in the development of enlightenment as catastrophic; utilitarianism signifies for Hegel complete spiritual abdication since it is a doctrine which assigns anew to the individual a central place. The inwardness of belief, the individual's haven of refuge from the self-alienation to which the world of culture condemns him, the process of enlightenment effectively undermines and finally destroys, replacing it by the secular tenet that all values of life derive their sole sanction from the universal principle of utility. Rationalistic clarification of religion removes from it all transcendent reference: its seat and fulcrum is the natural individual. This is simply a corollary from the thesis that everything, not excepting the will to believe, is related to some use ultimately beneficial to the individual. The cultured or artificial self thus reverts dialectically to a happy state of nature. How strikingly Hegel satirizes the optimism of the utilitarian individualist! He depicts him as if coming from the hand of God to walk the earth as in a garden planted for his enjoyment, a garden in which still blooms the tree of knowledge of good and evil, and eminently useful is the fruit thereof. Of particular use is the knowledge that enables him to draw a sharp line between his own gifts and powers and those of creatures belonging to lower species. In this earthly paradise all things exist to minister to the individual, and he, a child of nature, emerges as the measure of values hitherto deemed spiritual. Nor are men without use to one another. If things are serviceable in different ways, so are men, seeing that they are able to form various groups for their mutual advantage. The protection of one's interests often involves satisfying the interests of others, every individual using and being used by his fellows. "One hand washes the other"—thus pithily Hegel phrases the matter. Enlightened self-interest, test of individual and social conduct, thus comes to be proclaimed as wisdom's ultimate counsel. To minds unconverted to utilitarianism, such advice must seem unmitigated folly, Hegel's expression being abomination (*Greuel*). Is it any wonder that utilitarianism, aiming to promote the greatest happiness of the greatest number, should reveal itself as his pet bête noire? Hegel's idea of the good does not involve reference to egocentric beneficiaries, nor does it depend on arithmetic for measuring the good and counting its recipients. If on occasion he employs the dialectic as medium for the expression of his own view, this is done, as it were, in an aside. More often than not he advances comments designed, as he explicitly states, merely 'for us', comments not integral to the diagnosis of the chosen theme. Yes, the dialectical process runs, here as elsewhere, the same inevitable course: enlightenment, such as it appears in the context of the *Phenomenology,* must by its own inner logic be driven to a position too overweening to remain tenable.

Hardith: You have failed to remove the difficulty relating to perceptual experience on which Hegel lays here so much stress. Enlightenment, so definitely rationalistic, would seem to have left behind the dialectic of sensuous cognition. The light which reason sheds on human belief and behavior emanates from within consciousness and is not kindled by anything external to consciousness. What has the light by which reason achieves clear and distinct insights in common with the light by which the luminous sun renders visible the things we perceive? Yet the analogy between them is one by which Hegel sets much store.

Meredy: Hegel is aware that the light of reason—the *lumen naturale*—is a figure of speech, and figurative, too, are the cognate expressions, such as clarification, elucidation, enlightenment. How ingenious is his varied play on the tropes *Aufklärung* and *Einsicht!* There obviously is no true resemblance between the light by which we *think* and the light by which we *see*. The similarity lies in the immediacy

240

in which their claims to equal certitude are alleged to be rooted. The directness of intellectual intuition, though not reducible to, may nevertheless be considered parallel with, the directness of sensuous experience. Either form of cognitive directness proves in the end to beggar all description. As far as valuation is concerned, the relation of enlightenment to perception is more intimate. For the principle of utility can originally have no other objects of application than such as come within the purview of individual percipients. Things produced for consumption, to speak in economic terms, *are* things, things visible and tangible, never precluded from being present here and now, and while often extended to cover commodities not directly perceptible, those in actual use are always particular and palpable. What utilitarianism thus confers value on is everything the use of which affords satisfaction, and be the users ever so numerous, the satisfaction cannot be enjoyed save by each user separately. Utility and perception thus reveal themselves as true elective affinities; the useful must primarily appear in the form of an individual percept, and there is no percept which some percipient could not endow with usefulness. On the paradox this involves Hegel dwells more systematically in the section that follows.

The Truth of Enlightenment

Hardith: The title puzzles me. Does it express Hegel's intention to argue *for* the truth of enlightenment or merely to state the truth *about* enlightenment? The first alternative is of course precluded, seeing that the dialectic has already shown enlightenment to be a despiritualizing force, a phase of rationalism incorrigibly superficial and jejune. The second alternative, though more tenable, is hardly necessary, the truth about enlightenment being of the ambivalent sort such as the dialectic confers upon mind's every recurrent posture. To enlightened belief thus pertains the same truth intrinsically enjoyed by all the persuasions marshalled in the treatise; each persuasion, exemplifying as it does a determinate perspective of human experience, is relatively true, and, being the perspective it is, indefeasibly so. It is only when for any perspective the claim is made that it encompasses the entire truth, a claim Hegel asserts to be inevitable, that absurdity ensues, and the logically incongruous becomes the very steppingstone to a higher position in the truth of which it survives transfigured as an essential component. What then is the significance of the heading of the present section?

Meredy: The point you raise is perhaps too fine for us to be punctilious about. I wonder, however, whether the use of the title could not be justified in connection with the explicitly creedal controversy enlightenment precipitates. The insight that initially appears pure—an intellective vision purged of belief—becomes in the course of the dialectic transformed into a species of belief. Assuming the shape of a discursive philosophy, enlightenment comes to embrace within its purview issues relating to religion and metaphysics and ethics, its determinate position constituting a synthesis of agnosticism and materialism and utilitarianism. What ultimately develops is a clash of opposed beliefs, each involving the insight proper to it. And since

242

having a belief and believing it true go hand in hand, the conflict of rival beliefs is tantamount to a conflict between rival truth-claims. Hegel hints that the contending claims resemble in essence the incompatible laws central in the *Antigone;* in obvious allusion to the tragedy, he speaks of one claim as possessing a 'divine right' and of the other as enjoying but a 'human right'. With respect to the different creeds, too, recognition of the paramount right of one entails disregard of the other's. And of like quality is the pathos towards which the antithesis of equally rightful claims inevitably tends. Affinitive if not synonymous are here right and truth. The truth of belief under attack by enlightenment, like the certitude of belief impelling Antigone to defiance of the state, is not susceptible of discursive proof, its claim being one which reason can neither support nor subvert. The truth of enlightened belief, more cognate with the validity of the belief by which the ruler of the state is guided, invites and meets the challenge to justify its rightful appeal. It is the truth such as enlightenment claims for its position which constitutes the theme of the present section.

Hardith: Illuminating indeed is the analogy between the conflict of laws in the *Antigone* and the creedal truth-claims in cultural society. The analogy casts an oblique light not only on the opposed truth-claims but on their mutual dependence as well. As neither law can destroy the other without injury to the community, so can neither truth-claim deny the other without impairing the significance of belief. May I state the matter in my own fashion? Faith without criticism turns into fanaticism, criticism without faith surrenders to nihilism. Is this not the gist of the dialectic? The reciprocal relation of faith and criticism is clearly implicit in the conception of enlightened belief: it is belief patently not inimical to rational criticism. Nor is the notion of enlightenment intelligible unless unenlightened belief constitutes its preemptive subject matter. Above all, however, there can be no enlightened faith without faith in reason in which alone its doctrine or method can be grounded. This may in general be granted in terms quite other than Hegel's.

Meredy: You seem to forget that what in this section Hegel is concerned with is enlightened belief assuming the shape of a tripartite philosophy in articulate form. And it is the truth-claim staked out, as it were, by an enlightened philosophy to which the analysis is directed. Of the three major tenets which that philosophy comprises, theological agnosticism comes first. Although at war with beliefs resting on nonrational or irrational grounds, enlightenment does not exclude such religion as can be harmonized with faith in reason. In complete accord with it is that kind of religion the object of which is in

243

the anomalous position of admitting knowledge concerning its existence but not concerning its essence. The supreme being of rationalistic religion is a subject possessed of no other predicate than the predicate supreme, thus remaining in effect predicateless and hence unknowable. That one can know of the supreme being nothing more than that it is supreme derives plausibility from the assumption that every other qualification of it would be a limitation of it. Negative predication alone is accordingly permissible if absolute supremacy is not to be detracted from. And if enlightened judgments of existence are said to depend for their contents on objects of sense-experience, what else can be asserted of the existence of the supreme being but that its nature must be absolutely other than the nature pertaining to objects of perception? Such absolute otherness is ultimately the sole determination of which the religious object is susceptible. Agnosticism, a cardinal article of enlightened faith, strikingly exemplifies the difficulty of maintaining an absolute separation of existence and essence. It is Hegel's contention that no significance can be attached to any object of which nothing is affirmable save merely *that* it is.

Hardith: Yet refusal to define and thus confine the nature of the supreme being is consistent with a philosophy seeking to vindicate religion in nontheistic terms. If such refusal constitutes agnosticism, what is the alternative? Surely not gnosticism! Whence the repugnance to the conception of a subject resisting positive predication? Hegel's dialectic, which reduces the conception to absurdity, here merges entirely with his polemic. Two thinkers might be mentioned—and Hegel's opposition to them is notorious—who saw no anomaly in the possibility of affirming knowledge of existence of which the essence must remain unknowable. In referring to Spinoza, I have in mind chiefly his notion of infinite attributes. When stress is laid on their actual infinity, the statement that the order of things is the same as the order of ideas cannot have the universal applicability his conventional interpreters assume it to have. The statement is relevant only to the relation of thought and extension, the two attributes to which alone knowability is limited. Of the parallelism between thought and the attributes other than extension, no assertion is possible, though the universe be viewed under the form of eternity, for such assertion would presuppose familiarity with the infinity of attributes, demonstrable knowledge of which is restricted to their existence and cannot extend to their essence. I am aware of the paradox of including Spinoza among the champions of agnosticism, yet what else but agnostic should he be called in relation to all those unfathomable infinities that constitute the sum and substance of nature whose pious synonym is God? Kant's agnosticism is more radical and hence more obvious. His things-in-themselves, too, exemplify knowability of their existence but not of their essence. Their resemblance to Spinoza's substance is striking, differing from it in remaining totally predicateless. Kant is induced to posit a transcendent reality in order to provide a realistic underpinning for the matter of experience which, unlike the form of experience, has an extra-rational ground. His very theory of knowledge, strange to say, requires reference to the unknowable; the contents of experience derive from a source alien to mind, and of that source, transcending the mind-dependent order of experience, we must, in complete ignorance of its essence, affirm an indubitable existence. These are two impressive versions of agnosticism. And whatever be their internal difficulties, the dialectic as here propounded could scarce be said to render them vulnerable.

Meredy: I should not disagree with your contention if we were to debate on its merits the limits of human knowledge. Our concern, however, is not with the general theme of agnosticism but only with that special variation which enlightenment exemplifies. The supreme being averred by enlightened religion, whose existence alone may be vouched for, turns out to be an abstraction, ultimately identical with the abstraction of pure matter in which enlightened metaphysics culminates. What the ensuing development of the dialectic hinges on is precisely the way in which agnosticism and materialism become interchangeable.

What is pure matter? Not directly present in sense experience, the purity of matter can only be posited by thought. One thing is to denote objects from which we receive varied and variable sensations, quite another is to arrive at the notion of a material substratum. Of such substratum, admittedly not perceivable, we can only say that it is perceptual objectivity desensitized, being merely what remains over, as Hegel says, "when we abstract from seeing, feeling, tasting, etc." The existence of pure matter thus becomes apparent only when we analyze away from things perceptible the sensory qualities they are supposed to have, when, in short, we *dis*qualify them. In affirming the existence of an unqualifiable substratum, materialism becomes in principle indistinguishable from agnosticism, differing from it not in the abstraction reached but in the manner of reaching it. Between the supreme being, an object of religious reverence, and pure matter, a subject of metaphysical preoccupation, the line proves to be vanishing, each abstraction susceptible of reduction to the other.

The reduction is of course a reduction to the absurd. For after all the supreme being is but another name for a divine being, an intellectualized synonym for the traditional God, and the aura that clings to such a being remains undiminished in any consciousness however enlightened. Should it be said that the concept of God, be it ever so pale and thin, coincides in the end with pure matter? And would not pure matter, too, lose the sense attaching to it as a metaphysical or scientific concept if thought of as signifying an object with a sacred halo conducive to the sentiment of piety?

It thus becomes inevitable that there should arise within enlightenment a division between the beliefs of two parties. The party of the 'Right', so to speak, representing the religious interests, comes to look with horror upon the godlessness of a smug naturalism, while the party of the 'Left', intent upon safeguarding the interest of science, cannot but regard as folly faith in a *fainéant* deity rendered otiose by scepticism. If the two parties, as in effect Hegel comments, could rise above the verbal or formal level of their controversy, they would make the surprising discovery that the contents of their respective beliefs are completely compatible. Indeed, between the notion of a supreme being and the notion of pure matter the distinction reveals itself as a distinction without a difference. It is to this anomalous situation which Hegel's analysis is dramatically directed.

Hardith: To follow Hegel adequately in his all too brief analysis, one should be fully familiar with the views of the French Encyclopaedists, for it is they that furnish the requisite material for this section. An examination of these views would raise anew the question of the extent to which the dialectic has the validity merely of a generalization based on ideas culled from sources bearing the impress of their origin in a given age and culture. On ideas so patently selective Hegel grafts the form of a sequence and development the necessity of which they can obviously not prove but may only exemplify. Whence, for instance, the necessity of the process whereby agnosticism and materialism appear initially differentiable and subsequently interchangeable? It is a necessity certainly not inherent in the material; among the Encyclopaedists were men who succeeded in maintaining these positions separately with no apparent awareness of being committed to theses subject to mutual substitution. That they do admit of reduction to each other would seem to be a reflection on them made by an external critic. But, here as elsewhere, the dialectic depends for ideational content and appropriate idiom almost wholly on the very illustrations it is alleged to be independent of. What different features Hegel's portrait of enlightenment would have exhibited had he drawn it from models not exclusively French! I am simply reiterating a point that continues to baffle me. Be that as it may, however, and assuming enlightenment to have reached an impasse, how can the principle of utility serve as means of escape from its predicament? And in what sense does the ethics of enlightenment constitute an advance in its dialectical progress?

Meredy: Hegel's statement of utilitarianism is unfortunately very compact and abstruse. Being a transition to the next section, its full import can only appear thereafter. The kernel of the argument seems to be this: the emergence of utility, principally as a concept of value, marks the transcendence of vapid abstractions and a return to the subjective individual. Utility is of course itself an abstraction if hypostatized as a predicateless substantive. Abstracted from things useful and from persons who use them, utility is but a formal concept void of content. As unqualified or unqualifiable utility resembles in indeterminateness the supreme being and pure matter. But even in an abstract view utility has the advantage over them, for it implies more clearly the priority of its adjectival import. Basic to its connotation is the presupposition of objects denotable as useful to individual users. In utilitarianism, therefore, the abstractions that plagued enlightenment before are left behind: self-consciousness becomes again dialectically paradigmatic, since no object can qualify as useful except in relation to a subject. Nothing, in other words, is profitable unless somebody finds or makes it so. Hence Hegel's view of utilitarianism as representing a higher stage in the dialectic of enlightenment; the relation of using and being used, comparable to the relation of perceiving and being perceived, reinstates the supremacy of the principle of subjectivity. Just as the subject enjoys primacy in the cognitive sphere (and this is self-evident when cognition takes the form of self-consciousness), so in the domain of enlightened ethics, the subject conceived as user must be accorded a like paramountcy. Relativity of knowledge to the knower has thus its counterpart in the relativity of utility to the utilitarian. Momentous indeed, as Hegel shows, are the consequences that flow from this new subjectivism.

Hardith: Before proceeding to the next theme, one more issue needs to be raised. What precisely is the connection between the different theses advanced by enlightenment? Of its tripartite philosophy, deism and materialism have to do exclusively with judgments of existence, utilitarianism chiefly with judgments of value. To what extent do the latter judgments depend on the former? The dialectic requires that ideas internally discordant must not be entirely abandoned but must become incorporated as transfigured or *aufgehoben* in a wider perspective. In what form do the enlightened ways of thinking regarding ontology reappear in relation to ethics?

Meredy: The enlightening process traced is continuous, reaching journey's end, as it were, in defense of utilitarianism. The process, having its inception in the insight into the factitiousness of the world of culture where the individual's self-alienation is reflected in speech and conduct, effectively deepens the feeling of self-alienation by making the individual increasingly aware of the separation between his artificial self and natural self. As it grows in power and influence, the insight that illuminates and clarifies must needs arouse the hostility of those governed by the fixed beliefs in the prevailing culture. Insight and be-lief—thus Hegel dramatizes the situation—gradually engage in open conflict, the former aiming to bring about a transvaluation of values that would result in freeing society of false standards and the individual of the consciousness of self-estrangement. Of such transvaluation enlightenment is but initially a programmatic prophecy; what finds at first utterance in a sort of manifesto gradually develops into a full-fledged doctrine. By what name should the doctrine be distinguished? Naturalism would seem a fitting label for it. Nature and the natural, in their varying senses, now become deeply fundamental. Enlightened religion is natural religion representing a synthesis of deism and agnosticism; enlightened ontology is that of nature conceived as homogeneous, the pure matter of materialism being the stuff or substance of all perceptual things purged of their sensible qualities; enlightened morality centers on the interests of the natural man, utilitarian values presupposing individuals liberated *from* the yoke of culture and liberated *for* the pursuit of happiness as an end in itself. Enlightenment is of one piece; it seeks to reconcile nature and man, and by such reconciliation, as Hegel concludes this section, "to transplant heaven to the earth below."

Absolute Freedom and Terror

Hardith: The title is clearly 'loaded', alluding as it does to the intellectual ferment and the social upheaval attending the French Revolution. I am once again moved to question Hegel's procedure. Is enlightenment always of the sort in which revolution lies dormant? Must every revolution inevitably follow the pattern here exhibited? Of the revolutions historically recorded how many actually fit into the Hegelian dialectic? Whence the legitimacy of conceiving as logically generic a single species? After all, the revolution in France was the result of ideas and events without exact parallel elsewhere. It is only on the generic level—and such admittedly is the level of the *Phenomenology*—that revolutionary processes must necessarily occur in accordance with conditions dialectically determined, the special forms they may assume being due to diverse causes which, though empirically ascertainable with varying degrees of probability, are obviously beyond the ken of a priori speculation. Hegel, so it seems, invests with necessity not the general concept of revolution but solely a specific instance of it, as if here the universal and the particular could be made to coincide. For he lavishes his attention upon a dated phenomenon of which he delineates with assurance the genesis and outcome. Yet concerning its true causal explanation unanimity among historians is scarcely conspicuous. But the dialectic is of Hegel's own making, and so is the necessity he attributes to the emergence of a revolutionary process under conditions fixed beforehand in the course of mind's dialectical biography. As regards the necessity of its appearance *within* the dialectic, the operative conditions are both original and immediate, being implicit in the very conception of culture and explicitly related only to the principle of utility. The cultural ethos, itself conditioned by the estrangement between the individual's legal and extralegal personality, conditions in its turn a deeper consciousness of self-alienation,

249

and this serves as a condition of an enlightenment that moves inevitably towards its culmination in absolute freedom and supervening terror. It appears as though the terror to which the French Revolution gave rise were the end product of a series of dialectical movements having its inception in culture. Culture, in a word, must be viewed as containing within it the seeds of its ultimate subversion. But it is on the proximate condition on which Hegel lays his chief stress. That condition he looks for in the ethics of enlightenment. The basis of the claim for an absolute freedom that must ineluctably lead to a reign of terror he finds in the principle of utility as the measure of the greatest good. In the basket of utilitarianism, to speak facetiously, are thus to be laid all the revolutionary eggs. How weak in the dialectical chain is the link between enlightenment and utilitarianism! Assuming a nonutilitarian ethics to be equally compatible with the spirit of enlightenment, an assumption not impermissible, would not the revolutionary movement such as Hegel here traces either have been precluded or have taken a different direction?

Meredy: Your reiteration in a new form of a matter often urged before is challenging. Hegel here does depend far too much on his chosen example. Most of the details are drawn from sources that bear the stamp of a definite era. Yet the treatment of a theme so dated, though too sketchy and too slanted, is not lacking in symbolic verisimilitude. It is true, of course, that revolutionary outbursts are unlike one another, resulting as they do from multiple causes the specificity of which is relative to time and place. But they yield to comparison. Revolutions are as a rule impelled by desire for freedom from some state of affairs deemed intolerable; they usually explode into turbulence and violence; they generate the struggle for power among different factions; they tend to inspire open or hidden counterrevolutions; they lead to the spread of general fear and suspicion; and, though prone to forge new chains for old, more often than not they are followed by a spiritual emancipation and rebirth. Of these and other generic features of the revolutionary process Hegel's analysis is all compact, in spite of the heavy burden laid upon the details of his particular illustration. Many of the details, which may belong to this or to that atypical situation, are indeed misleading, justifying not a little the charge against him of having misconceived the specific as generic. Unless we adhere to the distinction between actual and symbolic verisimilitude, Hegel's apparent confusion of the topical with the typical must needs remain a stumbling block.

As for the posited necessary connection between enlightenment and utilitarianism, a position requisite for the dialectical passage to revolution, your comment on it does not militate against Hegel's thesis.

Utility is a principle Hegel could obviously not have borrowed from the English moralists. Chronology rules out his dependence on Jeremy Bentham or John Stuart Mill. Hegel simply 'deduces' the principle from the enlightened attitude to life and the world. What but enlightened self-interest, which Hegel's words *die Nützlichkeit* and *das Nützliche* signify, could receive moral sanction from a naturalism the related tenets of which include deism in religion, materialism in ontology, sensationalism in epistemology? Central in the philosophy of enlightenment is the natural individual whose perceptions and actions constitute the standard for judging all matters of fact and matters of value. The later theory of utilitarianism, could Hegel have known it, would have appeared to him as if made to order for his dialectical purpose. How remarkable that he should have not only anticipated the very principle of an ethical system so essentially English but that he should have considered it the dialectical bellwether of the French Revolution! This if nothing else should be a lesson not to mistake symbolic for literal verisimilitude.

Hardith: It seems anachronistic to saddle Hegel's words with philosophic connotations alien to them. The juxtaposition of an English system of morals and a French social upheaval, as if the former afforded passage to the latter, is too extravagant to be taken seriously. Nothing is to be gained by attributing to Hegel's procedure, which is paradoxical enough, a feat so fanciful. The dialectic, I take it, is chiefly concerned with the logical implications of utility conceived as predicate. What does the predicate signify and what does it presuppose? It is of course obvious that the description of anything as useful presupposes some user whether actual or potential in relation to whom alone the predicate may be said to acquire meaning. Here is an objective predicate—that is, a predicate affixed to objects—the origin of which is subjective and the application relative. Upon utility as thus understood Hegel lays the major emphasis. To connect it with a later system of ethics in the context of which utility plays a different part is to entertain, if I may say so, the notion of guilt by phonetic association. No, Mill's *Utilitarianism* is not chargeable with the dialectical delinquency of which in the *Phenomenology* the concept of utility is shown to be so culpable. After all, no revolution actually followed upon publication of Mill's work, and no revolution need actually ensue from Hegel's dialectic of utility.

Meredy: 'Guilt by phonetic association'—an admirable phrase, not inaccurately descriptive of Hegel's paronomastic diction. His diagnosis of many a persuasion is made to depend for the exhibition of its 'dialectical delinquency'—another felicitous expression—on a pun

251

deliberately designed to reveal the radical ambivalence implicit in it. On this, however, we need not expatiate further. As for the different uses of utility—such, for example, as Hegel's and Mill's— a congeneric sense clearly belongs to them. Whenever and however used, utility is a concept relative and ancillary to subjective interests. And herein lies precisely the latency of revolution. Incidentally, revolution is a word lending itself particularly to paronomasia, naming as it does a rotary motion as well as a social cataclysm. Without actually employing the term, Hegel retains its ambiguity in the analysis of the consequences to which the principle of utility gives rise, and since the Frence Revolution forms in fact the content of the analysis, to call the consequences revolutionary is no misnomer. From utility to revolution, then, the transition appears inevitable. Why? The answer is twofold. Utility is a principle the application of which proves to be precluded without revolving back to the centrality of the individual self, a revolution signifying a return to a superseded stage of the dialectic; and in becoming universal, utility is a principle on which every individual may assert a rightful claim, this revolution moving in the direction of changing society where men will be free and equal—free to use whatever they choose and equal in their right to do so. Of these two revolutions—reversion to subjective individualism and extension of freedom and equality to all—utility is the fount and origin.

Hardith: But the revolutions you speak of, if but derived by analysis from the concept of utility, can have no other status than that of abstract possibilities. The concept, considered fundamental to an enlightened theory of value, involves certain beliefs expressible in propositional form—to wit: nothing has value except that which is useful; things acquire or retain usefulness solely by the grace of those using them; everybody is free to endow with usefulness whatever he pleases; and to all alike belongs the same freedom. Absolute freedom, which Hegel singles out as the chief new desideratum, together with absolute equality as its corollary, is simply a logical inference from the concept of utility. Insight into the necessity of absolute freedom as inseparably bound up with the notion of utility thus becomes the crowning triumph of enlightenment. But being a product of logical inference, the necessity has but formal validity, such as belongs to all analytical statements. The inference might indeed appear revolutionary but only in thought and for thought and need as such produce no action. Whence its necessity to explode into deeds of violence culminating in a reign of terror?

Meredy: Since Hegel's allusions are nearly all to a revolution that actually occurred, and whereof he knows the intellectual sources as well as the calamitous results, the dialectic simply takes the form of

252

showing that the asserted belief in universal freedom and equality cannot be enacted: the enactment must necessarily contradict the assertion. What Hegel says in this connection cuts rather deep, raising anew the issue of the relation between the individual and the universal but couched principally in political terms. The main contention is briefly this: the belief in absolute freedom and equality invests with absoluteness the individual himself: the individual no longer represents the universal but becomes one with it. Broken away under the influence of enlightenment from the social and cultural bonds that bound him to a particular ethos, the individual now proclaims the right to speak and to act in the name of the universal. But since, alas, the right to be spokesman or agent for the universal none can in theory deny to others, the ensuing struggle for exclusive possession of the same right among different persons or factions promises to have dire consequences. What renders the struggle inevitable is the claim by each to reflect through his private will the will of all. Hence a dilemma: either the emphasis falls on the individual or it falls on the universal. If on the former, the anomaly lies in some individuals forcing their decisions upon all; if on the latter, the anomaly consists in the impossibility of justifying the general validity of any decisions unless initiated or executed by some individuals.

Hardith: References to Rousseau are evident throughout the section. Why does Hegel treat so lightly the distinction elaborated in the *Social Contract* between the general will and the will of all? Aware in one form or another of the dilemma mentioned, Rousseau shows how each individual, in theory if not in practice, may look upon himself as 'sovereign', in the sense of sharing in the general will and thus being entitled to exert power in and on its behalf.

Meredy: Curiously enough, in his later writings, Hegel held the distinction to merit praise, criticizing Rousseau only for not consistently adhering to it. Most of Hegel's references in the *Phenomenology* are disconcertingly oblique, and those relating to the *Social Contract* are no exception; they merely serve the purpose of illustrating the precarious relation between the individual and the universal, with special emphasis on the way it was understood—or misunderstood—by the French revolutionaries. What principally here concerns him is the paradox inherent in the necessity which the individual is under to be both a private person and a participant in the general will. Who has the right to act as another's deputy in voicing the intent of a general will supposedly incarnate in everyone? As Hegel says, "Where the self is but represented, or present only by proxy, the actual self is conspicuously absent." The very general will, alleged to be present in each and all,

253

would seem to preclude the assumption by any particular self of the authority to render decisions universally binding. And yet, if deeds in the name of the general will *are* to be done, they *can* only be done by these rather than those individuals. If these do the deeds, those are excluded from doing them, and, in being thus excluded, must needs find themselves deprived of their legitimate freedom. From this analysis Hegel concludes that "universal freedom can ultimately achieve nothing positive; there is left for it only negative action lashed into the fury of destruction."

Hardith: Not freedom as such but only its assumed absoluteness or universality is here subject to Hegel's dialectical indictment. The dialectic runs true to form: any concept must turn into its opposite when pushed to extreme lengths. Abstract freedom entertained by thought leads to action which in its very name results in the struggle of its votaries for the privilege of annihilating each other. It is thus that Hegel views the struggle among the leaders in the French Revolution. On behalf of everyone's freedom to share in the general will, the freedom of some equally entitled to participate in it must be drastically revoked. Complete silence of rival claims to equal freedom can here be brought about only through death of the claimants. No wonder Hegel can ironically speak of death as "the sole and only work and deed accomplished by universal freedom." Between men considered unconditionally free and equal no other relation appears possible. The death of all but one, if I may emulate Hegel's irony, would indeed realize the ultimate fusion of the individual with the universal, a consummation hardly to be wished, yet short of this, death loses its sting by becoming too commonplace, serving as a cold-blooded means for furthering the ends of a government by terror. In the triviality or meaninglessness of this syllable (*Plattheit dieser Silbe*) lies the sole wisdom of those who, in order to preserve the fruits of a revolution instituted for the liberation of mankind, must perforce turn into implacable terrorists! The dialectic is undeniably impressive. It is permissible to question, however, whether the dialectic would have taken precisely this curve without a biased reading of Rousseau and of French history.

Meredy: Hegel's reading is indeed biased, though the word selective, being less pejorative, would seem the more accurate. But it must be remembered that the topic, as the title indicates, has to do with the relation of freedom conceived as absolute and the ensuing reign of terror. Is there a necessary connection between them? The question, as Hegel shows, is ultimately bound up with another—namely, what kind of government is compatible with the postulate of absolute freedom? Choosing from his literary and historical material only such

254

features as are essential for the dialectical analysis of the question, the crucial argument is this. The government of a society composed of ideally free members should be no government at all or a government merely by a particular faction. No particular faction, however, regardless of how it achieves power, can be said to govern except by courtesy, and is thus always open to challenge by a different faction. The exercise of a power that belongs to it no more rightfully than to any other portends the eventual overthrow of every faction. Between the governors and the governed the relation must accordingly grow ever more precarious; naked force alone being the basis of the specious stability the community happens to enjoy, the agents and patients of force remain natural enemies, divided by mutual distrust, each chargeable with guilt. The guilt of the governing faction consists in usurpation of the right to govern, that is, in arrogating to itself exclusive jurisdiction over the lives of individuals all deemed free and equal. The governed, on the other hand, are held culpable of the crime of appearing unwilling to be governed. Even of being but suspected of such unwillingness serves as evidence sufficiently grave to merit punishment by death. 'Off with their heads'—this humorous phrase in *Alice's Adventures in Wonderland* becomes the grim order daily given to the executioner! Thus they are dealt with who can be accused of no iniquity greater than the iniquity of secretly harboring intentions to subvert the factional government in power. And is there a more effective way of exterminating intentions, if I too may indulge in irony, than to remove their fount and habitat? This of course is a reduction to the absurd of a putative conception of absolute freedom envisaged as if capable of political realization, the dialectical outcome being destruction of all freedom. The horror inherent in the situation is the horror of sheer negativity—death fortuitous and meaningless. And they who come face to face with death, their lord and master, confront at last the only power that can satisfy the desire for universal equality. The dead alone are absolutely equal.

Hardith: The argument against absolute freedom does not necessarily preclude arguments for relative freedom. For a deeper analysis and more adequate justification of freedom Hegel returns to the region of the inner life, dropping the concept as one of no further social significance. And yet the mutual opposition of freedom and control elaborated in this section cries out for dialectical union. Should not the dialectic, remaining true to form, strike some balance between them, such as democratic constitutions define in principle and which the social communities founded on them may achieve with varying degrees of approximation? Is it not curious that Hegel should at this stage

255

abandon further consideration of the crucial issues relating to the political state as if they were of little or no consequence in the biography of mind? The *Phenomenology* never resumes the discussion of freedom, a theme so momentous in the life of everyone living in an organized society. Is human experience under conditions of such freedom as the state makes possible inferior in spiritual dimension to human experience attainable in the spheres of morality and art and religion of which the treatise henceforth exhibits the dialectic? Could it be the same Hegel who later declared that "man must venerate the state as the divine on earth?"

Meredy: The matter you broach is puzzling only if we assume the *Phenomenology* to represent an historical biography of mind or a compendium of a systematic philosophy. On either view, the absence of a more extended development of the idea of freedom would seem difficult to explain. Hegel was of course aware that the revolution in France, despite the episodic government by terror, marked the beginning and not the end of human freedom. And did he not have a theory of the state altogether at variance with the political reflections contained in this book? His very neglect to dilate subsequently on freedom should suffice to show that it must not be held to constitute a life of mind subject to the demands of chronology or the author's intellectual autobiography, as if the typical persuasions examined coincided with his own. As far as the *Phenomenology* is concerned, the French Revolution exemplifies men's recurrent aspiration to *absolute* freedom and terrorism its necessary concomitant. *Relative* freedom, admittedly variable, involves no reconciliation but rather compromise with its opposite, the issues precipitated being more political or practical than speculative or dialectical.

The dialectical story of freedom here told is the story of a 'cyclic necessity', as Hegel calls it, representing the logical evolution of certain forms of organized society. The cycle begins with the city state (such as the Athenian), the internal instability of which dooms it to be superseded, and ends, after passing through intermediary and progressively more advanced social structures, with the society of culture (typified by the monarchy of Louis XIV). It is within a society of culture that enlightenment makes its appearance, and the consequences of its inevitable spread consist in undermining the foundations of the established order and in engendering in men's hearts the passion for a new freedom. This passion underlies the revolutionary gospel of absolute freedom resulting in terror. It is Hegel's contention that the same cycle of necessity would have to be traversed afresh and continually repeated whenever freedom initially limited becomes ultimately

purged of all limitation. Relative freedom can thus not serve as antidote to absolute freedom. Although freedom circumscribed by sundry
conditions and qualifications is the only freedom organized society
permits its members to claim or to enjoy, what society can debar them
from entertaining in the privacy of their minds thoughts of freedom
free of all restrictions?

In the reverse order, the dialectical story of freedom is also the
story of the progressive growth in the individual's consciousness of
self-alienation, depending on the conditions of his social life. His
feeling of estrangement becomes increasingly intensified as he advances
from simpler to more complex forms of social organization. And if
in the aftermath of revolution during a reign of terror, he reaches the
culminating point of self-estrangement, this very culminating point becomes its turning point. Chastened and deepened by the awesome
experience of revolution and terror, man awakens to a fresh knowledge
of his true position. And the knowledge is twofold: it is knowledge
that the general will and the single will are inseparable, and it is knowledge that absolute freedom and organized society are mutually exclusive. The assertion of absolute freedom is simply impossible of social
enactment. Yet the assertion is a spiritual necessity. It is the recognition of such necessity that drives the individual once more back upon
introspection. In the rediscoverable land of self-consciousness absolute
freedom loses its power to alienate and to destroy. But it is the inwardness of moral consciousness that must afford the habitation where the
individual and the universal may meet again as one.

The Moral Consciousness

1. The Concept of Morality

Hardith: Hegel's dialectical transitions from stage to stage differ in clarity and relevance, some being quite transparent, others more or less abstruse. The last statement in the analysis of any theme usually serves as intimation of what is to follow; but while the intended clue is often provided by a pun or some other obvious device, more often its expression appears at first somewhat mystifying. The passage, for instance, to this new theme, heralded by the closing words of the old, can hardly be said to constitute an illuminating introduction to it. Hegel speaks of what we are about to examine as 'the moral structure of spirit'. The significance of the adjective is far from evident. Whence the necessity of preempting it for designating the postrevolutionary stage of mind? Is the word prima facie the most apposite here? The passage in question might be stated in at least three different though related ways. (a) Passage from absolute freedom involving social anarchy to absolute freedom requisite for spiritual autarchy; (b) passage from the war of political factions to the reemergence of subjective individualism; (c) passage from the experience of self-estrangement to the experience of self-reconciliation. If moral consciousness requires the subject of it to be volitionally autonomous and singularly universal and completely self-assured, the term 'moral' would here seem to acquire a connotation strangely unwonted.

Meredy: That many of Hegel's terms are, in your phrase, 'strangely unwonted', is no secret and should by this time cause no surprise. In a technical disquisition on his work it would indeed be pertinent to expatiate at length on the author's linguistic peculiarities, a task we may safely leave to the specialists. But the label 'moral' affixed to the new type of consciousness, the theme of the present section, is clearly appropriate if we bear in mind the distinction here particularly important between volition and action. Even in common parlance the

258

label cannot be attached in the same sense to the will prompting the act and the act prompted by it. Should moral value be ascribed primarily to the will or to the act? For reasons to be considered Hegel assumes that morality is an attribute intrinsic to volition, the attribute related to action being derivative. He uses a different predicate in connection with certain types of conduct: 'ethical' (if this be the proper translation of *sittlich*) are those acts which group-conscious rather than self-conscious individuals perform spontaneously in compliance with laws bred by custom. The inescapable obligation to perform them Hegel regards as exemplified by the ethos and pathos of a social order presupposed and reflected in the tragic fate of Antigone. And the Sophoclean tragedy typifies for him a concrete world the spiritual quality of which lies precisely in the conflict of equally imperative duties. When in the *Phenomenology* we reach the theme of morality, the ingenuous society under fateful control of rival ethical forces has long been dialectically superseded. What we are now called upon to examine is not the spiritual form of a world but the form of a spiritual posture. Requisite for this posture is the antecedent persuasion that the postrevolutionary world, whatever social shape it may assume, can never be a world conducive to individual enjoyment of absolute freedom. Yet, such freedom, though not attainable in the world, is inexpungible from the sphere of the individual's moral consciousness. One thing is the ethical structure of the world, the basis of its particular ethos; quite another thing is the sense of morality, the habitat of which is not the world but the self, and hence its ineradicable subjectivity. The contrast between the ethical and the moral, as Hegel employs the terms, affords a measure of the distance that separate the later from the earlier stage of man's spiritual experience.

Hardith: I understand quite well why absolute freedom, an idea shown to entail anarchy, should be made to survive as an ideal of individual aspiration within reach beyond the compass of organized society. Where indeed could enjoyment of absolute freedom be sought and found if not in the depth of consciousness. This much seems clear. But whence the necessity of qualifying as moral the consciousness where alone complete freedom must have its seat and anchor? The argument derives plausibility from assigning to morality a meaning exclusively Kantian. If absolute freedom is the same as absolute autonomy of the will, and if moral consciousness signifies nothing but consciousness of duty, many of the details marshalled in the text effectively serve Hegel's purpose but it is a purpose principally polemical. It is as if the entire argument were constructed to give vent to his personal reflections on the principles and consequences of Kant's ethics. To

259

be sure, strictures on sundry and selected views of his predecessor appear in earlier parts of the work, but only as illustrations of certain persuasions relative to recurrent perspectives. But here the perspective is wholly and uniquely Kant's, and so prejudicially reproduced that its inner dialectic and external criticism become inseparably fused. Does Kant's theory of morality embody such a universal or typical aspect of experience that it must form a necessary chapter in the biography of mind? If so, one might expect the chapter to contain more of the story of mind than a compendium of the biographer's doctrinary prepossessions?

Meredy: The section on morality does indeed appear modeled on tenets with which Hegel's own are in fundamental disagreement. Kant's are not the only ones to which he refers. Allusions to Fichte are unmistakable. And allusions to other writers, notably to those belonging to the Romantic Movement, are easily detectable. Hegel is too close to his contemporaries to represent their ideas with the same relative detachment with which he portrays ideas more remote in time and interest. Intrusion into the representation of hostile criticism must needs detract from their importance. Hegel's histrionic efforts are more often than not producive of caricatures. Yet, the intent of the work is distinctly not autobiographical; it traces the dialectical development of the mind of the race, and in that development the moral perspective, comparable to the perceptual or sceptical or any other, emerges as typical and necessary. What Hegel here deals with is not a moral *theory* but a moral *attitude.* And the emphasis is clearly on a world assumed to be amenable to the demands of a moral consciousness. Basic to all this are certain postulates to a brief discussion of which I propose that we now turn.

2. The Moral Postulates

Hardith: In approaching the 'moral view of the world', as he calls it, Hegel contrives a situation palpably anomalous. He begins by giving a particular meaning to the world in which morality is to be realized and by attributing an equivocal meaning to the postulates requisite for its analysis. As for the world, its true synonym is here simply the order of existence or of nature. We must not forget that it is absolute freedom entailing social anarchy which necessitates transference of its conception from the political to the moral sphere. Not the order of society but the order of nature now becomes the center of attention, since only in relation to the latter can moral postulates be rendered intelligible. As Hegel chooses to state them, the postulates are demands made on nature. With the world and the postulates as thus construed, Hegel's dialectical triumph over the moral attitude is an easy one. He shows that it conceals but thinly a whole nest of contradictions, an expression Kant used in similar form in a different connection, one Hegel is not averse to quote.

Consider the first postulate. Hegel speaks of it as the harmony of morality and nature. What a curious demand! Although actually opposed, morality and nature must be assumed as ultimately conjoined. But a harmony enjoying no present but only eventual realization, belongs to an epicene species, one that partakes of being as well as of nonbeing. It represents the kind of desideratum of which we cannot say that it is but only that it ought to be. Were morality and nature in complete disharmony, the will to act in obedience to duty, in obedience, that is, to what ought to be operative in the natural world, would be doomed to everlasting frustration, and were their harmony an accomplished fact, every act performed would automatically come to possess a moral quality. The moral will cannot function at all except in a nature the moral neutrality of which must be taken for granted. Is the first postulate then nothing more than a hope that the relation of indifference between nature and morality may finally become transformed into one of concord? "To postulate a proposition," says Charles Peirce somewhere, "is no more than to hope it is true." Is this not consistent with Hegel's contention? If to a mere hope, and a hope infinitely deferred, the moral view of the world owes its sole support, what a fragile reed to lean on! Phrased thus, the postulate's absurdity is of course a foregone conclusion.

Meredy: 'Sentence first, verdict afterwards'—is this the gravamen of your charge against Hegel? The charge is not entirely unjust. For his exposition of the postulates is certainly too censorious, having little resemblance to their alluded prototypes. In the context of Kant's doctrine they appear in a different form and with an austere cogency of their own. But Hegel's allusive method is not amenable to principles of verisimilitude. Kant's name, strange to say, is actually nowhere mentioned; and if Hegel borrows the Kantian postulates, taking excessive liberties with their original formulation, he does so primarily with the intent of pointing up the difficulty of harmonizing by means of them antitheses antecedently posited.

For after all (confining ourselves to the first postulate), what is the relation between nature and morality? The natural, it is obvious, *must* initially be contrasted with the moral: there would be no need for morality without a prior bifurcation of the moral as the nonnatural and the natural as the nonmoral; yet the bifurcation cannot be taken seriously, since the moral would appear otiose unless deemed capable

261

of becoming manifest in the natural world, and such a manifestation would be patently precluded if the natural world were thought to be radically alien to morality. Hence a dilemma: either the bifurcation is real or unreal. If real, morality seems impossible; if unreal, morality seems unnecessary. This dilemma no postulate or hope of their ultimate harmony can logically resolve.

Apart from the allusion to Kant, is not Hegel's analysis germane to any system based on the distinction as well as the relation between what naturally is and what morally ought to be? And does not the previous dialectic of absolute freedom appear here in another form? If absolute freedom as a political conception entails social anarchy, absolute freedom on the moral level presupposes natural lawlessness. For only a natural world *not* determined by laws descriptive of its intrinsic structure and ways of operation can be said to conform to moral ideals or imperatives originating in volition conceived as absolutely autonomous. Yes, it is the same dialectic to which the demand for absolute freedom or autonomy is ever subject on whatever plane of human experience the demand is made.

Hardith: You have greatly clarified the dialectic involved in the first postulate by comparing absolute freedom of the individual in the social sphere with absolute autonomy of the will in the moral. But should not their difference be noted also? While the claim to absolute freedom by the individual is utterly irreconcilable with the possible existence of organized society, the claim to absolute autonomy by the moral agent may—postulably, at any rate—be harmonized with the existence of an external world the natural laws of which are merely indifferent to the demands of morality. Absolute freedom, denied co-existence with the social order, reemerges as absolute autonomy inherent in the consciousness of duty. If to the first postulate belongs the task of bridging the gulf separating nature and morality, the second postulate, reinforcing the first, has the function of dealing with the same issue in simpler and more concrete terms. Moral and natural now come to designate differentiable and conflicting aspects *within* individual consciousness, the problem shifting, as it were, from ontology to psychology. The new antithesis is between morality and the inward nature of man, a nature covering the whole gamut of sensibility. Man's sensuous nature, prone to countless impulses and desires, of which each is, so to speak, a law unto itself, would, but for his rational consciousness, remain in a state of perpetual anarchy: it is the aim of reason to establish over the chaos of natural inclinations the hegemony of moral duty. But in what precarious position does this leave morality! Short of abolishing all inclinations, the struggle of duty with them can never cease. Because the duality of inclination and duty appears at the outset as a stark dualism, and must so appear, such acts as are prompted by inclination fall outside the sphere of morality, and the label 'moral' can be affixed solely to deeds done in the teeth of inclination. Upon morality devolves the task of keeping the natural man in unremitting subjection, and the natural man retorts by continual rebellion against the dictates of morality.

In the struggle between reason and sensibility, as Hegel phrases it, reason is called upon to resolve the conflict and to restore the unity of self-consciousness. But this cannot be accomplished save on reason's own terms. Hence the insistent demand that sensibility ought to be in conformity with reason. Such a demand, which is contained in the postulate of harmony between inclination and duty, what is it but an expression of hope comparable to that voiced in the first postulate? There is, however, this notable difference. The struggle, not being between morality and nature but rather between man's natural sensuousness and moral consciousness, thus becomes transferred to the subjective level. It is a struggle carried on within everyone. To be always engaged in making progress in morality reveals itself as the true vocation of man, and all the truer because journey's end can never be reached.

Hegel's allusion to Kant's postulate of immortality is unmistakable. Since at no moment of existence in the sensible world can man's rational will achieve perfect accordance with the moral law, a perfection synonymous with holiness, approximation to it can only be found in an infinite progress. And if in an endless progress alone can perfect accordance with the moral law become attainable, does this not presuppose an endless duration of the existence and the personality of the same rational being? This is briefly Kant's famous proof of the immortality of the soul, proffered as nothing more than a postulate of Practical Reason. Hegel's caustic remarks relating to it seem gratuitous. Why the animus? My own interest in immortality, I hasten to confess, is less than warm, yet Kant's argument for it strikes me as no feebler than most.

Meredy: The second postulate, though differing from the first, shares with it a common dialectic. Nothing but this matters. Duty and inclination must of course be considered initially bifurcated, for if every inclination to act in a certain way were spontaneously moral, duty would simply remain a word signifying nothing. Yet the bifurcation must not be construed as complete, for how could any moral undertaking ever be carried out if inclination were absolutely unamenable to the call of duty? Thus once more a dilemma: the bifurcation is

263

either real or unreal. If real, duty seems impossible; if unreal, duty seems unnecessary. The postulated existence of their ultimate harmony impales morality on one of the dilemma's horns, since duty and inclination are assumed to approximate progressively a state of happy union. But the harmony is only postulated, remaining a hope infinitely deferred, and the conflict between man's sensuous nature and his moral consciousness must ever continue unabated.

As for Hegel's criticism of Kant's postulated immortality of the soul on which the possibility of moral perfectibility is made to depend, the criticism, though only oblique, is not extraneous. It is plainly in keeping with the dialectic to which any mere postulate lays itself open. Apart from condemning the moral consciousness to inevitable extinction in the dim distance of infinitude where it would reach perfection and thus cease to be perfectible, apart from this, Kant's postulate suffers from the contradiction of positing a goal, the attainment of which by a process admittedly endless cannot be other than a priori fictitious. Morality, in short, is involved in a process which both ought and ought not to be completed. Infinite continuity of moral progress is incompatible with the soul's aspiration after ultimate perfection. Final attainment of perfection removes the need for the soul's immortality. The ambivalence of Kant's postulate is too obvious to require further comment. My own interest in immortality, which resembles yours in lack of warmth, is neither here nor there. But of all the arguments in favor of it, Kant's seems to me the weakest, fully deserving Hegel's derision.

Hardith: The issues involved in the third postulate are too recondite to be handled without going too far afield. Here Hegel broaches a double theme, combining them by making use with considerable latitude of ideas embodied in Kant's final postulate which epitomizes an 'ethico-theology', a name by which in a different context Kant described his position. The first theme has to do with the plurality of duties, the second with the relation of morality to happiness.

The conflict between inclination and duty is now supplanted by the conflict of determinate duties, each duty excluding all the others. Yet, such as are excluded appear equally consonant with the principle of dutifulness. Indeed, what act could not be justified by acting as if the maxim of the action were by the agent's will willed to become a universal law of nature? Hegel simply reiterates a contention often urged that the categorical imperative can neither prescribe nor proscribe any particular deed. The moral command to do one's duty cannot by itself resolve the conflict between rival duties.

It is this which lies behind the impulsion to postulate the existence of a higher moral consciousness sanctioning by its supreme will whatever course of action the agent chooses dutifully to embark upon. Every moral agent is thus in harmony with a universal lawgiver whenever he acts in obedience to the only moral law which is absolutely binding—namely, the law that duty be done. And this postulated harmony between the moral law and a divine legislator receives final expression in connection with the postulated harmony between morality and happiness.

The existence of God thus averred has here no other basis than the demand that happiness should be eventually proportional to virtue: the divine legislator must also function as divine judge of moral desert. If the moral law commands that duty be done, it commands also that justice be done. The belief in the existence of a divine being as the guarantor of ultimate justice owes its validity to moral rather than logical necessity. To be sure, the will incited to action by the stern voice of duty is not a will bent on the pursuit of happiness. But actual indifference of duty to happiness does not entail prohibition of its possible enjoyment. Lack of correspondence between righteousness and a happy lot is only too apparent. Good fortune is but a fortuitous concomitant of moral conduct, the result, as it were, of grace. Consistent, however, with a true sense of justice is the hope that happiness will be ultimately distributed according to merit, for so only can the final triumph of morality be assured. And just as towards moral perfection the progress must be infinite, so equally infinite must be the progress towards the realization of happiness proportional to goodness. The postulate of the soul's immortality and the postulate of God's existence are thus bound together by mutual implication.

Kant's ethico-theological postulate, so candidly a confession of faith and hope, can of course not be treated as if it were an argument resting on irrefutable evidence. Its probative force is too vulnerable to be taken seriously. Why does Hegel misconceive the postulate as if it were a proposition with a claim on truth? How otherwise explain the harshness of the criticism he brings to bear upon it?

Meredy: Is a postulate a proposition, and in what sense; and has it a truth-claim, again in what sense? Such questions are irrelevant simply because Hegel is here not concerned with the subject matter of logic. 'Proposition' and 'truth' are words we had better eschew, substituting for them expressions more apposite in the present context. Moral postulates such as the Kantian are for Hegel but asserted beliefs rooted in the will, and the exhibition of their dialectical instability is what his analysis is intent upon. Thus the assertion of final harmony between nature and morality develops into an inescapable di-

265

lemma; and a cognate dilemma is latent in the affirmation of an ultimate harmony between inclination and duty. There is something seriously the matter with postulates the analysis of which yields the paradoxical results that morality is either not possible or not necessary. And is not the third postulate in the same predicament? And does it not likewise depend for its significance on a bifurcation of opposites at once real and unreal? Here the opposition is represented by a particular consciousness and a universal consciousness. The former is ever confronted by many inclinations and many duties. The struggle within and between separable spheres of the individual's inner life is incessant. Suppression of specific inclinations by specific duties is but a matter of contingency. Necessity pertains solely to the sovereignty of the moral law, the law commanding that duty should always prevail. The morality of any act lies not in its content but only in its form, and the absolute validity of the form hinges on the belief that a universal consciousness, a sacred lawgiver, is present in and sanctions a priori any duty performed in accordance with the autonomy of the moral will. Hence once more a dilemma: either the universal consciousness is or is not present in conflicting duties. If present, every act is dutiful; if not present, no act is dutiful.

I have simplified the third postulate and phrased the dilemma implicit in it chiefly with reference to the attempted reconciliation between man's moral consciousness subject to infinite perfectibility and the morally perfect consciousness of a superhuman legislator and judge. The attempt to reconcile morality and happiness, which depends explicitly on the existence of God, has its own dilemmatic difficulties. On these, however, there is no need to dilate. We have, I think, allowed ourselves altogether too often to be sidetracked by matters properly falling within the domain of exegesis. The moral point of view, resting on postulates, is now completely before us, as completely as our task requires. It has been necessary, following Hegel's procedure, to delineate the ideological structure of that point of view. But the moral posture is one thing, moral action is quite another. The postulates requisite for the posture are but visioned if not visionary harmonies, bound to be compromised in actual practice. Such compromises are dealt with in what follows. The transition to be made is from the formal representation of the postulates (their *Vorstellung*) to the betrayal of them through tergiversation (their *Verstellung*). The verbal play on which the analysis turns is quite felicitous.

3. *The Moral Makeshifts*

Hardith: Yes, this is certainly one of Hegel's better puns. It is unfortunate that for *Verstellung* no English equivalent can so subtly convey its strange ambiguity. And how many changes Hegel rings on a word signifying at once misplacement and dissimulation! Makeshift is perhaps the nearest approach to the original. But a change of position does not necessarily imply dissemblance or hypocrisy which Hegel's term is intended to connote. Here again an ambivalent expression is made to serve the purpose both of analysis and disparagement. The moral consciousness, forced under the stress of the dialectic to resort to makeshifts, thus becomes chargeable with deceit, as if a shift in attitude were the same as an attitude of shiftiness. There is nothing morally offensive, it would seem, in accepting the postulates with certain reservations. Why then should a modified view of them be stigmatized as the result of tergiversation?

Meredy: What Hegel does is merely to develop more fully the contradictions latent in the moral point of view grounded on postulates. Either the postulates preclude moral action or moral action belies the postulates. Their reduction to makeshifts simply proves that they cannot be taken seriously. No moral consciousness can adhere to them and remain moral. This tersely expresses Hegel's contention. For the prerequisites of moral action are not postulated harmonies but posited disharmonies, and the latter cannot be transformed into the former without condemning moral action to complete otiosity. The postulates, as already noted, all center on the demand that what is not should be: opposites must eventually surrender their opposition. The first postulate, for instance, demands the ultimate concordance of nature and morality, initially given as opposed. Although the concordance is what moral action aims at, it is their everlasting disharmony which moral action must inevitably contend with. Furthermore, to the contrast between the concordance as goal of morality and disharmony as its presupposition belongs no such fixity as the postulate implies. Each present deed gives the lie to the alleged ultimateness of the goal; in affording satisfaction to the moral agent, the deed may actually produce much good in the natural world, here and now, serving as instance of the very postulated harmony projected into the dim future. What is declared to be absent is in fact already present. Morality requires that a remote concordance be postulated the remoteness of which turns out to be fraudulent. The place assigned to the distant harmony becomes displaced in action, and this displacement places the moral consciousness in the following dilemma: either acquiescence in the postulate's ultimate aim to abolish the necessity of moral action, or else insistence on moral action as an end in itself in total disregard of the postulate. The dilemma, which involves final cessation or endless continuity of the moral struggle with nature, thus calls for resolution. This lies in the expedient of shifting frequently the location of the postulated harmony. Removing it from the empyreal sphere, the harmony may be sought on earth. And lo! it is here or there or anywhere though often nowhere. From such an egregious makeshift the earnest moralist cannot but recoil.

Hardith: The difficulty, it seems to me, lies in the word deliberately played upon to discredit the postulate. To speak of the harmony between nature and morality as displaceable is to think of it at the outset as discreditable. But for the word *Verstellung,* meaning the act of mislaying as well as the act of misleading, the moral postulate could scarce be made to appear so prejudicially open to moral censure. How typically Hegelian is the task of unmasking a moral postulate as subversive of morality! And how relished a task when the postulate is one sired by Kant! The dialectic strikes me as more verbal than real. The issue would hardly arise, certainly not in the same form, if the nomenclature adopted were not so designedly pejorative. Why not look upon the postulate as a hypothesis? And it seems to be one not contrary to fact. The belief in the harmony of nature and morality is not empirically unwarranted; the belief's validity hinges on such results as are undeniably achievable through action in conformity with it. Yes, the will to believe in the postulated or hypothesized harmony leads to performances of deeds redounding more often than not to its confirmation, a confirmation growing, as it were, by accretion. The various shifts and changes in the ways of rendering nature adaptable to morality prove natural stubbornness rather than moral delinquency.

Meredy: It is true of course that Hegel's approach to the Kantian postulates is not without bias but the bias is one sustained by internal criticism, the only sort comporting with the dialectical method. How could the postulates pass muster as empirical hypotheses, seeing that at the heart of Kant's ethics is the primacy of the will under the autonomous jurisdiction of the categorical imperative? So primary is the will and so categorical the imperative that we are expressly enjoined not to look for their support in the external and contingent consequences of action. Their support in the shape of postulates can only come from within, from the will itself, the only thing in the world unqualifiedly good. It is the dialectic of such support with which Hegel is chiefly concerned. The support given by the first postulate is shown to be unstable to withstand the assault of criticism. The second postulate reveals to analysis an even greater instability. What a formidable paradox lies embedded in the presumptive harmony of morality and sensibility! The paradox is briefly this. All moral endeavor is a struggle with sensibility. In every struggle ultimate victory is the principal desideratum. And here, as elsewhere, the struggle must cease when victory is attained. But the conception of morality involved in the postulate requires perpetual continuity of the struggle as well as its eventual termination. How reconcile the contradiction? Strictly speaking, there is no escape from it save by abandoning morality altogether, a result ensuing equally whichever alternative be chosen. If morality consists in everlasting struggle with sensibility, the postulated harmony presages a state of nonmorality or immorality; if the postulated harmony represents the absolute purpose of moral action, moral action is destined to become obsolete. Because, in other words, harmony is what morality aims at, the aim pursued is final abolition of morality. This ineluctably follows only if adherence to the postulate remains unqualified. But it does not so remain. That the purpose of morality to achieve harmony with sensibility cannot be taken earnestly is proved by the fact that its fulfillment must be infinitely postponed—shifted away, as it were, into a dim future or another world. By a singular dodge morality is doomed to a progress without end or to a progress towards its disappearance. Entailing or rather being such a dodge, the second postulate too reveals itself as resting on slippery ground.

Hardith: Your treatment of Hegel's criticism of the second postulate is a model of lucidity. But how much is it the result of oversimplification? I wonder why you choose to omit as if it were negligible all reference to the conflict between duty and inclination? Is not the postulate designed for the very purpose of resolving that conflict? Then, too, you soften, here as elsewhere, Hegel's persistent animus. The shiftiness he attributes to the postulate appears not merely logically reprehensible, a matter of exchanging one untenable position for another, but morally reprehensible as well, in the sense of becoming synonymous with hypocrisy. This you completely ignore. Why?

Meredy: The second postulate clearly admits of alternative formulations. The most general way of exhibiting it requires merely the distinction between morality and human (rather than external) nature, comprehending all the varieties of experience having their source in sensation and impulse. Substitution of duty for morality and inclination for sensibility involves clarification but no abandonment of the second postulate. The postulated harmony of duty and inclination does not differ from that of morality and sensibility except in greater concreteness of expression. In the less abstract alternative, too, the postulated harmony of the opposites is at loggerheads with the necessity of their endless opposition. Stricter adherence to the text alone determined my choice of the more abstract statement.

As for Hegel's animus, which you accuse me of ignoring or attenuating, its significance lies more in revealing the mind of the biographer than the mind of which the *Phenomenology* purports to be the biography. Hegel's biased opinions, often intrusive and impertinent, diminish instead of advance the putative cogency of the analysis. A case in point is the attribution of hypocrisy to the Kantian postulates. Has the attribution dialectical justification or is it sheer prejudice intervening in the argument? Now shifts in attitude do not necessarily constitute dissimulation. The dialectical movement is nothing but a movement of shifting positions; the position shifted away from appears only in retrospect as representing a state of self-deception. This is the dialectical story of mind as Hegel tells it, beginning with the position of sense-certainty. The shiftiness exemplified by the postulates would thus seem to be the universal rule rather than the exception. Why then does Hegel identify the particular form of their shiftiness with hypocrisy? It is a puzzling question to which I can only hazard an answer. Hypocrisy is obviously out of place in contexts involving no moral judgments. How absurd to speak of turpitude in connection with attitudinal shifts which a percipient or observer is called upon to make in the presence of new or altered data! Being a term of moral discourse, hypocrisy has no meaning in relation to ideas and beliefs falling outside the domain of ethical valuation. It is only when the text is concerned with moral consciousness that the term makes its appearance, and it does so with particular emphasis when the postulates come to be conceived as the buttresses of morality. And solely as such do they become amenable to moral and not merely to logical valuation. Is it Kant who deserves censure for having formulated makeshifts expressly to foster and to condone the vice of hypocrisy? Hegel's language is sufficiently ambiguous not to prohibit a construction so preposterous; in allusions to his predecessor, Hegel's animus seems indeed irrepressible. But is not the important point rather this, that the postulates contain within their very logical framework the mainspring of moral insincerity, so that conduct based on them becomes inevitably tainted with hypocrisy?

Hardith: Hegel's discovery of hypocrisy in the third postulate is particularly impressive. The harmonious goals of the preceding postulates prove not attainable at all or attainable only with the expiration of morality. The predicament in which morality thus comes to be placed is to remain forever in transition or to vanish altogether at journey's end. Yet this predicament has no bearing on *present* morality, whether in transition to a state continually stretching away into infinity or to a state beyond which there can be no further advance. The antinomy, which is but speculative, can of course not militate against the conception of moral perfectibility. The conception is not indefensible, Hegel's dialectic to the contrary notwithstanding. Be that as it may, the third postulate, which involves the accordance of a particular moral agent with a universal holy lawgiver, though sharing in the antinomies of its predecessors, is beset by antinomies of its own, such that even the view of morality as transitional, regardless of its ultimate status, ceases to be tenable. The opposition here postulated as harmonious is too radical not to appear absolutely recalcitrant. To put the matter bluntly, the opposition is between man's moral consciousness and God's. To assume their harmony is to saddle the divine being with responsibility for every act performed by every human individual at the command of duty. 'Let God's will be done!'—who could not thus sanctify whatever his own will prompts him to do? Who could not claim that the dictates of his conscience enjoy supernatural sanction? When hard pressed to justify a claim so stupendous, would not he that makes it be found to 'rationalize', as it were, his covert superstition or hypocrisy? The moral consciousness here examined, being an enlightened one, appears impervious to the charge of superstition. *Ergo. . . .*

Meredy: Your statement of the chief difficulty peculiar to the final postulate hits the nail on the head. Although an exemplary specimen of condensation, the statement is unfortunately too general to do justice to Hegel's intent. The dialectic of the postulate has many facets, and the anomalies of the preceding postulates serve to bolster the argument. The hypocrisy, latent before, now comes out of concealment. It is fully revealed in the demand for a universal legislator whose moral consciousness should at once surpass and remain present in all particular calls to duty. How unbridgeable is the gulf that divides the holy lawgiver's transcendent existence from his alleged immanence in a moral law which commands that duty be done, irrespective of the individuals natural inclinations and the inevitable consequences of his action? Consider again the plurality of mutually exclusive duties, each performable in accordance with the moral law. How could the universal legislator be the ground and sanction of each and every duty? Moreover, the moral consciousness on the human plane is affected and conditioned by outer nature and the nature of sensibility; the moral consciousness attributed to a superhuman being is presumably free from the limiting and vexing circumstances with which on the mundane level all duty must be always contending. For the human psyche, in short, duty is duty only when done in opposition to inclination, a higher consciousness remains a stranger to such moral struggle. And the attitude to happiness is here singularly vacillating. Inadmissible as a

271

moral incentive, happiness must nevertheless be postulated both as ultimately harmonious with duty and as its ultimate reward. Thus the natural propensity to seek happiness, the moralist's bête noire, triumphs over duty in the end; justice demands that duty shall not go unrewarded, the only reward here deemed appropriate, and this is the crowning irony, being its eventual accordance with happiness. The happiness which duty ought to shun will in God's good time ever attend it as recompense for the very act of shunning happiness! And precisely in the demand that happiness should be proportional to duty lies the ground for the belief in the reality of a just lawgiver. Kant's postulate relating to God's existence—and it is this which is here virtually caricatured—shows the lengths to which, according to Hegel, subterfuge may be carried: opposite positions are allowed to follow one after another, one position being displaced by its alternative, a displacement taking the place of the synthesis they are so desperately in need of. The final postulate, like those before it, turns out to be a syncretism of contradictions, as Hegel calls it, a fusion of makeshifts and back-slidings, betraying folly if adhered to in earnest, hypocrisy if the adherence is but pretended. Since it is the postulates which bring morality to this impasse, a sincere and ardent soul must flee from them in abhorrence. Not on such quicksands can the moral law be made to rest. It has an unshakable basis in the inmost spirit of the self. The voice of duty speaks directly and with the assurance that can dispense with shifting assumptions serving as spurious props. Man's conscience infallibly tells him what to do. Away then with postulates, let conscience be the guide.

Conscience

1. *Morality without Postulates*

Hardith: It is altogether in keeping with Hegel's sense of irony to develop from a morality depending for its support on postulates a morality grounded solely in individual conscience. For the conception of conscience here made central is partly Kantian and partly anti-Kantian. From the assumptions and principles of the *Critique of Practical Reason* we must necessarily pass to the ascendancy of romantic moods and mystic intuitions—such is the dialectical evolution of morality we are now bidden to follow. And here again a verbal play is required to do valiant service—the play upon *Gewissen* and *Gewissheit*. As Hegel manipulates the word, conscience comes to signify cognitive certainty within the domain of moral consciousness. The very connotation of the term thus foreshadows the result: morality reduced to conscience must exhibit the same paradoxes which the claim for cognitive certainty engenders in nonmoral spheres of experience. The paradoxes peculiar to moral certainty will be found to parallel those brought to light in connection with sense-certainty. For nothing but silence or contradiction can ensue from the appeal to immediacy. And if immediacy and discourse are mutually exclusive, the dictates of conscience alleged to be infallible are condemned a priori to share the ineffableness or self-inconsistency pertaining to the so-called indubitable data of sense-experience. To what extent then does the transfer of morality from postulates to conscience constitute an advance to a new theme? Does not the task ahead lie in the analysis of a certainty we know beforehand will prove incorrigibly anomalous? Is this not retrogression to a position already superseded?

Meredy: Every claim to immediacy must give rise to paradoxes akin to such as emerge from the analysis of sense-certainty the dialectic of which is indeed paradigmatic. If conscience were but a name for moral consciousness directly certain of its duty, conscience would in principle not differ from nonmoral consciousness immediately certain of its sensations. Although the dialectic of immediacy is generically the same, the forms of experience subject to it are not equatable. In sense-experience the immediacy experienced depends on things external to it; but nothing from without can impinge upon conscience, for that which it is certain of—its duty—has its habitat exclusively in the mind of the moral individual. The morality of conscience, abandoning as *de*moralizing, so to speak, all postulates, may accordingly be regarded as representing a higher stage in moral development. What we have here is a return to the earlier distinction between consciousness and self-consciousness; the former confronts some object other than itself, the latter's object is its own other. Conscience is but a synonym for moral self-consciousness, arising as it does from the dialectic of a moral consciousness involved in everlasting struggles with recalcitrant contents. Of the cessation of these struggles there is only a promise redeemable in Gods infinite time. Conscience has nothing to do with anything alien or transcendent, its dictates being entirely immanent and entirely autonomous. Just as the claim for *self*-certainty is stronger than the claim for *sense*-certainty, by the same token conscience outranks in moral force any and every postulate. Of moral self-consciousness assuming the name of conscience the present section is the detailed diagnosis.

Hardith: The distinction here re-introduced between consciousness and self-consciousness is certainly illuminating. A moral consciousness depending on postulates must ultimately depend on another consciousness, the consciousness of a divine legislator, for harmonizing the oppositions between duty and inclination, duty and happiness, duty and duty, and so on. Conscience, being moral self-consciousness, is self-legislating and thus self-dependent. Oppositions requiring reconciliation by postulates do not arise within the immediate experience of the moral agent. There can be no moral action not instigated by conscience and every deed done has the dutifulness conscience alone can sanction. The only thing absolutely good is held to be a good will—the will to obey with conviction what conscience commands. But if duty is by definition solely what conscience dictates, how absurd to speak of a plurality of contending duties! To speak thus is to saddle the moral agent with a plurality of warring consciences. For conscience and duty, like subject and object in self-consciousness, are not only mutually implicative, they also constitute a union of distinguishable but inseparable correlatives. And as the subject in self-consciousness, though one with its object, nevertheless enjoys priority, so in the moral individual his conscience is primary and his duty derivative. In a conscience which is single and undivided nothing but the duty acknowledged and prescribed by it can have title to the name. For it is conscience that must be considered determinative of duty, and not vice versa. All this follows ineluctably from the distinction between consciousness and self-consciousness applied to morality.

But consider the implications of the distinction. The 'other' to which consciousness is related, whether the consciousness is that of sensation or perception or understanding, remains other, in the sense of appearing external and incomprehensible. Such is the otherness the dialectic of which conditions the emergence of self-consciousness where subject and object are required to be kept distinct as well as united. The object, without losing its otherness, must cease being remote and impenetrable. And of the struggle with its own inexpungible other, self-consciousness constitutes a universal theme of which Hegel exhibits the different variations. But the struggle, taking place on the purely subjective level, need presuppose but a single individual. Reference to a social context is irrelevant or merely tangential to the dialectic. Awareness within self-consciousness of one's self by one's self may be treated as a phenomenon strictly psychological, and even the imaginary solipsist could be assumed to enjoy it. While the conception of a self-conscious solipsist is speculatively plausible, the conception of a conscientious solipsist would seem difficult to entertain. Conscience, though individual, is not preemptively personal; its possession is one which every individual concedes to every other, and its exercise depends for significance on the existence of some intersubjective community where deeds must be done of whose dutifulness the individual agent alone is alleged to be the supreme judge. Could conscience be regarded as attributable to a conceivable solipsist? If not, it would appear contradictory to assert that conscience exemplifies a mode of experience merely self-conscious. Self-consciousness as such is an experience open to everyone, not excepting the individual supposed hypothetically to be destitute of all social relations.

Meredy: To be conscientious is to be morally and not merely self-conscious, the choice of adverb being here most important. If the solipsist's self-consciousness must be said to be amoral, the moralist's, which is quite distinctive, can only have a superficial resemblance to it. Consciousness as well as self-consciousness appears throughout the text in many shapes and in various contexts. Morality is a late chapter in the life of mind, and depends for its emergence on the dialectic of the preceding stages of experience. As Hegel considers it, the moral consciousness grows out of the demand for absolute freedom. This

demand, leading to disaster—to revolution and terror—when introduced and spread in the world of culture, receives complete satisfaction
solely in man's inner consciousness of moral autonomy. Absolute freedom, impossible of achievement in the ordered life of social relations,
is a freedom which every individual assumes he has when, confronted
by a conflict of duties, his own will makes the decision untrammeled
by any other will. Morality, conceived as having its fount and origin
in the absolute freedom latent in the will of each and every individual,
becomes, so to speak, the spiritual heir of culture and enlightenment,
and the task devolving upon it is to preserve and deepen its dialectical
patrimony in sublimated form. But the moral consciousness, while thus
holding in solution the antinomies it inherits, generates antinomies of
its own, some of which we have already noted. The central issues in
relation to morality may be conveniently epitomized by the distinction
(for the pedantry of which I apologize) between consciousness of freedom and freedom of consciousness. The moral consciousness is indeed
free but it requires postulates to bolster or to rationalize its freedom in
the face of the nonmoral conditions that ever tend to frustrate its enjoyment. It is conscience and conscience alone that can lay claim to
absolute freedom, absolute in being freedom from the natural conditions thwarting its expression, and hence freedom from the necessity
of postulates. For conscience (*Gewissen*), as Hegel declares, is in
possession of immediate certainty (*Gewissheit*) of its own truth. Moral
self-consciousness thus concretely exercises the freedom present in
moral consciousness only as abstraction.

Hardith: In your statement of the distinction between consciousness of freedom and freedom of consciousness there is no hint that
more than one conscientious mind must exist to enjoy absolute freedom. Nor is there any allusion, if many such minds do exist, to the
kind of social relations obtaining between them. I thus come back to
the charge of solipsism. The privilege to exercise absolute freedom can
only be the privilege of an absolutely single self, paradoxical though the
qualification of it as moral would appear.

Meredy: The private nature of conscience does at first sight invite
comparison with solipsism, and this alone might suffice to discredit,
if judged on their merits, its claims to infallibility. But as dilated on in
the text, conscience is not a subject of independent analysis, divorced
from a dialectical background and foreground. Behind is the view of
morality depending on postulates which render it precarious and vulnerable, morality without postulates thus becoming the only alternative.
Conscience, if I may say so, seems like the answer to the moralist's
prayer, obviating as it does the necessity of postponing to infinity the

harmony of the actual disharmonies perennially experienced. Although conscience has its habitat in self-consciousness, the habitat is not the self-consciousness of a self solely real. Attempts to condemn conscience to the solitary confinement of solipsism must prove abortive. Taken in conjunction with what lies dialectically back of it, conscience appears as the common element of all individual self-consciousnesses, each recognizing in the others its presence and operation. Such universal recognition, indeed, makes possible the existence of a community of rational beings.

Echoes of Kant's categorical imperative, the unconditioned command of conscience, resounds throughout Hegel's analysis, showing that moral action to be strictly moral hinges on the presupposition that the will of every individual is equal in rationality to the will of every other individual. Action at the behest of conscience, whatever the ensuing consequences, derives its morality not from them but solely from the original motivation. No action is thus open to moral judgment unless it carries conviction of conscientiousness, alike to the agent and patients. All this is a far cry from solipsism.

Hardith: Morality without postulates, bearing the comprehensive name of conscience, appears of many elements all compact, and compact literally, since in their indissolubleness lies the differentia of this new form of spiritual experience. Thus conscience is self-consciousness on the moral plane; all action is moral that arises from conscience; the duty to perform a particular act is grounded in the conviction conscience has of its moral rightness. The same adjective 'moral' affixed in this sentence to different nouns has approximately the same connotation. Primary significance, however, belongs to it as applied to conscience. Somewhere in the present section Hegel expresses the essence of the new morality by asserting that not for the sake of the moral law does the self exist but it is rather the moral law which exists for the sake of the self. This is an illuminating dictum, true of everything here designated as moral, the designation having no validity save as sanctioned by a conscientious self. Of all the components entering into the complex notion of morality conscience plays the sovereign role: it is to his conscience the individual owes his moral self-certainty and it is to his conscience to which he must turn for the moral conviction that a particular deed ought to be done without regard to the consequences. What baffles me in all this is the double cognitive function conscience is called upon to discharge. On the one hand, *Gewissen* grows into *Gewissheit*—conscience comes to coincide with certainty, more specifically with self-certainty, and it is not at all clear to me whether the self's certainty is the certainty of having a conscience or of being one.

On the other hand, *Gewissen* goes under the different alias of *Überzeugung*—conscience breeds the conviction of the necessity to pursue heedless of results a definite course of action, and here again I am not clear whether conscience coalesces with conviction or only serves as its primary source. Of the two cognitive deliverances attributed to conscience which is the more credible? One thing is the knowledge involved in self-certainty, quite another is the knowledge inherent in the conviction of what must be done in a given situation. What a curious organ or faculty or mode of mind is conscience that can be so infallibly aware at once of the self as moral agent and of the action morally incumbent upon the agent!

Meredy: You subject conscience to a dialectic which, though not foreign to Hegel's, has an interesting slant entirely your own. I should certainly share your bafflement if we debated independently of Hegel a topic the vagueness of which is so notorious. As it appears in the text, however, the idea of conscience appears against a rich dialectical background; and it also serves the purpose of examining the issues raised by Kant's ethics, principally in the terms freely borrowed, as his allusions amply prove, from philosophical and literary writers of Hegel's time. Your criticism voiced on different occasions that Hegel often tends to draw the dialectic to the scale of a particular example, whether historical or fictional, thus jeopardizing its claim to generality, is here eminently justified. But for Kant's view of conscience and its subsequent transformations, many details of Hegel's analysis would seem superfluous or irrelevant. His treatment of the theme is obviously tailored to polemical considerations as well as dialectical. He subsumes under conscience a progressive order of sundry thoughts culled not without distortion from various sources with the intent of showing that escape from Kant's postulates resembles the process of jumping out of the frying pan into the fire. When concretely at work, this being the gist of its further analysis, conscience must inevitably lead to delusion and deception much more formidable. The crux of the matter lies indeed in the cognitive role which conscience is alleged to play. Now the immediate certainty of acting in accordance with duty—this being the definition of conscience—is evidently not identical with the superadded conviction—and this too is a differentia of conscience—that a specific duty, *this* and no other, is morally imperative. Clearly, the conviction relating to choice of a dutiful mode of behavior exceeds in extent the knowledge comprising nothing more than direct acquaintance with a feeling of conscientiousness capable of attaching itself to any content, no single deed having a preemptive claim on the sense of duty. To be sure, the knowledge vouched for by conviction is not knowledge of the generative conditions or the eventual fruits to which the deed done owes its existence in the natural order. Yet, how can a moral conviction be acted upon unless the agent does take cognizance of the natural circumstances related to action, since the very dutifulness of the conscientious deed consists in deliberate indifference to them? The conscientious agent, convinced that the moral value of his deed is not dependent on circumstances, must by the same token be aware of the circumstances the deed is morally independent of. The introduction of conviction into conscience, as Hegel develops the theme, stirs up a dialectical hornet's nest of considerable magnitude.

2. *Moral Judgment*

Hardith: If the condition for the possibility of moral action lies in the agent's conviction of having fulfilled his duty, is it a condition sufficient as well as necessary? If it were sufficient, moral action would presuppose but a single agent. Consciousness of duty, being private, is not sharable. The individual, at the bidding of his conscience, may thus endow with supreme dutifulness any particular deed. Whatever he decides to do in obedience to the prompting of his conscience, becomes at once imbued with moral value, seeing that moral value attaches not to the result but solely to the motive of behavior. Every individual, therefore, whose conduct is subject to no moral judgment save his own, may aspire to absolute goodness and absolute rightness in total disregard of the existence of other individuals or of the effect on them his conduct entails. To assert that moral judgments have their only basis in individual conscience, a basis deemed both essential and adequate, is simply to succumb once again to the solipsistic predicament.

Meredy: You anticipate in admirably clear but too condensed a fashion the dialectic which Hegel's subsequent analysis brings gradually to light. Obviously, conscience is not enough. Morality must sink to the level of individual caprice if nothing but conscience remains in which to ground the commands of duty. For duty, as Hegel reiterates, is a general form which any particular content may be made to assume. There is no conceivable conduct of whose righteousness the conscientious individual might not claim to have an infallible conviction. The agent unerringly knows that what he does is his duty, and, if his conscience is his only guide, this is all he needs to know. But of course he knows more than this. How could his conscience guide him aright without the conviction that a specific act to be performed is in absolute accordance with the categorical imperative in control of his rational will? For the object of the conviction is not duty as such, an abstract universal empty of content, but a concrete deed felt to be exclusively compelling.

279

Hardith: Of the alleged distinction here so central between conscience and conviction, I fail to grasp the exact difference. The certainty imputed to conscience, *Gewissen* being a species of *Gewissheit,* on which the individual depends for guidance in fulfillment of his duty, is self-sufficient and needs not the support of a supervening conviction. Either the conviction is but another name for conscience, in which case the distinction becomes superfluous, or else conscience surrenders its cognitive supremacy to a cognition with a greater claim on certainty, in which case conviction appears to supplant conscience. But if conviction is not other than conscience but conscience focused on a determinate course of action, is not the distinction too tenuous for the dialectical burden it is made to carry?

Meredy: The distinction, finespun though it seems, is indispensable for the dialectical development of morality grounded in conscience. It is one thing to speak of conscience as consciousness dominated by a sense of duty, it is quite another to speak of it as consciousness impelled to attribute exclusive dutifulness to a specific mode of behavior. And it is upon conviction that the task of such attribution devolves. No particular act can become dutiful unless and until conscience receives from conviction the impetus so to judge it. The adjectival use of duty, accordingly, may be said to define the cognitive function of conviction, a function essentially judicial.

Of special significance here is the conventional differentiation between judgments of facts and judgments of value. As a *fait accompli,* the dutiful deed done ceases to be the personal affair of the conscientious agent, entering as it does the world of objective existence. That which owes its origin to a private will becomes in a trice an overt datum big with consequences. As regards factual judgments pertinent to conscientious conduct there can be no difference in principle between agent and patient, since they are judgments the validity of which rests on outer circumstances within apprehensible reach of every inquiring mind. What distinguishes agent from patient is this, that the former deliberately discounts in advance the consequences of his behavior precisely because its morality is alleged to reside in nothing but the motive with which he alone is conversant. And it is this allegation which sets the stage for conflicting judgments of value.

Hardith: Once it is done the conscientious deed becomes of course a matter of fact amenable to causal judgments. Open to public inquiry are its originative conditions as well as its subsequent results. And its occurrence is subject to scientific description either without reference to the agent's private motive or with reference to it only as one of the explanatory circumstances. The adjective conscientious affixed to an externally observable deed is for causal explanation irrelevant unless reduced to or correlated with some datum or data capable of extrospection. Whence then the morality of the deed when it leaves the sphere of subjective volition to become an objective fact among other objective facts? We have on our hands the following dilemma. Either the agent cannot disregard the actual consequences his conscientious deed entails, in which case its dutifulness is not entirely derivable from inward conviction; or else his conscientious deed loses all moral value at the very moment it is accomplished, at the moment, that is, its accomplishment turns the deed into a natural event, in which case the concept of morality appears to have no bearing at all on human action.

Meredy: Of your ingeniously contrived dilemma the second horn is of course a reduction to the absurd of the concept of morality; application of morality solely to the will to act and not to the action itself simply absolves the agent from all significant responsibility. The first horn is indeed inescapable but not in the unqualified manner in which you phrase it. If action is held to possess moral worth irrespective of consequences, the consequences meant are such only as preclude anticipation or prediction. The agent, so Hegel notes, can have but slight acquaintance with the circumstances attending or following his action but incompleteness of knowledge does not diminish the strength of his conviction. Yet, action prompted by conviction hinges on judgment about some of the consequences the action is expected to bring in its train. Of certain circumstances the agent *must* take cognizance because they constitute the very desiderata from which action derives its dutifulness. Thus, to use Hegel's illustration, an individual considers it his duty to increase his wealth in order to maintain himself and his family in a state of economic security as well as to advance the purposes of philanthropic enterprises. Clearly, his duty is enmeshed in a net of calculable consequences. Convinced not only that this is his duty, his conviction extends also to the ways he employs in fulfilling it. To be sure, other people are not so convinced; they are apt to brand as fraudulent the pretension to clothe with the mantle of duty the pursuit of gold. Means and ends deemed morally justified by the agent thus come to be held suspect when viewed from without. The case mentioned is not singular. Who does not know that an act felt by the agent to be an act of courage may appear to others as one of cowardice? And how often the outsider sees selfishness in an act seemingly benevolent! Hegel has in mind different instances of acts ever at the mercy of conflicting valuations, depending upon whether the acts are judged *ab intra* or *ab extra*.

Hardith: How then are 'outsiders' to know whether a particular act reflects a morally good or a morally wicked conscience, seeing that none but the agent has direct awareness of his duty? Detached from the conscience to which it owes its genesis, the act alone remains open to moral valuation. What a yawning gulf there is between the subjective origin of the act and its objective manifestations! By what means can the gulf be bridged? Does a medium exist other than the act through which the secret of the agent's conscience may be divulged?

Meredy: Here again language appears as mediator, being the sole medium in which individual conscience present in a particular act can find universal expression. Conscience as such is dumb, hidden within the individual's inner life, and the deed done in obedience to it turns into an outer fact, bearing on its face, so to speak, no indelible sign of the agent's moral intent. But for language as universal vehicle of rational communication, morality would have its habitation either in the privacy of ineffable conviction behind action or in alien judgments to which perceived action and its concomitants are subject. From such a position between the Scylla of complete inwardness and the Charybdis of complete overtness morality must be rescued. And what except language can do this? For it is precisely the function of language to objectify in general terms the subjective contents of consciousness. Although conviction and action are both essential for the meaning of morality, either by itself proves entirely inadequate, the reason being that conviction has its roots exclusively in personal volition, and action invites criticism chiefly of its fruits. Now language is a form in which the life of mind becomes variously embodied, one self-consciousness revealing itself to another as differentiated from as well as united with it. This is a theme Hegel harps upon repeatedly. Here too, language is all-important, serving as antidote to the extreme subjectivism within which conscience is immured; for in the agent's spoken assurance that his action truly reflects his consciousness of duty lies the recognition of others as well as concern for their approbative judgments. When, as Hegel remarks, a man says that he is acting from conscience, he is stating what is true, his conscience involving cognitive certainty of what he must do. But it is essential that he should *say* so. Assurance through discourse that acts of conscience are acts impelled by conviction of duty thus comes to constitute the only ground of moral judgments.

Hardith: Can the translation of morality from the level of action to the level of language be said to meet the issue? If mere asseveration of duty, not covert conviction or overt performance, is to be made the basis of moral valuation, by what standard may its credibility be judged? How distinguish here at all between the valid and the invalid? Only on the assumption that all expressions of conviction are of equal validity can language mediate between the privacy of individual conscience and the publicity of ensuing action. And language is apparently able to do this because of its radical ambivalence, discourse being the very medium in which the dimensions of the intrapersonal and the interpersonal meet and cross. The two extremes mentioned are thus precluded from entering separately the sphere of morality: moral value attaches not to inner conscience or to outer conduct but only to the assurance of conscientiousness which individuals extend to one another. Must morality then be conceived as a sort of preestablished harmony between such mutual assurances? It would appear so; for how else defend as legitimate everyone's assertible assurances that purity of purpose guides his will, that his inner voice of duty is the voice divine, that his behavior derives its sanction exclusively from his inspired genius? Assurances so extravagant, and the privilege of asserting them so universal, can never be contradicted, there being no proof of their validity other than the individual's own word that they are valid. It is thus that Hegel introduces the theme of the 'beautiful soul' which he treats with such excessive irony that between polemic and dialectic the line tends to be vanishing. The transition between language as moral mediator to the conception of the 'beautiful soul' is abrupt and tenuous, producing the impression that its analysis is but incidental, a strange interlude enabling Hegel to give vent to animadversions on ideas he abhors. But the dialectical relevance of the conception seems remote, so remote indeed that its omission would, I think, have enhanced the cogency of the 'linguistic' argument.

3. *The Beautiful Soul*

Meredy: The discussion devoted to morality conceived in quasi-religious or quasi-aesthetic terms, though very compact, is richly laden with allusions to contemporary ideas to which Hegel is distinctly averse. Does the discussion represent but a polemical excursus or does it form an integral part of the dialectic? The answer is not easy. Polemic and dialectic are often commingled in the text, but it is generally possible to distinguish Hegel's intent to ferret out incongruities or contradictions latent in the subject under scrutiny from his own intervening or supervening strictures. Here, however, the censorious remarks, voicing his 'asides', are so intimately interwoven with the examination of the topic's 'inside' meaning that between dialectical analysis and polemical animus the distinction becomes almost imperceptible. It is thus not impermissible to regard the 'beautiful soul' as a theme more or less digressive in the present context. Yet there is much to be said for its dialectical necessity. The theme has many facets, each a variation on moral subjectivism, reemergence of which the 'linguistic' argument, as you call it, renders inevitable. Consider the mutual opposition of inclination and duty, so central in the Kantian view of conscience, the ultimate harmony of which being guaranteed by the grace of a postulate. A harmony infinitely delayed is precisely what a morality radically subjectified must reject, replacing it by a harmony present here and now, and present in every individual possessed of a pure will, a good intention, an ardent conviction, sources from which alone his conduct derives its moral worth. Whatever such an individual does may be always justified by the declaration that it is a spontaneous expression of a clear conscience. What else can make action good if not the goodness of the agent's heart? Yes, it is to a good heart alone to which pure goodness may properly be attributed. This, I take it, is the essence of morality involved in the dialectic of the beautiful soul; the egocentric position becomes inescapable on the assumption that moral value pertains to nothing but the harmony of conviction and action which language can bring about.

Hardith: The beautiful soul, if I understand you aright, enters the situation as the necessary antidote to the categorical imperative. Kant's moral rigorism must ultimately turn into moral aestheticism. Concepts drawn from art thus come to be grafted upon morality, and if harmony is essential to beauty, the soul called 'beautiful' must embody in its nature and conduct all those harmonies which in Kant assume the form of postulates. But harmonies appearing as mere postulates are admittedly not real, being but hopes resting on grounds to which morality itself can lend no support. The morality defended by Kant is clearly a morality which depends for its possibility on actual disharmonies, and these can only cease with the cessation of morality. Moral life cannot be assured of continuity except through perpetual struggle with recalcitrant elements. Contrasted with this is a vision of life intent upon a serenity attainable not by action but by contemplation. The harmonies but promised by Kant are fulfilled in aestheticism, and the disharmonies necessary for his stern morality simply do not exist for the beautiful soul. A dialectical somersault, indeed!

But this is not the whole story. There is also a religious side. Hegel's allusion to it is quite clear. Mystic self-absorption, though cognate with aesthetic, seems more complete. In contemplation of his soul is to be found the serenity sought, the source of the serenity being the mystic's conviction of his subliminal identity with the divine. Worship and service of God thus consists in unremitting concentration on this alleged identity, the beautiful soul now appearing in the garb of holiness. Moral mysticism, if I may so call it, while renouncing the ordinary self, the self of daily perception and thought, exalts the deeper self of feeling and intuition. A self so conceived lives a solitary life or in company with others in a conventual community. But, as Hegel speaks of him, he always remains in dread of staining the glory of his devout selfhood by contact with the actual world. To preserve the purity of his heart he must withdraw from secular affairs altogether. Hegel has many harsh things to say of the beautiful soul aspiring to be invested with a saint's halo; the light of the soul's inner and ineffable vision, so reads in summary his disparagement, "dims and dies within it, and disappears as a shapeless vapor dissolving into thin air." Thus does polemic usurp the function of dialectic! Conceding, however, the necessity of moral rigorism becoming its own other, is its proper antithesis moral aestheticism or moral mysticism?

Meredy: Between the aesthetic and mystic aspects of the beautiful soul there is in the text no sharp differentiation, nor is their relation exhibited as dialectical in the sense of one growing out of and superseding the other. Of the beautiful soul Hegel's portrait is distinctly composite, representing a blend of several models; the principal feature common to them being the recrudescence of individualism, the dialectic of which, while dealt with earlier, is here reiterated in connection with the theme of morality. What sets the stage for the dialectical emergence of the beautiful soul is a morality which has at its core a categorical imperative such as to enable the individual to think and to act in the name of the universal but which requires postulates to mitigate the severity of the conflicts on which its possibility actually depends. In Hegel's context, the beautiful soul is a pregnant phrase encapsulating a conception of morality according to which the single self must be considered central and sufficient, the sole claimant to the attribute of goodness, a stranger to that dualism between compelling impulse and impelling reason on which a rigoristic theory of morals such as the Kantian is founded, the postulates as harbinger of eventual freedom from inner bifurcation thus becoming completely otiose. Hegel did not invent the phrase; he found it in general circulation among the literati of his time. What a peculiar fascination it exerted on poets and philosophers alike! With the use made of it by different writers— for example, by Jacobi, Schiller, and Goethe—Hegel's familiarity may be taken for granted. *Die schöne Seele,* remarkably protean, assumed various shapes, appearing in classic guise as well as romantic, and serving with equal appositeness as paradigm in art and religion. More important, however, is the part it played in speculative thought. That Hegel should have seen in the beautiful soul a graphic image typifying in a new form the vindication of the self-contained individual is scarce surprising. Upon the dialectical method devolves the task of demonstrating the necessary appearance as well as the necessary supersession of the new individualism; the necessity of its appearance is simply the necessity of satisfying the demand for an antithesis to moral rigorism; but its dialectical destiny is the same implicit in every defense of the self-contained individual, regardless of the terms in which the defense is couched. If the individualism appearing under the figure of the beautiful soul appears to contravene the doctrine of man's divided and dolorous psyche, such individualism must be understood in a generic sense, compatible equally with moral aestheticism and moral mysticism. The soul is free to cultivate its moral beauty in different ways. Incidentally, moral mysticism, in the manner in which you express it, strikes me as misleading. What you have in mind is clearly the religious conduct of those living in cloistered seclusion from the world. This, I think, had better be called moral monasticism or monastic morality.

Hardith: You are placing in too favorable a light Hegel's treatment of the beautiful soul which, I still maintain, is more polemical than dialectical. What Hegel offers sounds like a travesty of a posture of mind which his method requires to be presented as representative. He speaks of the 'so-called' beautiful soul—how much disdain the adjective conveys! There is hardly a hint of its classical expressions—such, for example, embodied in Goethe's *Wilhelm Meister,* and notably in the part entitled *"Bekenntnisse einer schönen Seele."* Would that Hegel had approached these 'confessions' with the empathy he could evince on other occasions! The full-length portrait of a pure and irenic soul might have appeared to him as paradigmatic as other literary products on which the dialectic depends so strongly throughout the work. Consider *Antigone* and *Rameau's Nephew*—how profound is his interpretation of their significance as intimations of universal forms of experience! But ignoring the classical versions, Hegel proceeds as if the beautiful soul were a conception exclusively romantic, and venting his spleen on it, he resorts to impassioned invective. Thus he describes the beautiful soul as a subject related to a hollow object—namely, itself—and which can be filled only with the feeling of emptiness. Its sole activity consists in longing but only for what is unsubstantial and shadowy. The thing it longs for is ultimately longing itself. And in longing for longing, while thus retaining its vaunted purity, the beautiful soul remains rooted and fixed in self-absorption. Not having the strength to face concrete reality, it continues to exist in a sort of spiritual vacuum, ever distracted, near to madness, wasting itself in nostalgia, and languishing away in consumption. This, you must admit, is polemic in questionable taste. The allusion, obviously to Novalis, is too cruel to be condoned, the allusion especially to the cause of his death.

Meredy: You are very hard on Hegel. His criticism, though indeed merciless, must not be taken apart from the analysis of which it often, and here in particular, forms an integral part. It can hardly be reiterated too frequently that a discussion on its merits of any persuasion does not explicitly fall within the purview of the *Phenomenology*. Hegel's earlier statement on stoicism, to mention but one example, does not represent his personal opinion. What he is concerned with is some abstract or abstracted facet of it illustrative of the dialectic of self-consciousness. And so with the beautiful soul: in a study of the history of ideas it would naturally have to be considered as a theme with many variations. How could the variation depicted by Goethe fail to engross the historian? But this or any other classical version is here of no use to Hegel, not because it is unimportant but simply because it is irrelevant. The romantic versions alone are here pertinent and merely as illustrations of the dialectic of conscience. When moral worth is held to apply not to action but to the agent— and exclusively to the avowal of his conscientious intent—how can anyone's assurance be ever gainsaid that his action proceeded from the purest of motives? In a similar fashion, how can the artist be contradicted in asserting that beauty lies not in his product but in his imagination, his vision of it being too deep or too intense to receive embodiment in anything actual. It belongs to the essence of subjective individualism, moral as well as artistic, to rivet attention from action to the agent, making focal the creative intention instead of the intended result, the verbal declaration of motive rather than its incarnation in particular form. And in the beautiful soul where art and morality become one in principle, subjective individualism reaches a singularly triumphant stage. It is a soul, admitting no impediments to the true marriage of art and morality, which appears to Hegel restless and disenchanted, pining for what is not. Its everlasting longing, so Schlegel in his *Lucinde* epitomizes the romantic creed, is longing for longing. Or, *à la* Shelley, it aspires to emulate the West Wind in being the wild spirit which is moving everywhere, destroyer and preserver. In all this lies the importance of Hegel's treatment of the beautiful soul; principally dialectical, the treatment is unfortunately suffused with a polemic unusually venomous.

4. *Evil and its Forgiveness*

Hardith: After the assault on romanticism, which I cannot help believing to be digressive, the text returns to the dialectic of morality

287

in need of language to mediate between the extremes of secret conviction and open behavior. The accent on language is here essentially anomalous. The agent, convinced of his duty cannot justify his conduct except by merely averring his conviction. Averment of duty thus tends to usurp the moral value attributable to duty as directly felt or deliberately done. As Hegel phrases the anomaly, "Duty consists in nothing but words." Yet in such anomaly is supposed to lie the transition to the conception of moral evil. The transition, quite sudden and subtle, somehow eludes my grasp.

Meredy: The transition, though abrupt, is hardly subtle. It is latent in the fact that words no less than deeds are subject to misinterpretation. The words voicing conviction are not the speaker's own; as soon as uttered, they impinge upon the consciousness of others where they may be regarded as screening intentions quite at variance with those avowed by the speaker. How credible is one's neighbor's assurance that good intentions prompted his action? Should it be taken as self-evident or as open to doubt? And could scepticism be carried far enough to discredit the assurance altogether? If no assurance of the individual's private conviction can ever be made to sound fully convincing to others, speech can obviously not succeed in mediating between the extremes of intention and action. The crux of the matter lies in the capacity of words to breed suspicion instead of confidence.

Hardith: This is certainly true if not truistic. But the issue is not that the inner voice of duty precludes translation in a discursive medium. It is an old story that speech belies immediacy of experience or that its immediacy defies utterance. The story, beginning with sense-certainty, Hegel rehearses over and over again. The failure of discourse to convey to others the individual's intimate feeling of duty is but one of its variants. The issue is obviously deeper. What the language of conscience must inevitably lead to is not mere suspicion but moral evil. Is this not the crucial point on which the dialectic turns?

Meredy: Precisely. Between the language of conscience and moral evil there is a necessary connection. For the evil that men do and suffer has its beginning in the mere suspicion that adheres to the agent's insistence on the purity of his motives regardless of the condemnatory consequences the action produces. Can mistrust be ever removed by protestations of innocence? Once the possible discrepancy between noble utterances and despicable acts becomes the basis of moral judgment, the very nobility of the utterances tends to serve as evidence of hypocrisy. Rhetorical avowal of conscientiousness, apart from signifying disavowal of responsibility for the deed done, may be always rejected as a device for concealing in high-sounding phrases ignoble motives. Every man may thus be deemed morally evil whenever his inner intentions are suspected of being masked by their outer expressions, and to unmask their hypocrisy now appears as the chief moral desideratum. And since absence of hypocrisy is not susceptible of proof, mere suspicion of its presence is here sufficient, with the result that none can escape becoming suspect.

Hardith: But suspicion so universally extended would seem to abolish altogether the distinction between the evil type of consciousness and the nonevil. How could anyone defend his motives in the face of the reprehensible acts instigated by them without laying himself open to the accusation of hypocrisy? For the defense can only be carried on by means of words, and words are deceptive. He whose motives are questioned must thus perforce remain defenseless. Every base motive may be imputed to him, and who but himself can contradict the imputation? Alas, however, the contradiction is entirely bootless, seeing that it must be expressed in a medium a priori suspected of duplicity. Everyone is thus in danger of being considered intrinsically evil, not because of his palpable acts but solely because of his hidden motives. Is freedom to pass judgment on each other's motives the prerogative of all men? And is there no curb on such freedom?

Meredy: It is the dialectic of conscience which opens, as it were, the floodgates of reflection on the motives of each by each. On the view that *intended* action alone is amenable to moral valuation, the intention, closed as it is to minds other than the agent's, must needs remain the agent's secret until disclosed in words. And it is the words and not the intention on which attention can be directly focused, since the intention is but a datum of inference. Do words reveal or do they veil the speaker's meaning? Are they expressions of his noble or base character? The interest in words thus acquires priority over the interest in morals, and where conscience comes to grief is precisely in the realm of words. He who insists that his words should be received as proof of his honest convictions may be always challenged to show whether or not he is mistaking or falsifying their alleged honesty. And how could a challenge so formidable be met? Since every critic of another's convictions is also an agent, and thus liable to be hoist on his own petard, the general tendency to mistrust the purity of avowed motives becomes dialectically inevitable.

What Hegel has in mind may perhaps be clarified by an imaginary illustration. Consider the possibility of psychoanalysis growing into a universal method of dealing with motives revealed in speech, everybody, as it were, using it on everybody else. Consider further that in justifying his action the agent is apt by a process often unconscious to suppress many motivating desires or interests actually unjustifiable. And consider this, too, that as no man is a hero to his valet, so no person is a saint to his analyst; one's 'real' personality may be un-covered by the latter to harbor a variety of villainous impulses, ranging from the salacious to the criminal. Now in a society whose members are bent on psychoanalyzing each other, evil must indeed become rampant, this being the outcome of the dialectic of conscience when conscience is driven to assume objectivity in nothing but language. Hence to judge an act is to impugn without ruth the agent's stated motive. All moral valuation must perforce turn into disvaluation. In passing harsh judgments on one another, men thus reach the plane of equality in hypocrisy. Mutuality of recrimination unites them in a common bond. But what binds them together is evil. It is evil which every man inflicts and suffers, committing the sin of doing deliberate violence to his brother's conscience and having the same violence done to his. The dialectic of conscience thus ends in universal evil or sin crying out for forgiveness and reconciliation.

Hardith: The picture you draw of the moral evil from which the world would suffer if psychoanalysis became the universal mode of exposing men's hidden motives is scarcely flattering to its current practitioners. And it appears even less flattering by the comparison between the analyst and the hero's valet. Yet I find this ingenious as well as illuminating. No hero is indeed a hero to his valet, not, as Hegel comments, because the hero is not a hero, but simply because the valet is just the valet. A world in which psychoanalysis and valetry are in the ascendant, human motives must inevitably be at the mercy of cynical judgments; a fundamental mistrust of the purity or sincerity of purpose seems ineradicable from the minds of those whose vocation breeds too great a familiarity with contemptible foibles and aberrations. What deed done in the name of some noble ideal or high principle can escape denigration by the 'valets of the moral sphere' (*Kammerdiener der Moralität*), as Hegel calls them, an application not in-apposite to the new and secular believers in the 'confessional' as a method for probing the secrets of 'sinful' motivation? Of course, the evil which reduction of conscience to language is said to entail suffers from inordinate exaggeration; after all, the putative existence of actual heroes and saints must be presupposed for giving valets and analysts their occupational reason for being. The pessimism about human nature in which the dialectic culminates seems forced. The terminology is slanted to afford dialectical ingress into the next theme. For is it not religion which is held to offer remission of the evils that men do and

290

of the sins they commit? The passage from the moral to the religious consciousness strikes me again as more verbal than real.

Meredy: The text covering the transition is, alas, not free from obscurity; too much lies within its narrow compass. The terminology is exceedingly difficult, suited to the author's own doctrine to be adumbrated at the close of the book. The climax of mind's phenomenology consists in its apotheosis: the human subject of the biography becomes superhuman and puts on immortality. The apotheosized mind which is to arise is the object of worship present to the religious consciousness, appearing in the course of the immediately succeeding dialectic in progressively adequate forms. The religious persuasion, the theme of a protracted analysis, will reveal itself as the philosophic in embryo, God emerging transfigured in the Hegelian Absolute. Although very little can here be grasped of the import of Hegel's Absolute Spirit, his reference to it seems necessary to mark the difference between the moral sphere and the religious. The difference relates to the reality of the individual, on the one hand, and to that of evil, on the other. In morality as conscience, the *Phenomenology* reaches the last desperate attempt to make central the self-confined and self-contained single individual. It is only in religion, as Hegel teaches, that the ultimately real nature of the individual comes to be duly though imperfectly recognized, the religious consciousness presupposing an individual that has ceased to be self-centered, self-sufficient, and solitary. The problem of evil has different dimensions of which the moral is but one. Attentuation of moral evil, the evil considered in connection with the divorce of individual conscience from the objective consequence involved in the action it instigates, would indeed follow from universal relinquishment of separate selfhood. But in the spiritual life as conceived by religion the reality of evil is a necessary condition of its very spirituality. Spiritual values grow more exalted in the face of evil that threatens them. With the disappearance of evil would disappear the need for expiation and atonement and reconciliation. But the evil essential to the Hegelian Absolute demands treatment in terms transcending those of religion. All this lies ahead following the phenomenology of the religious consciousness. The story is long and intricate.

The Religious Consciousness

1. The Concept of Religion

Hardith: With the dialectic of religious experience we reach the penultimate stage of the *Phenomenology*. The final stage, concerned with what Hegel calls 'absolute knowledge', seems to serve as a sort of appendix, containing a preview, as it were, of mind's postphenomenological career. The logical categories, supposed to represent the union of thought and being, signifying that the real is the rational, and vice versa, differ of course from the varieties of human persuasion. The *Phenomenology,* the subject of whose inquiry is the subject of experience, can only foreshadow the content and form of objective knowledge. Your borrowed conception of the treatise as biography— borrowed from Royce—strikes me as admirably apposite. The story of mind it tells, though having but a dialectical sequence and development, is a story nevertheless, rich in allusions to dated persons, dated events, and dated currents of opinion in philosophy and literature, so that as regards some varieties of experience the dialectic often corresponds to the chronological order of the illustrative material on which the analysis is made to depend. But for the many cases where Hegel either ignores or reverses actual chronology, the dialectic of the *Phenomenology* might easily though mistakenly be construed as a dialectic of history. Consider, however, the transition from morality to religion. Historically speaking, the morality to which Hegel confines himself is strictly modern, and especially modern is the idea of absolute freedom upon which it follows. It is the Kantian view of morality that provides the primary content of the dialectic and against which Hegel's unremitting polemic is directed. And for the development of that view into extreme subjectivism Hegel depends on illustrations drawn chiefly from contemporary sources. The morality presupposed for religion has thus every earmark of a species exhausting the entire genus, the Kantian version alone forming the preemptive subject matter of the dialectic. Yet, how general in scope is religion to which the dialectic of morality gives rise! Representing different levels of experiences, the concept of religion comprehends many and various species, and the species the dialectic begins with appear logically simple and in strict correspondence with their historically early forms. Should we say then that the passage here is from Kant's theory of morals through its romantic subjectifications to the religious beliefs of primitive man? Should we consider a perspective of mind of recent origin as exemplifying a stage transitional to one bearing an ancient date?

Meredy: Your question is very important, showing the absurdity of equating logical sequence with temporal. The transition is clearly not from Kant's moralism to religious primitivism. So to view the transition is to look upon time in a topsy-turvy manner. The relation of morality to religion is primarily a relation of one general concept to another. Which is to be endowed with supremacy in the life of mind? Which outranks the other in spiritual value? That the highest instance of one concept is in spirituality inferior to the lowest of the other follows from Hegel's treatment of the religious theme as transcending in spiritual import all the previous themes.

Hardith: But how can a theme exemplifiable by its appropriate variations serve as variation of themes alien to it? Religion is a strange concept indeed if, in addition to being present in its own instances, it may be present also as an instance elsewhere, to wit, in concepts extraneous to religion. For Hegel distinguishes modes of religion involved in nonreligious types of experience, every type having the mode germane to it.

Meredy: What we must here bear in mind is the distinction between the adjectival use of a concept and its substantival meaning. For example, attribution of truth to a statement is one thing, quite another is truth as a special topic of inquiry. 'What is true?' and 'What is truth?' are clearly not equivalent questions. Again, to describe a phenomenon by its spatial or temporal properties is of course not the same as to explain the nature of space or of time. A similar ambivalence adheres to religion: this concept, too, occurring in diverse contexts, may function as predicate-term or as subject-term. Here likewise a religious quality, be it attributable to feeling or belief or attitude or conduct, differs markedly from religion as a determinate phenomenon amenable to study by various methods. The distinction, in other words, is between religion as an element in extrareligious complexes and religion as a definite complex involving nonreligious ingredients. And on the implications of the distinction the ensuing dialectic hinges.

Hegel shows the variable nature of the religious element as it appears on the preceding levels of experience. Even on the plane of mere consciousness, but only when its dialectic reaches the phase of the understanding, there is a religious element latent in the belief of a supersensible or imperceptible being hidden in the object of perception. On the plane of self-consciousness, when its dialectic culminates in the unhappy consciousness, the religious element is more pronounced, for the self's sorrowful search for unchangeable being is akin to that of the mystics. At the plane of reason, the religious element is conspicuously absent, because the abstract and formal and hence superficial equation of the real and the rational precludes the necessity of transcending the observable present. But it is on the plane of spirit that the different religious elements emerge in more recognizable shapes. Thus, in the world of the ethical order, the world typified by the *Antigone,* the religious attitude takes the form of loyalty to the underworld, based upon belief in the shadowy and mysterious governance of fate, and 'in the Eumenides of the spirit of the departed'. The worldliness of culture generates as antidote belief in an ultramundane sanctuary to which the self-estranged individual takes flight; but this religious haven of refuge becomes the object of destructive criticism by the enlightenment. This gives rise to morality, the religious concomitant of which comes to full fruition in the final phase of conscience. And conscience it is, representing the strange union of the self's certainty and the self's impotence, the source of sin and the longing for forgiveness, which ushers in religion proper.

Hardith: The distinctions between adjective and substantive and between element and complex are undeniably important and useful. But I am not sure of their relevance to the present text. In the opening passages of the introduction to the new subject Hegel does indeed draw attention to the place of religion in the types of experience previously examined. What he speaks of, however, is religion. Why split the term's meaning into subject and predicate, composite and component?

Meredy: The twofold distinction I have ventured to make cannot appear strictly germane until we note the equivocal position which religion occupies in the *Phenomenology.* The position is, so to speak, Janus-faced. On the one hand, religion exemplifies the final and overarching form of consciousness to which all the preceding forms are ancillary, and on the other, it represents more than a form of consciousness terminating mind's dialectical odyssey—it serves as a bridge that leads to the conception of absolute spirit free from myth and allegory. Looking before and after, as it were, the religious consciousness moves from lower to higher expressions until it reaches the stage that marks its transformation into a consciousness purely speculative. For the consciousness distinctly religious is cosmic in sweep; it appears on the scene only when the whole is envisaged in its wholeness. Not before adequate awareness of totality occurs can the religious consciousness be said to exist. Religious elements discernible in secular types of experience, being so vague and amorphous, are but religious by courtesy. Thus, the supersensible realm in which understanding of sensory perception culminates; the unchangeable selfhood which the unhappy individual seeks so desperately to attain; the law of the underworld obedience to which fatally undermines the stability of the ethical order; the belief in a supercultural heaven as an escape from the plight of self-alienation; the autonomous conscience as the ultimate arbiter of good and evil—all these are aspects pertaining to postures of mind essentially nonreligious. None in short, may be regarded as involving an explicit relation to the global integrity of things. If the truth is the whole, the formula into which Hegel compresses his doctrine, the content of religion, though not its form, is the same as the content of philosophy. And this is the argument of the text before us.

Hardith: I observe that you speak of religious consciousness more often than you do of religion. Is this due to inadvertence? Surely not. For you seem to have hit on a way of differentiating between religion relating to experience and religion as a prelude to philosophy. Is not Hegel's treatise, when it remains true to its title, the dialectical narrative of the phenomena of mind (or those of consciousness in its broadest sense)? Religion can of course be no exception; the term religious consciousness has an obviously subjective connotation. Not the intrinsic nature of the religious object is here focal, the object considered being such only as appears or must appear to human experience under different and variable conditions. Treatment of religion as a theological theme tends to detract from the preeminence which in the analysis of religious experience naturally pertains to the human psyche. When religion ceases to be but an episode, albeit a crowning one, in the life of mind, it reveals itself as a complex idea, the content of which includes the idea of an *ens realissimum,* a being emerging in the end as the Hegelian Absolute in disguise.

Meredy: The pages introductory to the section on religion serve indeed the double purpose you tersely indicate. Hence their difficulty. Hegel introduces the theme, to put the difficulty in a colloquial nutshell, as having one foot within phenomenology and the other without. As a type of experience, how can religion appear if not on a finite level? It comes last in the order of spiritual phenomena, following directly upon the dialectic of morality. No experience examined in the *Phenomenology,* whether the observational or the cultural or any other, can be thought of as occurring in a mind alleged to transcend the human. How grossly anthropomorphic to imagine the Hegelian Absolute perceiving things, living in a state of nature, becoming civilized and thus self-estranged, spreading enlightenment, instigating revolution, obeying the call of duty, and so on! Mind typically human plays here the role of subject, and its recurrent ways of experience constitute the only subject matter with which the book is concerned. Nevertheless, the phenomenology of religion is more than phenomenology. Unlike any other experience, the experience called religious enjoys a privileged status. The religious consciousness itself must regard the object experienced as endowed with an independent reality, independent, that is, of the experiencing mind. The religious object, if I may say so, though related to a subject, is not relative to it. This is a cryptic utterance, I know, yet how relevant to Hegel's analysis! But this can obviously not be shown in advance of a minute and subtle discussion.

2. The Structure of Religion

Hardith: I am aware that the distinction between the objective reference of religion and the subjectivism of religious experience can here be only stated and not justified. The justification obviously demands that phenomenology step outside the subjective circle to which it must needs be confined. Religion is either a spiritual phenomenon, remaining an incident in mind's biography, or it is a matter pertaining to ontology, thus coming within the domain of consciousness no more signally than any of its other contents. Phenomenology, in a word, echoing Jean Hyppolite, is not noumenology. No less curious than the privileged status assigned to religion within the life of mind is its formal structure. For religion as here considered is differentiable in accordance with the fourfold classification of mind, namely, consciousness (in the narrower sense as consciousness of 'things'), self-consciousness, reason, and spirit. These are names for the principal dimensions of the dialectic—Hegel calls them 'moments'—under which must be subsumed the entire spectrum of human experience. Religion, which is the final and complete expression of spirit, should logically mark, as it were, the end of an era, and with the attainment of religion the phenomenological task would seem to have been accomplished. But no, Hegel is intent upon proving that religion, while immanent in spirit, has an independent life of its own. Its biography will exemplify a recapitulation of the stages of mind's dialectical progress, religious phenomenology thus becoming a condensed or reduced replica of the phenomenology of human consciousness as a whole. Presupposing the types of secular consciousness that have run their dialectical course,

Hegel proposes to create in their images the varieties of religious experience. And he will manage to cull from history many a striking illustration. The program thus intimated certainly constitutes a tremendous *tour de force*.

Meredy: You seem to forget that it is the definition of religious experience which dictates that the phenomenology of religion be modeled on the phenomenology preceding it. But for that definition their parallelism would be quite unintelligible. The consciousness of totality —for thus in effect Hegel defines religion—can only arise as a consequence of mind's incessant struggle with the partial masquerading as the complete. The series of the prereligious types of experience serves as necessary background of religion in general; the difference between its sundry species is a difference in form rather than content. According to Hegel, then, no religion can appear without awareness however rudimentary of wholeness which the partial may symbolize but cannot simulate. The phenomenology of mind prior to religion contains in increasing measure the inevitable trend or nisus towards a totality which in religious experience alone can become the explicit object or objective. Between the two phenomenologies, to speak of them thus, the relation is of the organic sort; the larger is the condition for the emergence within it of the religious consciousness, while the smaller, in borrowing from the larger a comparable method and structure, sums up and vindicates mind's unremitting quest for a truth subject to continuous growth in internal coherence and concrete universality.

Hardith: You attenuate the extravagance of Hegel's language by greatly simplifying it. You speak as if the consciousness of totality as such were the differentia of his definition of religion. What he lays stress on is a totality absolutely unique. It is the totality embracive of all time and all existence to the comprehension of which no mind not superhuman may lay claim. Religion involves, for Hegel, not consciousness but self-consciousness—spirit knowing itself as spirit, the Absolute aware of its absoluteness. On this theme Hegel harps repeatedly throughout the introduction. It would thus follow that the object of religion, never present except to a commensurable subject, must lie beyond the ken of finite consciousness. Is God alone capable of being religious? The question, in spite of its facetious sound, is not altogether impertinent.

To be sure, the introduction is not intent upon demonstration of any thesis; it only conveys Hegel's comments on the previous dialectic and on the dialectic to come. The unashamed bias here revealed is remarkable. A metaphysical conception of religion—Hegel's own—

for which there can here be no proof, must result, so we are told in advance, from the investigation of religious phenomena as empirically or historically given; and the method guiding the investigation will be able to invest this singular conception with universal and necessary validity. All this would here seem to be out of place. What is one to make of utterances so enigmatic? And unlike earlier introductions, the present one is surprisingly unencumbered with polemic; containing dogmatic statements couched in esoteric diction, it is concerned not so much with the immediate task to be embarked upon as with the subsequent undertaking to turn phenomenology into noumenology.

Meredy: I would gladly concur with what you say if we had not agreed at the outset to eschew matters properly pertaining to a learned commentary. A critical explanation of Hegel's text is a scholar's concern. Our lay conversations can obviously not invade the field of the expert. Obscure minutiæ we may thus safely ignore, and arguments too complex we need not hesitate to simplify. What significant insights may we glean from a nonprofessional study of Hegel's treatise? Are such insights separable from the tortuous language in which the author clothed them? We are merely desirous of gaining whatever profit we may from a work admittedly profound but vexatiously difficult, refusing to be intimidated by the specialists with their different keys to the secret of Hegel. To discuss, for instance, the introduction to religion with scrupulous fidelity to Hegel's recondite thought and dark idiom would defeat our purpose. His notion of absolute spirit is a case in point. If I have deliberately failed to mention it, it is because the notion, though central in Hegel's own philosophy, is irrelevant to his comprehensive survey of the life of mind. For the subject of this biography is the human mind, a mind finite and mutable, given to overweening ideas entailing tragicomic issues, the necessity of whose apotheosis forms no part of the biography. Not until we reach the introduction to religion does Hegel bring into focus the apotheosized subject. Such a subject, however, is not essential to the phenomenology of religion; the primitive types, though exemplifying a vague feeling of totality, can scarcely be assumed to involve the consciousness of organic wholeness Hegel attributes to his Absolute. Within the phenomenological context the definition of religion as consciousness of totality is eminently sufficient, and reference to the doctrinary conception of a superhuman spirit becomes downright intrusive. The sense of totality, as the text will show, is present in differing degrees in different forms of religion, ranging from the crudest to the most refined.

Hardith: Yet there remains the division between the phenomenology of the nonreligious types of experience and that of the specifically religious, though the latter depends on the former for its stages and architectonic. The earlier phenomenology, so Hegel states the division, is dominated by the category of *substance* and that of the later by the category of *subject*. Here, I think, is the heart of the matter. Every variety of nonreligious experience, from perception to morality, must ultimately reveal itself as but an attribute of a pervasive substance. The recognition that all the species of consciousness presuppose a common genus can only come when the dialectic culminates in spirit as the concrete universal or the organic totality of the previously distinguished but inseparable forms of experience. Now acknowledgment of this spiritual substance, in which the entire gamut of nonreligious experience is found to be grounded, marks the transition to the phenomenology of religion. The substance, which sustains as attributes the various modes of consciousness, makes its appearance as subject in need of determination by suitable predicates. By what predicates should the subject be defined? No definition of it is possible Hegel insists, save by predicates derivable from nonreligious phenomenology. On the level of its special phenomenology religion must repeat the pattern of the preceding general phenomenology: the dimensions of religion, too, will be consciousness, self-consciousness, reason, and spirit, and the forms of experience comprehended under them will supply the terms requisite for tracing religion's dialectical evolution. Attributes of substance thus come to function as predicates of the subject, with this difference, however, that whereas the priority of substance over its attributes is a dialectical discovery the priority of the subject over its predicates becomes a dialectical axiom. How crucial is here the idea of subject! What precisely does it mean? It is one thing to speak of the putative subject of a putative biography of mind, it is quite another to posit a subject required for the religious metamorphosis of spirit. The same word *Geist,* notoriously ambiguous, does service for both. Where is the line between them to be drawn? And is there a line that does not prove to be blurred? We seem to be here confronted by a remarkable feat of dialectical transubstantiation: mind turning into spirit, spirit into God, God into the Absolute! The two phenomenologies, merging into one, thus come to constitute the biography of a single subject latent in all human experience, the aim of the dialectic being to trace the progress from mere latency to full and final revelation. But does not identification of the subject of a unitary phenomenology with the unique subject, the synonym of which is God or the Absolute, involve the absurdity of conceiving the divine self as the true subject of Hegel's biography? Are the finite forms of consciousness, from sense-certainty onward and upward, God's or the Absolute's intrinsic predicates?

Meredy: You lay too much stress, I think, on a distinction that occurs in the text but incidentally, an echo, perhaps, of the difference between his position and Spinoza's stated by Hegel in the preface. "In my opinion," he there says, "everything depends on grasping and expressing the ultimate truth not as substance but as subject as well." This shows that in the introduction to religion, no less than in the preface to the treatise, Hegel is intent on averring one of his fundamental tenets. But since you insist on raising the difficulty that attaches to his use of the term, a comment or two on its incorrigible ambivalence or rather multivalence might not be amiss. The term has at least three distinct meanings, namely, logical, epistemological, and metaphysical. Logically, the subject is a term of a proposition about which something is asserted, the term distinct from it being the predicate. Epistemologically, the subject is the term in the cognitive relation performing the office of knower, the term employed in distinction from it being that of object. And metaphysically, the subject is Hegel's synonym of the Absolute as the supreme category of reality. In the introduction the use made of all the three meanings is easily discernible.

(a) Religion constitutes the subject of a special phenomenology (or the subject matter of a particular chapter in the general biography of mind), having principally the significance of a substantive open to several adjectival determinations.

(b) Denoting one of the cognitive areas, religion involves the necessary interplay of knowing subject and knowable object. What indeed does the condensed phrase 'religious consciousness' mean if not the individual's awareness of some being or beings deemed sacred on some ground or other and thus worthy of worship? As Hegel considers it, religion does not appear until the subject, the finite individual, is face to face with the totality of things which alone can qualify as the distinctly religious object. This object, in its purely epistemological sense, is completely relative to the subject—relative, that is, to the subject's ways and conditions of experience. Incidentally, how could any epistemology question the assumption of the knower's priority and centrality without ceasing to be a theory of knowledge and becoming instead a theory of things? If phenomenology is differentiable from ontology, the object of the religious consciousness, being but an epistemic object, owes its objectivity chiefly to the point of view of the subject, though the objectivity attributed to it be that of an absolute spirit.

(c) Solely on the metaphysical level can absolute spirit, if this be the supposed object of religious experience, lose its relativity and win

true absoluteness. But on that level the subject undergoes radical transformation; no longer merely logical or epistemic, the subject passes
beyond the limits of phenomenology. The notion of the superhuman
subject, the adjective denoting preeminence of its reality, is the fount
and origin of the metaphysics of self-consciousness, Hegel speaking of
such subject as absolute spirit knowing itself both as spirit and as absolute. Its objectivity is not of the sort religious experience can vouch
for. That experience, being the experience of a finite subject in relation
to an object transcending it, in kind as well as degree, is clearly not
self-conscious in the ordinary sense. It would seem rather awkward to
define religion as consciousness of the self either in connection with the
experience of the finite individual or with that of the self-knowing
absolute spirit. The assumption that the essence of religion lies in the
consciousness of identity of subject and object, be the scale human
or superhuman, must inevitably reduce religion to narcissistic self-
worship.

Hardith: Alas, the three meanings of subject so carefully distinguished are in the text quite confused. The confusion, I admit, may
only exist in my head. But the confusion is there. As I read the introduction Hegel not only impersonates the absolute subject—he person-
ifies it. The absolute subject is presented throughout as if speaking in
its own behalf. Thus, it is not the author of the treatise who looks upon
the holistic object of religion as substantive (or substance) definable
by its predicates (or attributes), absolute spirit, reflecting on the earlier stages of its progress, appears to itself as logical subject. Nor does
the author on his own authority lay claim to knowledge of mind's dialectical evolution; absolute spirit itself is made to enact the part of
epistemic subject in relation to the series of protean objects confronting it. And when he dwells on the differentia of religion, author and
personified subject so merge together that the purported biography of
mind virtually becomes mind's autobiography, self-revelation of absolute spirit being the guiding principle from its inception to its completion.

This may be said to justify the view of Hegel's product as possessing
unity and continuity. Yes, but at the cost of converting phenomenology into metaphysics. And were it still construed as phenomenology,
because the phenomena depicted must necessarily be such as absolute
spirit requires for expressing the amplitude of its dynamic life, would
not the distinction between appearance and reality remain without a
difference? The alternative to all this would seem to lie in interpreting
Hegel's work as essentially divided, one part relating to the diversities
of prereligious experience, the other part having to do with prolegom-

enary arguments of Hegel's doctrine—the doctrine that between religion and philosophy the difference is one of form and not of content.

Meredy: There is of course the humanistic interpretation as the other alternative. In spite of Hegel's misleading language, it is not a superhuman subject of which the *Phenomenology* is the biography. Such a subject, if conceivable, can here be only a human conception. The religious consciousness *as* consciousness is man's and not God's. The appearance of religion, whether in the course of history or in the course of the dialectic, can appear nowhere but in the life of the race. There can in respect of its phenomenism be no difference between religion and, let us say, culture or morality. As regards all phenomenology, the apothegm of Terence may be given an inverse sense: *everything nonhuman is alien to it*. How then can there be one phenomenology of the nonreligious forms of consciousness, and another of the distinctly religious forms? There is but one phenomenology of human experience; of experience nonhuman or superhuman Hegel's treatise can afford no information. But his language, alas, is treacherous, presupposing the possibility of cognitive intimacy with absolute spirit. Discussion of this matter must, however, be deferred, being at present more or less premature. Let us first consider the various types or modes of religious consciousness.

Natural Religion

Hardith: The artificiality of the architectonic in connection with religion is striking. With its threefold division, and each division again subdivided, religion follows in its evolution the evolution of secular experience. The stages of the preceding dialectic are recapitulated in the dialectic of religion, religious experience thus appearing in modes corresponding to those serving as its models. We accordingly begin at the level of consciousness, which is the first major section of the *Phenomenology,* and these modes Hegel speaks of as belonging to Natural Religion. It is unfortunate that the descriptive name has in English parlance a distinctly modern flavor, and it is equally unfortunate that the only forms of religion based upon nature with which Hegel deals are chiefly Oriental in origin. This limitation obviously runs counter to the universality the dialectic is alleged to be intent upon. And militating also against the supposed claim to universality is the close identification of dialectical with historical sequence. The modes of experience at the level of consciousness, to wit, sense-certainty, perception, and understanding, which serve as paradigms in the phenomenology of religion, are undeniably universal: they appear always and everywhere, and the order of their development is not necessarily or uniformly chronological. Not so the religions exhibited as parallel to them; being but historical phenomena and not logically growing out of one another, their universality is highly dubious. The dialectical structure which Hegel grafts upon these early historical religions, ingenious though it is, seems nevertheless quite forced.

Meredy: It is true that here more than elsewhere dialectical and chronological relations go more or less hand in hand. Hegel selects for consideration types of religion he deems dialectically essential, taking for granted their actual historicity. To primitive religion in a prehistoric sense, a subject matter of anthropology, he makes no allusions.

303

The Oriental type with which he is concerned clearly belongs to history usually described as 'ancient'; assumed by him as antedating Greek religion, the type appears in different expressions and among different cultures. Of its varied causes and varied effects he could hardly lay claim to expert knowledge. His interest in early religious thoughts, not being scientific, lies exclusively in their direct affiliation with nature; this affiliation, their common denominator, has, according to Hegel, a dialectical development parallel with the historical. The treatment is inordinately abstruse and too sketchy to be more than suggestive, and the interpretation in terms of experience falling into the rubric of mere consciousness is, as you say, artificial and forced. The sketch is important notwithstanding, showing the possibility of subsuming under a generic tendency, a diversity of religious ideas, and of correlating the two orders to which their arrangement is amenable, the order of appearance and the order of significance. Thus, the different forms of natural religion exemplify, in history as well as in logic, a progressive series in the direction of anthropomorphism. The less its dependence on the powers of nature, the higher the religion. And the more religion comes to depend for its expression on human activity, the greater its spiritual advance. It is thus that Hegel traces the transition from Oriental to Greek religion. And it is thus also that the transition seems to him analogous to the transition from consciousness to self-consciousness. If natural religion finds attributes of divinity in the phenomena of nature open to perception, and if religion of art depends on human creation for its notions of the divine, the analogy is not implausible.

Hardith: How studiously you circumvent what Hegel actually asserts, and how admirably you express his thesis in such simple and lucid words! Could you not be accused of falsifying his argument by rendering it intelligible? For he does contend, and unmistakably, that in all religion, from the lowest to the highest, the self-conscious absolute spirit is always implicitly present. It is only at the highest level of the highest form of religion, which he identifies with Christianity, that the Absolute explicitly reveals itself, religion then passing into philosophy and becoming therein preserved and superseded, that is, *aufgehoben.* Conceiving religion as consciousness of the Absolute, Hegel reads this consciousness into even its earliest forms. We must accordingly ask—and the question is moot—whether, forsaking phenomenology, Hegel is not simply harping upon a preconception of which history must be forced to provide willy-nilly confirmatory illustrations.

Consider Zoroastrianism with which the analysis begins. Is light here the very embodiment of the divine essence, absolute spirit itself appearing in visible shape? We have here, so Hegel comments on the conception of God as Light, "the pure subject conscious of itself in its externalization as universal object, an object signifying the inter-penetration of all thought and all reality." Baffling language, this—and one wonders whether thus spake Zarathrustra! And how egregiously equivocal is here the use of the personal pronoun! Light, forsooth, the divine ego (*das reine Ich*), conscious of its pure egohood, is in con-tinual struggle with the Other, the principle of Darkness!

More in keeping with the phenomenological task is attribution of selfhood solely to the finite individual to whose inchoate religious thought light must appear as if possessed of a godlike character. The ambiguity is particularly glaring in view of Hegel's correlation of the first phase of natural religion with the first phase of natural conscious-ness. Religion, too, must initially pin its faith on the certainty of sense-experience, but a certainty, as Hegel says, the content of which is "filled with spirit." Is it not preposterous to think of absolute spirit, when appearing in the shape of light, as depending for the proof of its own existence on the testimony of the senses? Yet, absolute spirit, so Hegel emphatically declared, must see itself under the form of being, and under that form which pertains to the object of sense-certainty. To the human mind still in the early stages of religious development one may indeed legitimately ascribe the tendency to envisage God as incarnate in an object of sense of which the certainty is as immediate and as compelling as the presence of light. In short, when Hegel speaks of absolute spirit as subject or object of religion, in what sense does reality belong to it; and if immediate experience is the starting point of religious thought, whose experience must here be posited?

Meredy:　Let the pundits explain Hegel's enigmatic utterances, but, alas, they explain them differently and in ways often no less inscrutable. To save Hegel from the Hegelians—nay, from Hegel himself—is a task worth attempting. The insights that abound in the *Phenomenology* are more important than the occult vocabulary in which they lie em-bedded if not buried. The treatment of religion is a case in point. Failure to disentangle the phenomenology of religious experience from the metaphysical construction Hegel puts upon it must inevitably give rise to flagrant paradoxes. One of the lessons Hegel unwittingly teaches is never to mix analysis with indoctrination. And to such a mixture he himself is here peculiarly addicted. What could possibly be the meaning of the statement that the Absolute Spirit cannot know itself as absolute spirit without first knowing itself as Light, and that it must thus contemplate itself in the form of being such as belongs to the object of sense-experience? If the statement makes any sense, which I seriously doubt, it may perhaps do so when religion is considered at the level of Hegelian metaphysics. In a phenomenology of religious experience it is sheer nonsense. There is no warrant for the assumption that the consciousness *of* absolute spirit, conceding such consciousness to be definitional of religion, must be a consciousness possessed *by* absolute spirit. One might as well contend that one's consciousness of any object—a star or a flower, for example—is shared by the object. Why introduce in the first place the notion of absolute spirit in the analysis of religious consciousness? In the analysis of it free from dogmatic prepossessions, such as Hegel pretends to offer in the *Phenomenology,* the notion is entirely gratuitous. It seems to enter surreptitiously for the purpose of making religion ancillary to Hegelian ontology. Religious experience, as a phenomenon in the life of mind, makes its appearance as the experience of finite mind, distinguished from nonreligious experience by a consciousness of the total nature of things instinct with divinity. Religious vision, being synoptic, will see its comprehensive object in different shapes comporting with the different modes of seeing it which the dialectic calls for. Thus, religious phenomenology forms part of the phenomenology of all human experience. It too must have a simple or primitive origin. And here likewise historical illustrations must be available to justify the chosen point of departure.

What better example, therefore, than Zoroastrianism? What more immediate or more compelling a vision than light? When not eclipsed by darkness, how could light fail to appear totalistic and omnipresent? The struggle of light with its opposite must thus be construed as taking place on a cosmic scale. How natural then the apprehension of God as Light? And must not such divinity outrank dialectically every other in natural religion, seeing that the divine source of all that is visible manifests its own visibility, as attested by the certainty of sense-experience than which nothing can initially claim to be more certain? For with this claim mind's phenomenology begins, and since the phenomenology of religion is modeled on mind's prior evolution, it must obviously have a cognate beginning. It is thus that Hegel's procedure must be understood.

Hardith: But thus to understand it is to fly in the face of his categorical assertions. Does this not involve a drastic emendation of the text liable to be vigorously challenged by the specialists? What in effect you demand is that some of Hegel's most salient statements should be dismissed as either unintelligible or negligible. Explanation of the inexplicable you wisely leave to those you call pundits. As for me, I can but voice bewilderment in the presence of the opaque. The conception of an absolute spirit which experiences *in propria persona* all the variants of natural religion, to speak here only of these, produces in me a state of complete incomprehension. So I cannot but welcome the support you are lending to my feeling that Hegel's metaphysical speculations are here altogether misleading.

With the remaining material covered in this section we may accordingly deal quite briefly. Nothing indeed could be more cursory than Hegel's treatment of the early religions of India. He groups them together for the purpose of illustrating the process of deifying organic rather than inorganic nature. Plants and animals of various kinds now come to be looked upon as objects sacred to the religious consciousness. This, for Hegel, represents a higher stage in the phenomenology of religion, central here being the belief that the essence of the divine is incarnate in living forms and living powers. And because sundry specimens of organic life may be regarded as incarnations of divinity, the dialectic of the religious consciousness becomes one in principle with the dialectic of perceptual consciousness. Just as a sensory property is perceived as an object's own and shared with other objects, so the same sacred quality appears embodied uniquely as well as universally: to different animals different tribes attribute a peculiar odor of sanctity. And in their mutual hatred and warfare such tribes (*Völkergeister*) consciously adopt the singular ferocity of the several animals they severally venerate as sacred. This religion Hegel speaks of as "the religion of spiritual sense-perception," and, in keeping with his creedal bias, he also speaks of the process involved in dispersing so widely the quality of divinity as one of self-differentiation by the absolute spirit. All this is certainly ingenious—but how fanciful!

Meredy: Yes, fanciful, if what Hegel so slightly says about Indian religion be viewed out of context and in relation to his doctrinary prepossession. The theme here adumbrated serves but to illustrate a type of religious consciousness that must arise under the dialectical conditions definitely specified. Religion of sense-perception follows upon that of sense-certainty for reasons strictly architectonic. It is the earlier dialectic of mere consciousness which dictates the order in which the variants of natural religion make their appearance; the immediate vision of divinity in some sensory quality necessarily precedes the apprehension of it in some particular thing. Given the division within nature between physical and biological phenomena, a division which the dialectic of religion presupposes, what more 'natural' than that the initial object of the religious consciousness be deemed visible in inorganic shape? Religious experience moves to a higher plane when the object deified is seen to belong to the world of organic forms. And it happens that for the progress from physicalism to vitalism, if such terms here are not inappropriate, Hegel finds historical confirmation. But such confirmation, here as elsewhere, is merely tangential, the dialectical sequence resting on other grounds. This point, so often reiterated, needs no further emphasis.

In passing to the final phase of natural religion, Hegel goes to Egypt for relevant illustrations. For it is in Egypt that he discovers religion which, liberated from exclusive dependence on sensory qualities and perceivable things, owes its expressions to a laboring self. What the dialectic thus calls for is a species of religious consciousness whose object, ceasing to be merely physical or biological, becomes one that has the earmarks of human production. Because the human agent now enters the sphere of religion, Hegel entitles this part of the text "The Artificer" (*Der Werkmeister*), intimating that the activity exercised, while becoming progressively weaned from nature, is nevertheless incapable of reaching the level of art. Like the consciousness involved in understanding, struggling in vain to unite the opposed factors of which perception is the resultant—to wit, objective content and subjective form—and must therefore surrender the task to self-consciousness; so the consciousness implicit in Egyptian religion facing a similar problem, must in the end leave the solution to a more complex state of religious thought. It would be tedious to dwell on Hegel's treatment of Egyptian pyramids and obelisks, columns and statues, hieroglyphics and sphinxes, tinged as it is with his irrepressible bias. His tendency to intrude himself in the analysis apart, the dialectical significance of this type of religious consciousness is impressive. Here is the ultimate and inevitably equivocal version of natural religion. The religious object, instead of being sought in external phenomena, emerges as a thing made with hands to the construction of which nature must lend assistance. But the forms that go into the making of the product, those borrowed from nature and those conceived by the artificer, remain poles asunder. The polarity of the natural and the artificial, which here seems irreducible, corresponds to the play of polar forces at the level of understanding. And since the dialectic of understanding is here the paradigm, the transition of religious consciousness to religious self-consciousness becomes equally necessary. In the new context, however, such transition is one of advancing from the religious posture of the artificer to the religious posture of the artist. The work of the former, being a blend of incompatible forms, reflects the essence of divinity as if it were a strange riddle; the work of the latter, achieved by self-conscious thought, will represent in increasingly adequate forms the harmony of subject and object relating to religious experience.

Hardith: You again omit all reference to absolute spirit as the *fons et origo* of religion. I do not complain, for I find the dialectic without its ghostly presence more palatable as well as more convincing. Yet how great is your infidelity to the text! Every page belies your attempt to construe the argument in terms so completely humanistic. It is spirit, Hegel declares of the religion of Egypt, "which here appears in the shape of the artificer, and its action, when producing itself as object, but without having as yet grasped the thought of itself, is an instinctive kind of labor." With a stroke of the pen, as it were, all the works of Egyptian genius sink to the plane of pseudoart. Religious progress, so we are told in the same mystifying prose, consists in the exchange by the Spirit of the artificer's role for the role of the artist: *Der Geist ist Künstler.* Are we bound then to think of God or the Absolute as literally migrating from Egypt to Greece?

Meredy: Your irony is not misplaced. What indeed is one to make in this context of an absolute spirit alternately enacting and abandoning a series of histrionic parts? Whence the necessity of such a mythical being? Is it not here an embarrassing encumbrance? The dialectic of religion might be made to exhibit a high degree of generality independently of Hegel's creedal preconceptions and even of his historical illustrations. Let us conceive of the religious object as amenable to the variable predicates which the human subject—and in phenomenology there can be no other—must in the course of the dialectic attribute to it. And let us think of the predicates as forming a definite series, the first in the series denoting material forces, the second living organisms, the third human fabrications, and so on. The three phases of natural religion, corresponding to the adjectival differentiation of the subject, might then not inaptly be designated as religious physicalism, religious vitalism, and religious artifactualism. Does this sound odd? If to speak thus is to import into Hegel's text a strange vocabulary, the vocabulary is scarcely so strange as Hegel's own. Yet it does no injustice to the pregnant insight his analysis of natural religion actually affords with such remarkable acuity. Unless we disengage the analysis from the dubious contentions infused into it, the insight is apt to evade us. But enough of this. The sections that follow contain insights of much deeper significance.

Religion of Art

1. Concentric Spheres of Art and Religion

Hardith: A preliminary observation in connection with the section before us seems to me worth making. Hegel does not here consider art as a special subject matter; he regards it as but an aspect or 'moment' of religion. Only later do art and religion appear as distinguishable stages in the development of his systematic doctrine. In the early work, however, art occupies a singular position: one species alone—namely, Greek art—is singled out for analysis and dealt with solely in relation to Greek religion. Must this not present a formidable problem to those interpreters who read the book, not in its own peculiar terms, but principally in the light of the author's subsequent products? Where do we here find recognition that art, religion, and philosophy form a thematic trilogy, each of the themes individually distinct from as well as organically related to the others?

Meredy: The treatment of art as exclusively Greek and largely synonymous with Greek religion simply shows the difficulty of fitting the *Phenomenology* into the structural framework of the completed system. The attempt to extract from the early treatise arguments for Hegel's later major theses is bound to fail, despite his lapses from the original intent the treatise was designed to express, the intent clearly being to portray in dialectical progression the perennial types of men's attitudes to the world. Not until Hegel addresses himself to the types of religious postures does he conspicuously betray his method; instead of being as hitherto the vehicle of impersonal biography, it now becomes the instrument of special pleading. By a strange equivocation, particular kinds of religious experience now represent stages in the life of the Hegelian Absolute. Yet, the religious forms of consciousness, no less than the nonreligious forms preceding them, presuppose a human subject; and a superhuman mind, conceived as their object, is but a human conception, bred in sundry ways in the finite psyche under varying historical and social conditions. It is necessary to mention this again in order to renew the contention that phenomenology does not cease being phenomenology when the phenomena considered are those subsumed under religion. The issue is crucial. Without meeting it squarely, the distinction between dialectical procedure and the procedures of historian or metaphysician must needs remain blurred. Within the context of phenomenology, and within that context alone, Hegel is indeed justified in choosing only such particular illustrations as may enable him to set art in antithesis to nature as basic to religion, basic alike to the religious consciousness and the religious object. The illustrations, though drawn from history, are deliberately construed to suit the dialectic. Given the architectonic to which the dialectical sequence of forms of religion is amenable, the forms of natural religion must inevitably precede religion in the form of art. That Greek religion and Greek art happen to be bound each to each by mutual implication happens to be for Hegel a happy circumstance. Neither historical causation nor metaphysical grounds would in this context seem to be called for. The interfusion of art and religion which Hegel finds in Greece is simply the perfect example illustrative of a necessary phase of the dialectic. No absolute mind need be assumed as advancing from mere consciousness to self-consciousness in the transition traced by Hegel from the Egyptian artificer to the Greek artist. It is the dialectical method which requires that the latter's transparent achievements be regarded as contingent upon the hieroglyphic creations of the former. The Greek artist is here envisaged as bringing to fruition the incipient aspirations attributable to the Egyptian artificer. The historical allusions merely serve the purpose of exhibiting the passage from dialectical antecedent to dialectical consequent.

Hardith: The phenomenology of natural religion as corresponding to the phenomenology of mere consciousness presents, in the light of Hegel's architectonic, but little difficulty. The demonstration of the correspondence, cursory though it is, is not lacking in clearness. Not so clear to me is the conception of religion in the form of art as religion at the level of self-consciousness. Whose self-consciousness is involved in the creation of art concentric with religion? And what precisely does self-consciousness here signify? If we reject the untenable assumption of an absolute spirit in the role of self-conscious artist, the only artistry strictly self-conscious is strictly human. Now self-consciousness has here more than one connotation. If self-conscious art is art resulting from purposive activity, the finished product bearing the impress of its creator's intended design, how preposterous to limit its rise and dominance uniquely to a certain time or place! He who

311

can impose upon the raw material whatever form accords with his afflatus is always and everywhere a self-conscious artist. Hegel's judgment on the 'artifices' of Egypt as ensuing from an instinctive kind of labor, comparable to the labor of bees building their cells, hardly merits serious consideration. Can it be cogently maintained that an Egyptian pyramid is not a work of art or that it is less self-conscious a creation than a Greek temple? Is not deliberate activity *eo ipso* self-conscious activity? But there is another sense of self-consciousness which, though one would hesitate to use it in connection with ancient art, could apply to the products of Egypt no less than to those of Greece. Self-conscious art, it is often held, is more or less autobiographical; it is art which, when the self of the artist appears focal, not only embodies but reveals his visions and beliefs, his thoughts and sentiments. What I am endeavoring to do is to break down Hegel's dichotomy between artificer and artist, the latter alone operating at the level he deems higher, the level of self-consciousness. My point is that the work of the former too belongs to art and to art as self-conscious in the selfsame sense.

Meredy: To be sure art is human—and what more human than art definitely self-conscious? With the existence of a superhuman mind, save as posited by human thought, phenomenology, as we agree, can of course not be concerned. But the two meanings of self-consciousness you mention, though undeniably important, have no bearing on Hegel's text. The self-consciousness Hegel attributes to the religion of art has a sense chiefly cognitive, the sense in which the self as subject and the self as object are logically different but actually identical. Whereas for the analysis of self-consciousness, as self-consciousness first appears in the course of the dialectic, we need but assume a single and separate individual, for its analysis in connection with the concentricity of art and religion, we must conceive of the individual as explicitly social. It is Hegel's contention that neither religion nor art can be accounted for in terms purely personal, every form of either being the expression of a particular ethos involving a pathos relative to it. The contrast between artificer and artist is ultimately this. The work of the former, too, reflects the characteristic spirit informing his community; and if the community's religion is vague and mysterious, not expressible except in strange shapes, still beyond sound or speech, the artificer's work cannot present the religious object otherwise than as a 'thing' or 'force' alien to the mind and the heart of man. It is thus that the dialectic of Egyptian religion comes to resemble the dialectic of mere consciousness. The transition to the religion of art is transition to a higher ethos; the human and the divine, ceasing to be estranged, manifest the same union of difference and identity belonging to subject and object in self-consciousness. The religion of art, as Hegel shows, is essentially and deliberately anthropomorphic: in portraying the divine in human form, the Greek artist mirrors that ethos to which the concentric view of religion and art is fundamental. But this ethos must generate its own pathos. The story of the process is long. With remarkable empathy Hegel tells the story under three heads—the abstract work of art, the living work of art, the spiritual work of art.

2. *The Abstract Work of Art*

Hardith: "The first work of art," says Hegel, "because immediate, is abstract and individual." A cryptic sentence, this. If I read it aright, the artist is said to begin where the artificer ends, as if, speaking in view of the illustrations Hegel has in mind, the initial attempts of Greek artistry were intended to realize what remained but latent in the final products of Egyptian craftsmanship. The first work of art must thus appear as a particular thing, comparable to the artifice it dialectically grows out of, but a thing no longer exhibiting the odd intermixture of incompatible elements. The thing created, now serving as unambiguous image of the divine, derives its significance from being modeled on the human form, and it is in the sculptured god that the religion of art finds its primary expression. Upon sculpture, accordingly, devolves the task of starting the humanizing process of divinity; in representing in perceivable shape the anthropomorphic essence of the religious object, the artist produces in his work a reality cognate with his own. Is this then the sense in which sculpture exemplifies the religion of art at the level of self-consciousness? For a carved object, the product of self-conscious activity, portrays a divine personage all of whose visible aspects are typically human. Such individual portraiture would prima facie seem to belong to representational art. Why is it here designated as abstract?

Meredy: The art here considered is undeniably the art of sculpture, though not so named, the reference being to representations of the gods with forms distinctly human, no longer with forms half animal, half human. But despite all attempts at verisimilitude, the anthropomorphism sculpture aims at can never be anything but abstract. The raw material to which the artist is bound precludes faithful representation. The individuality imparted to a carved god, an individuality so inevitably external and so completely quiescent, differs radically from the individuality which the artist attributes to himself. The statue made to represent a divine personage remains a thing in perpetual repose, in absolute contrast with the dynamic personality of its self-conscious maker. Not by means of his particular art can the sculptor fashion a

313

reality akin to his own. This discovery becomes dialectically crucial. To represent the inwardness of the subject the artist must look for more adequate ways of production. It is thus necessary that the religion of art pass beyond the limitations inherent in the art of sculpture.

Hardith: I realize of course that matters properly aesthetic are here not strictly relevant. We are supposed to be concerned with religion in the form of art and not with art unrelated to religion. Nevertheless, the view of sculpture as abstract because its representations fall short of complete verisimilitude does raise an aesthetic issue. Why should abstractness be taken in a pejorative and representationalism in a eulogistic sense? That its forms are but imperfectly representational is surely no reason for relegating sculpture to the position of an inferior art. And does it follow that no art is truly representational unless its forms appear to resemble the forms of life or of consciousness? Movement, process, change—in short, all subjects of a dynamic or sensitive nature—do indeed defy verisimilar reproduction through sculpture, a fact which does not detract from its importance as a distinct art, distinct as regards requisite material and methods of formation. Must sculpture be deemed to end in failure simply because it is an art condemned by dialectical fiat to serve religion solely by exhibiting the gods in the frozen shapes of men? And is failure in one domain failure in every domain? Sculpture has many uses and its so-called abstractness is a virtue when judged as an art not subservient to religion.

Meredy: Your defense of sculpture as an independent art, though arresting, is more or less beside the point. To be sure, Hegel's phenomenology of religious experience is not, as remarked earlier, purely phenomenological; the sections devoted to religion contain many utterances heavy with references to his own doctrine. The label abstract affixed to art is here essentially ambivalent. It relates, in one sense, to the material limitations under which sculpture must labor to represent the gods as resembling ideal types of human individuals; the possibility of so representing them hinges on the necessity of removing or abstracting from the human models all but their bodily attributes. The sculptor's sole way of humanizing the divine lies in corporealizing it. In another sense, the label adheres to the separateness of the individual: abstraction means isolation. The individual god represented by sculpture is individual only as a single and solitary entity. That the detached individual is an abstract individual, a theme on which Hegel rings many changes, applies with particular force to the sculptor's statue: the image of a deity it exhibits is the image of a being in perpetual and self-sufficient solitude. The real nature of the deities wrought by sculpture—'real' in Hegel's metaphysical sense—must perforce suffer be-

314

trayal by an art incapable of representing individuality save such as pertains to monolithic things existing in a state of rest. Here we have another instance of Hegel's tendency to intermix in his analysis of religion phenomenological and ontological arguments. Apart from aesthetic and metaphysical considerations, which are extraneous to the phenomenology of religion, abstractness characterizes the art of sculpture in one sense only, in the sense, namely, that the religious object it portrays appears entirely divested of spiritual inwardness. The art germane to religion, as Hegel observes, requires another element for its expression, and this element, which he designates as higher, is that of language.

Hardith: How often language serves in the *Phenomenology* as turning point of the dialectic! And how various are its functions! Conducive to spiritual estrangement, it is also the means of spiritual enhancement. Language, being for Hegel the process whereby self-consciousness asserts its existence, now appears on the scene to express the inward nature of the religious object. Words are of course better instruments of communication than statues. It is curious, however, that Hegel should regard the hymn as the first work of art in this new element. Why the hymn? And why deem it abstract, seeing that the hymn constitutes the very antidote to sculpture?

Meredy: The principle of polarity governing the dialectic demands that one form of the religion of art be superseded by its opposite. The religious object exhibited in a state of silence and quietude must thus find expression in song of praise and devotion. How great is the contrast between the calm statue and the lyrical hymn! It is tempting to think, as does, for example, Hyppolite, that Hegel here anticipates the Nietzschean distinction between Apollonian and Dionysian art. Be that as it may, the hymn does have the advantage over sculpture in establishing a more intimate relation with the religious object. The god expressed in the medium of language, ecstatic and inspirational though the language be, comes to partake of the character of him who speaks it. What the sculptor's art cannot achieve, the hymnologist's brings to fruition. As embodied in the latter's art, the deity appears as if endowed with animation and soulfulness, thus ceasing to be an alien thing, alien, that is, to the artist's self-conscious activity. Besides, in forming part of the religious cult, the hymn unifies the separate selves to whom it is simultaneously communicated. But the hymn whereby the many become for the nonce one—by contagion, so to say, as Hegel calls it—remains abstract. Here, too, abstractness is synonymous with limitation. Sculpture and the hymn are equally subject to the restraining conditions of their respective material—one constrained to

315

corporealize the divine, the other to emotionalize it. The language of
the hymn not being ideational, Hegel speaks of it, playing again upon
the word, as *Andacht,* a form of adoration touched with thought. Not
by language that takes this form can the divine be revealed.

Hardith: From the language of the hymn we are thus compelled to
pass to a language more commensurable with the religious object. This
language, curiously enough, turns out to be the oracle. The transition
to it seems quite arbitrary. In every natural religion, and not only in the
religion of art, the oracle, as Hegel declares, is the first utterance supposed to issue from a divine being. If so, why should not the oracle
have dialectically preceded the hymn? And must not priority be accorded to the oracle because the language it employs, though vague
or equivocal, is nevertheless ideational? It does seem to be related more
or less explicitly to the sphere of reflection. For it is after all a response
to a question or entreaty; it gives advice regarding choice of action
that would in certain circumstances promote the welfare of the individual or the community. The oracle would thus appear to exemplify
a mode of expression more articulate than that involved in the impassioned hymn. But what has all this to do with the subject of art?

Meredy: Hegel introduces the oracle as being a kind of language
contrasted with that of universal self-consciousness characteristic of
the hymn. The oracle, it must be remembered, though alleged to have
a divine origin, issues through a medium, its form depending upon the
inspired priest or priestess conveying it. Unlike the voice of the hymn
which kindles in all whom it reaches kindred religious feelings, the
voice of the oracle is the voice of one individual moved to communicate to another the god's answer to a query. True it is that the oracle
is more articulate than the hymn, and in need of no other vehicle than
the vernacular idiom. Yes, articulate, but how enigmatic! The oracles
of Apollo, for instance, for all their supposititious intelligibility, were
often found to be appallingly capable of more than one meaning. The
divine author of statements so equivocal must perforce appear to the
religious consciousness deeply mysterious. It is inevitable that a being
speaking so ambiguously should come to be looked upon as itself infected with ambiguity, embodying at once the essence of nature and
the essence of spirit, foreign as well as akin to the individual self. The
transition from the univalent lyricism of the hymn to the ambivalent
prose of the oracle is quite in accord with the dialectic. The language
of inwardness must of necessity run its course and become its own
other. And oracular locution, too, no less than hymnal, is bound to develop into a distinct art.

Hardith: What *you* say makes sense. But does Hegel say it? I wonder. The discussion relating to oracles, highly prejudicial, reads as if it were an excursus designed to reduce them to absurdity. Oracles are consulted, Hegel holds, in fortuitous circumstances only, and the counsel they are alleged to impart seems unreflective and contingent. That sage of old, says Hegel, alluding to Socrates, while suffering his daimon to guide him in matters accidental and relatively trivial, searched in his own thought for answers to important questions such as have to do with the nature of the good and the true. Here reappear Hegel's tendencies to allow his historical illustrations to dictate the course of the dialectic and to introduce into it his biased opinions. But for the role which the oracle, and especially the Oracle of Delphi, played in Greek religion, Hegel would scarce have incorporated it in the dialectic. And his critical comment on it, made on doctrinary grounds, sounds quite gratuitous. But having repeatedly entered a caveat against these tendencies, I will not press the matter further. Assuming, however, the oracle to be dialectically inevitable, does it afford the necessary transition to the next stage in the development of the religion of art?

Meredy: Not the oracle serves as transition but the religious cult to which language is ancillary. The forms of speech so far considered, those of hymn and oracle, are opposites and are thus required by the dialectic to pass into some higher unity. The cult emerges as the process mediating between the inwardness of religious feeling contained in the hymn and the externality of the divine being involved in the oracle. It is in the practice of the cult that the two sides become mutually implicated. For rites and ceremonies are acts through which religion receives objective embodiment without which it would remain a matter of private experience. The cult, an art essentially transient, has a twofold purpose: it is conducive to an awareness of the god's immediate presence and it enables man to express in public his inner sentiments. Hegel dilates at some length on the development of the cult, showing it to be a configuration of several elements. He lays much stress on the ritual of sacrifice the analysis of which seems oversubtle. Sacrifice here means surrender of some object of value to a particular deity. It is offered up as an earnest of religious devotion to that divine being with which the object is peculiarly identified. Devoted to the god, the offering may be also feasted upon by the worshipers. There is here more than a hint that it is theophagy which unites the human and the divine: "the fruits consumed," as Hegel says, "are the actual living Ceres and Bacchus." We must leave to the exegetes the task of dealing with the significance which Hegel attributes to the sacrificial act. His treatment of the theme is recondite and not free from sophistry.

Inherent in the cult, which is a complex though still an abstract art, is the interaction of different factors, and this interaction lends to it a certain objectivity. Primarily a social product, it cannot be sustained save by the active devotion of each and all. Its diversified form depends on the work of many men: there are those who build the local habitation of the gods and those who mold the statuary for its adornment. Architecture and sculpture, requisite as they are for the cult's existence, thus lose their extreme abstractness and externality. (We have here the first and only indirect reference to architecture in connection with the religion of art.) Dedication to a common aspiration lifts the cult above mere outer rites and ceremonies. The sacred places created for the glory of the gods are also for the use of men, and the treasures laid up in them are ultimately their own. The honor accorded to the gods redounds to the honor of a people richly endowed with the genius of art. In homage of the gods, individuals at certain seasons adorn with grace and splendor their own dwellings and persons, receiving in return for such homage promise of divine favor. The harmony between human acts and divine gifts does not rest on a hope infinitely deferred but has its basis in enjoyment of present wealth and beauty.

3. The Living Work of Art

Hardith: But for the architectonic dominating the phenomenology of religion, Hegel might have considered the cult under the caption of the living work of art instead of under that of the abstract work of art. The cult can scarcely be said to exemplify the sort of abstractness attributable, let us say, to architecture or sculpture. Being a social product, whose production is governed by a certain ethos, the cult celebrates in action the kinship felt by the worshipers with the gods they worship. The cult, bringing to fruition this transient feeling, is not a thing made with hands or words; it represents rather at certain times and places an interplay of different actors performing different parts. There is of course no art not presupposing life, in the obvious sense that living beings must produce or practise it; the life presupposed for the cult has a particular meaning, seeing that it is the art of worship, and for such an art living persons alone can constitute the matter and form requisite for its existence. The cult would thus seem to be the very model of a living work of art.

Meredy: Consideration of the cult as an abstract work of art is indeed questionable, and you are right in questioning it. Why abstract? Apart from Hegel's special use of the term, we should not hesitate to describe as purely abstract that art which is purely formal. Some species of the art of the dance naturally suggest themselves. In analogous fashion, Hegel regards the cult as an art of worship practised in accordance with those formalized or stylized ways to which alone it owes distinctive existence and value. Although the culmination of the religion of art in abstract form, the cult is at the same time the transition to the religion of art in the form Hegel describes as living in a concrete sense.

Hardith: There seems to be an additional feature which prevents the cult from attaining the stature of a living art. Hegel speaks of it as lack of profundity. The spiritual substance or ethos of a people de-mands expression in ways more spontaneous than the ceremonial cult permits. You alluded earlier to the Dionysian strain present in the hymn. Living art, such as the celebration of the mysteries exemplifies, is indeed carried on with unrestrained freedom and ending in baccha-nalian revel and enthusiasm. Yet, this too is a cult depending on certain rituals of its own. How does it differ from the so-called abstract cult?

Meredy: Yes, a cult, but a cult at a deeper level. Rooted in myster-ies, the cult appears closely related to mysticism. Although mystical, the cult is not occult. There is nothing secretive about the enjoyment of the feasts celebrated in honor of the gods. Strangely enough, Hegel sees in the enjoyment a cognitive bond that binds the human cele-brants to the divine beings. The mysteries of Demeter and of Bacchus, to which Hegel alludes, are not enigmatic to those who take part in them. On the contrary, what the mystic rites generate in the initiates is an experience immediate and certain, the experience of being in harmony with the worshiped deities. Hegel develops the theme chiefly with the intent, it seems, of distinguishing Greek from Oriental mysti-cism: it is a mysticism implying affirmation and not negation of the joy of life. But the details are not particularly relevant to our purpose. What is important is the view that a mystery cult—for instance, the Dionysian—may be said to typify a living work of art, involving as it does exuberant acceptance of the gifts given by the Earth-Spirit, or, as Hegel describes it, "unconfined revelry of nature in self-conscious form."

Hardith: As the dialectic proceeds, however, the living work of art ceases to be a mystic cult and becomes instead a feat of skill, the center of attraction shifting from the deities to their human imper-sonators. Hegel refers again to the art of sculpture which cannot rep-resent the gods except in a state of complete repose. But man, capable of free mobility, can replace the statue and use his own figure as me-dium, more suitable than stone or any other inert material, for express-ing the essence of the divine. As paradigm of a living work of art Hegel singles out the individual who plays the part of torchbearer, a part that requires smooth movement of the body, graceful coordination of all

319

its members, and exhibition in equal measure of beauty and strength. It is the torchbearer who, as reward for a performance at once athletic and aesthetic, now receives the adornment formerly reserved for the statue. In the end any and every religious festival comes to be looked upon as if principally designed for the apotheosis of man. Is this to be viewed as transition to the spiritual work of art?

Meredy: Yes, this is here the transition. In what Hegel calls living art, the apotheosis is embodied in too external a form; absent from it is the fundamental element required for spiritual expression. And this element appears here again as language, a medium in which, as Hegel says, the inwardness is as external as the externality is inward. But the language now seen to be essential is not the ambiguous locution of the oracle or the laudatory voice of the hymn or the stammer of bacchantic frenzy. The language productive of the spiritual work of art must be clear and universal. Such language in which alone the religion of art can find its most perfect expression is, according to Hegel, the language of the Greek poets.

4. *The Spiritual Work of Art*

Hardith: In dwelling on the literary products of Greek genius, Hegel's intimate acquaintance with the requisite material is evident throughout. The material utilized, though it ranges far and wide, is adapted strictly to the main theme. Here the religion of art reaches its apex. The humanization of the divine appears to Hegel as a continuous process running through the entire course of Greek poetry. And it is this process of which he treats with almost excessive detail the dialectical development. If anthropomorphic representation of the gods constitutes the very differentia of the religion of art, representation of them through the art of poetry would seem to exemplify in its most complete form the affinity between the human and the divine. Is it permissible to speak of literary anthropomorphism in distinction from any other?

Meredy: You have coined a felicitous term which brings out sharply the difference in medium here under consideration. Language for Hegel is spirit's "native element and habitation." Linguistic rather than plastic or graphic portrayals of the divine thus come to dominate the phenomenology of the religion of art. And in accordance with the threefold division of that phenomenology Hegel discerns three distinct versions of literary anthropomorphism. He likens the epic to abstract art and tragedy to living art. In comedy alone he sees the flowering of spiritual art. Notwithstanding this structural division, the relation of the gods to men assumes in the epic a form markedly different from the form in which it appears in tragedy and comedy. Whether the form be called abstract or not would seem more or less unimportant. It is the kind of anthropomorphism involved in the epic that matters. Let us examine it briefly.

Hardith: Although for depicting the first type of literary anthropomorphism Hegel uses illustrations drawn exclusively from the Homeric poems, he lays his primary stress not on the poems themselves but on their contents such as they were chanted in many places by primitive minstrels. The credit for initiating anthropomorphism in literary form thus seems to belong to the minstrel (*Sänger*) in whose language, which Hegel regards as the earliest, the divine and the human appear distinct as well as united. Why consider the Homeric gods not as found in Homer but as portrayed in song by some minstrel before Homer?

Meredy: The minstrel has a special significance. He represents one extreme and the gods another, the middle term being represented by the people whose heroic age the minstrel's song is designed to recall. Hegel often likens the process of mediation between the universal and the individual to a dialectical syllogism. It is the minstrel who through his mnemonic language seeks to evoke those days of glory when the Olympian deities and the earthly heroes were bound together by bonds of wondrous intimacy. The minstrel's is but a chant of a single individual to be heard by others like him; what he expresses, however, communicates a collective pathos attending the memory of a vanished ethos. The ethos recalled is that of the harmony of gods and men once immediately present to consciousness. The harmony was so complete that the process of anthropomorphizing the several deities had as its correlate the process of apotheosizing certain mortals. The first appearance of literary anthropomorphism must indeed be regarded as contained in the epic; the epic, however, does not acquire religious significance—that is, does not become a spiritual work of art—unless its contents enter into a people's pious recollection through the instrumentality of the minstrel's muse.

Hardith: Here is another case where emphasis on a specific illustration militates against the supposed generality of the dialectic. The only matter here important is the contention that the Homeric poems involve a certain conception of the relation between the human and the divine, and it is this to which the epic owes its place in the phenomenology of the religion of art. The fact that some of the poems were initially chanted would seem to be entirely irrelevant. The origin of Homeric poetry, of great interest to the literary historian or critic, has no bearing on Hegel's task. "When and by whom were the Iliad and

321

the Odyssey written?" The question is one that has nothing to do with the epic as a spiritual work of art subject to analysis by the dialectical method. Hegel's references are not to the contents of early song but to those of the epic poetry generally attributed to Homer. That diverse material embodied in such poetry can be traced to primitive sources must remain a circumstance strictly extraneous to the dialectic. Why then so much ado about the minstrel?

Meredy: Your strictures would be pertinent if Hegel's conception of the epic were confined to a species of literature in written shape. He rather looks upon it as the manifestation of a distinct ethos, comprising the modes of life and attitude prevalent in a particular age among a people accustomed to heroic tradition and open to the seductive influence of the imagination. The epic is here treated as an epitome of a mental vision which has, so to speak, one eye on the forces of nature and the other on the events of the past. Time was when the world of the epic—a world where deified natural powers and archaic human aspirations appeared commingled—served as object of universal belief. This belief, having lost credibility, can only be recaptured in a recollection touched with nostalgia. If language, the organ and instrument of spirit, is to be the medium of such recollection, what more natural then that its first and immediate expression be the spontaneous song, the written poem being a later and deliberate effort? And since fragments of Homeric poetry are actually derivable from versions originally chanted, the role which Hegel assigns to a primitive minstrel, far from being extraneous, legitimately forms an integral part of the dialectic. But there is a deeper reason for his role. When the song is over, the minstrel disappears from the scene, joining the ranks of other individual persons who happen to compose the audience. Not his own self but only his muse is of importance. His sole function is to serve as the inspired singer of a glorious day, and it is the song and not the singer that matters. This is altogether different in comedy where the self of the actor is of greater significance than his part.

Hardith: What you say is plausible but not convincing. If the minstrel is dialectically necessary because of his anonymity, not the singer but the song being essential, is not the epic poet anonymous in precisely the same sense? The Iliad or the Odyssey by any other author would sound as impersonal. Homer, assuming him to be the sole creator of his poetry, keeps himself aloof, the chronicle rather than the chronicler preempting our interest. With the introduction of action into the epic to the analysis of which the text proceeds, the minstrel becomes the forgotten man, and all references hereafter are explicitly to the written poems. For it is action upon which the dialectic ultimately

322

turns, and its nature and development can hardly be dealt with in the compact language of the incidental song. But I do not wish to dilate on this further, so let it pass.

Meredy: We have, I think, given far too much attention to the minstrel whose part in the dialectic is but subordinate. What Hegel is here concerned with is the role which language plays in the phenomenology of the religion of art; the language of the epic, considered by him the earliest, thus comes to enjoy high priority. But since the literary epic contains portions initially chanted, the priority of the song is distinctly higher, and a priority not merely temporal, for its language is a simpler and a more direct mode of reviving the idyllic past. This is quite in keeping with the recurrent pattern of the dialectic which requires that the analysis of any theme proceed from its putative self-consistency to its discernible self-contradiction. Behind the literary epic, then, there is an ideal conception of an ethos, exemplifying a golden age remembered in song, but this conception involves internal instability and incongruity which only the full story as told in the written poems can fully disclose. What shatters the harmonious confusion of heaven and earth, the irenic intermixture of the divine and the human, is indeed action. Think of the absurdity that inheres in the relation between the gods and men as mutually implicated agents in the affairs of the world! With the exhibition of this absurdity the dialectic is chiefly preoccupied.

Hardith: The core of the matter, if I understand it aright, seems to lie in the unnecessary reduplication of causal agency for an identical effect. If a specific act is said to proceed from human volition, it would appear superfluous to invoke for it divine volition too. Should it be held that both gods and men intend and do one and the same thing? If a double genesis of a certain deed be deemed arbitrary, one source of its origin alone being sufficient, which source should be rejected as otiose and hence as dispensable? The question at issue becomes crucial. What men do either is or is not determined by interfering gods—if the former, human volition is illusory; if the latter, divine volition is impotent. Is this not the absurdity inherent in the divided unity of action as Hegel finds in the epic?

Meredy: The pathos of epic action has indeed its source in 'divided unity'. How divisible is an act if its specific character is due to the individuality of the agent? The divine agents, as depicted in the epic, are highly individualized beings, and each is supposed to possess undivided causative power in the production of any desired effect. What folly Hegel ascribes to the gods! Seriously and strenuously seeking to foster or to frustrate the pursuits of men, the gods act as if they them-

323

selves were not the moving forces of the world. And the light in which men appear is no less ludicrous: they strive and labor for ends they are powerless to achieve without efficient assistance from the gods. This singular relation of the human and the divine the epic reveals as singularly comic. Overzealous mortal creatures have the effrontery to offend and defy the gods; and the eternal deities of Olympus, aware of their impotence, derive sustenance from the gifts of men, and the most precious gift is the incentive to intervene in terrestrial affairs. Or, as Hegel ironically remarks, it is through men that the gods first find something to do. The relation of the two is simply without rhyme or reason.

Hardith: Taken apart from the dialectic which requires it, Hegel's conception of the epic has every earmark of a caricature. Is this, one wonders, all that he can find in Homeric poetry? But in view of his intent to confine the analysis to anthropomorphism in literary form, the gods in Homer seem as if made to order for Hegel's purpose. Although eternal and self-contained, existing in their calm abode removed from the flux of time and the influence of external circumstances, these Grecian deities possess the determinateness of individual selves, and their relations to one another resemble those discernible among the mortals here below. How nearly human is the life of the divine selves! Ever forgetful of their essential divinity, they comport themselves as if they were persons of the earth earthy, exemplifying all the natural impulses and passions that the flesh is heir to. Here indeed is anthropomorphism with a vengeance! But it is only in the epic that immortal beings are made to put on traits of mortality. Whatever happens in the world which the epic reflects must needs appear entirely contingent and deeply unintelligible. For the same blind necessity hovers over gods and men alike. Hence the difficulty inherent in the epic as a spiritual work of art; the confusion between the human and the divine is too fanciful and can appeal only to the religious consciousness still at a childlike level. Anthropomorphism, though essential to the religion of art, must assume the more adequate form in what Hegel calls a 'higher language'. Thus the transition to tragedy. Is it not curious that Hegel should so completely ignore the tragic elements in which the epic actually abounds?

Meredy: If Hegel disregards them, it is because they seem to him episodic and more or less irrelevant. Intimations of tragedy, and of comedy as well, are indeed implicitly present in the epic; there is no want in Homer of tragic situations and persons, nor of comic scenes and especially where the gods unwittingly cut absurd figures, but they merely serve as hints of works of art to emerge on a more spiritual plane. Tragedy and comedy proper, as Hegel interprets them, transcend the ambivalence of the relation between human and divine characteristics of the epic. In tragedy, the immortal gods recede more and more into the background, their place being taken by the mortal heroes. In comedy, the gods are shown to be fictions of the mind, no more substantial than clouds. But the religious significance of these genres of dramatic art is too important not to merit a separate dialogue.

Tragedy and Comedy

1. *Decline of the Gods*

Hardith: In his admirable work on the *Phenomenology,* Hyppolite epitomizes the transition from epic to tragic poetry by saying that the minstrel becomes the actor who directly enters the action of the drama (*L'aède devient l'acteur qui intervient directement dans le drame*). Language thus ceases to serve as but an impersonal vehicle of narrative. Uniting passion and action, the language of tragedy now appears dispersed among different speakers; and it must inevitably vary in conformity with the content to be expressed. The participants in the drama are accordingly made to speak as befits their different parts, for what they are required to represent would suffer complete distortion were they to exchange their respective modes of utterance. What, for example, the protagonist is called upon to say can obviously not be said by the chorus. Unlike the hero who in the epic is merely talked about, the tragic hero does his own talking: he appears before the audience as an actual human person conscious of himself as well as of the character he impersonates. He assumes for the nonce the speech and bearing of a different individual, asserting the righteousness of action in a given crisis, and asserting it expressly to free the principle of the action from the accidents of circumstance and from personal idiosyncrasy. Just as it is essential for the statue to be made by human hands, so is the human actor essential to his mask. The mask is nothing without the actor behind it, coming to life, as it were, only through the latter's rhetorical artistry. To the actor, it would seem, Hegel accords a spiritual function higher than pertains to the sculptor. Is histrionic impersonation of the heroic individual of greater religious significance than plastic representation of the divine being? What role do the gods play in tragedy?

Meredy: The gods, though present in tragedy, are present there only by proxy, so to speak. It is the chorus that generally represents them. Serving a double purpose, the chorus speaks for the assembled audience on the one hand, and the higher powers on the other. The spectators find in the chorus, as Hegel states, their image and counterpart, receiving from it an articulate reflection of their own desultory thoughts. And the thoughts they particularly recognize as their own are those relating to the divine rule of human life such as the epic depicts. It is as if through the diverse choric interludes the instinctive wisdom of the epic, which is the very wisdom of the people composing the audience, became incorporated into tragic poetry. Hegel's text dealing with this theme, though very compact, is quite clear. He interprets the chorus as voicing in dispersed fashion the varied richness and fullness of the divine life, each choric part constituting a separate recitative. Now one independent deity is the subject of hymnal honor and praise, now another. But when individual action portends calamity, resulting from the strife of intervening gods or from the clash of divine law with human, the chorus can do nothing but utter laments for the living, resorting to ineffectual rhetoric for the purpose of affording appeasement or consolation. The ultimate significance of the chorus lies in its constant reiteration of terror before the higher powers: terror before their mutual conflict and terror before the inexorable necessity by which they as well as the mortals in league with them are destined to be crushed. Mitigated by compassion for beings to which it is bound by natural affinity, the chorus has for its principal aim the expression of helpless horror of the catastrophic spectacle, all complaints seeming equally futile, and what remains in the end is the mere empty peace of resignation to necessity, the operations of which ensues neither from the deliberate conduct of the character nor from the processes inherent in the nature of things. Upon the scholars in this field devolves the task of tracing in detail Hegel's allusions to the Greek poets—notably Aeschylus and Sophocles. How close is he to the sources of his material? And how legitimate is the construction he imposes upon the material? Such questions are of course beyond our competence.

Hardith: As you phrase Hegel's view of it, the function of the chorus appears to be chiefly germane to the *Antigone*. To this tragedy, made use of previously in connection with the ingenuous society fatally divided by two irreconcilable laws, Hegel returns briefly in order to indicate its relation to religion. These laws, divine and human, law of the underworld and law of the upper world, one relating to the family and the other to government, comprehend in epitome that distinction between gods and men the ambivalence of whose mutual dependence enters so largely into the content of the epic. In Sophocles's work the conflict is simply between two categorical imperatives, religious and secular, and the imperative the heroine chooses to obey is but vague and mysterious, since no man knows whence it came, the invocation of Zeus and some of the other members belonging to the circle of the deities devolving upon the chorus. Not the persons of the drama but only the chorus and the audience the chorus speaks for identify the 'higher power' to which Antigone appeals with the popular gods of the epic. Of anthropomorphism in literary form, if we disregard the choric interludes, the tragedy proper is singularly free, the Olympians being conspicuously absent. In what sense then may it be said to exemplify a spiritual work of art?

Meredy: You put too heavy a stress on the *Antigone*. This is not the only work on which Hegel depends for attributing to tragedy a function specifically religious. What he seems to be chiefly intent upon is the contrast between epic and tragic poetry as regards the relation of the human to the divine. The bonds that bind mankind to the gods become in tragedy gradually weakened and ultimately loosened. It is this which makes inevitable the transition to comedy. Tragedy occupies in the *Phenomenology* a midway position between the epic and comedy: it transforms the Homeric gods and moves towards Aristophanic subversion of them. The gods involved in tragic poetry are but shadowy images of their epic prototypes, and when they become completely identified with the masks put on and dropped by the actors in comedy, the religion of art reaches its apex. The religious significance of tragic poetry lies for Hegel in the manner in which it radically changes the divinities whose comportment in the epic is so human, all-too-human. The illustrations to which he alludes are all variations upon this central theme. Thus from the *Antigone* he passes to the *Oedipus*. There are here allusions also to Aeschylus and even to Shakespeare. Although the treatment is too condensed not to seem cryptic, the main point is clearly this: the gods of the epic lose in tragedy their *exact* likeness to human selves: while *essentially* anthropomorphic, they remain nevertheless supernatural, beings apart and aloof, careless of mankind if not altogether hostile.

Hardith: Not negligible, however, is the positive theodicy which tragedy implies. Hegel's habit of lumping together such different authors as, for example, Aeschylus and Sophocles, not to mention others, militates against his generalization about tragedy as a whole. The reference to Phoebus, the sun god, who knows all and reveals all, can hardly be made to square with the conception of divine indifference or animosity. And how about Zeus, Apollo's father? His place in tragedy, as the text develops it, seems to run counter to the thesis that tragedy in degrading the divinities of the epic is but a steppingstone to their negation in comedy.

Meredy: Hegel often fuses into a single conception ideas having different origins. The reference to Phoebus is a case in point. Apollo as the god of light is one thing, Apollo as the god of the oracle is another. Hegel identifies these views in order to lay bare the paradox of the *Oedipus.* You evidently missed Hegel's reflection on the oracle. Why, thus in effect he asks, should not the oracle, since it emanates from so omnilucent a source, impart the truth without clothing it in language dauntingly obscure or ambiguous? Yet how deeply deceptive is the god's utterance issuing through the priestess! At the root of the notorious parricide lies, according to Hegel, divine deceitfulness. For unlike the opposition in the *Antigone* of two laws, the opposition in the *Oedipus* is between knowledge and ignorance. The tragedy turns on a crime unwittingly committed, foretold though it was by an oracle. In predicting the crime the oracle withheld all further information concerning it, leaving the future here completely in the dark. He who could solve the riddle of the Sphinx found himself powerless to unlock the riddle of the oracle, and was thus sent to his doom by the sly words of the son of Zeus. An evil spirit, so it must seem, was lurking in ambush to entrap its prey. Apollo's priestess resembles not a little those equivocal 'sisters of fate'—an allusion clearly to the witches in *Macbeth*—who drive their victim to crime by their misleading prophecies. How superior is the ghost of Hamlet's father in disarming doubt of its revelation by the probative force of the proffered evidence! The religious effect of a tragedy such as the *Oedipus,* the background of which is the devious prediction of divine origin, is to undermine faith in the ancient gods.

Hardith: Ground for mistrusting the gods lies not only in their chicanery but also in their revengefulness. Hegel refers to the Erinyes through whose agency the character obedient to one power, as in the *Antigone,* experiences the vengeful ire of the power rebelled against. The character in this drama, acting in conformity with but one law, acts of necessity in violation of the other. Action thus inevitably becomes charged with guilt, no matter which of the powers receives complete devotion, the agent's fate consisting in arousing the hostility of the Furies whose function it is to safeguard the right of the challenged power. In the *Antigone,* however, the heroine is fully aware of her divided loyalty, knowing, too, to which power she owes primary allegiance. In the *Oedipus,* the dramatic situation is quite different: the division is between knowledge and ignorance, and the avenging spirits do not visit their fury upon the hero until Apollo's oracle becomes, so to speak, verified. Prior to its verification, Apollo alone has foreknowledge of the predicted crime, and the Erinyes, remaining concealed and lurking in the background, are presumably ignorant of the actual events to occur. Knowledge and ignorance are thus divided among distinct divinities, the very division that determines the hero's fate. No wonder that the religious effect of tragedy—and principally with this, I take it, is Hegel concerned—should culminate in destroying implicit trust in the gods, seeing that the hero is ever at their mercy, subject to their wiles and spites. But there is Zeus. The 'depopulation of Heaven', as Hegel calls it, the ultimate expulsion of separate and independent deities, begins in tragedy, Zeus alone emerging as the acknowledged being from which everything derives its destiny.

Hegel adds a sort of coda in which he deals with the need of reconciling the fateful conflicts involved in tragedy, mentioning the Lethe of the nether world and the Lethe of the upper world, two forms of forgetfulness, one brought about by death and the other by absolution from crime. His remarks on Zeus and Lethe, and especially on the former, seem designed to purge tragedy of its epic heritage, so to say, and to invest it with a religious content exemplifying a greatly attenuated anthropomorphism. Whence then the necessity of the transition to comedy?

Meredy: The transition lies, I think, in the ambivalent character of Zeus. He is but one god among many, though the chief, and as such he appears to the chorus and to the spectators whose ideas and sentiments the chorus reflects. And to chorus and audience alike the King of the Immortals must perforce seem remote and alien, a being to fear and to propitiate. In tragedy proper, however, precisely because of his strangeness and aloofness, Zeus is simply synonymous with the abstract principle of necessity or the inscrutable web of destiny. Between necessity and destiny, indeed, no distinction can be drawn relating to tragic action. Whether determination of such action be ascribed to the machinations of a god or to the operations of fate leaves unresolved the ethical or religious issues connected with tragic poetry. Upon comedy devolves the task of resolving them. And this is accomplished by showing that they have their source in human fancy. Gods and heroes enjoy their sole existence as masks in a play. Behind the masks are the actors—persons of flesh and blood; it is their histrionicism which lends a semblance of reality to the mythical personages the masks represent. The actors, dropping their disguise, stand forth as the actual selves who have the power to simulate the imaginary figures disporting themselves on the stage, their art alone producing the illusion of an inexorable fate governing the lives both of gods and of men.

330

2. *Departure of the Gods*

Hardith: Is it not curious that Hegel should attribute a greater spiritual significance to comedy than to tragedy? Is this not a view that runs counter to the verdict of literary critics? The subject matter of tragedy is generally held to possess a grandeur and dignity absent from the subject matter of comedy. Tragedy is a revelation of the higher things in existence, comedy of the lower. One is elevating, the other entertaining. One is concerned with men's fate, the other with their folly. Can it be seriously maintained that sportive treatment of the graver issues of life is spiritually superior to a treatment of them especially designed to excite the passions of pity and awe? Is doubt really deeper than faith and theoclasm than theolatry?

Meredy: Where and how should the line be drawn that divides tragedy and comedy? In answer to this one looks in vain for unanimity among the authorities on poetics or aesthetics. With the distinction on its merits between the two species of dramatic art Hegel is here not concerned. Confining himself to a few specimens chosen exclusively from Greek literature, he considers the distinction particularly relevant in connection with the phenomenology of religion. It is only within its dialectical context that comedy may be said to occupy a more important place than tragedy.

Hardith: I find no inordinate difficulty in understanding the contention that religion of art attains its culmination in comedy, comparable to the argument that natural religion reaches its apex in the product of artificer. What seems baffling is this. From natural religion to the religion of art—from artificer to artist—the transition sounds fit and intelligible. Not so—at first sight, at least—appears the transition from religion of art to revealed religion, the transition that is, from humanistic scepticism to belief in supernaturalism. The passage from Comedian to Christian—how ingenious but also how preposterous!

Meredy: Yes, preposterous, but only so in the way in which one might read the text, as if Hegel intended to trace the passage from Aristophanes to Jesus! Hegel does indeed take comedy seriously but not because he interprets it as leading historically to the advent of religion transcending the forms of art. It is the logical implications of comedy which he regards as necessitating the dialectical emergence of a new stage in the phenomenology of religion. And Christianity provides illustrative material for this stage as Greek art furnishes it for the preceding one.

Hardith: One implication of comedy seems to be this: in the process of unmasking the gods, men who are engaged in the process unmask themselves too. How heavily Hegel leans on the word 'mask'! The actor, alternately donning and doffing his disguise, shows by such alternation how great is the contrast between his real self and his assumed self. From behind the mask his own countenance becomes suddenly visible, and the god or hero impersonated sinks to the level of the actor's ordinary person. The spirit animating comedy—and it is chiefly Aristophanes Hegel seems to have in mind—feeds on the incongruities inherent in imposing figures, whether divine or human, their farcical behavior forming the content of satire or caricature. The deities of the epic and the heroes of tragedy, seen in comic perspective, exhibit the frailties common to all mankind, arousing pity as well as derision. What, I wonder, has all this to do with religion?

Meredy: The religious aspect of comedy is not obvious, coming into full view only at the threshold of the final form of religion. Signposts to it alone are here to be looked for. The critical assault on the gods, characteristic of the new ethos, implies of course a corresponding pathos. And it is this pathos upon which Hegel lays his main stress. Scepticism of the gods is not the only result that must be laid at the door of comedy. Ideals and values previously acknowledged and honored are abandoned to scorn and ridicule. The ancient faiths are shown to be delusions, and the ancestral hopes fictions. All traditional ideas and beliefs, such in particular as relate to the beautiful and the good, now come to be exposed as idols and surrendered to the vulgar as objects to be laughed at. How pathetic is the reduction of the things of the spirit to a comic spectacle! What you speak of as theoclasm becomes included in a more universal idoloclasm. The very few Aristophanic plays to which Hegel alludes hardly suffice to justify a generalization so sweeping. This simply goes to show that his interest lies more in the comic vision conceived as rampant than in the episodic nature of the illustrative material. It belongs to the essence of comedy as Hegel pictures it to impugn what in a given culture has too long dominated and held captive human thought and aspiration.

Hardith: All this is quite in keeping with the dialectic the logic of which is essentially the logic of comedy. Dialectical and comical muses are kindred in the eye they cast on ideas and beliefs infected with internal inconsistency or contradiction. The function with which Hegel here endows the art of comedy is thus not to be wondered at. Be that as it may, what I find disconcerting is the difficulty of squaring comic atheism with the theological anthropomorphism of the religion of art. The process of humanizing the divine—this we have found to be the major theme of which, from sculpture on, Hegel traces the different variations in their order and connection. Of this theme comedy appears as a variation altogether anomalous. In what sense does comedy exemplify the continuity of anthropomorphic religion, seeing that, instead of humanizing the gods, comedy abolishes them?

Meredy: The question is pertinent. If comedy merely abolished the gods, its relation to religion would indeed be entirely negative. For in losing its objects of worship, the sense of the sacred must eventually become atrophied. To be sure, loss of the ancient deities entails also loss of the dread they arouse. Their departure has as necessary concomitant liberation from their meddling in the affairs of mankind. Freedom from everything external and alien brings with it a feeling of rational contentment found nowhere but in the sort of comedy that banishes from the world the incubus of the fear of the gods of old. In this lies the positive outcome of comedy. *The gods are no more; men alone are real.* Mutually implicative, these two propositions sum up the phase in which religion of art must ultimately culminate. And is this not anthropomorphism with a vengeance? But it must be understood as having a significance much broader than previously expressed. In replacing the gods by men comedy proclaims that 'human forms' in all their variety, now become universally paradigmatic; they and they alone can serve as the measure of things. That the anthropomorphism of the earlier stages should reach its zenith in the anthropocentrism of comedy Hegel considers dialectically inevitable. And equally inevitable is the emergence of a new form of religion which will reveal the depth of meaning implicit in both the theoclasm and the anthropolatry of comedy.

Revealed Religion

1. *The Ambivalence of Revelation*

Hardith: Hegel's approach to the new type of religion is gradual. He first reviews the entire process of religious experience, evoking its previous expressions as background for the rise of religion at a level he considers the highest. Speaking in parables, he assembles the former manifestations of religion as if present at its revelation in final form. "In a highly dramatic passage," so Royce paraphrases the text, "Hegel now depicts how about the birth-place of this new form of consciousness there gather, like the wise men from the East, some of the most significant of the *Gestalten* so far represented: Stoicism is there, proclaiming the dignity of the self as the universal reason, but knowing not who the self is; the unhappy consciousness is there, seeking its lost Lord; the social spirit of the ancient state is there, lamenting the loss of its departed spirit: all these forms wait and long for the new birth. And the new birth comes thus: That it is the faith of the world that the Absolute, even as an Absolute that was hidden, has now revealed itself as an individual man, and has become incarnate." The passage is typical. Here we have the epitome of the elements that enter into Hegel's treatment of Christianity, to wit, the metaphorical, the diagnostic, and the doctrinary. The use of the term birth-place with its allusion to Bethlehem, the analysis of the new religion as implicit in antecedent versions, and the thesis that the Absolute finds its true embodiment in Christianity, clearly involve modes of utterance that are not interchangeable. The language of allegory is distinct from the language of logic; and if the phenomenology differs from metaphysics, the language of logic can obviously not be the same as the language of ontology. When Hegel comes to deal with revealed religion these distinctions are more honored in the breach than the observance. It is difficult to tell when allegory ends and logic begins, and when phenomenology masquerades as metaphysics.

Meredy: Linguistic heterogeneity is characteristic of Hegel's conception of religion. This appears in a dual fashion.

First, there is his tendency to consider religion as containing in embryo his idea of the Absolute. Of the Absolute he sees diverse disguises in all the varieties of religious experience, and not until the sundry images and symbols representing it undergo dialectical supersedure can the Absolute become completely unveiled. What he does through the medium of a multivocal vocabulary especially designed for the purpose is to disclose the nisus in all religion towards Hegelianism. This markedly vitiates the intent to deal with the religious consciousness as a recurrent phenomenon in the life of mind. Hegel's metaphysical bias injected into religion clearly contravenes the aim of phenomenology.

But the confusion of tongues to which Hegel resorts in connection with revealed religion seems to have a more legitimate justification. For the confusion belongs to the very essence of Christianity as he interprets it. Take, for example, the notion of birth as applied to Christ. In what sense is it to be understood? To Christ's historical nativity no literal meaning could be attached without reducing to meaninglessness the claim of Christ's eternal divinity. Of the divine one can obviously not speak in terms strictly biological. Born of an actual mother, Christ is believed to have had no earthly father. (Of the spiritual founder of the new religion it must be said, in Hegel's own cryptic words, *"dass er eine wirkliche Mutter, aber einen ansichseienden Vater hat."*) The assumed union of God and man in Christ requires for its expression a diction essentially heterogeneous in purport. All literalness must here be abandoned. The idioms of allegory, logic, and ontology must perforce remain inextricably mixed.

Hardith: What you say appears in even stronger light in connection with the idea of death. If God and man are united in Christ, who dies on the Cross? Here biological terminology is at once literal and symbolic. Only the human organism can die but not the divine spirit of which it is the incarnation. The death of Jesus, abstracted from his divinity, has no greater significance than the death of any other martyr; as God incarnate, however, his death, hardly a natural phenomenon, goes beyond mere martyrdom. How Christ, being God himself made man, could perish, perish as man but not as God, constitutes a mystery, subject to different interpretations. Here indeed allegory lies cheek by jowl with theology and metaphysics.

Meredy: What language free from equivocation can interpret such mysteries as the birth and death of Christ? Hegel's allusions to Christianity—and but allusions they are—must be taken as having primarily an illustrative use. But here as elsewhere—here in fact more than else-

335

where—he tends to adapt the dialectic to the historical examples, and not vice versa. It is important to remember, however, that the rise of a new conception of man, in consequence of the departure of the gods, constitutes the outcome of comedy as the culmination of the religion of art. The sharp antithesis, precipitated by comic art, between the human and the divine, leading to the sacrifice of the divine upon the altar of humanism, serves as transition to a singular kind of self, the self of a God-man. The idea of a being thus hyphened, which emerges as a result of the theoclastic spirit of comedy, is historically exemplified by the idea of Christ. If religion of art ends with the death of the gods, inducing man to embrace the belief in the absoluteness of his own self-hood, revealed religion begins with the birth of God in man. The mystery of such birth, to which Christian doctrine assigns a major role, Hegel, viewing it in the larger perspective of religious phenomenology, seeks to divest of mysteriousness. Central here is the revelation of a self absolutely unique, that of the incarnate God, and to the detailed analysis of its implications the present section is devoted.

Hardith: One matter of great importance here is the play upon the word revelation. For it enables Hegel to consider the new religion on two distinct levels which he does not permit to remain distinct. On the dialectical level, it is clear, the word signifies the process of rendering manifest in explicit form the creed to which the religion of art is ultimately driven. The creed, inherent in comedy, Hegel condenses into the statements that 'the self is absolute' and that 'God is dead'. Expressed with a light heart, as it were, they sum up and vindicate the happy frame of mind induced by the persuasion that man alone is real. But such happy consciousness must turn into its opposite when the comic spirit succeeds in expelling from heaven all its divine denizens and in dissolving the sacred bonds that bind together men on earth. What pathos must in the end be engendered in the presence of the destruction by ridicule of hallowed rites, venerable traditions, inveterate loyalties, treasured faiths! The judgment that values heretofore deemed immutable and inviolable are as insubstantial as clouds must of necessity lead to spiritual despair. And the more pervasive the judgment, the more universal the despair. The advent of the new religious consciousness thus becomes dialectically inevitable. This is the consciousness of a being capable of comprehending within its nature the attributes of humanity and divinity. Such consciousness alone, it may be contended, can overcome as well as justify the creed which in the religion of art finds final expression. Man's absoluteness and God's death, propositions playfully adumbrated in comedy, become in the new religion soberly transfigured. They are utterances the truth of which can at once be superseded and preserved—that is, *aufgehoben*. This is revelation on the dialectical plane, and any being conceived as God incarnate in man might serve to exemplify it.

But Hegel chooses to illustrate revelation wholly in terms drawn from the context of a particular religion. It is the Christ of Christianity he has solely in mind—a God-man alleged to be revealed through Scripture or the Church. For the general problem of incarnation, which the dialectic demands, he substitutes the problem of Christology, a problem belonging to a special historical religion. What then are we to understand by revelation? Is it the name for a process of making explicit consequences which the logic of comedy entails? And does the logic of comedy necessitate the historical transition to a religious consciousness exclusively Christian? What, in short, is here said to be revealed—a stage in the phenomenology of mind or an ultimate expression of religious truth?

Meredy: Your emphasis on the equivocation in Hegel's use of revelation is not misplaced. The equivocation, fundamental as it is to his argument, is of course deliberate. Borrowing the term from the context of a special religion in which it has a unique meaning, he enlarges it in two directions. There is nothing unique about revelation as a dialectical process: the progressive development of religion in the form of art is a progressive revelation of the divine in human form. Anthropomorphism belongs to the very essence of the religion of art. From sculpture to comedy, representation of the gods in the image of men advances from the static to the dynamic, acquiring ever greater inwardness and refinement. It is in comedy that anthropomorphism receives its pregnant expression: the image of the divine, assuming the shape of a mask displayed at dramatic spectacles, reveals itself as having no other than imaginary existence. That man alone is real and God but a figment of his fancy sums up the dialectical revelation rendered explicit at the apex of the religion of art. It is this which affords the passage to a revelation of a higher order. The human and the divine, which comic art exhibits as so mutually estranged that God must die for the exaltation of the power of man, reveal themselves as united in the doctrine of incarnation. The belief in the birth and death and resurrection of a divine being inspires a new religious consciousness emerging from but moving beyond that phase of religion in which theoclasm and anthropolatry go hand in hand. The special revelation, revealing the union of God and man in Christ, seems indeed a mystery that passes understanding. But recalcitrance to reason is here merely the form and not the content. Expressed in language congruous with its ideational import, the special revelation reveals itself as universal in scope and in accord with rational thought. What ultimately revealed religion reveals, when disentangled from metaphor and myth and allegory in which its historical formulation lies enmeshed, is a speculative vision of the world. It is a sphere beyond religion to which religion itself points the way. Dialectically embryonic in comedy, the revelation of revealed religion entails transition to philosophy—the Hegelian, of course!

Hardith: The double view of revealed religion is certainly singular. Can one seriously maintain that Christianity, the only historical religion here considered, has its dialectical source in Aristophanic comedy and its dialectical realization in Hegelian philosophy? What an extravagant play of ideas! The necessity which the gods are under to die in order that man might inherit their claim to absoluteness—and this Hegel takes to be the religious meaning of comedy—is a necessity purely imaginative if not imaginary. What are we to make of the supposed death to which comedy condemns the gods? Are we perchance to think of it as a biological phenomenon? We are here entirely in the realm of metaphor. Yet the juxtaposition of the assertions, which Hegel declares comedy implies—namely, God is dead and the self is absolute —serves as transition to a religion founded on the beliefs in the absoluteness of that individual self in whom the divine has become incarnate and in God's death as an actual event that occurred to redeem mankind! From metaphor to event, and from man as a natural to man as a supernatural being, the passage seems both verbal and arbitrary. Does it not sound preposterous to say that in comic art the Christian religion lies dialectically prefigured?

Meredy: Preposterous only if we confuse phenomenology with history. Unfortunately Hegel abets the confusion. Between certain types of consciousness and their historical illustrations the line is often so tenuous that dialectical and temporal succession tend to coincide. Although Hegel appears to identify revealed religion with but one historical species, what he is chiefly concerned with is the logical evolution of the idea of revelation, the sequence of which is singularly free from chronology. Consider again the relation of revealed religion to comedy. What historian would commit the absurdity of attempting to trace a causal connection between the doctrine of incarnation and Aristophanic writings? It would be rash to charge Hegel with such egregious folly. In a phenomenology, however, it is quite proper to look upon religion called revealed as following logically from religion of art, just as religion of art may be seen logically to derive from natural religion. Chronology is here irrelevant. And this Hegel shows by viewing revealed religion itself as constituting a distinct phenomenology the phases of whose development are not conceived by him as forming a temporal order.

338

Hardith: Very well. Phenomenology of religion is not history of religion. Yet, it is particular expressions of religion culled from history which serve as subject matter of the analysis; religion in the shape of art is here exclusively Greek and religion based on revelation exclusively Christian. Hegel's preoccupation is thus not with religion as a phenomenon universally human but only with certain species of it that originated and flourished under given conditions in a dated past and geographical regions. Do the illustrations chosen, if but illustrations they are, illustrate anything else than themselves? But I will not press the point. Assuming Hegel's choice of illustrative material justifiable on one ground or another, in what sense may the development of Christianity, for instance, be construed as following a nonchronological course?

2. *The Stages of Revelation*

Meredy: We must not forget Hegel's architectonic. The detailed development of revealed religion is in stages, and the stages are like those of the preceding forms of experience. Every form has its initial phase in immediacy, the immediacy of sense-experience serving as paradigm. Divine revelation, too, must thus make its first appearance in a 'sense-certainty' proper to it. Was not Christ once perceived in the flesh? Did he not show himself as a man to be seen and felt and heard? His life and death and resurrection, events supposed to have been actually witnessed, thus come to be accepted by the believing mind as if resting on 'empirical' evidence, so to speak, having been certified as veridical in the inspired records of the Gospels. The certainty of revelation, the certainty of God's presence to direct experience, is simply analogous to the certainty of the presence to immediate awareness of any and every sensum. And this certainty constitutes the primary phenomenon in the dialectical evolution of Christianity.

Hardith: If revealed religion is an act through which the divine communicates its presence to the believing mind, it will of course assume different forms in accordance with the demands of the dialectic. The initial revelation, considered to be inevitably immediate, must thus inevitably become transcended at a higher level. Revealed religion, which constitutes a chapter in the phenomenology of mind, will perforce recapitulate the process of development every other chapter has been found to exemplify. That revealed religion should arise in a consciousness attached to apparitions is not surprising. What religious visionary could not invoke the testimony of his senses in support of his vision? "I saw Eternity the other night," declares the poet, and proceeds to liken it to a "great ring of pure and endless light." And he expatiates on the theme with an abundance of sensuous imagery. But Hegel is concerned not with a poetic vision of the Eternal but with alleged events attesting its appearance in incarnate and sensible shape. He frequently alludes to the Evangelists who variously rehearse the story of Christ as he comported himself as an actual man. The sensory data made use of by Vaughan, symbolizing the Eternal, remain symbolic; the events narrated in the Gospels, are not treated by Hegel as figments of inspiration. Accepted by the believing mind as indubitably historical, the incarnation of the Eternal in the person of Jesus is shown to conceal a metaphysical doctrine which only speculation transcending religion can bring to light. The phase of sense-certainty which revealed religion is said to illustrate can scarcely be taken seriously. Does it do more than satisfy the needs of the architectonic?

Meredy: Religious symbolism, and especially of the mystic kind, is here not under consideration. Mysticism, tending as it does to abolish the difference between vision and the visioned, is an affront to discursive thought and becomes dialectically vulnerable with a vengeance. Between vision and the visioned there must always be a distinction and relation. The claim to immediacy is a claim that leaves all experience, nonreligious as well as religious, completely inexpressible or expressible in the language of abstract universals. So if revealed religion is said to have an incipient phase comparable to sense-certainty, that phase must either lead to ineffable mysticism or else to a phase in which the divine being, analogous to an object of perception, becomes definable in terms of its attributes. It is thus that God comes to be spoken of as the good, the righteous, the holy, creator of heaven and earth. Such and similar predicates are of course universals. And as long as they alone are fastened upon, the unique subject to which they belong and by which they are sustained escapes understanding no less than a particular percept described by qualities generally applicable.

Hardith: Assuming the dialectic of revealed religion to resemble in its preliminary phases the dialectic of consciousness, we should expect description of God's nature to be followed by explanation of his mode of being. One thing is to enumerate God's essential predicates, another is to grasp God as their real subject. As perception leads to understanding, so should religious consciousness pass from knowledge of the divine attributes to knowledge of the divine self omnipresent in them. I fail to find in the text such a clear-cut transition.

Meredy: It is true that the principle of similitude relating to the dialectic of the various stages of human experience is not always applied by Hegel with sufficient definiteness. The development of religious consciousness as analogous to nonreligious does not receive in the text adequate attention. From the perceptual to the conceptual perspective in ordinary consciousness the transition is certainly exemplary. Analysis of perception reveals distinctions latent in perception with which perception is unable to cope: its objects, though present to be seen and touched, are under the dominance of abstract concepts. Either the percipient ignores them, in which case what he perceives is purely sensory, and his awareness of it remains ineffable, or else he takes full cognizance of them, and in that case what he perceives is open to description by mutually exclusive terms of discourse. It is thus that the perceptual situation cries out for explanation by the understanding. But the understanding, as Hegel shows, since it must needs employ the very polar terms perception entails, can explain nothing until explanatory operations are discovered to be relevant to its own nature rather than to the nature of external things. The polar opposites, for instance, involved in the concept of force, must find their explanation in other polar opposites, and these in others, and so on. There is but one case of polarization that appears self-explanatory, namely, the self-polarization such as self-consciousness exemplifies. For self-consciousness is a form of knowledge the object of which is at once other than and identical with its subject. Of the transition from consciousness to self-consciousness revealed religion, at its own level and in its own terms, affords a pregnant expression.

Hardith: But does not this change Hegel's procedure? The divine being of revealed religion seems at the outset to be modeled on self-consciousness. That Absolute Spirit, to quote Hegel's own words, has assumed the form of self-consciousness, that of an actual human individual, "this appears now as the belief of the world." It is, in short, the belief in God's incarnation which belongs to the very essence of revealed religion. In view of Hegel's explicit assertion that the Christian God cannot reveal himself other than self-conscious, how account for the necessity of prior revelations analogous to the phases of cognition comprehended under consciousness? Here the architectonic would seem to have broken down. The passage is clearly not from consciousness to self-consciousness. Are you not inclined in the interest of structural uniformity to reverse the order in which the dialectic is worked out in the text? Is the matter really important?

Meredy: What I consider here especially important is not to confuse, as Hegel unfortunately does, phenomenology with noumenology. Hegel often seems to forget that the subject of the dialectic is mind believing and not the intrinsic nature of the objects believed in. Throughout the phenomenology of religion, the equivocation of Hegel's language is too consistent not to be intentional. The language is made to sound as if the religious experience examined were God's experience rather than man's. And as regards revealed religion in particular, the phenomenology of it is couched in terms so ambivalent that its conversion into Hegelianism becomes a foregone conclusion: the Christian God is unmistakably the Hegelian Absolute in disguise, the task of the dialectic consisting in removing the disguise. Does the Absolute Spirit, which in revealed religion appears as God incarnate, enjoy *esse in re* or merely *esse in intellectu?* The scholastic distinction is here singularly pertinent: with being in the first sense noumenology alone can be concerned; phenomenology has to do solely with being in the second sense. Identification of the religious object, having its origin in mind, with the Absolute Spirit knowing itself as Absolute Spirit, passes beyond the sphere of religion: the metaphysical conception of an *ens realissimum* supplants the pious vision of God. If to the visioned God the believing mind attributes self-consciousness, can the attribution be other than subjective? As long as mind of which the *Phenomenology* purports to be the biography remains human, all the forms of its experience, not exempting the religious, are incorrigibly relative and finite and mutable.

Hardith: Your criticism of Hegel that the dialectic of religion is designed to harmonize with his philosophic preconceptions seems to me unexceptionable. I am not clear, however, about the correctives you have in mind. You surely do not propose a reconstruction of religious phenomenology on a basis other than Hegel's. Such an undertaking can hardly be ours. What you contend for, I take it, is the necessity of restoring Hegel's true intent by purging his language of its distortive ambiguities.

Meredy: What needs to be done is of course nothing more drastic than a consistent interpretation of Hegel's thought, seeing that the peculiar diction in which it is clothed more often than not hinders rather than aids comprehension. If revealed religion is an integral part of mind's biography, how can it be conceived as revealing in absolute fashion the objective nature of divine existence? From the point of view of phenomenology, every persuasion reflects primarily the human perspective. To speak of the divine perspective as transcending the human, a perspective alleged to belong to God's consciousness of himself as absolute spirit, is to abandon phenomenology. It is within the context of phenomenology alone—that is, within the context of human consciousness—that the divine appears to be amenable to description and explanation in ways analogous to the ways encountered at the level of prereligious experience. The stages of revealed religion will accordingly recapitulate the dialectical progress of the previous forms of con-

342

sciousness. No wonder then that the initial criteria concerning God's incarnation should be drawn from sense-certainty, perception, and understanding. It is the inadequacy of these criteria that renders necessary the introduction of the believer's self-consciousness as model for God's.

Hardith: We must, it seems, take the architectonic seriously if the phenomenology of revealed religion is to be saved from becoming non-phenomenological. How faithful is Hegel's adherence to the parallelism in structure between religious consciousness and prereligious? Specifically, in what sense does the dialectic of the understanding serve here as transition to self-consciousness?

Meredy: The entire section on revealed religion may be said to be concerned with that transition. Freely interpreted, the problem of incarnation, analogous to the problem of perception, confronts thought with the necessity of coping with the logical polarities it entails. The hyphened conception of a God-man constitutes the chief polarity with which revealed religion is burdened, all the others being corollaries from it. How understand, for example, the union of opposites ascribed to Christ, such as his natural and supernatural origin, his temporal and eternal life, his death and resurrection? How explain the relation of space and time to the infinitude of his being? How harmonize revelation as a dated event occurring in a specific locality with the teaching of it by the Church as enjoying an absolute truth independent of history and geography? In its various attempts to meet the challenge of reconciling antitheses so formidable, religious thought, so Hegel contends, struggles in vain until the language of philosophy comes to replace the language of religion.

Hardith: But why should religion be required to convey the experience it vouches for in the discursive forms amenable to logical criteria? To the demand that religion be explained the retort is always open that religion passes understanding. Revealed religion in particular is full of mysteries for the acceptance of which an autonomous faith transcending the jurisdiction of reason must serve as the ultimate court of appeal. It is thus possible to decline altogether to speak whereof nothing intelligible can be said or, satisfying the need of communication, to resort to utterances deliberately figurative or analogical. Whence the necessity of introducing here ways of understanding modeled on those which in prereligious experience appeared intermediary between perception and self-consciousness?

Meredy: The first alternative, namely, to avoid speech in matters of religious belief, is simply to fall back on immediate experience, the dialectic of which, like that of sense-certainty, proves it untenable. Ineffable faith, regarding which nothing can be said or gainsaid, is obviously impervious to dialectic and thus seems invulnerable. Is this not irrelevant here? If God is supposed to manifest his presence to a mystic vision, the vision remains the mystic's silent secret, and nothing but its mute secretiveness can render the vision free from logical encroachment. And immunity from dialectical attack derives from the occult nature of the object visioned as well as from the private vision of it. What the mystic seeks to become engulfed in is a reality absolutely unique, a reality undivided, unqualified, indeterminate. Such a reality, as Hegel remarks elsewhere, is the night where all cows are black. To the mystic's way of *seeing* or to what is thus *seen* by him none armed with discursive weapons can have access. It is only if and when the mystic breaks silence and divulges the secret of the vision and the visioned, be the form in which the secret is communicated ever so figurative or analogical, that the dialectic enters upon its diagnostic labor.

3. *Revelation of God as Trinitarian*

Hardith: Hegel's hostility to mysticism, apparent throughout the text, receives added emphasis in connection with the discussion of the doctrine of the trinity. Apart from the mystic's negative theology, which consists of divesting the divine being of all positive attributes, his spiritual ambition is to achieve ineffable oneness with the nameless One. The correlatives of unity and multiplicity, together with all other distinctions of reason, disappear in the ecstasy of the mystic's experience. The unity of which he speaks, whenever he does speak, is unity pure and simple, unity without parts and variations. The religion with which Hegel is here preoccupied, a religion solely Christian, explicitly recognizes the two persons of Christ, the human and the divine, their indivisible union comprehended in a third. The conception of three persons in one, though mysterious, is clearly nonmystic. A divine being assertible as triune is evidently incompatible with a divine being having no definable or differentiable nature. Yet it is not impertinent to ask whether the former notion is more intelligible than the latter.

Meredy: Basic indeed is the contrast between Hegelianism and mysticism, and the idea of the trinity broached in the text deliberately exemplifies it. That mystic revelation is proof against indictment by the dialectical method is obvious: outside the discursive level the method ceases to be applicable. How charge with contradiction a position eschewing diction? But a revelation not ineffable, the revelation of God as triune, invites different interpretations and is thus not closed to the dialectic. Of the trinity, as a conception capable of utterance, Hegel's analysis serves a threefold aim. One is to show the total inadequacy of the terms in which revealed religion renders the trinity amenable to understanding; another is to rid the trinity of mysteriousness by assimilating it with the universal experience of self-consciousness; and still another is to find the philosophic rationale of the trinity in the triadic pattern of dialectical logic. The first two aims are not inconsistent with the intent of exhibiting revealed religion as a spiritual phenomenon. The third goes beyond phenomenology; here Hegel treats revealed religion as steppingstone to his ontology. These aims are unfortunately so fused by him that one seeks in vain to keep them clearly apart. Yet distinguish them we must lest the fusion be construed as confusion.

Hardith: In the structure of revealed religion, corresponding to that of prereligious consciousness, the stage of understanding is represented, I take it, by the descriptions of the trinity in the terms borrowed from the different disciplines of arithmetic and biology. The description resting on arithmetic involves not only the notion of three persons in one but the notion also of their hierarchy: first, second, and third. The numerals employed are thus both cardinal and ordinal. The description based on biology resorts to nomenclature drawn from the natural process of generation, the relation of the first to the second person of the trinity being called the relation of father to son, though as regards the position of the third person the biological analogy seems rather remote. Of course the view of understanding must be considerably stretched to accommodate the trinity to ways of thinking so distinctly metaphorical. But metaphors have their intellectual uses; and if elsewhere they often facilitate understanding, why not here too?

Meredy: But the metaphors are so crass. Indeed they deepen the mystery that clings to the trinity instead of attenuating it. Consider the arithmetical conception. To speak of the sum of three as being one is literally to speak in riddles. Either the persons of the trinity are not subject to the process of counting or else the result arrived at cannot run counter to the rules governing addition. Here we encounter again the polarity of mutually exclusive ideas with which understanding is unable to cope. Whether taken in a cardinal or ordinal sense, trinity and unity remain inequatable and can thus never be made to coincide. The same holds of the biological conception. Here too the polar terms resist rational assimilation. Fatherhood and sonship, the latter biologically derivative, denote typically asymmetrical relations possible only between separate persons. But if the persons of the trinity are actually believed to be not only indivisible but identical, nothing prevents one from thinking that the father is his own son or the son his own father. An absurd thought indeed—absurd both logically and biologically!

345

And can the idea of incarnation be said to mitigate the absurdity? Hardly. For if God's incarnation is viewed as a dated event to which the son of God owes his existence, the absence of the second person prior to the incarnation clearly contravenes the assumed eternal oneness of the trinity.

Hardith: Yet, some understanding of God's threefold nature seems dialectically necessary, be the idiom in which it is couched ever so strange, unless the believing mind, taking refuge in mysticism, declares God to be completely wrapped in impenetrable mystery. Any analogy or simile may make partly intelligible what the mystic considers totally incommunicable. It is curious, however, that at this stage of the phenomenology of revealed religion, surrender to mysticism can only be eschewed by the use of myths and metaphors. Granted the folly of taking them literally. Yet to view them as merely symbolic is to limit their claim to intelligibility. How profoundly enigmatic the trinity remains despite all allegorical attempts to explain it!

Meredy: Allegorical comprehension constitutes at this stage the sole corrective of mystic condemnation of discourse. Recognition of unity that does not exclude plurality, as well as recognition of the power of speech however pictorial to serve the purpose of understanding, is a signal departure from mysticism. But useless indeed is here explanation by figurative language. The language of arithmetic or biology, for example, concerned as it is with classes of objects, classes of numbers or classes of organisms, would seem altogether inapposite to the trinity conceived as an object absolutely unique. This must inevitably precipitate in the believing mind a formidable dilemma. Either the notion of the trinity, the union of three in one, is not at all singular, the theological version of it being a particular instance of a universal form, or else the notion applies exclusively to the triune God, in which case it must be considered ultimately incomprehensible, and the mystic's attitude to its ineffable mysteriousness admits no challenge. The crucial difficulty involved in the dilemma is evident.

Hardith: The mystic's attitude representing one horn of the dilemma, rejection of it necessarily entails acquiescence in the other. And this acquiescence appears to provide passage to a new phase in the dialectic of revealed religion. Comporting with the dialectic of prereligious consciousness, the new phase must perforce parallel that phase to which the analysis of understanding gives rise, and this of course is self-consciousness. Now self-consciousness, an experience scarcely unusual, could without too heavy a linguistic strain be properly described as trinitarian. For involved in that experience are three selves, so to speak, at once distinguishable and inseparable: the subject-self, the

346

object-self, and the self overarching them and constituting their actual identity. Here is a union of three in one, but the 'three' are not differentiable numerically or biologically, nor does the 'one' connote their sum or cognation. It is a trinity of aspects—Hegel calls them moments —logically discernible instead of being countable as units or derivable as persons from a common lineage. All the analogies and metaphors used in connection with the trinity in its theological form lose their esoteric character when translated to the dimension of self-conscious experience. But the implications of such translation seem rather startling. If the religious idea of the trinity is reducible to a secular level, in the sense of exemplifying in strange fashion a notion of familiar experience, does not the term religious cease to have a distinct meaning? If God's threefold nature is assumed to be comparable to human self-consciousness, the latter indeed serving as its paradigm, does not the assumption signify a reversion to anthropomorphism? Is it ultimately this which revealed religion is the revelation of?

Meredy: Your questions touch the nerve of the difficulty inherent in Hegel's treatment of religion and of revealed religion in particular. The ambivalence pervading it seems incorrigible. The terminology serves throughout a double purpose, suitable alike for depicting religious experience as an episode in the life of mind and for disclosing the intrinsic nature of the object of religious devotion. This linguistic syncretism enables Hegel to pass almost surreptitiously from phenomenology to ontology. What, you rightly ask, is revealed religion the revelation of? What indeed?

In the context of phenomenology, primacy belongs to the religious consciousness, the object appearing in forms such as accord with the stages of mind's evolution. The varieties of religion, from Zoroastrianism to Christianity, constitute a spiritual hierarchy, the significance of each becoming revealed in the mode succeeding it, precisely as in nonreligious consciousness the significance of sense-certainty is revealed in perception, that of perception in understanding, and so on. Viewed thus, revelation is a general principle governing the progressive advance of the dialectical process. No religion can accordingly fail to reveal its import at a later and more comprehensive level. Religion in the form of art, for instance, of which comedy is the ultimate manifestation, discloses its full meaning in a form involving the mutually implicative beliefs in God's incarnation and man's apotheosis. Such is phenomenology without ontology: every form of consciousness, including the religious, is a revelation, in the sense that it contains a disclosure of the relative truth hidden in its predecessor's isolated and overweening posture.

But what a radical transformation religion undergoes when its reve-lation is proclaimed to be special and exclusive! The emphasis then falls not so much on the kind of consciousness to which the disclosure is vouchsafed as on the disclosed finality of the truth of God's existence and essence. What henceforth comes to occupy the focus of attention is God's assumed supernatural self-revelation to man rather than man's natural belief about it, natural, that is, under the given conditions, whether historical or dialectical. And since Christianity is here re-garded as the only religion entitled to be called revealed, that and no other provides Hegel with the requisite material of analysis, chief among the themes being the incarnation and the trinity. From Chris-tian theology to Hegelian metaphysics the transition receives from these two doctrines its dialectical impetus.

In the end, Hegel's description of religion as revealed appears extra-phenomenological in meaning in two interrelated ways. It applies pri-marily to a particular historical religion assumed to have a preemptive claim on universal and timeless truth. Solely on the assumption that Christianity is the absolute religion containing the assurance of God's self-revelation to mankind can Hegel endow the description with philo-sophic significance. The intrinsic content of revealed religion, so he contends, can be truly disclosed only through the method and idiom of his ideology. Religious revelation thus becomes revelation in embryo of Hegel's doctrine. The Christian God turns into the Absolute Spirit and the trinity into an illustration of the triadic pattern of dialectical logic. Religion in its ultimate expression prefigures, as it were, the necessary passage from figurative to nonfigurative thought, thus pre-paring the process of transfiguring the form in which the religious object must appear.

4. Christianity and Hegelianism

Hardith: The attempt to extract from Hegel's linguistic syncretism, as you aptly call it, what does or does not belong to phenomenology, would seem to require considerable emendation of the text, an opera-tion that would result, if I too may indulge in verbal playfulness, in its disfigurement. The discussion of revealed religion reads as if designed to leave the outcome in suspense. Could Hegel's attitude to Christianity be ever acquitted of deliberate ambiguity? We need only to think of the division of his school, originally on theological grounds, into two wings, the 'right' and the 'left'. The conservative group interpreted Hegel in the orthodox sense, regarding his philosophy as the very bulwark of theism, while the liberal group sought and found in it vindication of a spiritualistic pantheism. Apart, however, from the controversies that caused and deepened the rift among his followers, the religious ambiguity, to name it thus, is conspicuously present in the *Phenomenology*. What are we to understand by the transformation of the divine being into a metaphysical entity? Is the change but nominal or does it imply a new creedal position? Is the Hegelian Absolute the Christian God or is the Christian God the Hegelian Absolute? If the Absolute is God under another name, Hegel may rightly be looked upon as defender of the Christian faith, the analysis of revealed religion serving to justify and fortify that faith. If, on the other hand, God is the Absolute, the Logos conceived as the governing principle of dialectical necessity and organic wholeness, Hegel appears rather as critic of all supernaturalism, his preoccupation with revealed religion having for its purpose to exhibit the universal mind as becoming conscious in mankind and incarnate in the world. Between theism and pantheism the distinction is after all not without a difference.

Meredy: The issue is certainly crucial and seemingly insoluble on lines strictly phenomenological. How problematic is Hegel's transition from religious experience to metaphysical speculation! It is one thing to speak of God as the object of a type of consciousness advancing to higher levels of spirituality at the different stages of its development, it is quite another thing to speak of a self-revealing God as the ultimate object of speculative thought. The varieties of religious experience of which Hegel traces the logical order and connection cannot as such vouch for God's actual existence or essential nature; the dialectical method has for its basis the priority of consciousness the object of which is invariably misconceived, each subjective form requiring another where the misconception becomes superseded. Until Hegel reaches the theme of religion the confusion of phenomenology with ontology is but incidental; the subject remains in the ascendant, the object being real solely in relation to consciousness. Ontological beliefs, in short, vary with the variations of their phenomenological conditions. Religious consciousness, however, appears exceptional and thus exceptionable. The phenomenology of religious experience is relative to the ontology of the religious object, and not vice versa. Primacy belongs to the reality of a divine being conceived at the outset as Absolute Spirit. The different modes of apprehending the Absolute are determined by the metaphysical necessity which the Absolute is under to reveal itself in progressive stages. When religious consciousness attains its climax in revealed religion—that is, in Christianity—the Absolute's self-revelation becomes complete. The relation of Hegel's Absolute to the Christian God, the ambiguity of which you state so clearly, presents a baffling problem defying solution until we approach the phenomenology of religion free from syncretism of thought and language.

Hardith: We have been assuming that phenomenology and ontology are antipodal. How valid is the assumption? Why split religion in particular into polar aspects? Is not misunderstanding of Hegel's intent traceable directly to such polarization? Does not all human experience involve the relation of consciousness to some object having its habitat in some realm of being? Is not mind saturated with being, if I may say so, the very subject of Hegel's biography? Interpretation of the treatise as biography demands only that the main accent be placed on mind's various postures rather than on the real world in which they arise and to which they are germane. But the emphasis may be shifted from the postures to their occasions or contexts; when focused on the latter, the life of mind appears so intermixed with objective facts and events shaping and controlling it that phenomenology must be held not only to entail but to require reference to ontology. Hegel's argument that the God of revealed religion is in essence the Absolute, an object of metaphysical thought, while vulnerable on different grounds, cannot be rejected as fallacious merely because it is alleged to rest on what you call his syncretism.

Meredy: What you say is pertinent, meriting serious consideration. Unfortunately, the points you touch upon call for the sort of technical discussion we have agreed to forgo. It is true of course that no biography can disregard such objective circumstances as are relevant to the subject's character and development. Nor does Hegel's treatise ignore the circumambient world relating to the various forms of consciousness. But the matter at issue is not quite so simple. Granted that biography, whether of the individual or of the race, is bound up, so to speak, with ontography. The important question is one of priority. It is not for their own sake that the biographer dwells on the sundry conditions and influences affecting the nature of his subject; whatever objectivity they possess outside the context of his story is simply irrelevant. He is concerned chiefly if not exclusively with such external data as are determinative of his subject's personality and career. Is this not true also of Hegel's work? Rehearsing principally the life of mind, the *Phenomenology* ascribes reality to the world so far as it impinges upon the subject. Study of the world apart from any relation to the subject is one with which the biographer can obviously not be occupied. It is clearly the self whose primacy must here be acknowledged, the world of which he is aware and in which he lives thus becoming ontologically derivative.

Allusion in this connection to Spinoza can hardly be avoided, for it is his conception of substance which Hegel deliberately sought to supplant by that of subject. If, as Hegel remarks in the preface, to an earlier generation the identification of God with substance appeared revolting, the reason lay partly in the feeling that self-consciousness was simply submerged. In the *Phenomenology* the role of self-consciousness is preserved with a vengeance. It emerges throughout to grow more and more exalted, celebrating its ultimate triumph in revealed religion. For does not the God of that religion resemble in form most closely the form of self-consciousness? His trinity, held to be a unique and sacred mystery, the self-consciousness of each and every human being daily exemplifies. Such language alone would seem consistent with phenomenology. But to speak of God's self-consciousness as that of an Absolute Spirit in whose self-revelation lies the key to all reality is to commit the fallacy of transforming biography into ontography.

Hardith: You must be aware that the attempt to separate the phenomenology of religion from the ontology with which Hegel expressly blends it is rather audacious. For the object of each and every form in religious consciousness he defines as the Absolute Being. And in approximation to the metaphysical notion of the Absolute Being lies for him the standard for marking the progressive development of the religious consciousness. In revealed religion he accordingly finds the promise of the prophecy contained in the earliest manifestations of religious experience. The object worshiped, however strange its shape, is simply an arcane appearance of the Absolute Being. And when the Absolute Being becomes truly revealed as spirit knowing itself as spirit, the implicit ontology to which the phenomenology of religion owes its sequence and direction requires formulation and defense in terms transcending religion. Such seems the indivisible union of phenomenology and ontology in Hegel's actual treatment of religious experience.

Consider now the consequences to which their supposed divorce would give rise. What kind of subject matter could phenomenology as such be here concerned with? The religious objects—and they must be spoken of as plural—must appear in pure phenomenology as but creatures of human imagination and thought, having no existence save in mind that breeds them. The hypothesis that mind is the generative source of many and different gods is hardly contrary to fact. This Hegel himself seems to confirm when he forgets his thesis that the Absolute Being lies concealed in every one of mankind's fabled deities. As long as phenomenology is allowed to remain divided from ontology, the principle of subjectivity must be endowed with supremacy and its applicability with universality. The God of revealed religion too, when

351

dispossessed of the privileged status assigned to him, must be assumed to owe his being to mind's inventive genius. From the point of view strictly phenomenological, the divine self-consciousness, upon which Hegel lays so much stress, can have no other origin than human experience, and on that experience it appears to be actually modeled. The sovereignty of self-consciousness, so central in revealed religion, exemplifies anew the irrepressible aspect of anthropomorphism. From the worship of 'sticks and stones' to the worship of beings like unto men the evolutionary process is continuous, reaching its climax in Christianity. And what is Christianity the ultimate revelation of? Can it reveal aught else than the insight that human self-consciousness is the absolute measure of God's divinity? Would this not be the outcome of the dialectic if from the phenomenology of religion the ontology it is made to hinge on could be completely eliminated?

Meredy: Strict adherence to the conception of the *Phenomenology* as a treatise on Mind precludes consideration of any other tenable outcome. There is no reason—and Hegel gives none—that the mind constituting the subject matter of the inquiry is not the subject of human experience. All the forms of consciousness examined, from sense-certainty to revealed religion, are forms definitely characteristic of the race. It is not, for example, a global and infinite spirit, lying concealed in a pure sensorium, which sets the dialectic in motion. Nor is it an Absolute Being, attaining self-consciousness in a particular historical religion, which brings the dialectic to a close. Would it not be absurd to speak of the subject of sense-experience as a superhuman mind equipped with a psycho-physical apparatus for receiving impressions? No less egregious is the absurdity of conceiving of the subject of religious experience as the Absolute Being worshiping in succession its own image in the series of religions from Zoroastrianism to Christianity. The principle of subjectivity remains in force as long as phenomenological analysis is germane to nothing but postures of mind. The religious posture is no exception. The evolution of God's own religious consciousness is not a theme open to scrutiny by the dialectical method. The vision of God's mind—or of the Absolute's— is a human vision, and no other is possible from the perspective of a study under the dominance of the principle of subjectivity. The self-consciousness attributed to God—or to the Absolute—must thus necessarily be cognate if not identical with the self-consciousness experienced on the human level. Hence the anthropomorphism which revealed religion may be said to illustrate. The humanization of the divine, begun in religion of art, becomes more pronounced in the later idea of incarnation. Ultimately, however, what stamps revealed religion as anthropomorphic is the

352

assumed affinity in self-consciousness between God and man. But for the confusion of phenomenology with ontology, the anthropomorphism of Christianity, though subtle and refined, would appear logically continuous and essentially congeneric with the anthropomorphism of Greek religion, so intimately does Hegel relate to the form of self-consciousness the major features he discerns in the final phase of the religious consciousness. With the apotheosis of self-consciousness religious phenomenology properly ends, and what follows contains a sort of prelude to speculative thought. Hegel entitles the last section 'Absolute Knowledge'. What does knowledge here mean, and in what sense is it absolute?

The Philosophical Consciousness

1. A Chapter in the Life of Mind

Hardith: The concluding section hardly lends itself to a general discussion. It is too forbidding. Excessive condensation and inexcusable obscurity must sorely try every reader's patience. Within its brief compass the thoughts and thinkers alluded to are bewilderingly numerous. And so cursory are the allusions that they are apt to elude all but the most learned. Concerning much that is here involved a discreet silence on our part would seem to be called for. Some aspects, however, are perhaps not too esoteric for our consideration. What interests me especially is the relation of the present theme to the study of the prior forms of consciousness. To what extent is the theme integral and to what extent extraneous to phenomenology?

Meredy: Falling partly inside and partly outside phenomenology, the theme remains in the same equivocal position in which Hegel leaves the topic of religion. The analysis of the latter is couched in a diction so syncretistic that the religious type of consciousness appears blended with an incipient version of the metaphysics of the Absolute. We now encounter a syncretism equally incorrigible: a mode of consciousness and a doctrine of being are presented as interfused. In the generic sense, consciousness appears throughout the treatise in different species; each of them, from sensory experience to religious experience, Hegel designates as a *Gestalt des Bewusstseins*. The philosophic consciousness, like as well as unlike the religious, has a rightful place in phenomenology, the place being indeed the highest, since it is a form that absorbs and transmutes all the others. Misleading therefore, is the title given to the book's final section. 'Absolute Knowledge' is an expression of which we must presently note some serious ambiguities. I feel quite justified in changing the heading in order to focus attention on Hegel's actual contention that in the dialectical development of the life of mind philosophy is at once posterior and superior to religion.

Hardith: Since you have taken so many liberties with other portions of the text, your present justification of not adhering to it with greater scrupulousness strikes me as amusing. The title replacing Hegel's is certainly ingenious; it clearly epitomizes the view that philosophic consciousness has a legitimate foothold in phenomenology, and its superiority to the preceding forms can obviously not be regarded as constituting a breach in dialectical continuity, seeing that every posterior form is superior to the form antecedent to it. But there is the foothold in the sphere transcending phenomenology which Hegel's title emphasizes and yours ignores. For not as consciousness does the consciousness labelled philosophic differ generically from any other. Does not its differentia lie principally in the possession of a peculiar object? The philosophic consciousness, as Hegel contrasts it with the religions, is cognitively related to an object the content and form of which turn out to be congruent or homologous. The transition, in other words, instead of being from one stage of phenomenology to the next higher stage, now becomes the transition from the phenomenological level of inquiry to an altogether different level. This is the level Hegel calls logic but a logic which in principle is one with metaphysics. It is an onto-logic; the felicitous hyphen used by Hyppolite clarifies admirably the difference between what is and what is not germane to the field of consciousness. The term absolute knowledge seems expressly designed to indicate a topic pertaining chiefly to speculative thought.

Meredy: Absolute knowledge, as Hegel manipulates the expression, is alleged to be the outcome of phenomenology, thus undeniably coming within its definable range. It serves, as it were, as a sort of finale or coda. With the objective of the philosophic consciousness phenomenology is concerned no less than with the objective of another. Absolute knowledge, in its varying senses, represents the conclusion of a dialectical argument of which the analysis of sense-certainty constitutes the beginning. The terminal phase of the argument is part and parcel of it as much as the initial. Do we not generally view the result of an inquiry, though liable to subsequent modification, as continuous with and inseparable from the inquiring process? If the nisus of the dialectical movement is towards absolute knowledge, the relation of such knowledge to the movement conditioning it must of course be internal. To be sure, absolute knowledge is the objective also of the investigation belonging to onto-logic (how singularly pat is Hyppolite's hyphen!) of which the phenomenological dénouement contains the preview. This, however, cannot expunge its significance as desideratum of the philosophic consciousness. Unfortunately, the term is too big with ambiguity to be illuminating. Absolute knowledge as goal of speculative thought tends to overshadow its place as climax of mind's dialectical odyssey.

Hardith: Until the senses attributable to absolute knowledge, which you speak of as varying, are clearly discriminated, it is hardly profitable to discuss whether or not such knowledge is involved in phenomenology. If excluded from it in one sense, need the exclusion extend to every other? Leaving aside for the moment the question of knowledge, since sundry ways of knowing actually determine the course of the life of mind, the point at issue centers in the description of it as absolute. It is the adjective and not the noun which is here the operative word. Now one of the adjective's antonyms here crucial is the term relative. Because the kind of knowledge with which phenomenology is concerned proves upon analysis to be nonabsolute, phenomenology must be followed by an inquiry which has for its explicit aim the attainment of knowledge demonstrably nonrelative. The very dialectic by which our ordinary cognitions are condemned to inevitable relativity necessitates as antidote the process of investing with absoluteness the nature of philosophic cognition. Phenomenology, in other words, serves as ineluctable transition to noumenology, the opposite in which it becomes superseded and transfigured.

Meredy: What you say is of course true of the dialectic generally, requiring as it does transition of everything to something else. All opposites, regarded as correlatives, are in Hegel's view so internally conjoined that each depends on the other for its essential meaning. And if phenomenology and noumenology are such opposites, they must necessarily exemplify the same interdependence. The particular bearing of this on the distinction between the relative and the absolute is obvious. Prima facie, these terms too, being opposites, must be taken as mutually implicative. Phenomenological relativity of knowledge is the point at issue. Is the relativity assumed or proved? The principle that proof of relativity hinges on prior assumption of absoluteness is one on which the entire phenomenology of mind is grounded: every mode of consciousness makes its appearance with a claim on certainty that cannot be set aside except by immanent criticism. The experience of sense-certainty which starts the dialectical ball rolling is archetypal. All subsequent certainties, such as those relating to self-consciousness, reason, culture, conscience, religion, have their beginning in the assertion of absoluteness only to end as relative to a truth more comprehensive. The notion of absolute knowledge, far from being alien to phenomenology, is its very soul and leaven.

Hardith: That any assertion must pass into its opposite sounds anomalous only if we reject the method to which such passage owes its necessity. What the method itself renders anomalous is the meaning of absolute knowledge not within but without the confines of phenomenology. Sense-certainty and self-certainty, for instance, must, within their respective contexts, exchange initial absoluteness for ultimate relativity. The movement from one extreme to another is in perfect accordance with the method. What seems a definite betrayal of it is the claim to the kind of absolute knowledge presaged in the closing chapter of the treatise. Such a claim can scarce be made without invalidating the method in conformity with which all opposites in all contexts must be shown to be related by mutual implication. Since absolute absoluteness, so to say, is dialectically precluded, any and every claim to it must of necessity become yoked to its own other.

Meredy: You succinctly point up the ambiguity with which the closing chapter is singularly burdened. What is the chapter's essential purpose? Does it or does it not belong to phenomenology? Does it contain the conclusion *drawn from* the series of the antecedently exhibited forms of consciousness or is its aim rather to serve as *transition to* an investigation by the same method of the objective ways of being instead of the subjective ways of knowing? Should the chapter be read as epilogue or as prologue? In the former sense, it provides an all-inclusive vision of the variable certainties and truths characteristic of the development of the life of mind; in the latter sense, it opens up the vista of the bloodless categories required for a systematic onto-logic. How deplorably double-faced Hegel here appears! He looks before and after, intent at once on consummation and anticipation. Since he faces in it in opposite directions, the chapter lends itself to different interpretations, depending on which direction one chooses as the more apposite. It is accordingly not unjustifiable to interpret the final chapter as an integral part of phenomenology in which the synoptic form of consciousness clearly emerges. Is the designation of it as the philosophic consciousness a misnomer? Does not such consciouness generally seek to contemplate the world under the aspect of wholeness? Nor is it altogether illegitimate to speak of the knowledge which philosophy embarks upon as absolute. So to call it is simply to indicate the perspective to which the prior and inferior cognitions must ultimately prove to be relative. The philosophic consciousness, having for its objective the concretion or distillation of the objectives of the lesser consciousnesses, thus comes to depend on them for its proper function. As far as phenomenology is concerned, the so-called absoluteness of philosophic knowledge is inescapably relative, relative, that is, to all that makes its claim to absoluteness dialectically possible. This, though in Hegel's spirit, is completely at loggerheads with his letter.

Hardith: But it is not philosophic consciousness in general towards which all the other forms are said to be tending. The consciousness finally arrived at is a special one. Only a singular philosophy—namely, the Hegelian—appears as heir and beneficiary of the preceding modes of experience. It alone asserts a preemptive claim on truth. Does this not militate against the view that in reaching the conception of absolute knowledge we need not forsake the level of phenomenology, Hegel's explicit statements to the contrary notwithstanding? Since on that level absoluteness is the objective of every form of consciousness, the philosophic form would seem to be no more final or immune from supersession than any other. How ironical a result! Is Hegel's text to be distorted to challenge Hegelianism?

Meredy: I am merely attempting to show that absolute knowledge, in its absolute sense, so to speak, can receive no support from arguments drawn from phenomenology. What happens to the conception of such knowledge outside and beyond phenomenology is of course another matter. Assuming, however, that the absoluteness contended for in the final chapter is susceptible of interpretation in terms consistent with the dialectical process to which all forms of experience are amenable, what could possibly be said of the absoluteness alleged to belong to philosophic knowledge? Absoluteness, an attribute to which each and every way of knowing may lay claim until the claim reveals itself as impugnable, must obviously apply to the philosophic way of knowing too, but in no differential or privileged manner. As long as phenomenology is kept distinct—distinct, that is, from noumenology—the absoluteness ascribed to the philosophic consciousness remains no less relative than the absoluteness imputed to any other. The closing chapter of Hegel's work can scarcely be held to foreclose the emergence of further modes of experience in the life of mind.

Hardith: Yet, an indefeasible distinction must be made, even at the level of phenomenology, between absolute knowledge and the limited persuasions anterior to it. The relation of knowledge to the different persuasions it comprises is comparable to the relation of an organism to its members. Does not the idea of absolute knowledge in which the treatise culminates exemplify an epistemic version of the concrete universal so central in the dialectical development of the various postures of mind? Comprehensiveness here clearly serves as one of the synonyms of absoluteness. Affixed to the synoptic way of knowing, which results from the synthesis of the separate cognitive efforts, the label absolute seems unexceptionable. Of the *Phenomenology* it might accordingly be said that it furnishes on the plane of human experience confirmation of the principle proclaimed in the preface as the very impelling force of the dialectic—the principle that the truth is the whole. With the conception of absolute knowledge—knowledge integral and complete—the holistic theory of truth thus receives verification in purely phenomenological or subjective terms. But this way of stating the case for Hegel precipitates a formidable difficulty. If all knowledge presupposes a subject in pursuit or possession of it, what subject is capable not only of seeking but of attaining the totality of knowledge in which alone its truth resides?

2. The Ambiguous Subject of Absolute Knowledge

Meredy: The question you raise is crucial. The difficulty involved in the conception of absolute knowledge is far surpassed by the difficulty relating to the conception of the subject needed for such knowledge. To what conception may credibility be accorded? Is the subject to be identified with the mind of the race of which the *Phenomenology* contains the biography? True it is that the human mind is ever prone to lay claim to absolute knowledge at every stage of its evolution. This the treatise fully demonstrates. But the claim, and this too the treatise amply shows, is invariably and repeatedly open to invalidation. Can we really speak of the knowledge ultimately vouchsafed to the human subject as enjoying that degree of absoluteness preclusive of further accretion? This of course is contrary to fact as well as to the principle of dialectical continuity. As long as the dialectical process continues, no consummation of the process, however incontrovertibly absolute it appears, can escape the necessity of becoming impugned and transmuted.

Another view, no less baffling, suggests itself. The subject of absolute knowledge, not extensible to the generic mind of Hegel's biography, may be confined to the specific mind of the biographer. It is Hegel alone (or the convinced reader of his life of mind) who arrives at absolute knowledge, in the sense that he infallibly discerns the conditions by which such knowledge is determined, the conditions being implicit in the very modes of cognition whose claims on absoluteness reveal themselves as pseudoclaims. But this conception, which Hegel reaches at the conclusion of his 'voyage of discovery', is merely Hegel's, its cogency depending upon the use of a certain method adaptable to a previsioned end. Another method, another result. To attribute to Hegel the pretension of being in possession of absolute knowledge is of course preposterous. What man could seriously maintain that absolute knowledge becomes his with the completion of an inquiry? Within the compass of phenomenology, knowledge described as absolute can only appear in the shape of an ideal. Of knowledge all-inclusive and all-conclusive no finite mind whether generically human or specifically Hegelian can actually serve as knowing subject.

Hardith: That absolute knowledge is an ideal outrunning every claim made to it in the course of the *Phenomenology* is true of all but the terminal type of consciousness. The theme broached in the concluding chapter is of absolute knowledge as realized. The problem here central relates to the necessity of conceiving the knowing subject as commensurate with the knowledge it is the subject of. It is this principle of commensurability which militates against the possibility of regarding finite mind as subject of absolute knowledge. None but the absolute mind, so Hegel intimates, could perform the office of absolute knower. The argument for absolute knowledge thus becomes the basis of the Hegelian argument for the necessary existence of an absolute knower. The absoluteness of the one and the absoluteness of the other are bound together by reciprocal involvement. This, it seems to me, is the sum and substance of the outcome of the dialectic. The metaphysical deduction of the Absolute, revealing itself as the *ens relissimum,* justifies the interpretation of phenomenology as the necessary transition to ontology, the latter beginning where the former ends. Your insistence on *pure* phenomenology—phenomenology purged of ontology—indicates an attitude more anti-Hegelian than Hegelian.

Meredy: What is and what is not strictly Hegelian is something enigmatic, a secret, as some wit has declared, that has been well kept. Interpreters of Hegel, so said one of them, "have contradicted each other, almost as variously, as the several commentators on the Bible." This remark would be hard to gainsay. Be that as it may, we are not concerned with the sort of interpretation preempted by the commentators. The relation of the *Phenomenology* to the *Logic* presents a special problem to the specialists. Let them settle the question of whether the section on absolute knowledge does or does not contain the demonstration of an absolute knower. Ours is a task definitely limited to an exploration of Hegel's early work for the purpose of extracting from it the principal insights deeply embedded in an esoteric idiom. Not all the insights can be made accessible to a nomenclature not his own. Nor can even such as are amenable to a different linguistic medium be shown to have the subtler shades of meaning expressed in their original form. Yet avoidance of his forbidding diction is one way of gaining entrance into Hegel's treatise; liberated from verbal obfuscation, it emerges as a treasure house of ideas rich in variety and wide in range. The *Phenomenology* may indeed be looked upon as a confluence of the major persuasions of mankind, appearing here in universal array and redolent of actuality. Whatever its worth as the embodiment of a philosophic argument, the work makes its appeal to the imagination also, in conception as well as treatment, and so to consider it provides another convenient means of ingress. Viewed thus, its resemblance to biography—on a vast scale and of a generic subject—allies the work with a species of literary art. But the biography is of the human and not of the absolute mind. It can hardly be spoken of as autobiography whether Hegel's or God's. In the light of all this, reference to absolute knowledge as entailing proof of an absolute knower is here quite clearly out of place, unless the reference arises within the context of a determinate form of consciousness called philosophic. But this form is as such no less subjective than any other falling within the purview of phenomenology.

Hardith: But there seems to be a natural continuity between phenomenology and ontology involving no breach of the principle of subjectivity. Does not Hegel constantly harp upon self-consciousness as the key to the operation of the dialectic? It is a form of experience which appears throughout the *Phenomenology* in many variations and with different emphases. Exemplifying the dynamic relation of opposites within the unity of a triadic pattern, self-consciousness serves as dialectical prototype of every subsequent type of human persuasion. Even the theological persuasion of the trinity becomes translatable in its terms. Now if all persuasions exhibit upon examination a trivalent structure and cyclic process cognate with the structure and process intrinsic to self-conscious experience, does not that experience supply the link connecting phenomenology and ontology? For the distinguishing mark of self-consciousness regarded as a species of cognition lies in the subject's priority over the object. This priority, debatable elsewhere, is here axiomatic. Although other than the subject, the object derives from and remains one with it. If the subject alone enjoys primary reality, an ontologically secondary meaning must thus pertain to the object. Of course between subject and object within self-consciousness the distinction cannot become separation save in extreme cases, as, for example, in schizophrenia. But considered not only a normal mode of experience but the supreme cognitive norm, self-consciousness depends for its possibility on the inseverable correlatives of subject and object, the subject having the logically prior status. In self-consciousness, it seems, we have the clue to the sort of ontology consonant with phenomenology. With self-consciousness as universal model, subjectivity emerges as the principle determinative of all that appears to lay claim to objectivity. No object unless it be the subject's own. Phenomenology, in short, far from excluding ontology, does in fact entail it. But it is the ontology of the kind said to be peculiar to idealism. The subject dominant in self-consciousness lends itself to limitless generalization and infinite extension. When Hegel so generalizes and extends it, the subject becomes the absolute subject, and the object, which comprehends all reality, is differentiable from as well as identifiable with it.

Meredy: What you say may be readily challenged if the passage from human to superhuman self-consciousness is but the result of analogical reasoning. How close should the analogy here be? If too close, the absolute mind is but an enlarged edition of the human; if too remote, the argument loses much if not all of its probative force. Analogical reasoning is too vulnerable to be convincing, and I am not sure whether Hegel's conception of the Absolute does not heavily rest on fragile inference. The inference of an absolute knower based on the progression of the modes of human experience marshalled in the *Phenomenology* remains logically suspect. Stated hypothetically, the contention in favor of such a knower might perhaps pass muster; *if* there were authenticated knowledge such as Hegel deems absolute, a subject commensurate with its holistic structure would be no implausible inference. But do the varieties of mind's postures which the treatise depicts add up to absolute completeness? The hypothesis is open to attack on two grounds: premise and conclusion are equally doubtful. Who can seriously maintain that at the end of the phenomenological pilgrimage all human persuasions form an absolute totality requiring for comprehension an absolute spirit? And does it follow that none but the Hegelian Absolute may thus be proved to exist for the purpose of grasping and encompassing in synthesis the dialectical gyrations of mankind's inordinately assertive beliefs? 'Not proven' must of course be the Scotch verdict. Another premise, another conclusion; and even from the same premise differing conclusions are permissible. Phenomenology can culminate in nothing else than the appearance of a new form of consciousness; it deserves to be called philosophic simply because such consciousness alone can survey in synoptic fashion the gamut of human experience by means of varying speculative hypotheses, none absolute in the sense of possessing the final and incontrovertible truth.

Hardith: There is admirable irony in your attempt to purge Hegel's phenomenology of Hegel's ontology. But the attempt, even if it be considered successful, is relevant solely to the ontology involving the deduction presumably categorical of a superhuman mind, the dialectical structure of whose eternal reason becomes revealed in the progressive evolution of human experience. Phenomenology, you say, provides no basis for it. In turning a supposititious deduction into a possible hypothesis of questionable validity, you adroitly condemn Hegel out of his own mouth. But what is Hegel without his Absolute? Their separation is not unlike the proverbial divorce of Hamlet from the Prince of Denmark. But I am not disposed to defend the Hegelian theory of being from which the Absolute is logically inseverable. Such a theory, admittedly nonphenomenological, does not concern us. Granted that to a nonphenomenological ontology phenomenology can lend no support. But there is another kind implied in and harmonious with phenomenology. I mentioned its feasible derivation from the nature of self-consciousness. Is the theme so unworthy of attention that it could be dismissed outright?

3. *The Twofold Ontology*

Meredy: The distinction between the two ontologies is highly important, requiring serious discussion. But we should have to go too far afield to do it justice. It could be scarcely dealt with in relation to the early treatise exclusively. And the issues which the distinction implies are crucial generally. All the recurrent problems having to do with the contrast and connection between epistemology and metaphysics are suggested by the double ontology. Far then from dismissing the distinction lightly, I am so much aware of its deep significance that I hesitate to dilate on it in the present context.

Hardith: The distinction is here too fundamental to be ignored. Phenomenological ontology must clearly make central the knowing subject as its source and fulcrum. To be is to be experienced—is this not, taking experience in the broadest conceivable sense, an apothegm suitably expressive of the tenor of the *Phenomenology?* Throughout the treatise, it is always on some posture of mind that the object under consideration depends for its being, a dependence which in self-consciousness appears with irrefutable obviousness. Is it any wonder that self-consciousness should emerge as foundation of a theory of being according to which the subject of experience must be accorded a self-evident priority over its object? But it is not primarily experience from which nonphenomenological ontology receives impetus and direction: categories of pure thought, in principle the same as categories of objective being, have a different origin and setting. A subjectivistic ontology and an absolutistic one are, at least prima facie, not equatable or interchangeable; the human subject suffices for the former, the latter requires a subject transcending the human. Are they mutually exclusive or mutually implicative? The concluding chapter of the early work leaves the question unresolved. Does it culminate in a duality ultimately irreducible or reducible only by the process of conceiving the superhuman subject as analogous to the human, a conception you have already shown to be impugnable?

Meredy: In distinguishing so sharply the two ontologies you put your finger on a major difficulty. The matter is of course quite technical and should in all conscience be eschewed. A learned interpreter of the *Phenomenology* might not inaptly see in it an attempt on a grand scale to combine articles of doctrine held by Kant to be at sixes and sevens. The argument for objectivity comporting with the Critical theory of knowledge is one thing; quite another is the objectivity vouched for by would-be metaphysics. Kant too has his two ontologies. The ontology immanent in his theory of knowledge is secure but phenomenalistic; the ontology transcending it is indemonstrable and thus problematic. Crucial, however, in this connection is his view of the knowing subject, the famous transcendental unity of apperception. The epistemological ego, though universal and necessary, is but an indispensable postulate requisite for the possibility of experience, not lending itself to hypostatization as a spirit with a divine halo. What an impressive net of flagrant paradoxes and fallacies Kant shows those to be enmeshed in who would treat a methodological postulate as if it were an existential entity! The contrast between epistemology and metaphysics, so basic to the *Critique,* disappears in the *Phenomenology* by mutual assimilation. When broaching the theme of absolute knowledge, Hegel tends to identify the subject of such knowledge with the Absolute Spirit but imperfectly present in revealed religion. What at last becomes truly revealed is the Absolute as *ens realissimum,* the ground of an ontology which, implicit in phenomenology, becomes explicit in a logical system of categories embodying the union of thought and being. The two ontologies of Kant thus merge into one; the objectivity latent in the series of human persuasions appears as truly objective only when it proves amenable to the forms and ways of operation whereby the Absolute manifests itself to the philosophic consciousness. How far a cry this is from Kant's position! But the relation of Hegel to his predecessor is a problem with which the specialists alone are competent to cope. My reference to it is too cursory to carry much weight.

Hardith: Yet, incidental though you take it to be, your allusion to Kant throws an oblique light on the principle of subjectivity dominant in the *Phenomenology.* The principle, while in the ascendant throughout, has a dual sense. It is noteworthy that reference to an Absolute Spirit occurs but seldom if at all in the analysis of the prereligious forms of consciousness, their phenomenology according perfectly with the conception of finite subjectivity. With the exception of the theme of religion, the work consists of a study of sundry postures of mind explicitly human. No superhuman subject need be invoked for the sort of experience the evolution of whose dialectic we are bidden to follow—the experience, for example, of him who perceives or doubts, grieves over his divided self or rejoices in nature's adaptability to his reason, regards his personality neglected in a legalized society or feels alienated in the world of culture, acts in open rebellion against the established order or seeks absolute freedom in the inviolable sanctuary of conscience. It is the human psyche with which alone we are concerned at the level of consciousness preceding religion. But what a radical change finite subjectivity undergoes in connection with religious phenomenology! The center of the stage now comes to be occupied by the Absolute. God's consciousness must now be found to lie hidden in man's. It is accordingly the Absolute that appears as if present in arcane fashion in all the successive modes of religious experience until, manifest in revealed religion, its ultimately true *self*-revelation marks the transition from religion to philosophy. Does not prereligious phenomenology seem to resemble Kant's epistemology in which the subject of experience is not ancillary to metaphysics and enjoys but a circumscribed universality? And does not, therefore, the passage to a metaphysical subject, one absolute in extent and superhuman in quality, look like a leap in illicit speculation? Is it possible seriously to maintain that the absolute subject of absolute knowledge can be incontrovertibly demonstrated by the dialectical method without ascribing to that method a power almost preternatural? By making or by seeming to make a claim so excessive if not arrogant Hegel greatly detracts from the value of his important insights which the book so richly affords.

Meredy: I am not disposed to quarrel with you. What you say is certainly pertinent. But the issue is too complex to be treated in so cavalier a manner. What lends significance to the issue is the ambiguous role which the dialectic is called upon to play. Many of the difficulties to which the work gives rise may be traced to the use made of the method as one chiefly relevant to consciousness. Now consciousness— or its synonym experience—presupposes a subject, and the question must inevitably be raised regarding its individuality. No particular man is the hero of Hegel's chronicle; nor is every man a fair sample of Everyman. Should we identify the subject with mankind in general? Is it the race as such of which Hegel rehearses the different stages of spiritual development? If so, the sequence of the stages is but incidentally historical. Requisite for the series of experience dialectically marshalled is a putative mind, its conception being the combined product of generalization and postulation. The forms of consciousness have a sufficiently recognizable verisimilitude to justify the generalization; but lacking, as they only too often do, actual exemplifiability, their ascription to a postulated subject is not unwarranted. The subject of the *Phenomenology,* its lineage derivable from reason as well as imagination, acquires absoluteness solely on the ground that all the forms of consciousness must be conceived as forms of a single self-conscious being. And it is the plenitude of these forms to which Hegel's Absolute owes, so to speak, its deduction. But for the notion of a totality of all possible modes of experience, so internally related that they must all be successively enacted and successively superseded, there would be no necessity for positing an absolute subject. The mind needed for grasping and realizing an infinite totality must of course be commensurately infinite. The whole, which alone Hegel avers to be wholly true, is here simply the whole of experience. Upon the dialectical method, in one of its functions, thus devolves the task of proving in the *Phenomenology* the truth of the apothegm that 'the truth is the whole'. And absolute knowledge, entailing an absolute knower, the culmination of the phenomenological saga, may be taken as but another name for absolute experience.

4. *The Anomalies of Absoluteness*

Hardith: On the view of the dialectic as the logic of experience certain comments naturally suggest themselves. One has to do with the signal importance of self-consciousness which receives in the work reiterated emphasis. This would seem greatly to bolster your contention. For in self-consciousness the subject is not compelled to look beyond itself for an object indubitably real. But the absoluteness which Hegel ascribes to it is not exclusively an attribute of his self-conscious Absolute. On a limited scale, absolute is everyone's self-conscious experience, seeing that the experience is one in which the object, though other than the subject, is the subject's very own, complete assurance of its existence being thus always within the subject's reach. Absoluteness characteristic of self-conscious experience, whether limited or unlimited, goes hand in hand with solipsism. Since it presupposes a being affirming in isolation its self-existence, solipsism may be exemplified at one extreme by any finite individual and on the other by an infinite spirit. Is the difference between them simply a matter of dimension or degree? As long as, comparable to Leibnizian monads, solipsists remain self-enclosed, they each and all have an indefeasible claim on absoluteness. Because of the wide open windows, so to speak, enabling them actually to communicate with one another, separate would-be solipsists must inevitably suffer loss of faith in the validity of their respective claims. The one and only true solipsist is the Hegelian Absolute. Having no rivals, since by hypothesis there are none, this Supreme Monad alone can legitimately be conscious of containing within itself the wholeness of reality. By a tremendous *tour de force,* the escape from finite solipsism which self-consciousness as such countenances, seems possible only by exchanging it for a solipsism on an infinite scale.

Meredy: You have succeeded admirably in sharpening as well as clarifying the issue by showing that solipsism is necessarily the outcome of the dialectic considered primarily as the logic of experience. How indeed can solipsism be avoided if self-consciousness serves as the one archetypal consciousness, a consciousness which so distinctly exemplifies, even in complete privacy, the logical triad on which dialectical discourse depends? The difficulties that ensue from positing a finite specimen of solipsism Hegel seeks to evade by the notion of the Absolute, a spirit infinite and sovereign, the sole subject of the apprehended and apprehensible world. But can they actually be evaded? If all arguments for solipsism derive from the logic of self-consciousness, the Supreme Solipsist can have no advantage over those of lesser breed. Is there or is there not some resemblance or continuity between the Absolute's self-conscious experience and man's? If the Absolute's self-conscious experience is *sui generis,* one without analogue to that of mortal beings, the argument from phenomenology falls to the ground. An experience altogether transcending the human remains a mystery, not repugnant to religious sentiment, but impervious to rational thought. But if superhuman experience is cognate with human, the Absolute, to put it bluntly, appears but man writ large, and anthropomorphism, which Hegel shows to be inexpungible from religion, attaches likewise to his philosophy, as far as he intimates it in the discussion of absolute knowledge directly following from the phenomenology of religion and crowning the phenomenology of all experience preceding the religious. All this is simply implicit in the choice of self-consciousness as paradigm of a dialectic exclusively germane to experience.

Hardith: I wonder whether we are not undermining the very foundation of Hegel's idealism by challenging his use of the dialectic as relevant principally to experience. For in drawing the line between Spinoza's philosophy and his own, Hegel distinguishes the conception of subject from that of substance, assigning primacy to the former. And subject—in the *Phenomenology,* at any rate—denotes mind in which self-consciousness is paramount. Absolute knowledge, the terminus of the entire phenomenological process, turns out to be the Absolute's knowledge of itself as the substance of all that exists. To assail then the necessity of an Absolute aware of its own status as spiritual substance is to strike a fatal blow at the Hegelian doctrine here foreshadowed. Can one seriously defend the dialectical method without defending what ineluctably seems to ensue from its operation? After all, does not Hegel's idealism ultimately depend on the method alleged to contain within it the irrepressible nisus towards the Absolute?

Meredy: There unfortunately are in the early work two distinct trains of thought not easy to harmonize, one absolutistic and the other humanistic. The terms do not matter; more suitable names marking the distinction are no doubt available. But by any other names the distinction would be important. The dialectic as ancillary to spiritual growth and progress is one thing, quite another is the dialectic in the service of objective observation and analysis. Does not the argument for an Absolute hinge on the use of the dialectic in the first sense? Mind is shown to advance as if on a Jacob's ladder to ever higher forms of consciousness, and only in the course of such ascensive effort does mind reveal itself as absolute. No finite mind, however catholic, can appropriate and encompass the series of the modes of experience depicted in the *Phenomenology,* a series each member of which survives as an essential ingredient in its more comprehensive successor. Incidentally, the ideology of romanticism against which Hegel so harshly fulminates in certain parts of the text becomes eminently vindicated when raised to the level of the Absolute. His Absolute, indeed, which depends for its self-development on the continual process of shedding one form of consciousness in favor of another, is the very exemplar of the romantic spirit. Be that as it may, the subject of Hegel's biography, being nothing if not protean, retains self-sameness in all the multiform and heterogeneous attitudes it assumes. The proof of the idealistic thesis is bound up with the conception of experience so omnivorous that 'its irrepressible nisus towards the Absolute', as you aptly put it, has the force of logical necessity. So much for the first trend of the dialectic.

The distinguishing feature of the humanistic trend lies in the possibility of dispensing with the necessity for an Absolute. Until the text reaches the theme of religion, the subject of the forms of consciousness preceding it, is one the reader never suspects of being other than human. Involved here, as noted in our earliest dialogue, are in fact two subjects both clearly finite—the subject of which the treatise is the putative biography and the subject authoring the treatise. The latter is Hegel who, impersonating each and every form of consciousness in the order and connection his method demands, employs the method for purposes principally diagnostic. The method is in essence contrapuntal, as it were, requiring for its application 'empathetic' vision of any claim to truth as asserted by its supposed claimant and detached examination of the alleged grounds held in support of the claim. Such, in brief is the second strain of the dialectic as Hegel exemplifies it by his treatment of the ways of mind from sensuous perception to religious worship.

Hardith: Is the *Phenomenology* but a critique of the ways of mind? Are we doing justice to it by laying our emphasis chiefly on the negative side? Because the whole truth comprehends within its scope all the areas of human experience and reflection, no single area can be singled out as prerogative. This is true enough. Hegel exhibits the unavoidable tendency of particular ideas and beliefs to grow overweening and to overreach themselves, thus eventually passing into their opposites. The task of the dialectic simply consists in impugning the extravagant claims made for any and every special perspective. But such *via negativa* goes hand in hand with the denigration of mind conceived as merely human. The *Phenomenology* is indeed a critique of mankind's recurring illusions of perspective. Are not all the forms of consciousness Hegel portrays veritable idols of the mind? Do we not have here a remarkable likeness of Hegel to Bacon? But whereas the Baconian idols are corrigible, the Hegelian are inescapable. The human mind is shown to be inevitably at their mercy precisely because it *is* human. Being more radical and more exhaustive than Bacon's, Hegel's idolology, in default of some corrective, must perforce give rise to unmitigated scepticism and pessimism. What can save the *Phenomenology* from assuming the character of unrelievable tragedy? The answer proffered is the conception of the Absolute. A superhuman mind becomes dialectically necessary to hold in solution all the mundane struggles and defeats. Expressing itself in all forms of finite consciousness, the superhuman mind can reconcile them by its eternal reason. This superhuman being, requiring for its dynamic life all that passes as error and evil on the human plane, may thus be always invoked to justify in advance things as they are. Hegel's dialectical master stroke lies in the contention that in the Absolute human unreason itself becomes ultimately rational. To eliminate the Absolute is to be left with a phenomenology containing nothing more than a systematic diagnosis of quasi-Baconian idols but without the empirical philosophy to which they owe their definition and correction.

Meredy: Your allusion to Bacon is ingenious. Phenomenology as idolology—this not inaptly epitomizes the nonabsolutistic trend of the dialectic. There is nothing in Hegel's text, with the exception of his frequent asides and intrusions, to preclude reading into it a survey, encyclopedic in scope, of the deceptive images of the world, analogous to that attempted on a smaller scale by Bacon. Yet the analogy seems at first remote. Idols as impediments to scientific knowledge and idols

369

as products of speculative thought have nothing in common save their deceptiveness. The very definition of idols is relative and variable. Opinions proved false by one method may be deemed trustworthy by another. Idols cannot be labelled as such except in connection with a particular methodic activity. What special procedure can escape being impugnable as source of deception? The empirical procedure, for example, is such a source for Hegel, and for Bacon (as well as for Hegel) it is the Aristotelian. In general, however, Hegelian idolology bears some resemblance to the Baconian if the forms of consciousness Hegel depicts are viewed as revealing nothing more than the perverse postures and absurd contentions to which the race of men is only too prone. Are they not each and all 'idols of the tribe'? But whence the necessity of regarding them as fundamental to Hegelian idealism? Can the argument for the Absolute be made to follow ineluctably from the dialectical assay of the ever-recurring 'humors of partisans'? Correction of the idols by Hegel's idealism, involving ascent to a superhuman form of experience in which all human error and human evil will find their sublimation or sublation, can hardly be said to constitute correction in any real sense. The various modes of consciousness appearing on the human level must always remain what humanly they are, to wit, incurably 'idolatrous', their putative transformation by an Absolute having no effect on their phenomenological status. Hegel's idealism whatever its justification, which is not our concern, can receive little support from phenomenology, this being here the sole issue. The introduction of the Absolute into the life of mind initially conceived as but human seems completely otiose. It does not detract from the importance of Hegel's tragicomic biography to dispense with the Absolute altogether or to disparage the role Hegel assigns to it as one belonging to a *deus ex machina*.

Hardith: Ours not being the office of commentators, we may perhaps have gone too far afield in discussing the concluding section of the *Phenomenology*. By the learned our opinions will be adjudged superficial and by the uninitiated recondite. The conception is so ambiguous that the very attempt to state what the ambiguity consists in must lead beyond the limits we have resolved to set to our dialogue. I for one am willing to forgo for the present further consideration of Hegelian subtleties. Let us close the debate at this point. But let us, when we meet again, go more deeply into such of Hegel's insights as we have touched upon rather lightly.

Meredy: Yes, the theme of absolute knowledge is too abstruse for lay discussion. Yet we must dwell on it if only to speak in cursory fashion of the glaring incongruity between the dialectical method and the final result it is alleged to produce. The section devoted to absolute knowledge, though marking the end of one kind of inquiry, serves also as necessary transition to another kind. As long as we remain inside the phenomenological context, the term absolute knowledge is emphatically a misnomer. What the dialectic proves can be nothing else than the necessity of a new mode of consciousness succeeding and superseding the religious. Philosophy, growing out of religion, must indeed grow beyond it, but only in form and not in content. Within phenomenology, the necessity of the philosophic consciousness does not differ from the necessity pertaining to any and every form preceding it. It is a consciousness no less generically human than those forms logically conditioning its advent in the life of mind. And in universality, too, it is cognate with them, in the sense that it requires exemplifiability in various ways. Identification of the philosophic consciousness with but a single expression of it is, of course, preposterous, preposterous, that is, if held to ensue exclusively from the operation of the dialectical process. To be sure, Hegel cryptically alludes to philosophic tenets of his predecessors, leaving no doubt, however, that he regards them as constituting moments of a logical hierarchy ending in his particular brand of idealism. Now this is an outcome which the dialectical method would seem definitely to proscribe. Strictly applied, the method enjoins any form of consciousness from closing the circle of conflicts or contradictions generated by the antecedent forms. Such a feat can be attributed to the method only by forcibly arresting its operations. The method itself can attain no end, whether in a sense temporal or nontemporal, simply because the law under which it operates demands that any result produce by an immanent process its own opposite. The argument that the only end which the method can achieve is absolute knowledge, such as an absolute knower alone must enjoy, rests on a betrayal of the very method to which the argument owes its supposed cogency. Dialectic and absoluteness are ultimately at loggerheads. One excludes the other. There is nothing mysterious about the method. That it is an important and fertile instrument of thought the *Phenomenology* richly attests until the Absolute makes its surreptitious appearance. The task of separating the exoteric from the esoteric uses of Hegel's dialectic is formidable. We have endeavored to show how it might be done. But this is only a beginning. Let us by all means resume our conversations with fresh minds at a later date.

Index

A

Absolute knowledge, variable in meaning, 356; objective *vs.* object of, 357; anomalies regarding its subject, 366 ff.

Adolescence, 104–106, 115.

Aeschylus, 327.

Agnosticism, in relation to enlightened belief, 243 f, 248; Spinoza's, 244; Kant's, 244 f.

Alice's Adventures in Wonderland, 255.

Alienation, consciousness of, by the 'unhappy self', 97 ff; under 'legalism', 206 ff; under culture, 209; under reign of terror, 257.

Allegory, 334 f.

Analogy, reasoning by, 126.

Anarchy, 258 f.

Animalism, in the life of mind, 168 ff.

Anthropocentrism, 333.

Anthropolatry, 333.

Anthropomorphism, 304, 313, 320, 324, 328, 332 f, 337, 347, 352, 367.

Antigone, 183, 191, 193 ff, 243, 268, 294, 327, 328.

Apollo, 316, 328 f.

Architecture, 318.

Aristophanes, 331 ff, 338.

Aristotle, 110, 370.

Arithmetic, 346.

Art, religious forms of, abstract, 313–318; Apollonian *vs.* Dionys-ian, 315; living, 318 ff; spiritual, 320–333.

Artifact, man's resemblance to, 210.

Artifactualism, 309.

Artificer, 308.

Asceticism, 110 f.

Asymmetrical relationship, twofold, between master and slave, 86–91.

Autarchy, 258.

B

Bacchus, 317, 319.

Bacon, 369 ff; his idolology *vs.* Hegel's, 370.

Beautiful soul, aesthetic and moral aspects of, 285 ff.

Behaviorism, 148.

Belief and insight, mutually implicative, 227 ff; amenable to clarification, 230 ff; enlightened version of, 238–241.

Bentham, 251.

Berkeley, 73.

Bethlehem, 334.

'Body and its members', metaphor of, 188.

C

Caesar, 205.

Categorical imperative, 175, 178, 182, 264, 285.

Categories, Kantian, 117.

Cerebral localization, 147.

Ceres, 317.

Certainty, social, parallel with cognitive, 189.

Chorus, significance of, 327 ff.

Christ, 334 f, 337, 339, 343 f.

Christianity, 331, 334 f, 337 ff, 347 ff.
Christology, 337.
Clarification, distortive aspects of, 236 ff.
Comedy, of sense-certainty, 37 f; religious meaning of, 331; gods and heroes as masks in, 332; exemplifies union of theoclasm and anthropolatry, 333.
Common sense, 42, 49 f, 58, 60.
Communism, 180, 182.
Comte, Auguste, 67.
Conscience, and absolute freedom, 276 ff; its relation to solipsism, 277; ambiguity of, 278; issues in connection with, 279; and the beautiful soul, 283 ff; role of language in, 288; as source of evil, 289 f.
Creon, 197.
Cult, religious, 317 f.
Culture, contrasted with nature, 212, 216; related to power of state and wealth, 213 ff.

D

Death, 86, 192, 219, 254, 334 ff.
Deism, 247 f.
Demeter, 319.
Depersonalization, spiritual, 211.
Dialectical Method, via negativa of, 11; its initial scepticism, 12; union of empathy and detachment, 15; as 'experimental', 15 f; antidote to dogmatism, 16; cognate with histrionic art, 17; disclosure of inward discrepancies in impersonated phenomena, 18; nonabsolutistic and humanistic aspects of, 369 f.
Dialogues from Delphi, xii.
Diderot, 209, 217, 224.
Disintegration, language of, 224 f.
Dualism, of powers, related to ethos and pathos of *Antigone,* 197 ff.

E

'Economic royalists', 224.
Electricity, 69 f.

Egypt, religion of, 305 f.
Encyclopaedists, French, 246.
Enlightenment, cultural origin of, 226 ff; relation to belief and insight, 227 ff; struggle with superstition, 231; beliefs compatible with, 238 f; its tripartite philosophy, 243–248.
Ens realissimum, 295, 360, 364.
Environment, influence of, on individual, 140 f.
Epic, the, the world of, 322 ff; its pathos, 322.
Epistemology, abstract, criticism of, 8 ff; relation to metaphysics, 363; Kant's restricted view of, 364; ontology derivable from, 365.
Esse in intellectu and *esse in re,* 342.
Ethico-theology, Kant's, 264.
Être suprême, 238.
Evangelists, 340.
Evil, problem of, 291.
Existence, proof of God's, 265.

F

Factions, government by, 255 f.
Fatalism, 157, 159.
Father, God as, 345.
Faust, Goethe's, 155 ff.
Fettered Master, 87 f.
Fichte, 118, 260.
Flattery, process of alienation, 221 ff.
Force, polarization of, 64 ff.
Formal logic, criticism of, 137; basic to logic of observation, 137.
Freedom, absolute, 252 ff; relative, 255 ff; as autonomy of the will, 259.
Freedom of thought, the stoic's 91–93; the sceptic's, 93–96.

G

Gedankenexperimente, 15.
Geist, ambivalence of, 186, 299.
God, 245, 265 f, 271 f, 291, 297, 299, 302, 305 f, 309, 335 ff, 340, 342, 344, 348 ff, 361.
God-Man, 336 ff.
Gods, Homeric, 321, 324; in tragedy

and comedy, 326–333.
Goethe, 155, 158, 285 ff.
Gravitation, 69, 126.
Guilt, inherent in dualism of imperatives, 198.

H

Hamlet, 329, 363.
Headhunting, 86.
Hedonism, 154 ff.
Heroism, of service, 218 ff; of death, 219; through language, 220; of flattery, 221 ff.
Holmes, Edmond, 101.
Homer, 172, 321 ff.
Human law, strictly male, 194.
Hylozoism, 135.
Hymn, the, 315 f.
Hypocrisy, in self-abnegation, 109; as culture's achievement, 224; exposed by enlightenment, 232; involved in moral postulates, 270; of asseverated conscientiousness, 288 f.
Hyppolite, Jean, 296, 315, 326, 355.

I

Idealism, 32, 115 ff, 367 f, 370 f.
Idolatry, 237 f.
Idoloclasm, 332.
Iliad, the, 321 f.
Immortality, 263 f.
Incarnation, 338, 341, 346 f, 352.
India, religions of, 307.
Individual, the, as universal, 174 ff.
Individualism, abstract and concrete, 152 ff; pseudo-objective, 167–174; legal, 203.
Individuation, principle of, 169, 187 ff.
Influences, hunt for, in literary studies, 142.
Instinct of reason, 120 ff.
Introduction, Hegel's, to the *Phenomenology*, 8 ff.

J

Jacobi, 285.
James, William, 36, 99, 107.
Jesus, 331, 335, 340.

Jurisprudence, Roman, 202 ff.

K

Kant, 19, 62, 65 f, 73, 117 f, 126, 174, 177 f, 196 f, 244 f, 259 ff, 277 f, 284 f, 292 f, 364 ff.
Knowledge, natural, dialectical starting-place, 10; absolute, dialectical halting-place, 355 ff.

L

Language, bearing on culture, 220 f; as source of alienation, 221 f; basis of heroism of flattery, 222 ff; function of, in mediating between the extremes of privacy of conscience and publicity of action, 283, 288 ff.
Law, human *vs.* divine, 190 f.
Laws of thought, as frozen universals, 137; in affinity with logic of observation, 137; grounded in introspective psychology, 138.
Lectures on Modern Idealism, x.
Legalism, analogous to stoicism, 204.
L'état c'est moi, 223.
Lichtenberg, 145.
Light, God as, 305.
Literary anthropomorphism, 320, 324.
Loewenberg, Bert James, xii.
Logos, 349.
Lordship and Bondage, linked by a pair of asymmetrical relations, 89 f.
Louis XIV, 209, 211, 217, 256.
Lucinde, 287.
Lumen naturale, 239 f.

M

Macbeth, 329.
Male, the primary sex, 194; source of human law, 194.
Materialism, 245.
Mechanism *vs.* vitalism, 134.
Mental traits, of individuals, observed in external form, 142–149; exemplified in physiognomy and

phrenology, 144–148; behaviorism as modern example, 148.
Metaphysics of religion, 297, 334.
Mill, John Stuart, 251 f.
Minstrel, 321 f.
Monads, 366.
Monasticism, 106–110, 286.
Moore, Stanley, xii.
Morality, defense of absolute freedom in terms of, 259 ff; its postulates, 260–266; its makeshifts, 266–272; of volition *vs.* action, 279 ff; identification with conscience, 273 ff; language as vehicle of conscientiousness, 282.
Mystery, Dionysian, 319.
Mysticism, 100–104; moral, 245; Greek, 319; in relation to religion, 340.

N

Naturalism, 246, 248.
Necessity, interchangeable with law, 68; related to process of explanation, 70; at variance with hedonistic aspiration, 157; sentimental rationalization of, 158; spiritual, in connection with absolute freedom, 257.
Newton, 69.
Nietzsche, 315.
Nobility, contrasted with baseness, 216; synonymous with conformity, 217; related to sycophancy, 222.
Noumenology, 296, 298, 341, 385.
Novalis, 287.

O

Observation, as *perception with a purpose*, 121; involving principle of selection, 124 ff; of inorganic nature, 123–128; of organic nature, 128–135; confined to individual organisms, 130 ff, and limited to their overt and fixed structures, 132 ff; bearing on distinction between physics and biology, 134 f.
Odyssey, the, 322.

Oedipus, 199 f, 328 ff.
Ontography, 350 f.
Onto-logic, 355, 357.
Ontology, objective, not implied in phenomenology, 360; subjective, compatible with phenomenology, 361; twofold, in relation to Kant, 364.

P

Pantheism, 349.
Pathos, in *Antigone,* related to determinate ethos, 197 ff.
Peirce, Charles, 261.
Penates, 193.
Perception, receptive, 46 ff; reflective, 50 ff; unstable, 54 ff.
Person, actual *vs.* juridical, 188, 203 f; the abstract subject of abstract rights and duties, 204 ff; absolute, 205.
Persuasions, synonym of 'forms of consciousness', x, 25.
Phoebus, 329.
Poetry, Homeric, 321 ff.
Preacher, 'Knight of virtue', 162–166; reformed reformer, 163; disguised individualist, 164; quixotic type, 165.
Pre-Darwinian hints, of evolutionary process, 130.
Preface, Hegel's, to the *Phenomenology,* program of philosophic system, 4; not directly related to treatise, 7; its threefold guidepost, 8.
Present, the specious, 36 ff.
Pre-Socratics, 63.
Priority, question of, relating to sense-certainty, 25 ff; as regards duality of subject and object in perception, 43 ff.
Properties, of perceived things, paradoxical status of, 43 ff.
Property, laws of, 180; rights of, 182.
Pseudo-objectivism, 167 f.
Psychoanalysis, 289 ff.
Psychology, laws of, inferred from observation, 139–149.

Q

Quixotism, in defense of abstract virtue, 162–166.

R

Rameau's Nephew, 210 f, 286.
Rationalism, 115, 179, 234, 238, 242.
Real, the, and the rational, equation of, 116 ff, 120.
'Realm of error', threefold, 233 ff.
Reformation, 209.
Reformer, in accordance with 'law of the heart', 158 ff.
Religion, natural, 303–309; of art, 310–333; revealed, 334–349.
Religious consciousness, its modes, 293; its phenomenology, 294; its cosmic vision, 295; its non-phenomenological aspects, 297 ff.
Renaissance, 209.
Revolution, French, 209 f, 249 ff; symbolic verisimilitude of, 250; its ambivalence, 252; in relation to absolute freedom, 252 ff.
Robbers, Schiller's, 158, 161.
Roman Empire, transition to, from Greek City state, 202 ff.
Romanticism, 108, 260, 286 f, 368.
Rousseau, 158, 253 f.
Royce, Josiah, x, 86, 168, 292, 334.

S

Sache, multivalence of, 172 f.
Saint Denis, 41.
Santayana, George, 26, 93–96.
Scepticism, 12, 93–96, 332, 369.
Schelling, 62.
Schlegel, 107, 287.
Schiller, 158, 161, 285.
Schizophrenia, 97 ff, 361.
Scientific methodology, crucial difficulty involved in, observational distinction between structure and function, 128–135.
Sculpture, 313 ff, 326, 332.
Sensationalism, 251.
Sex, related to ingenuous society, 193 ff.

Shakespeare, 328.
Shaw, Bernard, 151.
Shelley, 287.
Simmel, 104.
Sister, ethical significance of, 194.
Smith, Adam, 215.
Society, ingenious vs. ingenuous, 204–206; artificial, 209.
Socrates, 20, 317.
Solipsism, 32, 34 f, 84, 276 f, 366 f.
Sophocles, 183, 190 ff, 199, 259, 327 f.
Spinoza, 6, 62, 78, 244, 300, 350, 367.
Stoicism, 91–93, 204, 334.
Strauss, David, ix.
Superstition, enlightenment in struggle with, 231 ff.
Syncretism, 348, 350, 354.
Symbolism, religious, 340.
Symposium, 20.

T

Tautology, bearing on explanatory work of the understanding, 71.
Teleology, 131 ff.
Tennyson, 228.
Terence, 302.
Theism, 349.
Theoclasm, 331 ff.
Theophagy, 317.
Torchbearer, 319.
Tragedy, language of, 326; function of chorus in, 327; midway between the epic and comedy, 328; its theodicy, 328; ambivalent place of Zeus in, 330.
Transcendental Unity of Apperception, 117, 364.
Transubstantiation, 299.
Trichotomy, 111.
Trinity, 344 ff, 351, 361.

U

Unhappy consciousness, characterized by dichotomous split within it, 98 ff; a form of self-estrangement, 102 ff; variously exemplifiable, 97–110; transition from dichotomous structure to trichotomous function, 111; under legalism, 205.

Universals, abstract and concrete; 38, 82, 152, 186.

Utilitarianism, Mill's, 251.

Utility, principle of, 239; related to perception, 241; basic to enlightened ethics, 247, 250 ff.

V

Values, economic, 180.

Vaughan, 340.

Versailles, 211.

Vicariousness, experiment in, 17 ff.

Virtue, abstract and subjective, 162–166.

Vitalism *vs.* physicalism, 308.

W

Wallace, William, ix.

Werther, Goethe's, 188.

Wilhelm Meister, 286.

Windelband, W., ix.

Woman, secondary sex, 194; 'irony in life of society', 200.

Work, ambiguity of, 171.

'World-forms', 188.

Z

Zarathrustra, 305.

Zeus, 328 ff.

Zoroastrianism, 304, 306, 347.